Long Live Atahualpa

Long Live Atahualpa

Indigenous Politics, Justice, and Democracy in the Northern Andes

Emma Cervone

Duke University Press
Durham and London
2012

Printed in the United States of America
on acid-free paper ♾
Designed by Charles Ellertson.
Typeset in Arnhem by Tseng Information Systems, Inc.
Library of Congress Cataloging-in-Publication Data
appear on the last printed page of this book.

To my son, Mattias,
and to my family

"Thousands of Indians armed with truth and fire, with shame and dignity
Shook the country awake
from its sweet dream of modernity
'That is enough' their voices scream, enough of dreams, enough of nightmares."

—Subcomandante Marcos, 2 September 1994, *La Jornada*

Contents

Acknowledgments

Like so many books, this one is a point of arrival and of departure, and I hope it conveys some of the many lessons I learned en route to its publication. My research project and fieldwork in Ecuador started all at once and without the benefit of preliminary visits to acquaint me with what was for me unknown intellectual and human terrain. A few months before I left Scotland, where I was a graduate student at the University of St. Andrews, my advisor told me that the experience I was about to start would profoundly change the way I looked at life. He responded to my concern that I was not ready for fieldwork by pointing out that no one is ever prepared for life. I left for Ecuador with these words in mind and the name of my sole contact in my pocket, and I tried to prepare myself for both an intellectual anthropological journey and an existential one. Years later, after many travels back and forth from Ecuador, Italy, and Scotland, I realized how much I had come to appreciate life's grey areas—instances when ambiguities, contradictions, and tensions inherent in human experience reveal themselves and show the immense creativity individuals and collectivities use to make sense of their existence.

The first person to thank, therefore, is my doctoral advisor, Tristan Platt, who helped me to open my eyes and my mind to life. Second, and only in chronological order, are all the people from the Inca Atahualpa and the Quichua communities in Tixán, who with a mixture of laughter, pathos, and serenity not only allowed me to work with them but gave me their trust and their friendship. I am especially grateful to Juana, A. L., and Javier, with whom I shared all the intensity and beauty of my two years in Tixán. Their friendship and affection are precious and unforgettable.

I also want to thank all the other members of the *equipo técnico* of the time and Father Torres for sharing with me their ideals, their worries, and their dreams, and for the endless nights we spent discussing how we could really help the organization and the people we worked with. In particular I want to thank Luc and Amelie, with whom I shared the life-changing experience of living in Tixán as "gringos," which was symbolized by Gringo Huasi (the house of the gringos), as people in town called our home. I am very grateful to M. P., P. B., and Taita L. B. for allowing me to work on and reconstruct the history of the Inca Atahualpa. I hope that despite the name changes I have made to protect privacy—all names in this volume are pseudonyms—all those I have written about will recognize themselves in the pages of this book. My deepest gratitude in memoriam is to Taita Pedro Marcatoma and Taita Espiritu Vargas, whose wisdom and memories guided my research into the past of indigenous political struggle in Tixán.

Many colleagues and friends supported me during this long, yet exciting process. In Ecuador I had the great good fortune of sharing Patricio Guerrero's friendship and the depths of his intellectual sensibility. His comments on the earliest drafts of my dissertation were crucial in appeasing some of my intellectual quandaries of that moment. Special thanks go to Father Juan Bottasso and my colleagues at the Salesian University and Abya-Yala in Quito, who have been for me in fact much more than colleagues; they are people with whom I have shared political sensibilities, intellectual curiosity, and the hope for a brighter and more just future. I also thank my friends Cecilia Castelnuovo and Marcia Maluf for opening up to me their worlds and their intellects, and for navigating with me the intricacies of the *quiteño* work environment.

I am very grateful to all the friends and colleagues who shared insightful comments on drafts of this project, in particular Amalia Pallares, Andrés Guerrero, Carlos Diaz, Pepe Almeida, Michael Hanchard, Juan Obarrio, Deborah Poole, Jan French, Jane Adams, Charles Hale, and Veronica Shield, as well the anonymous reviewers.

A very special thanks goes to Lise McKean, whose dedication, accuracy, and savvy in copyediting my work were crucial. My thanks to Lacey Forman for helping with the editing of the bibliography. I also want to thank J. Reynolds Smith, Valerie Millholland, Miriam Angress, and the staff at Duke University Press for their help and guidance during the book's editorial and publication process.

I could never end this list without expressing my immense gratitude to my son, Mattias, my mother, father, and brother, my extended family and folks, and my sisterly friend Roberta for being there for me during this entire process. Their endless love, closeness, and energy have given me a sense of purpose and have helped me to keep my focus and balance despite the turbulence that inevitably accompanies life.

INTRODUCTION

Redefining Indigenous Politics

June 1990 marked a turning point for Ecuadorian politics, with events that changed Ecuadorian political culture and redefined the way different social forces related to the state. A large number of indigenous people from all over the country gathered in the streets of the capital Quito and in many other provincial capitals to claim their rights as ethnically and culturally diverse citizens. This powerful *levantamiento* (uprising), which paralyzed major roads and commercial activities for an entire week, was neither a sudden outburst, nor a chaotic and random protest. It was the result of almost a century of indigenous political organizing in a country in which, as in many others in Latin America, racial and ethnic discrimination has endured since the colonial era.

Equality in Diversity

As in other Andean countries, the process of formation of ethnic militancy in Ecuador began, in the early twentieth century, under the influence of left-wing parties and ideologies. As early as the 1920s, some indigenous activists, mostly in the highlands, presented the state with their first formal demands for education and against what they identified as mistreatment and abuse. The process of indigenous organizing consolidated in the 1950s around the struggle for agrarian reform laws, which gradually led to the formation of indigenous grassroots organizations, federations, and confederations, which in turn led to the formation of what scholars and activists define as the Ecuadorian indigenous movement. The levantamiento of 1990 marked the maturation of this political mobilization, officially elevating indigenous political presence to the national level and making visible indigenous peoples' quest for recognition as Ecuadorian citizens with rights to cultural and ethnic diversity, as well as with rights to equal access to resources and political participation.

The movement's struggle for recognition continued in the following years and marked what Ecuadorian social scientists have defined as the "won decade" (*la década ganada*) (Ramón Valarezo 1992). The constitutional reform of 1998 supposedly represented the completion of this process, since it officially recognized Ecuador's ethnic and cultural diversity by declaring the country multicultural and pluriethnic. Yet, rather than signifying a point of arrival, the multicultural era, inaugurated by the constitutional reform of 1998 and reinforced by the constitution approved in 2008, has signified for the indigenous movement a point of departure, the beginning of a new political phase. The postrecognition phase, as I call it, has posed new and unexpected challenges to both the movement and the Ecuadorian state. The political impasse and crisis that indigenous activism has faced since 1998, as it has consolidated its political presence within the state structure, underline the complexity of ethnic protest in the multicultural era. Due to the shift from the heightened ethnic focus of the 1990s to the postrecognition phase, the indigenous struggle cannot be pursued or contained within the limits of ethnicity. Indigenous activists have acknowledged that such a conjuncture was nevertheless propitious for forging new alliances with nonindigenous actors of Ecuadorian society, given that indigenous citizens were not alone in being adversely affected by neoliberal economics.

How, then, to best understand the different meanings, scopes, and possibilities of indigenous politics in contemporary Ecuador in this changed context? The Ecuadorian case offers an opportunity to examine the challenges that political participation poses to the indigenous movement and its constituency in a society where the contingency of economic neoliberalism and the endurance of the "coloniality of power" undermine the possibility for a more democratic exercise of power (Mignolo 2000; Moraña, Dussel, and Jáuregui 2008; Quijano 2000). My analysis of indigenous politics in Ecuador before, during, and after the implementation of economic and political measures under neoliberal agendas reveals that indigeneity cannot be reduced either to a matter of class or to a generalized fight against poverty. Such approaches do not address the protracted racial and ethnic discrimination that indigenous and Afro-descent citizens continue to suffer. The affirmation of indigenous rights becomes, therefore, a highly contested terrain in which different meanings of social justice and nation are disputed.

This book highlights the contours of the politicization of ethnic identity and the process of political organizing, by reconstructing the various contested arenas and conjunctures in which indigenous struggle emerged, became meaningful, and promoted change. My analysis traces the mobilization of the Quichuas of the Ecuadorian highland parish of Tixán and the formation of their organization, Inca Atahualpa, within the national context of the politicization of ethnic identity. Rather than pursuing a historical trajectory, I have taken into account all those elements, past and present, that Quichua activists and inhabitants in the parish indicated as pivotal and meaningful in the process of formation of their political consciousness and militancy, then analyzed how such elements spoke to the larger context of indigenous political organizing nationally. I explore the extent to which the Ecuadorian indigenous movement has redefined both nationally and locally its relationship with the state and nonindigenous society by creating venues for indigenous participation in decision making.

My analysis draws on eight years of uninterrupted experience, reflection, work, and collaboration with indigenous activists. During those years, I assumed various roles—researcher, university professor, consultant. I first arrived in Ecuador in January 1991, with a research project on the indigenous movement, a largely understudied topic at the time. I was not only interested in the movement's political discourse, but also particularly in deconstructing the traditions and ideologies constituting its political inspiration and practice. Many Ecuadorian scholars I met joked about the timing of my arrival, which they characterized as a missed opportunity to have witnessed the historical levantamiento of 1990. Notwithstanding, I tried to learn as much as I could from press reports and a selection of articles that the publisher Abya-Yala, directed by Father Juan Bottasso, had compiled in a series of volumes titled *Kipu* (1990) to document those extraordinary events. From this material, I clearly recognized that it was specifically the language of ethnic rights in which indigenous demands had been articulated. Yet it also seemed that such specificity was rather fluid and open to constant reinterpretation. Ethnic rights were not limited to the defense of an abstract and disembodied notion of indigenous culture, but rather linked to economic and social policies meant to redefine the position of subordination that indigenous peoples, referred to as nationalities, had suffered since the colonial time. Therefore, in order to

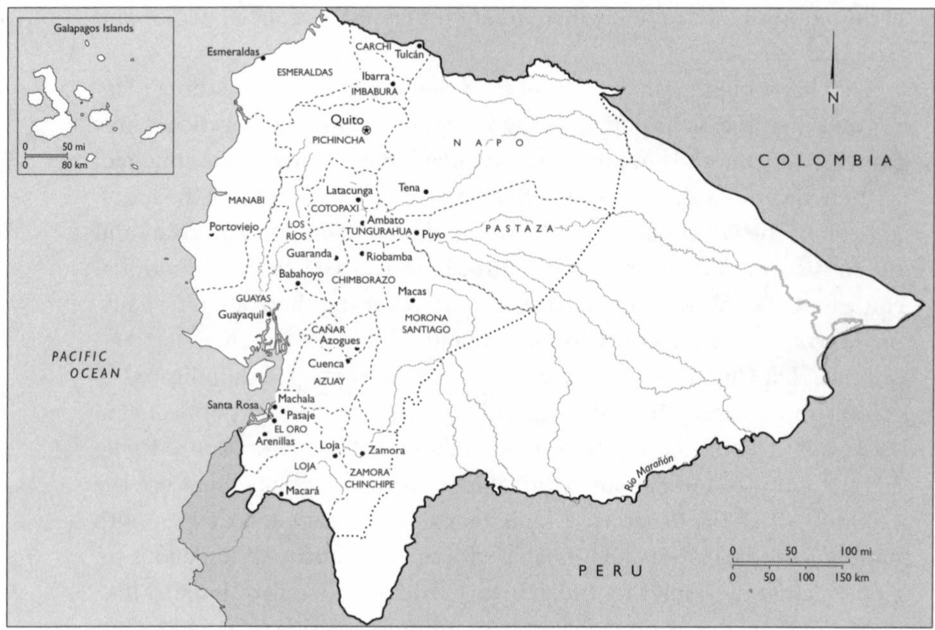

Map 1. Ecuador. Prepared by Bill Nelson.

understand the multifaceted ways in which indigeneity was produced and performed in political practice, I needed also to understand the circumstances in which it had emerged as well as the ways in which it was lived in quotidian practices.

The Ecuadorian sociologist Andrés Guerrero, who later became one of my mentors, told me about the Inca Atahualpa, a grassroots indigenous organization regarded as having been highly successful in negotiating power and in controlling abuses and racism locally. By the end of 1991, I had made my way to Tixán, a rural parish in the central highland province of Chimborazo, with one of the highest percentages of Quichua indigenous people.[1] In Tixán I worked, for two years, with the Inca Atahualpa leaders and residents of its affiliated communities, offering assistance in preparing an oral history on the formation of the organization and as a witness of its accomplishments. This journey took me from an examination of daily life interactions among indigenous and nonindigenous people, to the administration of indigenous justice in the parish, to the representation of indigenous cultural forms in ritual contexts. My analysis thus specifically explores the realm of cultural politics, self-determination, and application of hybrid discourses on human rights and indigenous justice and their implication for social change.

Such ethnographic immersion in the local dimension, at the micro-level, also gave me the opportunity to explore how indigenous politics intertwined at the local, regional, and national levels. As emphasized in other studies of indigenous movements, it is impossible to understand indigenous activism in Latin America without accounting for the many levels and networks (what Bret Gustafson defines as scales) in which indigenous activists and people operate.[2] Accordingly, I took advantage of my uninterrupted stay in Ecuador from 1991 to 1998 (and the shorter trips to Ecuador I made after 2000) to reinterpret the political experience of the Inca Atahualpa within the context of indigenous politics at the national level. At the end of 1993, after my intense and indelible experience of living in Tixán, I returned to Quito to talk to national activists and to learn more about the complexities of national politics, multilateral agencies, and the percolating effects of transnational discourses on human rights, diversity, and indigeneity. Although I maintained my contacts with Tixán, during the next five years I focused primarily on the national dimension of indigenous struggle, often working as a consultant for national nongovernmental organizations (NGOs) collaborating with the indigenous movement and for agencies such as UNICEF and the Inter-American Development Bank, all of which had fully incorporated the language of ethnic rights and diversity in their agendas.

By then the indigenous movement was cresting, fully pursuing participation in the state structure via national elections. In 1996 indigenous candidates of the newly founded Pachakutik movement won seats in local administrations and gained representation in the national government. This political presence gave the movement the opportunity to push forward its agenda for constitutional reform, a measure that had already been adopted by other countries in the region, specifically the neighboring Colombia and Peru. The 1998 constitution was heralded as a pivotal moment in the history of Ecuadorian politics, a significant step forward in the process of democratization that had inaugurated the era of multiculturalism in the country. My analysis of the postrecognition phase is a depiction of such a process and of the multicultural shift, which came about because of the participation and efforts of many other grassroots organizations like the Inca Atahualpa.

What led indigenous activists around the country to proclaim a historical victory were the 2002 national elections, when the alliance of the movement with the independent presidential candidate Lucio Gutiérrez (after the fall of two presidents) resulted in indigenous activists holding three cabinet ministries in the newly formed government, an achievement unprecedented in Ecuadorian political history. Yet my examination of the postrecognition phase reveals the many ambiguities of this process and the extent to which ethnic protest and the pursuit of political empowerment and social change are not only contested, but also contradictory.

During the nineteen years in which I have been engaged with the study of indigenous politics in Ecuador, the main focus of my anthropological interest has remained the intricate and complex process by which indigenous identity has been politicized, and the methodological and epistemological challenges thus posed to the discipline of anthropology. The complexity I encountered in the field also challenged my training as an anthropologist. At stake are ethical and methodological claims of detachment and objectivity, as well as anthropological notions of culture and identity that, while contesting essentialist renderings of indigeneity and indigenous politics, got trapped in formulaic notions of strategic essentialism or fluidity, failing to foreground the perceived immanent and overarching nature of cultural claims in the life of indigenous people.

Redefining Indigenous Politics

My analysis of grassroots indigenous politics is part of a more recent focus within anthropological studies of ethnicity in Latin America. The process of politicization of ethnic identity that clearly emerged during the commemoration, in 1992, of five hundred years of indigenous resistance has led to a shift in anthropological research interests and methodologies (Rappaport 1994, 17). Since the early 1990s, anthropological studies of indigeneity have moved beyond the synchronic analyses of indigenous societies as isolated entities to focus instead on the construction of political movements and identities among indigenous people.[3] Urban's and Sherzer's (1991) emphasis on the politicization of ethnic identity in Latin America paved the way for new studies of indigeneity, which focus on the complex and ever-changing nature of a political process that involved both indigenous actors and states. Even studies that do not center on political organizing examine indigenous societies in interaction with economic policies and social changes at the national and transnational levels.[4] Accordingly, microlevel analyses are linked to larger national and global contexts in order to demonstrate how indigenous groups are constantly trying to redefine their position of subordination vis-à-vis states and nonindigenous societies.

My examination of the process of formation and expansion of the Inca Atahualpa highlights features of the highly complex process of political mobilization known within the social sciences as indigenous movements. As indigenous activists have stressed repeatedly, especially in the context of the celebrations in 1992, the struggle of indigenous peoples has been a long-standing one, dating to the Spanish conquest, when they struggled to preserve their social and cultural integrity in the face of colonial abuse. However, during the twentieth century, with the emergence of the modern nation-state and with state-led modernization, indigenous resistance gradually coalesced into political movements representing the voices of the indigenous population—in Ecuador, approximately 35 percent of the citizens (see CONAIE 1989).[5]

Starting in the 1980s, indigenous movements in Ecuador, Bolivia, Colombia, Guatemala, and later Peru foregrounded and further reinforced the ethnic component of indigenous struggles.[6] In this context, the politicization of historical and cultural identity became key for redefining the structures of ethnic and racial domination. The right to self-determination that has become the central and highly contested demand of indigenous movements in the last three decades symbolically capitalizes on the injustice and discrimination suffered by the native peoples of the continent since the conquest. Their quest for recognition of their collective rights as *pueblos* (peoples) within the framework of citizenship rights has challenged both liberal notions of individual rights and the construction of monolithic and culturally homogenous national identities.[7]

Arturo Escobar and Sonia Alvarez (1992) have characterized this political phenomenon in terms of new social movements that formulate political demands based on cultural and social identities other than class. They contextualize this shift internationally as one of the many political changes of the post–Cold War era. Geopolitics have been profoundly altered by the implosion of the socialist bloc since the end of the 1980s. New social movements, therefore, are an expression of these changes in transnational alliances and equilibrium, and a response to global economic forces whose negative impacts are widely and variously denounced. In this context, human rights, women's rights, indigenous rights, and ecological principles have become powerful moral and ideological inspiration for transnational forms of mobilization against poverty and inequality.[8]

Scholars of ethnic and social movements have framed this transition in terms of the politics of identity to emphasize the protagonist role that identities—whether defined by race, ethnicity, or gender—have acquired in the struggle of political actors who attempt to reverse conditions of domination.[9] As cogently discussed by Kay Warren (1998) in her analysis of Pan-Maya activism in Guatemala, cultural distinctiveness has become the specific base for both indigenous political identity and practice in Latin America. Recent studies of contemporary ethnic struggles in the region show, however, that this transition from the old to the new paradigm is a highly complex and contested terrain that resists the simplification of ethnic versus class struggle. Both these dimensions have a distinctive role in defining the position of indigenous people in national society as well as their relationship with the state. As studies show, indigenous activists have stressed either of these two dimensions in response to political and social change affecting their subject position in society as well as their relationship to the state without treating them as mutually exclusive.[10] In his seminal work on indigenous peasantry, Michael Kearney (1996) argues that indigenous economic strategies not only have redefined the divide between ethnicity and class, but also have expanded the boundaries of those social identities beyond national frontiers when indigenous people became global citizens who incorporated transnational migration into their economic strategies.

This book addresses the intricacies related to this process of constant redefinition of identity by examining the intersection of culture and power, and the interplay between cultural and political distinctiveness. In other words, how do we approach and interpret the specificity of indigenous politics, and what challenges does it pose to anthropological studies of identity? I discuss here the major implications posed by the study of identity politics for both indigenous political struggle and for the production of anthropological knowledge.

Cultural Distinctiveness in Political Practice

The politicization of ethnicity in Latin America is a contested process in which indigenous citizens negotiate space, resources, and political participation with the state, political parties, NGOs, religious institutions, and other competitive local organizations.[11] Indigenous activists and leaders, therefore, are exposed to a broad spectrum of forces and political interests, as are activists and political leaders of labor unions, political parties, and other grassroots organizations at large. Thus, indigenous political affiliations and ascriptions are often multifaceted and situational (Warren and Jackson 2002, 11). Yet what are the specific implications of cultural distinctiveness for political practice? One primary implication relates to the multiplication of political subject positions within the same movement and the consequences of that. Because such movements focus on cultural distinctiveness, both as *indígenas* and as nationalities—that is, as distinctive ethnic groups within the broader racialized category of indigenous—the range of diversification and ethnic heterogeneity is further amplified within indigenous movements.

The highly heterogeneous composition of indigenous ethnic identities can provoke divergences based on cultural and social distinctions. As the account, presented in chapter 2, of the formation of the Inca reveals, this process of mobilization and identity formation does not rely on an uncomplicated and univocal understanding of oppression. Factors related to the production and reproduction of specific ethnic boundaries involving *páramo* (moorland) communities and lower land (valley) communities prompted Quichuas in Tixán to mobilize and ultimately create two competing organizations: the Inca Atahualpa and the Association of Autonomous Workers of the Zula Mines of Chimborazo (ATAMZICH).[12] In the context of political mobilization, these cultural and symbolic dimensions can acquire divergent political meanings, shaping intraethnic factions and alliances that connect to wider contexts of ethnic politicization in multifarious and sometimes contradictory ways.[13]

A second implication is the risk of internal political fragmentation. In Ecuador, for example, the regional specificities expressed in terms of state policies, local social networks, and economies generate substantial differences between the political agendas of highland indigenous organizations and of those of the Amazon basin. Often articulated as differences in demands over land and territory, these distinctions create discrepancies within the movement at both national and local levels of political action. Some scholars have suggested that this political multivocality is a danger that can lead indigenous movements to atomization (Van Cott 2002). For example, in her discussion of constitutional reforms in Ecuador, Donna Lee Van Cott highlights the risks that the ethnically based project of the country's leading indigenous federation, Confederación de Nacionalidades Indígenas del Ecuador (CONAIE), represents for the unity of the movement (ibid, 64). In an effort to gain control over rival national organizations, CONAIE rushed to restructure its internal structure as well as the structure of Consejo de Desarrollo de Nacionalidades y Pueblos del Ecuador (CODENPE).[14] According to Van Cott, the redefinition of both CONAIE's and CODENPE's constituencies not by organization but by nationality and peoples—that is, specific ethnic identities within the larger ethnic groups—further reinforced divisions within the movement and hindered the potential for direct representation of indigenous actors who, especially in the highlands, had joined peasant or evangelical organizations.[15]

Ethnic and cultural distinctiveness force indigenous actors to negotiate with multiple identities—racial as Indian, class as peasant, and ethnic in terms of their sociocultural membership—and create internal fragmentation. Researchers analyzing these complexities face many questions. How, for example, do we measure the impact of internal divisions on political practice today? Many of the rivalries Van Cott mentions are historical rivalries (Amazon and highland, regional and national federations) that have been reframed and reshaped along different ideological matrices and political practices over time, possibly dating as far back as the pre-Colombian period.[16] Studies show that these diverse internal discourses can be considered as expressions of different strategies of empowerment adopted by indigenous actors in specific circumstances in order to access resources.[17] Therefore, affiliations with multiethnic organizations, even if antagonistic to the CONAIE model, do not necessarily imply atomization per se, since they may represent a different channel for accessing resources and power. This was evident in Ecuador's national elections in 1992, when many indigenous grassroots organizations chose to present their candidates despite CONAIE's mandate not to participate in the electoral process; when I discussed this with indigenous grassroots activists, they made it clear that local politics required different strategies and that their decisions were not to be understood as attempts to undermine CONAIE's legitimacy.

This tension between fragmentation and unity deriving from the politicization of cultural distinctiveness is a feature of ethnic struggle in contemporary Latin America. I therefore do not treat unity and fragmentation as contradictory or mutually exclusive. As maintained by Charles Hale in his analysis of racial ambivalence in Guatemala, the study of tensions cannot provide clear answers, but can instead allow for the different modes to "disrupt and trouble each other" (Hale 2008, 17). If cultural and ethnic heterogeneity can lead to heterogeneous political choices and strategies of empowerment, internal fragmentation and unity can be treated as situational forces that exist simultaneously, rather than as mutually exclusive and reified political realities. While not denying that internal heterogeneity has the potential to fragment and disrupt the indigenous movement, I do not treat it as an intrinsic force leading to atomization, but rather argue that it is important to understand the specific circumstances and conditions under which such heterogeneity becomes disempowering for indigenous activism.

Furthermore, if indigenous political identities within their movement are heterogeneous and contested, how does one reconcile their quest for what at times appears to be a totalizing rendering of indigenous cultures and their related rights? Constructivist critiques of indigenous politics emphasize the risks of adopting essentialist notions of indigenous identity in political action. Such immutable understandings of ethnic and cultural specificity are seen as exclusionary and therefore as undermining indigenous movements' capacity to promote social change on behalf of nonindigenous people (Radcliffe, Laurie, and Andolina 2002). The underlying assumption in such antiessentialist critiques is that indigenous politics are by definition inclusive, cohesive, and ultimately egalitarian, simply because they fight against exclusion and oppression—a political noble savage. But such antiessentialist critiques are problematic in their own terms. They downplay the cultural, social, and historical variation under which indigenous movements operate. Such distinctions are key to understanding and contextualizing the conditions of production of such supposedly essentialist formulations. Paradoxically, this antiessentialist critique essentializes and idealizes the realm of indigenous politics and underestimates the political maturity of indigenous activists as well as the ability of subaltern political actors, indigenous and otherwise, to constantly reshape their alliances and defend their integrity. Moreover, as I discuss later in relation to ethics and methodology, the deconstruction of indigenous activism's political and cultural discourse can have consequences that affect the foundations of indigenous struggle.

Democratic Distinctiveness

The intertwining of cultural and political distinctiveness has, therefore, further implications. If fragmentation and unity are understood as a tension rather than a dichotomy, how do we understand the political and social changes that these multifaceted and culturally distinctive movements are promoting? Or, as many scholars of social movements wonder, how can we measure the success of these movements without simply assuming or anticipating their political goals and projects?

As suggested by Doug McAdam, John McCarthy, and Mayer Zald (1988) and by more recent ethnographic studies (see, among others, Gustafson 2009; Speed 2008b; Viatori 2010), it is important to distinguish between the macrolevel and microlevel of indigenous politics, where the former engages with national and transnational complexities, and the latter with local complexities. Albeit profoundly intertwined, these dimensions present different sets of challenges and predicaments to which indigenous activists and people must respond. The quest for inclusion and recognition as formulated by many national indigenous federations in Latin America constitutes the general ideological foundation of indigenous movements when negotiating with the state, political parties, and other entities representing national and international nonindigenous society for a more democratic and equitable redistribution of resources and power. Although these claims serve as frames for the political agenda at macro- and microlevels, in practice the strategies and goals of indigenous activists vary according to the specific circumstances of different sectors of the indigenous population. Thus, when comparing indigenous movements across Latin America, it is important also to take into account the broad variety of their political strategies (Postero and Zamosc 2004, 25). These variations depend on the historical specificities of ethnic relations in each country and, as Deborah Yashar (2005) argues when comparing indigenous movements in the Andean region, on the way Indian-state relations have been shaped and redefined over time.

What, then, are the meanings of democratization and social change when applied to indigenous politics at large? An examination of different arenas of indigenous political practice shows a lack of agreement about the process of democratization. The process occurs in a contested terrain, where the struggle to participate in defining the political rules may present contradictory outcomes. The contradictions between human rights and cultural rights that emerged in a community in Western Mexico offer an excellent example (de la Peña 2002). In this case, a conflict arose when indigenous authorities of the Santa Catarina Cuexomatitlán community in Jalisco decided to expel all the members of an extended family who had converted to evangelism. Because of their conversion, the family members no longer were able to properly fulfill ritual obligations. The normative principles of equality and inclusion defended by indigenous activists in their language of contention vis-à-vis the state became irrelevant when applied to intracommunity politics. The freedom of religion included among the ethnic specificities to be respected by state policies was perceived as a threat to the integrity of the sociocultural life of the immediate community and was therefore denied. Thus, an understanding of democratization does not merely refer to the issues of governability and stability of the formal political institutions (Alvarez, Dagnino, and Escobar 1998, 11–13). Nor does it refer only to a univocal strategy for gaining access to the decision-making process.

Democratization in multicultural societies is a highly contextual and multifaceted political process in which multiple meanings are expressed and negotiated while multiple allegiances are established (Kymlicka and Wayne 2000). The language of contention used by indigenous activists to negotiate power and resources with the state is incorporated but utterly redefined when applied to community affairs and negotiations with local authorities. The articulation of normative principles with political practice, therefore, varies according to the specific fields of force or contexts in which indigenous actors operate. In the realm of the politicization of ethnicity, analyses of political change have to incorporate the multiple levels and conditions under which changes occur. As the analysis of the western Mexican case shows, the need to defend both their political legitimacy and the integrity of their cultural distinctiveness pushed indigenous activists to adopt measures—namely, the expulsion of the evangelical family—that other social actors considered as contradictory or even unpopular. In the field of indigenous politics, different definitions of democracy and democratic practice are produced. The various meanings that democracy can acquire highlight the tension between collective and individual rights, the latter being the guiding principle of the universal definition of human rights. Yet both dimensions of rights implicit in the affirmation—and even in the essentializing—of indigenous cultural distinctiveness are principles deployed by indigenous activists in order to reverse their subaltern position vis-à-vis the state and nonindigenous society. In this case, cultural and political distinctiveness entails redefining liberal notions of citizenship and democratization.

At the macropolitical level, democratic change transcends the boundaries of intraethnic politics. Although the contradictions pertaining to community affairs are often indirectly related to indigenous people's subordinate position nationally, state and society are directly implicated in the democratization process at large in the case of macropolitics. In state and elite discourses, forceful political measures (such as armed struggle in Chiapas Mexico, and coups in Ecuador and Bolivia) have been considered contradictory to indigenous politics for movements that fight for a more democratic exercise of power in their own countries.[18] Yet these contradictions are embedded within another set of contradictions intrinsic to state projects. Although substantially different, the examples of Chiapas, Ecuador, and Bolivia have a common denominator: the negative impact of neoliberal economic policies on indigenous economic and social stability since the late 1980s.[19] At the same time, different and long-standing processes of mobilization have led to the formation and affirmation of an indigenous intelligentsia and leadership whose voice cannot be silenced or ignored. Additionally, in Ecuador and Bolivia constitutional reforms officially recognized the right of indigenous people to self-determination. Indigenous activists adopted forceful political measures after state authorities ignored popular protests against economic measures that drastically increased the cost of living for most of the population. The contradictory combination of multicultural recognition with neoliberal economics presents challenges, both to indigenous movements and to the state, for containing ethnic protest within the boundaries of democracy. Furthermore, the profound discrepancies and lack of consensus among ruling elites in many Latin American countries make democratization and political stability a more difficult task.[20]

The Fluidity of Identity

The complexity of the process of politicization of ethnic identity promoted by indigenous movements in Latin America and elsewhere (including Australia, Canada, and the United States) has prompted anthropologists to redefine their analytical categories and epistemologies related to the study of identity. Kay Warren and Jean Jackson (2005) offer a cogent synthesis of anthropological debate on this topic. Arguing that the two main dichotomies in this debate focus on essentialism and authenticity and their corresponding opposites, they take the lead in questioning fixed notions of "culture," "indigenous," or "development" understood as immutable essences characterizing the "authentic" identity of indigenous people and their lifeways. Since the 1990s, scholars and anthropologists of ethnicity and indigenous movements have emphasized the socially and historically constructed, and ever-changing, nature of social identities. Accordingly, the focus of analysis has shifted from defining identities to asking how identities were forged and produced, and by whom. Such poststructuralist analytical approaches have centered on deconstructing the elements and processes that produce identity, thereby underscoring the complex and often contradictory nature of identity formation, and the many actors and situated discourses that participate in the forging of a given identity.

As a similarly situated discourse, the forging of indigeneity has its roots in the specific histories of social interactions between different ethnic groups and the states (or the colonial administrations) that have ruled over them, and it therefore varies according to such histories (Hodgson 2002). In her analysis of multiculturalism in Australia, Elizabeth Povinelli (2002) cogently discussed the extent to which the Australian state contributed to the production of a specific "authentic" aborigine identity by establishing legal parameters according to which such populations could or could not prove their rights to lands. In the indigenous case in Latin America, the forging of the colonial category of Indian changed over time to acquire different meanings according the context and actors involved. With the process of modern nation building and throughout the twentieth century, dominant notions of indigenousness depicted indigenous cultures as cradles of tradition and primordialism, where tradition was equated with backwardness and antimodernity.[21] Such notions competed with left-wing and reformist discourses that held the regimes that exploited the peasantry to be the main cause hindering the development of indigenous people as modern citizens and with humanitarian views of indigenous people as victims of discrimination and violence, as promoted by the progressive Catholic Church. More recently, the politicized discourse on ethnic identity, as produced by indigenous activists and intellectuals themselves, rejected discriminatory rendering of their cultures by resignifying the notions of tradition and modernity as not mutually exclusive. Since the late 1980s, another competing discourse, channeled through transnational networks and NGOs, has also introduced the notion of rights, under the definition of human rights and collective rights. Accordingly, indigeneity became not only a platform for asserting rights, but also, at times, a romanticized alternative to the destructive and damaging individualism of capitalism or of Western societies in general (de la Cadena and Starn 2007).

Anthropological studies of identity formation in Latin America, therefore, came to terms with the situated and political nature of such processes (Warren and Jackson 2005). Many ethnographic analyses of indigenous identity formation emphasize the multivocality of such processes, whereby different actors and institutions participate in defining what is and is not to be considered authentically "indigenous."[22] The emphasis on the relational and on interconnectedness in identity formation also debunked the dichotomy of authenticity and inauthenticity, including in this approach a critique to the poststructuralist claim of "invented traditions," which was found to be problematic, for it potentially delegitimized the political struggle of indigenous movements. Drawing on Gayatri Chakravorty Spivak's notion of strategic essentialism (1988), such critiques often demonstrated the extent to which cultural claims had to be understood as political strategies adopted by movements in order to access resources and political participation from which they were otherwise excluded on account of their "backwardness." Yet the notion of strategic essentialism also proved to be too close to instrumentalist views of ethnicity, according to which identities are reduced to tools that political actors manipulate for specific ends (Govers and Vermeulen 1997). As argued by Shannon Speed (2008a) in her analysis of Zapatista political struggles, such an approach has been contested by indigenous political actors engaged in the struggle for social justice; they have maintained that their indigenous identity is not an opportunistic or new invention, but a practice rooted in their history and integrity as a people. Ever-changing and strategic notions of identity in anthropology, therefore, are insufficient for conveying the vitality and complexity of indigenous cultures and politics.

In her analysis of essentialism and authenticity among indigenous Nasa intellectuals in Colombia, Joanne Rappaport argues that indigenous culture is conceived by such intellectuals less as a preexisting immutable essence than as "a tool for delineating a project within which people can build an ethnic polity protected from the hegemonic forces that surround them" (2005, 38). In these political processes different actors reinterpret, represent, and redefine their identity in order to gain access to or defend resources and power—and ultimately to maintain their own sense of integrity and purpose. Indigenous identities become contested terrains in which different meanings and values are produced. Beyond notions of strategic essentialism, therefore, indigenous identity becomes a political project that defines difference and at the same time is subject to change and redefinition. For example, the United Nations Declaration on the Rights of Indigenous Peoples, adopted in 2007, has served as an international framework by which many ethnic groups not traditionally self-identified as indigenous have adopted the language of indigeneity to frame their claims over resources and land. Indigenous identity, therefore, "is not natural or inevitable, but neither is it simply invented, adopted, or imposed. It is rather a *positioning* which draws upon historically sedimented practices, landscapes, and repertoires of meaning, and emerges through particular patterns of engagements and struggles" (Murray Li 2000, 151).

In his critique of poststructuralism, Jonathan Friedman (1994) argues that the emphasis on the constructed and shifting nature of identity runs the risk of trivializing values and beliefs that are "deadly serious" for those who subscribe to them. In the ongoing debate around the production and politicization of indigenous identity and cultures, the concept of "fluidity" has been introduced to address these complex, shifting, yet vital elements. This concept moves beyond the notion of constructed identity and strategic essentialism to foreground not only the continuously changing process of identity formation, but also the dynamic coexistence within such processes of multiple and sometimes supposedly contradictory tropes of modernity, tradition, urban, rural, local, and global.[23] Yet not even the notion of fluidity resolves the ephemeral and slippery nature attributed to identity as it has been contested either vocally by indigenous activists (see Speed 2008a) or in the lived experience of many indigenous people. How, therefore, can the anthropological study of indigenous politics do justice to the "seriousness" and relevance of identity for indigenous people?

Identity, Politics, and the Everyday

The study of politics and the everyday offers an opportunity to overcome such disconnects in anthropological theories of identity politics, and to argue for a rendering of political identity that is about "becoming" as much as it is about "being" (Hall 1995, 8, 14). Many studies of the politicization of indigenous identity have privileged analyses of indigenous movements and the ideological discourses and practices as produced by indigenous activists and organizations over the dynamics of the quotidian experience of subscribing to and living a specific identity in asymmetrical relationships. My fieldwork on indigenous politics in Tixán, however, made me keenly aware of two intrinsically related dimensions of the politicization of identity in antidiscrimination struggles. Organized political actions and strategies constituted only one component in the complex mapping of the Quichuas' political practice. The everyday lived experience of domination and its related responses as based on a perceived identity were its complementary component. I quickly realized that these two aspects of the Quichuas' experience of ethnic struggle locally were so interdependent that political actions and the ideological premises on which they were based could not be understood unless analyzed in connection with the quotidian dealings of the interethnic conflict. By building on the local history of political mobilization, the political discourse of the Inca Atahualpa was the manifest and visible form of a less visible, more indecipherable political practice which rests in the everyday. These two dimensions were connected by what I call a mutual boomerang response, according to which the organization and its constituency respond to each other when they mobilize and negotiate their political values in the public square as well as in "so called apolitical locations" such as shops, markets, ritual kinship, and canteens (Alvarez, Dagnino, and Escobar 1998, 14). To paraphrase Stuart Hall, the ethnographic examination of political actions in articulation with everyday practices allows one to go beyond both the supposed fixity of identity and its critique to underline the conditions that make the forging of indigenous identity possible. Such articulation, or set of articulations, underscores the historical memory, the multiple voices, and the constraints that all participate in indigenous people's self-identification as a way of making sense of their life and of their struggle.

What are the implications for the anthropological study of identity politics when one focuses on the articulation of politics with the quotidian expressions and manifestations of social conflict in spaces where this conflict is apparently dormant? Beyond notions of fluidity and strategic essentialism, it is precisely in the quotidian sociality of this conflict that the relevance of identity politics emerges and make sense. The combined study of indigenous politics and the everyday can shed light on the way in which identities are constructed, lived, and "cast in stone" (Sutton 1998).

The political relevance of the everyday has been foregrounded by scholars such as James Scott, Michel de Certeau, and Pierre Bourdieu. More recently, in his analysis of quotidian politics, Michael Hanchard affirms that "imagination, organization and will more than rational choice and deliberation are the foundational nonprocedural bases of politics" (2006, 6). As the Gramscian understanding of the role of ideologies and culture suggests, ideas have a fundamental relevance in the dealings of everyday life. Political ideologies, therefore, have social and affective aspects that extend beyond their use by political institutions or organizations. My study, therefore, works at the frontier of culture, identity, and power to explore the meanings generated in the everyday by the people who resist domination. My analysis of interethnic conflict in Tixán claims that the performative, affective, and reiterated aspects of identity politics in the everyday contribute to validating a specific identity and culture for political action. In this realm the elements, dynamics, and behavioral codes deployed in quotidian interactions have a history and a materiality that constitute identity's "seriousness" and its perceived continuity against claims of endless reinventions.

A goal of my anthropological study of indigenous politics is, then, to reveal the connections between the lived and affective dimensions of identity in quotidian politics as expressed by Quichuas in Tixán and the political actions and strategies led by their grassroots organizations—what it means for the people involved in these political processes to live their perceived identity and ideals and act on them both in their political practice and in the "normality" of their everyday existence. This connection works as a boomerang, according to which the discourse of the Inca Atahualpa and the Quichuas' politics of the quotidian nurture and feed each other to generate political meanings. In my examination of the Inca and of the Quichuas' and *tixaneños*' interactions in markets, shops, festive occasions, and in ritual kinship relations, I combine Bourdieu's concept of habitus and its correlated *docta ignorancia* (Bourdieu 1977; Bourdieu 1990, 53) with de Certeau's distinction between tactics and strategies. I do this in order to discuss to what extent the domain of everyday life in Tixán acquires political meanings and how a habitus of resistance (Brechtian resistance or Scott's weapons of the weak) constitutes a form of political "capital" that allows a grassroots organization such as the Inca Atahualpa to effectively fight against domination and abuses, and enable the redistribution of power and resources. There are moments when words, acts, and attitudes are consciously directed to a specific interlocutor with a specific goal, which de Certeau defines as strategies (1988, xix). Yet in other moments people are responding to circumstances as they arise, making choices and defending their integrity based on their own sense of truth and value, or acting within a habitus that has a social history whose goals are not necessarily disclosed or manifested (*docta ignorancia*). Thus, even if the dominated know they are dominated, awareness of their condition not only is perceived as a potential motivation for political action, but also is cognitively and affectively incorporated as part of ordinary life (Das 2007; Scott 1992).

In his analysis of the Gramscian notion of hegemony, William Roseberry argues that the ways in which subordinate populations either accommodate or resist domination "are shaped by the process of domination itself" (1994, 361). The same condition of domination renders culturally defined codes of interaction and social values from within available repertoires more attuned to the conditions and the feelings experienced by dominated individuals and collectivities. In Raymond Williams's terms (1977), the structural condition of domination generates a "structure of feeling" that informs how the dominated imagine, act, socialize, and make sense of their lives. Domination is incorporated into their imaginations of what constitutes the ordinary in their lives. The "normality" of daily life is thereby established according to different parameters than those indicated in hegemonic narratives on social and cultural values and norms by dominant, middle-class, bourgeois, and white society. As the case of indigenous people in Tixán shows, the lived experience of domination implies a constant process of negotiation between two major affective poles: those of acceptance and of rejection of both the status quo and dominant values. This structure of feeling pervades the political actions of the dominated, as well as their leisure time, sense of humor, and intimate relations, such that either acceptance or rejection of being dominated is made recognizable especially to those who share the same condition. The lived experience of domination makes the personal into the social and political by generating a community of people who share the same "structure of feeling" and a "perceived commonality of subordination," thus rendering the affective experience of political struggle meaningful to anthropological studies of identity politics (Hanchard 2006, 34; Williams 1977, 131).

Accordingly, if domination is not limited to its structural dimension, then claims of authenticity are not limited to their political purposes—

that is, directed toward achieving a specific goal—but also are related to affects through which people attempt to make sense of their world and their position in it (Warren and Jackson 2002, 10). Quichuas' culture and identity are not simply fluid and ever-changing, but have an affective and situated component, expressed, for example, in the materiality of "traditional" clothing in the celebration of the harvest festival in Tixán (which I analyze in chapter 6). What makes the clothing traditional or "authentically" indigenous in that context is less a disembodied and monolithic notion of culture and identity than a "dressed" history engraved in the family histories of those who continued to wear such clothing in different moments and circumstances of their own lives. In my analysis of cultural politics in Tixán, rather than rendering identity as constantly reinvented, redefined, fluid, and reshaped according to the circumstances, I analyze claims of cultural "authenticity" as affective practices that go beyond their political dimension. Clothing in the context of a political struggle foregrounding ethnic identity connects to personal histories, awakens feelings of familiarity and belonging, and functions as a reminder of cultural as well as human integrity that goes beyond the institutionalized discourse of empowerment as produced by the Inca Atahualpa. The "apolitical" clothing of the past thus becomes political and relevant to the individual and collective sense of self for people who identify themselves as indigenous today.

At issue, therefore, is to understand the contexts and conditions in which claims of authenticity become meaningful or contested and lead people and collectivities to make political choices. Similarly, deconstructive analyses of identity politics also limit our understanding of the elements that prompt people to mobilize, manifest, and protest. As cogently argued by Elias Canetti (1984), collective action is powerful not only because of the morality and consistency of political discourses, but also because of the physical and emotional resonances of such action. Forms of physical contact with strangers that one might avoid when traveling on a bus become fundamental when they occur in a crowd unified by a common goal (Canetti 1984, 15–16). Marching together in the streets can be exciting and invigorating. Indigenous people protesting in the streets of Ecuador in the 1990 uprising vividly addressed this component: "It was like a dream, all together, we were strong, everybody with ponchos and hats, *reeeeed* [red]!" (in León 1994, 34).[24] In the context of the harvest festival in Tixán for example, deconstructing the elements that are assembled together in a festival to represent indigeneity does not necessarily explain what prompts participants to join the festive dancing, singing, or competitions. Beyond the manifest politicization of their identity, people are motivated to participate by the social and affective aspect of the celebration, the specific joy of the celebration, and the participants' experiences of sharing, showing off, and feeling creative and alive. An analytical perspective that focuses on the politicization of indigenous identity in its intertwining of political actions and the everyday sheds light on elements that have the potential to motivate individuals and collectivities to engage in or withdraw from political action. In some circumstances it is the political reification or essentializing of elements that is considered the "authentic" component of an identity and culture that motivates individuals as well as collectivities to act and mobilize.

The emphasis on "structure of feelings" and political struggle also helps to clarify the discourse of those who are identified as and act in the position of political leaders. Studies of indigenous politics and identity in Latin America have mostly focused on leaders and activists who have thought of indigenous identity from their subject positions as formally educated and trained activists (see Pallares 2002; Sawyer 2004; Rappaport 2005; Kay Warren 1998). In her cogent discussion of the role of Nasa indigenous intelligentsia in Colombia, Rappaport draws on Du Bois's notion of double consciousness in order to explain the position of such leaders, who see themselves as frontier individuals affectively placed between two cultural universes and functioning as mediators. Political leaders always occupy a position that is somehow at the frontier. Yet the notion of frontier is relational, since the position of mediation it implies varies according to the specificity of the spheres with which leaders intersect. Nasa intellectuals' analysis of their identity is complex and nuanced since it reflects their own predicament of belonging. Their analysis also addresses different interlocutors—the indigenous people of the communities, state and NGOs representatives, and a heterogeneous crowd of *colaboradores*—and the way those actors perceive them as different, more "modern" and emancipated than rural indigenous inhabitants.

The case I analyze in this volume presents a different perspective, that of grassroots activists, the vast majority of whom have not had more than primary education, and who are mostly self-trained in political activism. They belong to a generation who did not experience the intervention of the first indigenous national coalition, the Federation of Ecuadorian Indians (FEI), or of any other union, and largely learned about the conundrums of activism by evoking and reinterpreting the legacy of the native *cabecillas* (political leaders) of earlier times.[25] Such re-evocation represents to grassroots activists the path to the political continuity of their struggle locally, as well as the acknowledgment of its translocal dimension.

I have examined elsewhere the extent to which the difference in the political discourses, strategies, and actions of indigenous female leaders relates to the specific challenges that both grassroots and national leaders face in exercising their leadership (Cervone 2002). Similarly, the Inca Atahualpa leaders' discourse on justice, political change, and indigenous culture responds to the specific environment in which they operate and therefore participates in those narratives that are intelligible to their direct interlocutors. These grassroots leaders remain strongly tied to the lived experience of domination posed by the local distribution of power and resources and to local networks of social relations. They can still be considered to occupy a position at the frontier when compared to indigenous commoners since they interact with the nonindigenous world and negotiate for resources on behalf of their affiliated communities. Yet, in these interactions, nonindigenous people do not perceive these grassroots leaders as being different or more "modern" than the rest of the local indigenous population. In the midst of different narratives on indigenous identity and on the place of indigenous people in politics and the national economy, grassroots leaders therefore share a subject position that is similar to the subject position of other local Quichuas, all of whom nonindigenous people view in terms of the brutish Indian stereotype. These indigenous leaders share the same lived experience of domination with the rest of the indigenous population. Thus, their subject position does not involve the mediation of different cultural universes, but rather the revalorization of the most immediate evidence of their identity.

As a result, in their representation of indigeneity—that is, in their application of *derecho propio* (literally, "our own law") and in their ritual display of Quichua identity—the leaders of the Inca Atahualpa do not reproduce the same complexity and heterogeneity of and about indigenous identity that is found in the discourse of national or urbanized indigenous leaders. Yet they often capitalize on hegemonic notions of modernity and indigenous identity. For example, they understand modernity as linked to degrees of literacy and to a more general notion of technical ability—"we know how to . . . (read, write, control crime, make profits, progress)"—while their representation of indigenous identity relates to images of traditional authenticity that become almost folkloric, such as the display of indigeneity during the harvest festival. This apparent simplification is not to be understood as a lack of sophistication, but rather as a communicative choice in the production of their political discourse that responds to a specific asymmetric interethnic context.

Contextualizing Indigenous Politics

Tixán is a rural parish in the canton of Alausí, in Chimborazo Province. Its capital is a small town in the Ecuadorian Andes situated 2,900 meters above sea level and surrounded by two Andean ranges, the western and the eastern *cordilleras*. According to the 2001 census, the majority of the 9,203 inhabitants of Tixán parish live in the surrounding mountains.[26] Rural inhabitants are divided among twenty-nine communities and four autonomous peasants' and workers' associations.[27] Although the town dwellers, tixaneños, are mostly nonindigenous, rural inhabitants are indigenous and nonindigenous farmers and peasants, either self-identified as Quichuas or known as *chagras* in the case of nonindigenous rural dwellers. The presence of chagras in the area dates to the first half of the twentieth century, when they worked either as administrators or waged peons on behalf of the local landowners.

My analysis follows both Quichuas and the Inca Atahualpa as they interact with tixaneños, chagras, local authorities, the Catholic Church, and other different social actors in order to achieve control over their lives as individuals, as communities, and as Quichuas. Historical reconstructions of the initial phase of indigenous activism nationally have focused on the northern province of Imbabura, around the figures of Tránsito Amaguaña and Dolores Cacuango, indigenous women leaders who concentrated their struggle around issues of literacy and against discrimination. However, mobilization against abuses and the exploitation of indigenous labor and land under the landed-estate regime (*hacienda*) also interested other highland and coastal provinces and eventually culminated in the agrarian reform struggle of the 1960s (see Becker 1997; Pallares 2002; Prieto 1980; Yashar 2005). In chapters 1 and 2, I present a historical account of the process of formation of modern highland societies and their hierarchies by looking at the restructuring of social relations in Tixán following the disintegration of the hacienda regime and the mobilization that led to the agrarian reform laws. I focus on the major changes in the parish follow-

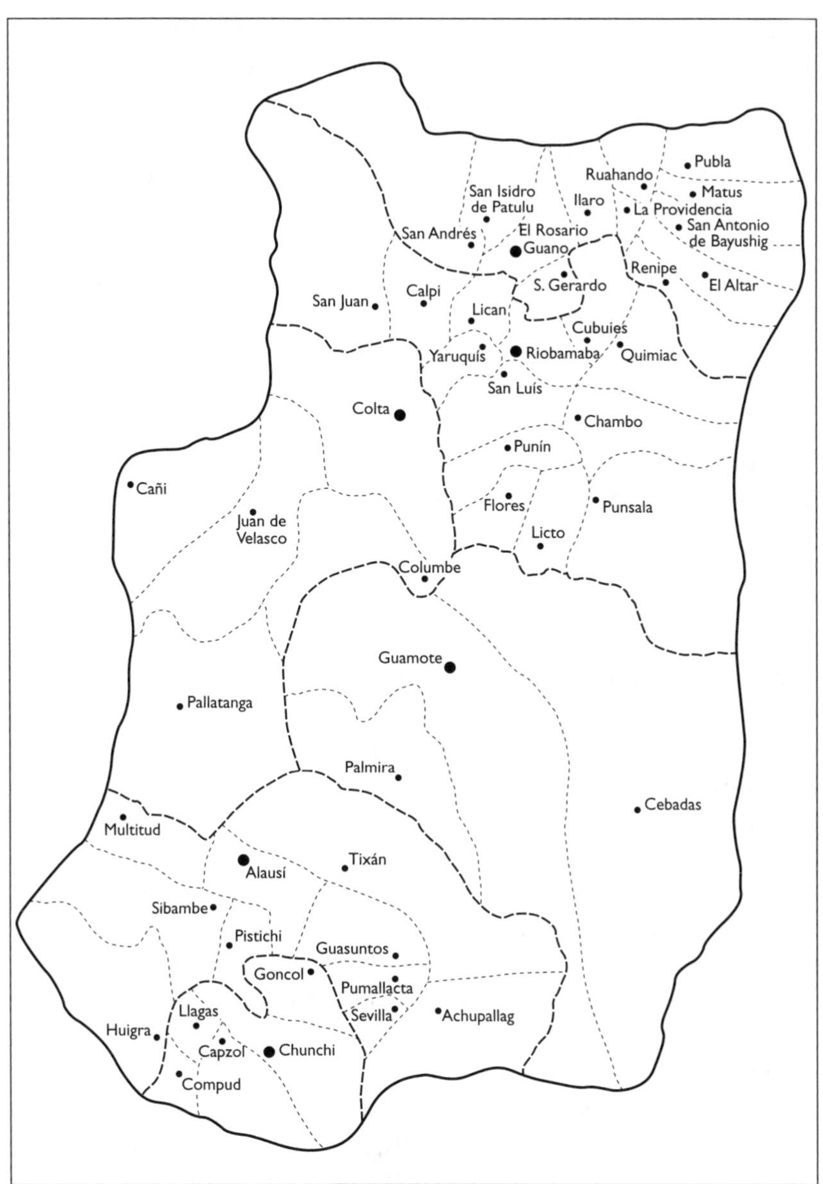

Map 2. Cantons and parishes, Chimborazo. Prepared by Bill Nelson.

ing the agrarian reform, their implications on the reconfiguration of local hierarchies, and the principles on which they were premised.

The Tixán case exemplifies the process of formation of subaltern politics in Ecuador. The partition of the local hacienda Moyocancha among the Salem family's younger generation in the late 1930s, well before the passing of the agrarian reform laws, did not alter the regime of exploitation of indigenous labor and resources. Recurrent abuses, coupled with the lack of knowledge of basic indigenous cultural codes among the young Salem landowners, fueled indigenous mobilization for land and labor rights. The mobilization continued during the 1980s throughout the province in the form of protracted land conflicts whose resolution sometimes required extralegal means. This phase led to the formation of many grassroots organizations in the province. As I analyze in greater detail in chapter 2, the role of a renewed and progressive Catholic Church was pivotal for consolidating this process of mobilization at both the local and national levels.

The permanent state of potential insurgency begun by the agrarian struggle functioned as a fertile ground for indigenous actors to fight against both new and old enemies: racism and the inequitable distribution of land and resources. In many rural towns in the Andean highlands, the slow process of land tenure readjustment that started in the 1960s with the agrarian reform laws led to a profound redefinition of the local power structure. In Tixán, the gradual extinction of the landowning regime created new opportunities for indigenous people to gain access to land, to the detriment of non-elite tixaneño families who found themselves depending increasingly on indigenous agricultural production and land. At the same time, the chagras took advantage of the agrarian reforms by adopting the community status required by the agrarian legislation in order to buy land.

The new distribution of resources also led to the creation of different conditions and spaces for interethnic interaction. Slowly but surely the local indigenous population started to exert control over its own production and fair market prices. Additionally, they gained access to another important resource, transportation, by acquiring control over the traditional practice of interethnic ritual kinship, *compadrazgo*, which had previously functioned as a mechanism to exploit indigenous labor and production. Drawing on de Certeau's analysis of everyday life tactics, I explore, in chapter 3, "so-called apolitical locations," which in the case of Tixán refer to spaces of quotidian life where local interethnic conflict takes place (de Certeau 1988; Alvarez, Dagnino, and Escobar 1998, 14). Marketplaces, shops, and a variety of communal spaces became arenas for the "art of the weak." By using their opponents' cultural and symbolic codes and behaviors as tactics that encroach on their territory, the Quichuas succeeded in temporarily reversing their "weaker" position (de Certeau 1998, 37).

The tactics of this quotidian conflict acquired greater significance after the formation of the Inca Atahualpa and the other three local indigenous organizations (ATAMZICH, General Rumiñahui, and the Federation of Achupallas), which came to represent public affirmation and consolidation of local indigenous power. A combination of the post-agrarian reform structural readjustments and the long-lasting habitus of ethnic resistance gradually led indigenous activists to gain control over power and resources at the local level. Within the general framework of the politicization of ethnic identity, the Inca Atahualpa gradually became the major producer of cultural identity on behalf of the local indigenous population. As I analyze in chapters 4, 5, and 6, the organization institutionalized the reshaping of ethnic identity in political, social, and cultural terms for use as a tool in local consolidation of indigenous power. In chapter 4, I analyze the processes of affirmation and consolidation of the Inca Atahualpa. The organization's role as mediator of land conflicts allowed the Inca Atahualpa not only to become the canton's most powerful organization, but also to define the parameters for a new modern indigenous leadership. In chapter 5, I further examine the Inca Atahualpa's political performance, analyzing the extent to which its role as justice maker at the parish level challenged state sovereignty by "invading" the jurisdiction of state authorities. The Inca Atahualpa became a powerful alternative to the local authorities for the resolution of local conflicts for indigenous and non-elite tixaneños alike. However, the controversial and contradictory applications of customary rights (derecho propio) analyzed in chapter 5 underscore the intricacies of ethnic politicization in multicultural societies. The examination of the Inca Atahualpa's political strategies also discloses the implications of cultural distinctiveness for political practice and the risks of fragmentation. The cultural and ethnic distinctions that led to the formation of the Inca Atahualpa and the ATAMZICH defined a state of intraethnic competition in which four local organizations fought for power and control. On the occasion discussed in chapter 5, the administration of indigenous justice became the arena for the articulation of this power struggle involving all four indigenous organizations. In this context, redundant punishment to address the robbery of a tractor violated principles that many local and national indigenous activists regard as foundations of their justice system.

The case study highlights complexities related to the institutionalization of indigenous politics. The contradictions evinced resemble those in western Mexico, analyzed by Guillermo de la Peña. The redundant punishment in this case contradicted basic principles of human rights, the same principles that the indigenous movement nationally claims as the framework of its own quest for recognition. The difference is that in the Tixán case the infringement of those rights was not for safeguarding the integrity of the community. It was, rather, a consequence of the power struggle among competing grassroots organizations that risked discrediting their political legitimacy. The discussion of indigenous justice here highlights the question of the extent to which grassroots organizations can contribute to the democratization of the local power structure despite interorganizational rivalries.

The harvest festival discussed in chapter 6 allows investigation of the semantics of cultural politics. Although the festival in its current form is a recent creation that involves several indigenous communities, activists, and the Catholic Church, it incorporates elements of indigenous harvest practices and celebrations that have been transmitted from generation to generation in different local ethnic groups. With the Inca Atahualpa gradually assuming leadership in the festival's organization, indigenous practices became exemplary of the local *costumbre indígena* (indigenous custom) and were publicly performed in the town square for an audience of tixaneños, local and provincial authorities, representatives of NGOs, and indigenous guests from other parishes. At the intersection of culture and power, the display of indigenous custom not only affirms cultural distinctiveness; as a concrete political body exercising power, the Inca Atahualpa also adopts strategies and discourses that prioritize its own reproduction as an institution of power, beyond the achievement of its major cause, that is, the well-being of the affiliated communities and their development. Music, songs, costumes, and other performances become a way of celebrating not only the empowerment of the local Quichuas, but also the organization that empowered them. Thus, the harvest festival becomes an act celebrating the harvest, local indigenous culture, and the Inca Atahualpa at large.

The intervention of the Inca Atahualpa in the production of Quichua identity highlights the extent to which indigenous culture is understood as a political project rather than as an immutable essence. The politicization of culture allowed Quichuas in Tixán to redefine power relations and, at a more symbolic level, to transform the hegemonic and racist imagery that portrayed Indians as brutish, ignorant, and premodern. Inclusion and exclusion are simultaneously at work here. If exclusiveness is constructed around "essentialized" notions of costumbre indígena as represented in the harvest festival, in areas such as the administration of justice, derecho propio has given opportunities to nonindigenous people to escape the network of local elites and their elitist politics. Therefore, the production of cultural and ethnic identities in this case is not only related to culture, but also to social relations and to the process of creation of new political subjects.

The political practice of a grassroots organization such as the Inca Atahualpa must be contextualized within the national process of ethnic mobilization. Whatever the specific motivations leading to the formation of the Inca Atahualpa, the organization incorporated the demands formulated nationally by the indigenous movement and adapted them to its local reality. While integrating my analysis of the local political struggle, in chapter 7 I present a reconstruction of the process of mobilization at the national level and highlight the many challenges that the indigenous movement faces in relation to larger dimensions of conflict involving national and transnational forces. The clash between the constitutional recognition of indigenous rights, in 1998, and the adoption of neoliberal economic measures, which further impoverished indigenous and nonindigenous marginal sectors, reveals the ambiguities and contradictions of official multicultural rhetoric and projects. In this context the recognition of indigenous rights appears to be instrumental to the neoliberal restructuring of state functions, rather than derived from an attempt to democratize Ecuadorian society and its power structure. Although multicultural recognition represents an accomplishment of historical proportions for the indigenous movement, indigenous citizens have still had to struggle against a society that has remained profoundly undemocratic and racist.

The participation of CONAIE in the coup that overthrew the democratically elected president Jamil Mahuad, in January 2000, intensified the debate on issues of democratization and the role of the indigenous movement in that process. Unlike other collective actions organized by the indigenous movement throughout the 1990s that generated a consensus of public opinion, in the case of the attempted coup indigenous activists were publicly accused of destabilizing the country and impeding an already difficult path to national economic and political recovery.[28] Ironically, one of the colonels who led the military faction that joined the condemned coup, Lucio Gutiérrez, was elected president, in 2002.

In chapter 7 I also discuss the limitations of multicultural recognition in light of the participation of Ecuadorian indigenous activists in the Gutiérrez government (2002–2005). By August 2003, the political alliance that had been established between indigenous activists and Gutiérrez during the electoral campaign was broken. A variety of factors pushed indigenous activists to the opposition. Yet Gutiérrez's attempt to delegitimize indigenous leadership by interfering in areas in which indigenous leaders had full decision-making powers exacerbated the confrontation.

The Ecuadorian case underscores the tensions and contradictions of multiculturalism. The constitutional recognition of indigenous rights to difference formulated by many Latin American countries during the 1990s does not automatically result in enacting these rights in political practice (Van Cott 2002). Official inclusion of indigenous people and their institutions under the umbrella of multiculturalism seems to be less an indication of the maturity of Ecuadorian society and its political structure regarding issues of ethnic discrimination, and more a neoliberal political device for streamlining the public sector and public spending via decentralization. Within the framework of devolution of state functions and responsibilities to local government, opportunistic recognition of indigenous authorities is useful in areas densely populated by indigenous people. In practice, however, the latter still have to fight against attitudes and behaviors that limit, control, and undermine their political participation and the full exercise of their rights as citizens (Hale 2002; Hale 2008b).

Such multicultural ambiguities also affected the Ecuadorian indigenous movement in its capacity to formulate a new political project. Inconsistencies between the inclusiveness expressed in constitutional rhetoric and the exclusiveness of political practice made it difficult for indigenous leadership to envision a viable and diverse society and state. As self-critically expressed by the indigenous intellectual Luis Maldonado, a significant challenge for the movement is to formulate a feasible social project that can solve the country's problems: "The experience of co-governing has shown us that once we assumed the responsibility of conducting the state and governing, we did not have viable and specific projects that could lead to effective and positive resolutions of complex national problems" (Maldonado 2003). Maldonado's statement expresses the challenges facing the indigenous movement, not only to consolidate its recognition in political practice, but also to democratize Ecuadorian society.

The ambiguity of the multicultural shift in Ecuador resonates with other cases in Latin America (Hale 2008b; Hooker 2005; Van Cott 2002). Recognition of multiple social identities is not synonymous with equality among different groups. As discussed by Hale in the case of Guatemala, neoliberal multiculturalism has brought about new forms of governance according to which indigenous subjects are at once recognized and domesticated (Hale 2002; Hale 2008b, 35). As I argue in chapter 7, new multicultural governance also meant the establishment of a hierarchy of cultures and knowledge systems according to which the "national" one is left unquestioned. The challenges facing indigenous activism, therefore, are not simplistically related to internal tensions within the movement. It is necessary to contextualize these tensions within a broader analytical framework in order to understand how and in what circumstances tensions, contradictions, and divergences undermine and advance indigenous politics.

My analysis of indigenous politics underscores the different faces and phases of indigenous struggle for equality, and therefore points to different manifestations of power contention. I have therefore intercalated the sequence of the chapters with quotes that introduce different types of tactics in power struggles and the everyday (as seen by Canetti), which evocatively suggest the changing subject position and characteristics of the parties involved in the struggle.

Engaging Methodology

Along with many colleagues who have been involved in the study of indigenous struggle in Latin America, I, too, have come to embrace and defend a form of methodology and anthropological practice that I define in general terms as politically engaged.[29] My positioning is a response founded on my personal formation and my fieldwork experience.

When I was about to start my fieldwork in Tixán, another foreign anthropologist already had begun research in the same area, on a comparative study of land tenure in Ecuador and Peru. Both of our research proposals received the requisite approval by the Inca Atahualpa. A few months later, I learned from a friend collaborating with the Inca Atahualpa on behalf of an Ecuadorian NGO that the other anthropologist had left at the request of the leaders of the organization, who had found out that the topic under study was not land tenure but indigenous movements. The president of the Inca Atahualpa at that time informed me that I need not worry, but at the same time he made sure that I knew he had questioned the Inca Atahualpa's relationship with foreign researchers: "These gringos still believe they can do what they please. Well, now we are the ones who decide what we want them to do" (M. P., 1992).

Studying processes of politicization of ethnicity poses serious methodological and ethical dilemmas for researchers by renewing past unresolved debates about the conditions of production of scientific knowledge and its impact on society (Cervone 2007; Hale 2008a; Speed 2008a). As I have analyzed elsewhere in greater detail, despite the existence of a significant body of literature that exploded the fiction of value-free, detached research practice in social science, this debate reappeared at the end of the 1990s with the proposition that engagement in anthropological practice cannot lead to "excellence" (Gross and Plattner 2002). Discarded as social work or advocacy, rather than representing excellence in anthropology, political engagement was portrayed as the opposite of "objectivity" and therefore as biased and subjective rather than scientific. At stake here is not the dichotomy objective versus subjective, and the related values attached to them, but definition of objectivity itself. Engaged anthropology is objective insofar as it exhibits methodological rigor rather than an abstract and self-contained notion of empirical "Truth" (Cervone 2007; Hale 2008a; Fabian 2001).

This debate has to be understood as situated and mostly rooted in the North American and European anthropological community. Thus they respond to preoccupations and debates as they emerge in milieus in which anthropology, situated mostly as an academic discipline, often has been deemed irreconcilable with political engagement and even more so with activism. However, since the 1970s, in the context of the growing power of dictatorships in Latin America, social scientists in the region have positioned themselves politically. Most of them have done so by defending the need to decolonize their disciplines and to fight for justice and democracy in their countries. Such commitment has endured, taking different methodological forms known as action research or participatory research. It has become common for social scientists in Latin America to fill a range of roles—as academics, activists, public intellectuals, NGO members—

without feeling that any of them jeopardize their legitimacy as producers of knowledge.

During my eight years in Ecuador, I came to consider my engagement inevitable. As a member of the North American anthropological community, like many of my colleagues I felt compelled not only to defend knowledge produced by engaged forms of anthropological practice, but also to address the conditions that led us to embrace engagement versus detachment in our profession. What does engagement means in anthropological practice? Although the defense of engagement in anthropological practice originated in the debate about the need to decolonialize the discipline (Asad 1973; Berreman, Gjessing, and Gough 1968; Stavenhagen 1971), I have argued elsewhere that this is not necessarily or exclusively a form of anthropological inquiry based on a preexisting commitment to political activism (activist anthropology as formulated in Hale 2001). It is a form of inquiry that often is the result of a longer process of fieldwork in which anthropologists and study communities gradually build a mutual relationship of trust and forge a common political understanding. In the course of such interactions members of the study community become research partners rather than informants; research topics and methodologies are discussed and formulated collaboratively.

Although the different forms of political engagement in anthropology (activism, collaborative, participatory, etc.) have in common the repositioning of the anthropologist and the study community as research partners who develop research and produce knowledge together and in support of social justice, there is no one formula for political engagement. My case, for example, resonates more with the path followed by Gustafson than with the one described by Speed (2008b). Unlike Speed's commitment, which stemmed from a long personal history of political activism, my own commitment resulted from a combination of the political views I had formed in the effervescent political environment to which I was exposed as a high-school student in the late 1970s in Italy and the ethical questions raised in my discipline when I was a graduate student in the early 1990s, a period when debates on subjectivity and reflexivity were questioning anthropological "Truth" and methodologies. Although I arrived in the field laden with open-ended questions and uncertainties, once I was there it quickly became clear, as M. P.'s statement blatantly indicates, that a neutral or detached research practice involving indigenous societies would be both unethical and epistemologically unsustainable.

Undertaking fieldwork in Tixán was not simply a matter of asking for approval, but an occasion for acting on the understanding that research topics need to serve the interests of the community involved in the project. Without this previous agreement, researchers would not be permitted access to data key to understanding the processes under study. Engagement, then, became for me not only necessary but inevitable, if "excellence" in anthropology were to be achieved. This implies a drastic change in the subject position of the researcher in his or her research practice. Research practice is now under the other's gaze, constantly scrutinized by the study community (Warren and Jackson 2002).

During my two years of fieldwork in Tixán, I gradually established a relationship of mutual trust and collaboration with the Inca Atahualpa and other indigenous activists with whom I worked.[30] Many complex dynamics shaped these relationships. The legacy of decades of anthropological practice that objectified indigenous people still percolates in imageries and discourses of fieldwork practice. After I had been in Tixán for over one year, everybody in town and in the communities of the area knew who I was—*compañera* or *comrade* to some, *gringa* or *gringuita* to others.[31] Less commonly known or understood by people not directly involved in my research project was what exactly I was doing there. Yet echoes of my collaboration with the Inca Atahualpa in an oral-history project on the formation of the organization had reached the communities of the ATAMZICH.

One of the leaders of that organization at the time asked my NGO friend if he knew anybody who could help them prepare a history of their organization. When my friend told him that I was an anthropologist working on this same topic with the Inca Atahualpa, his interlocutor, rather puzzled, replied: "Really? I thought gringa anthropologists studied the sex [*sic*] of the Indians." Aside from this highly sexualized perception of the relationship between a female anthropologist and her supposed male object of study, possibly fueled by rumors about romantic interactions between gringa researchers and indigenous national activists, the comment underscores the perception of a relationship that is imposed on indigenous subjects, regardless of the possible responses to the imposition. The sexual innuendo of the comment points to the breach of intimacy as perceived by those who have been denied the right to decide what knowledge about themselves—if any at all—is produced.

Misinformation or simple denial are common responses to this form of symbolic aggression and are a control mechanism over unwanted disclosure of knowledge. I believe that even if it does not eliminate this type of negative response, engagement leads to more unambiguous agreement about the boundaries that may or may not be crossed. As Craig Calhoun declares, "activist scholarship is a matter of critique not of advocacy" (in Hale 2008a, xxv). In a more general sense, therefore, engaged forms of anthropological practice have questioned the power imbalance inherent in modernist fieldwork practices by trying to redefine the outsider-insider dichotomy. These two dimensions, expressed in my situation by the terms *gringa* and *compañera*, are not fixed categories, but identities that can be negotiated in the field. By the end of my fieldwork, my allegiances were clear, and it had become known that I had not been studying the "sex of the Indians" (read either as indigenous sexual habits or otherwise). I did not engage in any personal relationship with any indigenous man, and the fact that I had become a compañera did not erase my identity as a foreigner, which continued to give rise to jokes, laughter, and, in isolated cases, mistrust.

Thus, redefining the power relations implicit in engaged forms of anthropological practice is not an uncomplicated task. The balance of power in fieldwork practice can only be negotiated at the level of individual and interpersonal relationships. Such relationships are rewarding yet rarely straightforward encounters between individuals who may or may not share common ideals and interests. The individual dimension of this experience should not create an illusion of equality in anthropological practice; it does not erase the inequalities that characterize relationships between the societies anthropologists represent and those they work in. During my second year in Tixán, I worked in close contact with other colaboradores (nonindigenous supporters) (see Rappaport 2005, 55–82). Javier worked with the Inca on behalf of the Ecuadorian NGO Center for Studies and Social Diffusion (CEDIS) based in Quito. Alfonso was an agronomy student at the Polytechnic in Riobamba, and Luc and Ameliè were two Canadian volunteers, who worked respectively on irrigation-systems design and on early childhood education. All of us comprised what the leaders of the Inca came to term as the *equipo técnico* (technical team). As foreigners living in Tixán, Luc, Amelìè, and I were reminded by the local people on many different occasions of our position as privileged citizens from rich countries. In somewhat simplistic yet still powerful terms, the hierarchies of the world order were demonstrated not only in obvious economic differences, but also more profoundly in the ease of our international travel compared to the legal impediments of visa requirements that make persons from developing countries second- and third-class world citizens.

Engagement in anthropology also poses dilemmas for knowledge production. Engaged anthropology seems to be trapped by its own predicament of split loyalties: scientific "excellence" on the one side, and political and ethical commitment on the other. One question addresses the public aspect of knowledge production: how do we render the complexity of the political process we study while making sure that the critical information we may disclose is not used against the people we work with?[32] The question remains open, for example, about the impacts on the political legitimacy of indigenous movements when deconstructing claims to cultural authenticity. The argument that such claims in indigenous political discourse are problematic because identities are not immutable essences can also disempower indigenous movements (Friedman 1994; Thomas 1994).

For example, in the early 1990s in Ecuador, the landowning sector started to push toward revitalizing the land market. The main target of their efforts was indigenous land, since its inalienable and indivisible nature as defined by law made it unsuitable for the land market. By borrowing from social-science discourses and methodologies, the powerful landowning lobby created the Institute of Agrarian Studies (IDEA), which sponsored research on land tenure in the highlands. This research claimed that the concept of indigenous communities and identity as being tied to collective lands was flawed, since in practice indigenous people divided their land among individuals. This "scientific" discovery was later used as ideological justification for the proposed Law of Agrarian Modernization (Ley de Modernización Agraria), which would have allowed indigenous lands to be sold on the market. Strictly speaking, IDEA researchers deconstructed the concept of an ethnic identity built on collective identity, in this case applied to collective land tenure, which is used in indigenous political discourse to legitimate access to land and agricultural resources. Heavily biased in favor of the landowning sector, in this case deconstruction of indigenous discourse attempted to delegitimize and discredit indigenous political struggle by dismantling the foundations of its cultural distinctiveness.

Another question refers to the potential conflict between political commitment and professional ethics. In his study of racial ambivalence among Ladinos in Guatemala, Hale (2008b) reveals the challenges that he faced as an activist anthropologist allied with the Mayan indigenous movement's cause when embarking on fieldwork practice with the supposed dominants. He argues that neoliberal multiculturalism, with its ambiguities, has allowed for different understandings of racial politics among Ladinos, therefore rendering their positioning toward Mayas more complex, ranging from racist prejudices to a declared commitment to cultural equality. In working with Ladinos along such a wide spectrum, Hale seems to suggest that his overt and clear positioning as a Maya supporter and the disengagement from his analysis of those voices who did not give permission to be revealed were enough to safeguard his activist stand. Yet his account reveals that political commitment in anthropological practice in circumstances like those he describes can conflict with professional ethics by establishing different ethical standards for research involving those who retain power and privileges in society. Even if anonymous, the unwilling voices of Ladinos are indeed reported. The old proposal by Rodolfo Stavenhagen (1971) to decolonialize anthropology by doing research on the "powerful" appears thus more complex than expected.

Although complicated, engagement is a form anthropological inquiry that allows for a redefinition of power relations in anthropological practice. This book is the result of my collaboration with many indigenous activists and friends. This collaboration enabled me to encounter the importance of conviviality in indigenous people's struggles in Tixán and emphasize the vitality and humanity of their struggles. This dimension of political activism highlights the extent to which quotidian victories are found not so much in the subversion of the status quo as in people's ability to make sense of their quotidian existence no matter the circumstances. This affective dimension allows people engaged in political struggle to make sense of who they are, to move ahead, to keep on struggling and to win battles, and to lose some without being defeated.

CHAPTER ONE

The Time of the Lords

The social history of a small rural town such as Tixán is emblematic of the process of formation of modern Ecuadorian highland society and its hierarchies. Tixán's social structure was profoundly shaped by the hacienda regime and later by its disintegration. The point of departure for my examination of the local development of political mobilization is, therefore, life under the landlords of the haciendas. Through the act of remembering that my questions would bring about for the elders who had lived in the haciendas, it was my intention to evoke the affective dimension that the memory of this lived experience was able to revitalize, extending beyond a descriptive narration of life and work in the hacienda. What was left of the complexity of this human experience, which I already knew (from my readings and hearsay) had been marked by exploitation and abuse? What was the affective response that allowed the past, the political struggle, and the everyday to come together and make sense of the present and of the possibilities for the future?

Injustice and Resilience

Taita Xavier Buñay claimed to be over one hundred years old when I interviewed him for the first time.[1] Although there was no birth or baptismal certificate to prove this claim, he was certainly the oldest living Quichua in Tixán. He would, therefore, offer an ideal opportunity to learn about processes of change that had occurred over the previous century. With my developing Quichua, his broken Spanish, and the help of an interpreter, we engaged in a series of conversations. His words and narrations, however, differed markedly from the factual and politically informed discourse of other elders that I would interview in the course of my work. From our very first encounter, Taita Xavier declared he only wanted to talk to me about "las cositas de Dios" (God's little things), which he proudly affirmed to know well. To my question on the life in the haciendas, he first responded, "There were two men—to the white one, God said, 'I give you science,' to the indigenous one, He said, 'I give you patience.' And so the white man built the machines and the indigenous man worked the land. But then the white man wanted the indigenous man to do everything and so the indigenous man said no and stopped working the land" (Taita Xavier, 1992).[2]

Although other activists did not consider Taita Xavier as having been active in the political struggle, he was regarded as living proof of the traditional indigenous life of the past. Despite his age, he still went barefoot in his community and walked twenty miles to the market of Guamote every Thursday to beg. Some of the youngest in his community regarded him as senile and at times made fun of him for accounts that sounded nonsensical to them. Yet, in religious terms, Taita Xavier articulated the same sense of injustice and resilience that later came out in interviews with others on the same topic. *Cabecillas* (a word formerly used to identified prestigious leaders and chiefs), activists, and commoners of different generations, who had participated in different political processes, articulated their own links between the past and the present. When these otherwise diachronic voices are connected, their past and present experiences converge in one common perception—that of injustice and resilience. The understanding of what constitutes an injustice is closely related to the lived experience of the speaker and therefore associated with different moral codes and social relationships. Taita Xavier applied a mixture of Catholicism and indigenous religious beliefs to make sense of his world. In his words, the breach came when the white man refused to comply with the destiny assigned by God, and this disobedience was met by the disobedience of the indigenous man, who in turn refused to keep doing what he was supposed to. This response was motivated by the injustice of being assigned tasks that did not correspond to his duty by the white man, who pretended to have attributes of God.

The Almighty Patrones

At the beginning of the twentieth century, two large landed estates on the eastern side of the cordillera and one estate on the western slopes defined the local economic and social landscape. On the eastern side, the Aña

Chaupiloma Moyocancha estate belonged to the Salem family, a powerful family of uncertain origins; the Zula estate extended to the adjacent parish of Achupallas and was owned by the diocese of Riobamba. On the western side was the hacienda Galte-Tipín, which belonged to the Borja family. Following independence at the beginning of the twentieth century, the liberals expropriated all properties owned by the Catholic Church. All church estates were transformed into state properties, Asistencia Pública (Public Assistance), and were rented to individuals, *arrendatarios*. Being a church property, Zula was expropriated by the state and in 1969 was granted to different indigenous communities, whereas the other two haciendas remained in the hands of the powerful Salem and Borja families until the agrarian reform. I focus here mainly on the hacienda Moyocancha, since the Salem family dominated the political and economic life of the parish until the second agrarian reform, in 1973. However, the local agrarian struggle was initiated by the peons of Galte-Tipín.

The internal relations that regulated labor within the haciendas were no different from the type of precapitalist relations existing in other highland haciendas in the Andean region. Indigenous families who lived on Moyocancha land were considered part of the estate. Indigenous workers received no compensation for domestic (*huasicamía*), agricultural, and pastoral (*huagracamía*) work, except for a small plot of land, called *huasipungo*, whose production was meant for their household subsistence. One of the sons of an indigenous peon from the Salem's hacienda remembered: "The owner made my dad work from Monday to Saturday from seven in the morning to five in the afternoon. And only gave a glass of *trago* [sugarcane alcohol], no food. Sometimes he would throw the workers five cents [*reales*]" (Taita Anselmo Estrada, 1993). Another common source of unpaid labor was provided by the *arrimados* (literally, "stuck on") and levied on *huasipungueros*' extended family members, who came to the hacienda from other areas in search of work. Landowners demanded this unpaid labor in exchange for permission to stay on the hacienda. However, the inhabitants of the *anejos* in the high plateau of the *páramo* land, which were not included in the perimeter of the hacienda, were said to be "free," meaning that their relationship to the hacienda was regulated not by access to cultivable land, but by access to other resources, such as pasture, water, and wood located on an estate's land.[3] Known as *sitiajeros* and *yanaperos*, such "free" indigenous workers from the sector called today Pachamama worked for the Salem family in exchange for pasturing herds and gathering water or wood on Moyocancha.[4]

During the post-independence period, many large estates in Ecuador were given or sold to foreigners in recognition of their service during the war or postwar reconstruction.[5] Moyocancha may be one such case. I was unable to find detailed documentation regarding the origin of Moyocancha, and the oral accounts I collected are at times discrepant. Townsfolk said that the land, over 10,000 hectares, previously belonged to a foreign gentleman from Quito, whose name nobody seemed to remember. This detail is confirmed in the accounts of several indigenous elders, who identified the first owner as "Zambrano" and said he was not Ecuadorian. The townsfolk version narrates that when the first owner (Zambrano) was on his deathbed, the *mayordomo* (field foreman) of the hacienda, Julio César Salem, of Colombian descent, paid a lawyer to prepare a false will, stating that the landlord had left the property to his faithful mayordomo in gratitude for his service. According to Taita Xavier Buñay, however, Julio César Salem had married Zambrano's daughter, María and thereby inherited the property.

On 7 January 1935 Julio César Salem divided his estate among his legitimate offspring, four daughters and one son.[6] The partition of the hacienda did not signify for the related anejos anything more than a change of landlord, since it did not modify the labor regime; the huasipungaje remained along with the system of yanapería and sitiaje. Indigenous peons would fight later against these five haciendas—La Pacífica, of Pacífica Salem de Polanco; Moyocancha, of Rosa Mathilde Salem de Gallegos; San Carlos, of Mercedes Salem, widow of Polanco; La Ermita, of Julia Salem, widow of Banderas; and Santa Lucila and Pachamama, of Julio Teodoro Salem.[7] Each hacienda was a law unto itself, where relations of asymmetrical exchange varied with the inclinations of the landlord and his or her nature, whether kind and generous or brutal and greedy (see Guerrero 1991b). Some elders, for example, narrated that in the hacienda of Pacífica Salem, they could resort to sharecropping in addition to the huasipungo. Taita L. B., from the community of Pachagsí, identified sharecropping as the principal labor arrangement for the people of that anejo.

Although mingled with nostalgic evocations resembling the "well-fed herds, good production of grains and the splendour of the festivals in the hacienda times" mentioned by Carola Lentz, exploitation and abuse characterized the prevailing memory of the hacienda system among the Quichuas I talked with in Tixán (Lentz 1986, 191). When remembering the *patrones timpu* (time of the lords), all of the elders whom I interviewed described the various forms of mistreatment they had suffered at the hand of hacienda owners and administrators. Taita Anselmo Estrada grew up in the Pishillig sector under the Salem family with the specter of such abuse: "With clubs, with whips, with sticks, the patrón treated the people, this is how the rich treated the poor. The patrones did not give food, did not pay, they mistreated the poor indigenous workers such as my father" (Taita Anselmo Estrada, 1993).

In addition to engaging in physical abuse and labor exploitation, some landlords and hacienda administrators took advantage of their huasipungueros' and workers' harvests and produce. One of the key figures in the reconstruction of this period was Taita Pedro Marcatoma, a former huasipunguero from Galte-Tipín, who became one of the most respected leaders of the area including Tixán. When I was seeking elders to interview, many suggested that he would be the perfect person to talk with about the haciendas and agrarian struggle. From direct experience, Taita Pedro remembered: "The patrones mistreated me, beating me, blaming me, charging me: when we counted the harvest they said it was missing, grain was missing and charged and blamed us for stealing and so they charged us and took away our grain. . . . At Carnival they said we had to salute the patrones and had to give them a chicken, at least three or four guinea pigs and so then they would give us a small glass of trago or a small plate of food" (Taita Pedro Marcatoma, 1992). Even those involved in sharecropping were often subjected to the greed and abuse of field foremen and administrators. Taita R. L. worked mostly as a sharecropper, as did many people from the community of Pachagsí, formerly part of a Salem property. As he recalled, "The *mayordomos* were really bad, beating up, cursing, kicking. They did not give us what we were to have of the harvest, the portion we should have had and if I were to say something they would beat us up and blame us and insult us, 'Indian liar, beast.' They didn't give any food, sometimes only a handful of tasteless barley for the whole day and nothing, nothing else" (Taita R. L., 1992).

The annexation of Pachamama Chico is another example of the abuse by the all-powerful *terratenientes*, who, this time in the person of Julio Teodoro Salem, used violence and coercion to impose control over indigenous lands. This specific abuse is engraved in the popular memory of both Quichuas and Tixán dwellers. According to various people, Julio Teodoro arrived "*bravísimo*" (furiously) in the Pachamama sector on his horse, accompanied by his men. Taita Espiritu Vargas remembered that vividly. As a highly respected cabecilla of the Pachamama sector, he knew well all of Julio Teodoro's vexations: "Coming one day with other *mishus*, armed, shooting in the air he said those lands were his, *carajo*" (Taita Espiritu Vargas, 1992). The de facto usurped lands were later transformed into a legitimately owned property. Of the two communities known today as Pachamama Chico and Pachamama Grande, the former became part of the hacienda, while the latter was under a regime of sitiaje.[8]

The daily life of the Quichua population of the parish revolved around the hacienda. Farming, cattle and sheep raising, and domestic service, the huasicamía, constituted the huasipungueros' basic socioeconomic activities. A former huasipunguero from La Pacífica explained, "Everybody worked for the patron for free, like slaves. My wife served in his house and my children helped with the animals. I worked from four in the morning till eight at night on the patron's lands. If I don't go, 'lazy,' they say and beat [me] up" (Taita G. G., 1992). In the case of sitiajeros and yanaperos, the bond with the hacienda was less omnipresent, although it remained vital for their economic stability.

The subsistence requirements of households at that time devoted only a little surplus production to the market. By bartering with members of their extended families, indigenous peasants were able to acquire the agricultural surplus of other ecological niches such as the lower valleys, where corn could be cultivated.[9] Generally, in order to gain access to more resources, especially for ritual occasions such as weddings, funerals, and festivals, the huasipungueros and the arrimados asked for *socorros* (subsistence doles), a kind of symbolic loan in goods that the peons received from the landowner. They owed nothing in an immediate sense, yet they were often tied to the hacienda for life in order to avoid imprisonment for debt. Known nationally as the *concertaje* system, this permanent state of indebtedness guaranteed on the one hand the availability of labor for the landowner and, on the other, the fulfillment of traditional ritual obligations for the peons.[10]

Gathered in the smoky communal house of Pachamama Chico, five elders from various communities reminisced about the patrones timpu. Unlike the interviews I had conducted with individual elders in their community, this collective remembering induced an outflow of memories made more vivid by the act of sharing them. This was the first occasion on which I heard discussion of the distribution of socorros in the area. Even if it was not always easy to reach agreement on the details of how and when, they agreed on the fact that it was customary for the mayordomos to summon the peons to the yard of the hacienda mansion every two weeks and to distribute socorros (potatoes or barley) to those who asked for it. However, such "generosity" was not always forthcoming. Taita M. G., a former huasipunguero from the hacienda La Pacífica, lamented that the new Gallegos landowners had started to refuse socorros to their workers: "Those Gallegos were tight-fisted. They would give nothing." Taita M. G.'s remark sparked immediate response among the other former huasipungueros, all of whom expressed similar complaints, usually referring to the landlords they had had immediately prior to the agrarian reform, younger landlords anxious to make their farming more profitable. The new landowning generation was frequently accused of ignoring customary rights (Clark 1992, 29). In order to reduce expenditures and control production, the new landowners ignored the obligation of generosity epitomized by socorros under the hacienda regime of unequal reciprocity. Moreover, according to the five elders, not all terratenientes of the past had been "generous." Taita Pedro Marcatoma emphatically lamented the lack of generosity of the Galte-Tipín landlord Luis Borja: "The patron did not give anything. If we asked, he gave nothing. 'Abusive,' he said to us, 'you already are taking my land and many things.' He said, 'What do you have to do with us?' . . . Some other patrones they gave, they gave socorros as they called them, yes, some rational patrones gave that, but not our patrones here in Tipín, they gave nothing" (1992). Such a lack of generosity, which Taita Pedro considered a form of irrational behavior, rendered the abuse and exploitation even more unbearable. And it was the peons of Galte-Tipín who, under the leadership of Ambrosio Laso, initiated agrarian struggle throughout the area, including Tixán.

In terms of ethnic administration, the terrateniente, the parish priest, and the *teniente político* (parish civil officer) constituted the "trilogy of power" of the hacienda regime (Sylva 1986). They publicly legitimized the internal power structure of the Quichua world. In Tixán, the landowner appointed indigenous authorities within the hacienda: the *alcaldes* and the *mayorales* were the indigenous authorities, the former being in charge of the administration of justice in the anejos, the latter being a hacienda employee who supervised the workers, especially during sowing and harvesting season. Taita A. V. explained to me how that worked. Although not a huasipunguero, Taita A. V. was appointed mayoral in the hacienda San Carlos under Mercedes Salem: "Alcalde, mayoral, mayordomos, that's what existed then but out of the will of the patrón and against us, the *naturales* [natives]. I was mayoral. Mayorales gave orders to the people, the harvest, tending the potatoes fields, the plowing, everything that needed to be done. The patrón gave me orders and I gave them to the workers to make them work" (Taita A. V., 1992). The priest appointed other indigenous authorities such as *regidores* (staff holders), who were responsible for organizing the festivals and rituals. The teniente político appointed the *gobernadores* from among the most prestigious *caciques* of the whole area. The gobernadores were in charge of regulating the *mitas* (forced labor) imposed on the anejos by the parish or cantonal authorities for specific tasks, such as cleaning lanes, maintaining secondary roads, and clearing irrigation channels.

Hacienda masters also violated the intimacy of indigenous life: "Masters even had laws to make the poor marry; they took one bachelor and one single woman and they locked them in a room in the hacienda and forced them to get married even without knowing each other, even without being in love" (Taita M. G., 1992).

In addition to suffering the exploitation of their land and labor, indigenous peons were also subjected to forms of physical violence. The hacienda authorities—the mayordomos, generally nonindigenous, and the mayorales, usually indigenous—were those who most often mistreated and physically harmed the workers. Sometimes the owners did not even live in the hacienda or (such as the case of La Pacífica) and hired different administrators. The mayordomos were superior to the mayorales and conveyed the landlord's orders to all the others. In a voice charged with anger, Taita A. V. recounted, "They beat us up, called us bloody Indians, *mitayos*, thieves. If we say some word, they pushed us on the floor, pulling by the hair, kicking in the mouth, on the nose, whipping like a donkey" (1992).

The words of Taita A. V. echo other accounts of extreme cruelty committed on the haciendas—a recurrent theme in Ecuadorian popular memory. Diego Bonifaz, son of the owners of the former hacienda Guachalá, in Imbabura Province, showed no reluctance to talk about the verbal and physical abuse of indigenous workers in many haciendas: "Indians could not talk, not even raising their eyes; otherwise they would face corporal punishment and beatings with whips or clubs" (1995).[11] Some haciendas were believed to have had torture chambers. In a climate permeated by punishment and violence, it is plausible that mayorales mistreated their own people in order to avoid being punished themselves: "If someone would not go to work, they called him to the hacienda house to whip him or to take some of his animals as pawn. In order to ransom the animals, one had to bring an extra peon to work. All this the mayorales would do, the same people from the anejo" (Taita G. G., 1992).

The testimony of Taita A. V. reveals many facets of life under domination. As mayoral—whether he had been abusive, he did not say—Taita A. V. got in trouble with his own people. When one of Taita A. V.'s relatives accused him of stealing, the mayordomo avenged the alleged theft: "They stole fifty-five sheep from me, beating me up, saying they were theirs, saying that 'you sell them big and buy them small, you're getting rich,' someone said from outside of La Merced. So losing respect, the same family and the same blood as my wife said I abused Polanco himself, said 'You're getting rich selling the hacienda's sheep.' It was not true; he said it out of envy" (1992).

As a consequence of this incident and from losing face, Taita A. V. was forced to leave the hacienda, which was possible because he was not a huasipunguero and thus was not indebted to the landowner. After fruitlessly looking for a living somewhere else, he came back to the hacienda: "The employee, the mayordomo, the tractor driver said, 'The patrón wants to talk with you,' so then I said, 'Good morning.' 'Good morning Andrés, why did you leave?' he said. So I said, 'Patrón, with what could I make a living, take care of my wife, get clothing? All you said was not true. [My relative] accused me, saying I was getting rich but it was not true. And so I came back" (1992). Once he had returned to the hacienda, A. V. met Ambrosio Laso, who had started a campaign to mobilize peons against landowners and their abuses, and A. V., too, organized his people against the patrón.

Among Indians, Chagras, and "Amitos"

The overwhelming power of the Salem family also informed its relationships with the local nonindigenous inhabitants. In my interviews with both indigenous people and tixaneños, Julio César, the first of the Salems, was mentioned only occasionlly, in contrast with the dominant presence of his son, Julio Teodoro, who was remembered as "The" landlord of the hacienda. His sisters, who owned vast tracts of land, were less well remembered. Julio Teodoro exemplifies the type of terratenientes rooted in the province. The landowning elite in Chimborazo consisted of powerful families who maintained their dominance by means of political connections within the state, for example as ministers, members of parliament, and judicial officers.[12] They also upheld absolute political power at the provincial level by controlling both the cantonal and parish power structures (Sylva 1986). Julio Teodoro was a member of parliament and remained in constant contact with the canton's political authorities. Everybody knew him because he was always present at village festivals, hosting the bullfights, which were highly popular. Additionally, he was remembered as a large, physically imposing character. Some elders from the town, of the same generation as Julio Teodoro, remembered having attended his banquets. With a mixture of nostalgia, admiration, fear, and disdain—recurring sentiments when Tixán townsfolk speak of Julio Teodoro—Don D. B., who was from a supposedly "good" family of the town, described him as "a big man, aggressive and powerful; he alone was capable of downing a whole leg of *hornado*" (personal communication, Tixán, 1992).[13]

The words of Alberto Borja, an illustrious writer from Chimborazo Province, portray landowners in the Tixán area as ruthless representatives of "a caste of lady-killers and brave men" (Borja 1953, 22). In Borja's works, the gatherings of these powerful landlords are characterized by a strong dose of cynicism and irony. The display of prestige and power required one to surprise, frighten, and amuse one's guests. For the powerful landlords, ridicule was a sure way of demonstrating their superiority. Their unpredictability, their ability to surprise and even to scare, made them unique in the eyes of others. They led the game.

Borja's vivid representations were powerfully validated in oral testimonies from elders of the same generation as Julio Teodoro. Many tixaneño families were wholly subordinate to the Salem family. Julio Teodoro, in particular, used his arrogance and power to dominate townspeople. According to Don A. H., Julio Teodoro once went down to the village of Tixán to invite his young friends to a party at his hacienda. To refuse would have been an insult to the host, so when the horses were ready, the invitees set out for the event. Once there, the guests were welcomed with customary hospitality: food in abundance and a lot of strong alcohol, of the highest quality. With the banquet barely over and the fire of the last *canario*, a strong drink made of sugarcane alcohol and eggs, not yet burning their stomachs and confusing their minds, charging bulls were let loose into the room, causing havoc and inducing panic among the guests, all to the hearty laughter of their diabolical host. As if to beg forgiveness, Julio Teodoro then led his guests to another room, where curtains covered the back wall. The curiosity of the guests was promptly satisfied: the curtains opened to reveal young indigenous girls, between eleven and fifteen years old, "well bathed and dolled up" for the satisfaction of the young gentlemen. Don A. H., who happened to be one of those guests, narrated the story with visible indignation. As a member of the Misión Andina of Ecuador, he had worked with indigenous people and as such he claimed to know their suffering.[14] Raising the tone of his voice during the interview, Don A. H. enacted the indignation that he had felt that night, how he had left the house without hiding his ire. The day after the banquet, he denounced the happenings to the press, which earned him the enmity of the Salem family. "Pero yo nunca les pedí disculpas" (But I never apologized for it).[15]

Violence and virility are two inextricable attributes of *gamonalismo*, past and present (see Poole 1994). Indeed, Julio Teodoro had all the qualities of a *gamonal*: arrogant and despotic, often violently imposing his overwhelming power.[16] In colloquial language, *gamonalismo* refers to a local economic and political system founded on quasi-feudal social relationships of inequality that are maintained by arbitrary and abusive force and violence (Poole 1988). Furthermore, the gamonal lives on his own terms and refuses to convert his wealth into capitalist investment. In the Ecuadorian case, Hernán Ibarra argues, *gamonal* referred, until the beginning of the twentieth century, to local functionaries, such as the parish civil officers or medium-sized landowners of peasant origin, who oppressed the Indians. After the 1930s, *gamonal* referred to aristocratic landowners (Ibarra 1992, 35).

Although Don A. H.'s indignation colors the story, the episode he narrated exemplifies the relationship between the terrateniente and the tixaneños, on the one hand, and the Quichuas on the other. Even townspeople belonging to wealthy families lived in subordination to the wealthy and all-powerful lord. Agricultural produce was sold mainly to the coast via railroad transportation. At that time, there was little land that was not controlled by the large Salem estates. Smaller properties in the sector called Pueblo Viejo, on the western side of the cordillera, were in the hands of a few families, known as the town's "good" families. By and large, many of the remaining Tixán families depended on the hacienda either as *piqueros* or as *piareros*. The former bought potato beds from the local haciendas, divided them into plots, and assigned less well-off townsfolk to harvest them. The large potatoes were kept by the piqueros, and the smaller ones were payment to the harvesters. The railway that passed through the town transported the produce of these harvests to the coastal market in Guayaquil. This trade was also a source of employment for the piareros. Using their own mules or animals hired from the Quichuas, the piareros transported the potatoes from the haciendas to the railway station.[17] The hierarchy of local families was based on their relationship with the haciendas, with the piareros ranked near the bottom, just above the chagras and the natives.

The overwhelming political power of the Salem family hindered the expansion of the good families' prestige beyond the parish. However, at the parish level, the trilogy of power of the hacienda regime included the dominant local group. Most parish civil officers were elected from among the local elite. At least within the parish perimeter, the good families always managed to assert their higher status over medium- and low-ranking families, mostly piqueros and piareros, and of course over indigenous people and chagras. The political power these good families exerted in the parish articulated with their racial and economic supremacy, with whiteness clearly defining the local ruling class: the lower the rank, the more "contaminated" the color line and the more multifaceted the identities of those called mestizos.[18] The same contempt directed at the indigenous was also directed at the chagras and poor nonindigenous people in general. The chagras, although they were not Quichuas, were poor peasants, and as such could not be admitted to the category of *blancos* (whites). As clearly expressed by Don T. G., tixaneños considered chagras to be "Indians who believe they are white" (Indios que se creen blancos). Don T. G. belonged to a family of piqueros and boasted of his family's Spanish descent, an element that constituted for him undeniable proof of his whiteness. For him, the hybrid identity of chagras as "not Indian and not white" was based on the combination of their occupation, their speech, their living conditions, and their proximity to and supposed descent from the indigenous population.

At that time, interactions between Quichuas and tixaneños were generally limited to weekend encounters and to the St. Peter and St. John festivals celebrated in June. The subsistence economy of indigenous households was guaranteed by the hacienda regime, and the town constituted the periphery of their economic activity and served as the source for their supplies. The naturales (the supposedly neutral term tixaneños often used

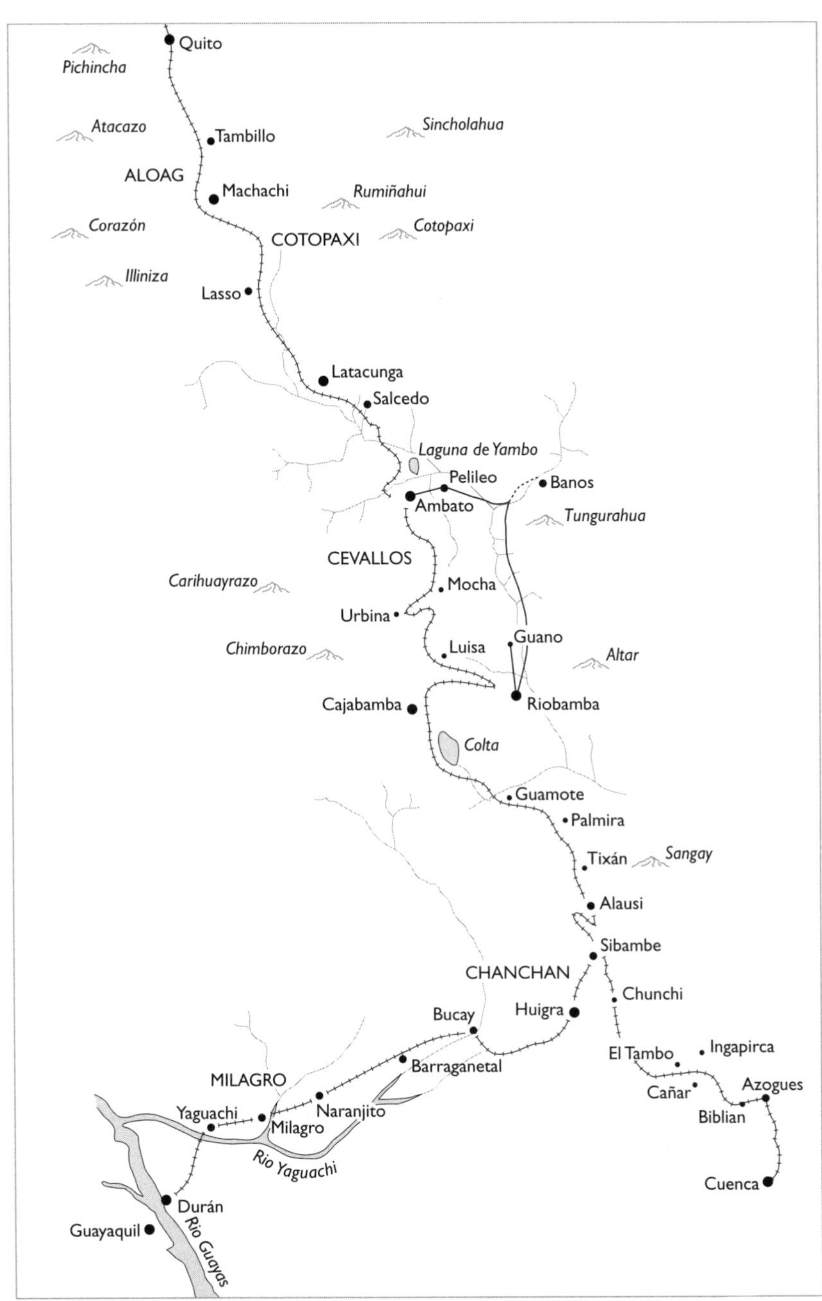

Map 3. Railroad Quito-Guayaquil. Prepared by Bill Nelson.

for the Quichuas) sold their products to the town dwellers before the actual harvest, when cash was needed, especially for purchasing animals. This system was particularly advantageous for the townsfolk, since the prices they paid before the harvest were always below market value. The only advantage for the Indians was that the system responded to their immediate need for cash, preventing them from resorting to a moneylender (*chulquero*). Even when indigenous people resisted this form of exploitation, the local power structure protected the interests of tixaneños. According to records in the archive of the Tixán parish civil office, disputes between tixaneños and Quichuas always fell in favor of the *mishu* (a derogatory term Quichuas use to refer to whites). A. L., a young activist and one of the founders of the Inca Atahualpa, considered this type of abuse to have been customary in public offices: "They [the parish civil officers] would solve problems of fights, robberies, land, and divorces. The people would always go to them because they were the appointed authority. . . . The authorities always had a grip on marginalized people, and stupid people, too; we indigenous people, we're stupid, too, this is my opinion. In truth we went bearing eggs, hens, even sheep we went to give *camaris* so they would listen. So I think that, in addition to their salary, they had camaris. If they were given a sheep, they had fifteen days of meat" (A. L., 1992).[19]

Taverns were another site for interaction and abuse. Enrique Bazante, a Communist Party activist who knew Alausí canton well, spoke passionately when remembering his work as an activist with the Ecuadorian Federation of Indians (FEI): "Tixán was the center for the distribution of booze; there were tanks of it. The Indians used to go down on Saturdays and Sundays to go shopping and go to Mass; then they got into a drinking session and paid with barley or a sheep for a liter of drink. Once they were drunk, they were robbed of everything and, when they came round, they thought they'd spent everything and got into debt for another drink. I know because I have seen it happen many times" (1993).

There were two types of taverns in the town, all owned by townsfolk: the cantinas serving the townsfolk and the *chicherías*, which sold the traditional indigenous corn beer *chicha* and were patronized only by indigenous people. Quichuas would meet relatives during their weekend visits to town in chicherías, which were infamous throughout the highlands as places where indigenous people were mistreated and abused (see Burgos 1977). The memory of the *chicha huevona* is still widespread in many highland provinces. Whether real or legendary, this term refers to a drink sold as chicha, but that in fact contained little chicha. I heard many people of different backgrounds, in cities as well as rural towns, describe chicha huevona as being made from low-quality grain, with the addition of bones and even, some said, of human excrement and other kinds of garbage, which were supposed to accelerate fermentation and increase the alcoholic content. It was understood that chicha huevona could even be toxic. Due to modernization and its emphasis on hygiene, chicherías were closed by council decree and *estancos* law beginning in the 1970s.

Some indigenous elders confirmed Bazante's claims that Indians would lose money and sometimes even property at chicherías. Taita A. V. reported, "Suddenly one, well drunk, would wake up in the morning like this, without poncho, without hat, there in the street; they would steal everything" (1992). When indigenous customers did not have enough money to continue drinking, they would become indebted to bar owners, who demanded collateral (*prendas*). According to the parish priest Father Torres many indigenous families from free anejos, such as Chalahuán, Gusniag, and Quislag, lost their land, having used it to secure loans that they could not repay.

The condition of expanded indebtedness to the townsfolk created another form of dependency, in the guise of interethnic ritual kinship of compadrazgo, usually established between two families on the occasion of a baptism, or of *padrinazgo*, in the case of a marriage. According to Father Torres, interethnic relations were usually condemned by Quichuas, who would establish endogamous networks of compadrazgo. However, indebtedness spurred some of them to look for *compadres* in the town, who could help them pay their debts. The son of D. B., Don B. B. already in his fifties when we talked, explained to me, "I have more than eighty *ahijados* (godsons). That's because, in the old days, they [the Indians] were well-disposed to their white compadres who helped them out financially. They even drank together; they would kiss your hand and offer you a drink, and if you did not accept, you were considered a bad compadre" (1993).

It is interesting that an indigenous person's need for financial support was interpreted by Don B. B. as a sign that that person was favorably disposed to the white compadres. Don B. B.'s nostalgic reconstruction of the past underscores the loss of power and prestige experienced by many tixaneño families from the 1960s on. Their sense of loss is expressed in their characterization of present-day Indians as rebellious, in contrast to the submissive attitudes they formerly exhibited in what Don B. B. and others remembered as peaceful interethnic relationships (Crespi 1981, 487). I heard many tixaneños complain about this purported change in attitude, referring to today's indigenous people as *alzamenteros* (rebellious).

Following David Theo Goldberg (1990), I define racism as a text that can be deconstructed in order to unmask and reveal the utterances of which it is composed. The Tixán case highlights the ways textual expressions of racism can be engraved in body language. As Don B. B. mentioned, *los indios* used to kiss the hands of whites as a sign of respect. Yet they were also required to avoid direct skin contact by covering their hands with their ponchos when shaking hands with whites. Some elders of the hacienda generation persisted in observing this behavioral norm of the past, greeting me and other tixaneños with poncho-covered hands. As underscored by Timothy Burke (1996) in the context of colonial Africa and by Ann Stoler (2002) in Indonesia, imperial regimes produced a racist discourse at the end of the nineteenth century that lasted through the mid-twentieth century; in this discourse, hygiene was racialized as a feature of civilization that the alleged inferior races lacked. In Ecuador, the emphasis on hygiene became pivotal in the 1930s for the modernizing state project that sought to resolve the "Indian problem" by means of education and hygiene (see Clark 1998). As the Tixán case shows, los indios were considered too dirty even to expose their hands when touching whites. Younger generations are clearly aware of the racist implication of that specific gesture. A. L. explained to me that the Inca Atahualpa worked to raise awareness (*concientizar*) of these implications among the elders.

Social and hierarchical distance was also reflected in the terms *amito* (my lord) or *patroncito* (my patron), used indiscriminately to address white people, not only the *hacendados*. Therefore, those terms did not simply refer to material property or to a labor relationship, but rather to the asymmetrical relationship between whites and Quichuas by implying an abstract possession of the person, whether or not the indigenous person in question was a white man's peon or servant.

According to the local hierarchy, poor locals and chagras also occupied the lower ranks among the nonindigenous population. The chagras were both racially and socioeconomically hybrid. As peasants, they lived in communities in the countryside and worked in direct contact with indigenous folks. They could understand and speak Quichua, even if they never used it. However, they were not huasipungueros, and they mostly worked for small local landowners. In the anejos of the eastern cordillera, in the

Pishillig area, some chagra families owned land and lived off it. They did not have much interaction with the tixaneños, as their outlets were mainly the Alausí and Guamote markets. Their relationship with Julio Teodoro Salem depended on the sitiaje regime, although, like everyone else, they were subjected to his omnipotence. The situation of the chagras of the western cordillera was notably different. They settled in the indigenous area of Sanganao, which extended as far as Pueblo Viejo and now borders the Pan-American Highway. These chagras worked as paid laborers or as sharecroppers for wealthy tixaneños landowners. Thus, they engaged in a type of patron-client relationship different than that engaged in by the indigenous peons on the haciendas.

People in town considered all chagras to be ignorant peasants of humble origin who were neither Indians nor whites. The terms that chagras used to address their employers, *señor* or *señor patrón*, generally indicated a labor relationship. Yet even when it was not directed at an actual landowner, the term *señor patrón* maintained hierarchy and difference: the señor patrón was the boss, the white master who lived in the town, whereas the chagras, although they might have had their own plots of land, were peasants.

Behavioral and speech codes reveal a state of racialized symbolic violence in Tixán, according to which the system of dominant values and the criteria imposed by local elites was apparently understood and followed by the dominated. Words like *indio*, *lluchu*, *chagra*, *mitayo*, *rocoto*, *callomicuc*, and *traposo* were used as insults in the old hacienda days, provoking quarrels even among tixaneños.[20] However, insulting terms, such as those that refer to the "dirty Indian" or to the "ignorant chagra," remain widespread and in current use across Ecuador. In Quito I often heard urban, middle-class residents use *chagra* as synonymous with "bad taste," "rural," and "of dubious aesthetic quality." One Saturday afternoon in Tixán, I was walking toward the house of A. L. on Panamericana Street, near the highway that leads to town. As was common on weekend afternoons, many of the indigenous families in Tixán gathered along this street, chatting outside of the little stores where they stopped to drink trago. On that particular Saturday afternoon, two indigenous men who were obviously drunk started to fight. In addition to using their fists, they insulted each other with slurs such as *indio* and *rocoto*. According to Frantz Fanon, the internalization of prejudice generates an inferiority complex that characterizes colonized peoples: "Every colonized people—in other words, every people in whose soul an inferiority complex has been created by the death and burial of its local cultural originality—finds itself faced with the language of the civilising nation; that is, with the culture of the mother country" (1986, 18).

In this highly racialized, hierarchical context, relationships between Quichuas and chagras were and are no less problematic and abusive. According to testimony, it would seem that squabbles and fights between the two groups have always existed. During the hacienda period, especially on the eastern cordillera, where chagras and Quichuas lived sometimes within the same space, interactions among them were often marked by mutual mistrust.[21] Despite the ability of chagras to understand and speak Quichua and their close proximity to Quichuas, from whom some of them even descended, chagras did not identify themselves as Quichuas, toward whom they seem to have adopted arrogant and often aggressive attitudes. Although outnumbered by the indigenous people, the chagras nevertheless wanted to establish power over them. Indigenous elders lamented the arrogance and aggression of chagras, who would laugh at them, harass them, and steal from them, especially their livestock. As Taita Espiritu Vargas explained, "Chagras are not Indians. They always mistreated us, suddenly pushing some of us in the ravine or insulting without a reason. They come from somewhere else" (1993). Even tixaneños recalled that some chagra families from Pishillig has reputations as thieves.

Chagras were perceived by their indigenous neighbors as a disturbing presence that would turn up suddenly and threaten the fabric of the whole anejo. Taita Espiritu likened them to the *huairapamushca* (literally, "brought by the wind"): "The huairapamushca is someone who comes here to do wrong *like the chagra*, who gets here already adult through marriage and thinks he's the bees knees; we do not like that kind. There was one here before, not brought up round here. He came because another boss had mistreated him, so he was looking for somewhere to work and he came here. Now there aren't any, we're all from the same community; there are no outsiders now" (1993, emphasis added). The word *huairapamushca* in this testimony defines alien status, not belonging, and the word *chagra* is assimilated into the same category. Although in the past the term stressed the geographical connotations of ethnicity by identifying those who did not belong to the anejo, today it indicates a broader ethnic boundary, referring not only to differences among indigenous people on the basis of their geographical origin, but also to people who are not Quichuas.

It would seem that chagra arrogance and aggressiveness was related to the generalized racist attitudes to which they themselves were also exposed. Arrogance, insults, mistreatment, even thieving were techniques of domination against those who were considered inferior, and directed by chagras against those who were responsible for their exclusion from the dominant.

The Beginning of the Struggle

The process of mobilization against the hacienda regime in the parish of Tixán reflects the widespread political ferment that was germinating throughout the country since the late 1920s, the decade when the Ecuadorian Socialist and Communist Parties started to mobilize both urban workers and the indigenous and nonindigenous peasantry. Based on the principles of class struggle, the early demands of the peasant movement were literacy, particularly for the indigenous masses, and labor rights. The Ecuadorian Communist Party in its early days was pivotal in the formulation of these demands. Its activists worked to channel the discontent of the Quichua peasantry, aiming at the creation of a rural unionist movement. The creation of the Federación Ecuatorian de Indios (FEI), in 1944, was an important step in this process. The FEI focused its political activity in rural highlands areas. During this phase of the struggle, lawyers committed to the cause helped their indigenous *compañeros* (comrades) with all kinds of legal work related to wage claims. Communities involved in the claims joined the federation.

The northern province of Imbabura became nationally known for its high level of political mobilization (Becker 1997). With its sizeable proportion of large estates, the province of Chimborazo was close behind. According to the data of the National Institute of Statistics and Census (INEC), in 1954 Chimborazo had 47.5 percent of total cultivable land, and only 16.6 percent of cultivable land was made up of holdings of under five hectares; the rest were hacienda lands. Due to the coexistence of large estates and smallholdings, in 1965 the report of the Inter-American Committee for Agricultural Development (CIDA) defined Chimborazo land tenure as extremely "parasitic."

The first steps toward mobilization in Tixán were taken in the late 1930s. An indigenous man, Pascual Estrada Miranda, from the eastern sector of Pishillig, began his own fight against Julio Teodoro's abuses and to obtain a school for his anejo. A schoolboy from Estrada's same community told his story at the storytelling competition I organized at Tixán's primary and secondary schools in 1993. Although I inquired about him, no one I spoke to remembered him—not even the people of neighboring indigenous communities. The area where Estrada lived after marrying is today a community of chagras. Although his parents were both Quichuas from a neighboring anejo, he was considered nonindigenous. Even his sons whom I interviewed considered themselves nonindigenous—“white” in their own words. Estrada’s real or perceived ethnic identity apparently made him unfit to become a local symbol of the indigenous struggle. Nonetheless, Estrada did exist, and the interviews with his sons added details to his story.

The story of Pascual Estrada brings to light all the components that intervened in the mobilization process. The people of the anejos under Julio Teodoro, both huasipungueros and free, were protesting against mistreatment, against the lack of respect, and against Teodoro’s gratuitous violence. While the demands Estrada’s lawyers presented to the ministry of labor against the landowner focused mainly on wage issues, his lawsuit, initiated in 1937, also denounced mistreatment. His son Victor narrated with emotion.

> He [Julio Teodoro] believed he was the owner of the world. He used to hit and mistreat my father for no reason; he used to make us work from seven to five with no food; anyone passing had to leave quickly or he set them to work, people from the town, anyone. Beating, whipping, clubbing, the landlord got people out to work; that’s how the rich treated the poor. A certain Mr. Mogollón, I remember well, did the papers of the case for the ministry of labor, stating that the landlords could no longer crush people for no reason, and if they needed people to work, then they should pay them, not abuse them and get away with it, and after that my father, who was involved in this fight, opened the school for everyone in Pachamama Grande, Pishillig, Quislag and Cherlo. . . . The lawsuit upheld that the landlord mustn’t crush the people, mustn’t go into the anejos, mustn’t beat us when he felt like it, and mustn’t come and throw a glass of booze out of spite into the plates one was eating from. (Victor Estrada, 1993)

Victor repeatedly returned to the issue of mistreatment by the landlords. As he himself mentioned, the people of his father’s anejo were not huasipungueros. Some of the families were nonindigenous and had come from north of Riobamba because they had bought land or had married into the area. Nevertheless, it appears that Julio Teodoro would use any excuse to trespass on their lands and force them to work for him.

This was the "crushing for no reason" that Victor Estrada spoke about. People believed that Julio Teodoro had no right to go into the anejos and force people out, ruining their meals with liquor, to compel them to work for him for free. He did not own the land; the owners had documents to prove it. What motivated the protest, it seems, was the abusive nature of the landlord. As Victor Estrada recounted, Julio Teodoro was abusive, but his father, Julio César, had not bothered people, nor had the landlord before him, Zambrano, who "left the land abandoned and did not do anything, just like the Spaniards." Julio Teodoro, on the contrary, being a member of the parliament, thought he was "the owner of the world" and thus broke the rules of social relations, bringing strife wherever he went. Thus, whereas the people had acquiesced to the hacienda system under Julio César and Zambrano, it did not take long for them to rebel once Julio Teodoro took control.[22] A previous claim for the school seems to have been complementary to all this, as the two pivots of the fight melded into a single package of claims.

Ambrosio Laso and Agrarian Reform

On his trips to the city, Pascual Estrada came into contact with a leader from Imbabura, Dolores Cacuango, and with a leader from his own area, Taita Ambrosio Laso, who is remembered by all the elders in the communities of Tixán for his fight against the landlords. Taita Ambrosio used to talk with Estrada about the exploitation and mistreatment of the people of the anejos, and about what the lawyers in Quito and Riobamba said. Estrada's son told me, "When my dad had started to go about, he met this man Ambrosio Laso. He was also a fighter in the provinces against those who treated people badly like that; he was a workmate, and they went around walking everywhere, as there were not cars at that time" (Victor Estrada, 1993).

Taita Ambrosio was a huasipunguero from the hacienda Galte-Tipín, on the western mountain range, which was part of the parish of Palmira, adjacent to Tixán.[23] The owner of this estate, Luís Borja Moncayo, did not provide food or socorros, and his mayordomos were particularly abusive to workers. Taita Ambrosio decided not to remain quiet and started to talk with his own people, attempting to wake them up to the fight against injustice. Taita Pedro Marcatoma, who soon became Taita Ambrosio's right-hand man, recalled,

> We poor, we were suffering under the landlords and we worked since 1952 against the patrón. . . . Before there was the five days of work and the Huambra Doctrina, as they called it, that made young people and free people work five days and Taita Ambrosio Laso started to fight against this. So we organized with the help of the union, of the FEI, we made that go away and also take away one day of work and take back all the animals and things that the patrones had taken away as pawns for no reason. . . . We met among ourselves, indigenous as we say, as huasipungueros, as we were before, and so meeting we started to demand. We met in hiding at night in the mountains, this way, hiding that's it. From there we walked to Quito by foot, because in Guamote, in Cajabamba, in Riobamba, they all tried not to let us go to Quito, so we could pass through only by foot. It was the patrones and the authorities who did not let us go and so they would take us to jail. (Taita Pedro Marcatoma, 1992)

Gradually echoes of the mobilization, although clandestine, spread throughout local anejos. One channel of information was Taita Pascual. The anejos under Julio Teodoro Salem's control—Quislag, Pishillig, and Pachamama Chico—had already joined Taita Pascual's protest against the abusive landlord. Soon the anejos of the other Salem haciendas got wind of their neighbors' discontent, and they, too, joined the rebellion. The first ones to join were those under the control of the Polanco and Gallegos families, terratenientes known for being tight-fisted. Remembering Ambrosio Laso, Taita L. B., one of the founders of the Pachagsí community, explained,

> Because I did not know how to read and write then, as I was a young lad, but I had my head screwed on, I used to go around with two bottles of booze while he was asking people questions, and all night from five in the afternoon till eight in the morning, we would talk the whole night, only sleep for a little bit. We talked about how to make a community, how to speak about the landlords, how to speak about the injustices. He would say, "Yes, yes, of course, but we have to be one, talk like one, get organized, unite." Then he would ask us, "How many times have you got together?" "Twice." Then, he said, "go and talk to the ministry of social welfare or somebody to make it public, to unite the community, and do all the legal paperwork."

These secret meetings, held at night, started to spread. Yet with the help of the FEI, leaders such as Laso also traveled out of their anejos, with places such as public offices and the FEI headquarters becoming meeting points. Taita A. V., who claims he was the first to start mobilizing in the Tixán area, met with Ambrosio Laso in Riobamba, where Taita A. V. used to travel to meet his sharecropping partner. "In Riobamba we talked with the rest-in-peace comrade Ambrosio Laso. 'Where are you from?,' he said. 'I am from San Carlos,' I said. 'And how is the patron behaving?,' he asked. 'They are bad, they mistreat me and I can't do nothing,' I said, and so we talked of reforma agraria and that we had to go to the ministry of social welfare, that Ecuador is for all Ecuadorians, and we had to fight for rights and against patrones. And so we organized to put an end to the mistreatments" (Taita A. V., 1992).

Kinship ties were another powerful means for disseminating the struggle. By means of extended family bonds that crossed the anejos boundaries, people learned that their relatives were already involved in the fight and followed their example: "Some other sectors were already taking plots, so others followed and followed, through relatives here and there, and so they followed from La Ermita, Santa Lucía, Pachamama, La Pacífica, and all that of San Carlos" (Taita A. V., 1992).

There is much confusion concerning the order in which these anejos rebelled. Two factors contribute to this confusion. First, each of the elderly leaders interviewed claimed to be the local initiator of the movement—second only to Taita Ambrosio. Second, the grassroots reaction to such mobilizing efforts was not always positive. Fear of reprisals from the landlords created hesitation and often paralyzed people. Eloquence and persuasiveness were qualities crucial to being a rebel leader, for success in mobilizing followers depended largely on rhetorical skills. In cases where legal recognition of the commune was necessary in order to claim the land, people would resist the census, a Quichua idiosyncrasy associated with many past uprisings (see Moreno Yánez 1985). "Before, as the people did not believe, they did not know, there were only a few people, I arranged maybe thirty-five I.D. cards and with four property documents. . . . Because they did not know, the people always thought I was going to take them away. I talked, I explained, I told them I was only going to take them for the census, and I had to send them to Quito. Then we did the census house by house, we made neat copies and sent them to Quito. One month later the statutes came back. That's how we got this legal record in Pachagsí community" (Taita L. B., 1992).

The FEI offered indigenous protesters guidance for formulating and presenting their claims to the authorities, as well as help in getting indigenous people released from prison. The landlords' strategies to control the protest did not bear fruit: "I initiated to follow demands against patrones to defend the people, and so for this he said to me, 'You are rational, I love you as a son,' but he lied, 'I will give you a house, make you work with the tractor.' So he tried to trick me so that I would not follow with the demand, but I knew it was a lie" (Taita A. V., 1992). Once the struggle started and the protesters had demonstrated their immunity to the persuasive tactics of the landlords, repressive measures were taken. Therefore, as Taita Pedro Marcatoma narrated, activists used to leave the haciendas at night, unseen by the landlords, and to walk all the way to the cities in order to meet with their FEI comrades.[24] The possibility of attack by the police, who sided with the landlords, made these trips highly dangerous. "The patrones brought the military, and they brought them in I don't know how many trucks of the military, who came armed in order to scare people. And we left, taking our children and women up to the mountain to hide them but knowing that we wanted to fight the military. How sad life was to see all those people suffering and scared coming and going, but we also were armed, even though with what—sticks, clubs, machetes, and even stones. Patrones wanted to catch at night those who were organizing; it was a terrible turmoil in those days" (Taita M. G., 1992).

Many cabecillas (protest leaders) such as Taita Pedro were arrested more than once, but were released due to the support of the FEI. "They arrested me and made me confess to robbery. They took me to Alausí and from there to Riobamba. So there they said, 'What does the law teach, you communists, abusing the poor patrones; now you have to die here, rocotos, so that you respect the poor patrones that are more than God, owners of the lands. You are alzamenteros.' This is how police used to treat me. And so they bit me up because those days there were nobody defending us in the canton. They kept me in jail in Riobamba three or four months. From there we, thanking God, all united, we did not let them abuse us. Comrade Modesto Rivera from FEI with the lawyer in Quito helped getting us out of jail; once all the reports and all the wage [demands] with the labor inspector were ready, we came out. It was 1955, 1956, or 1957, more or less. They took me to jail five times while we were forming the union. . . . This is how we lived" (Taita Pedro Marcatoma, 1992).

During this phase Taita Ambrosio Laso became the primary leader for the whole area, including Tixán: "[He] was the Colonel, so they called him, the colonel of the peasants, an authority for all the communes. He gave orders like a colonel and was like Luis Macas is today; he talked to the government, to ministers, to everyone. At that time there was not any specific law, but he talked all the same" (Taita L. B., 1992). Taita Ambrosio's popularity grew to the point of generating legendary accounts of his capture: "Our comrade Ambrosio Laso, from the community of Galte, went to all the congresses, fighting for a land law, but the landowners pursued him and wanted to kill him. On one occasion they kidnapped him and sent him in a box to Galápagos, but he came back one year later, thanks to the help of the poor peasants of Galápagos, who put him on a plane back to Quito" (Taita M. G., 1992). Many elders from the local communities recalled this episode, but the details varied. In any case, he survived and on his return kept up the fight. With his support, the people eventually obtained their land.

Even his death is veiled in mystery. According to Taita Pedro Marcatoma, Taita Ambrosio was about to sell himself to the landowners, accepting money in exchange for putting an end to the hostilities. According to Taita Pedro's narration, one day during the Carnival festival, a drunken Taita Ambrosio fell asleep in the sun and never woke up again: "And so he died because of that protest." Two elders from La Merced and Pachagsí offered a more detailed version: "He died because he was just a troublemaker, they say: he died for defending the land; they [the patrones] poisoned him." While it may be hard to believe that such a revered rebel leader—after nearly thirty years of fighting—would sell out to the landowners, it is nevertheless possible that Taita Ambrosio was about to do so. One plausible explanation for his alleged betrayal is that his incredible power to mobilize people earned him external as well as internal rivals and enemies, who may have spread false rumors to discredit him and thus justify his murder. One noteworthy detail that could corroborate this hypothesis of a complot against him is that, according to Taita Pedro and others, Taita Ambrosio died during Carnival, a tension-filled festival when anyone who has a personal vendetta trembles: Carnival is traditionally the time for settling scores and for revenge.

Like examples from other highland provinces (see Guerrero 1991b), the case under discussion shows that indigenous understanding of abuse was not necessarily related to a Marxist notion of capitalist exploitation. As Brooke Larson (1991) argues, the moral economy of the peasant community is not always moved by what James Scott (1976) defines as the "subsistence ethic." In Ecuador, the whole hacienda structure was based on a symbolic pact of reciprocity, which can be defined as a moral pact when interpreting the Indian-colony relationship and taxation (Platt 1982, 100). The loss of access to the socorros implied not only loss of access to goods, but also a breach of the moral pact. A similar infringement occurred during the transition to capitalism in Bolivia, where the modernization of agricultural production provoked the breach of an "unwritten pact" of reciprocity, traditionally manifested in ritual exchanges of produce between landowners and peons (Langer 1985, 264). However, this kind of infraction was not merely a byproduct of modernization (Larson 1991, 477–78). Indigenous people have rebelled against the breach of reciprocity pacts since colonial times.

In the hacienda system, although they were dealing with a regime of inequality, the huasipungueros relied on the obligation of generosity in order to have the landlord respect the rules of asymmetric reciprocity, what Guerrero (1991b) defines as the semantics of domination. This shared cultural and political language derived from the combination of dominant and subaltern cultural systems. The fragile balance of these different cultural codes secured the entire dominant structure of the hacienda system—a specific type of domination that proved to be less invincible than it appeared. The rejection and defeat of this dominant system resulted partially from a struggle over the production of social and cultural values. Furthermore, free and nonindigenous peasants who were not directly affected by the landlords' lack of generosity also mobilized to participate in this struggle. Their motivation is likely to be found in the excessively abusive nature of their specific landlord, Julio Teodoro, and not only in the structure of domination that the hacienda regime represented. In both cases, therefore, the breach of a moral agreement motivated people to insurgency.

As in the case of the Miskitus analyzed by Charles Hale, it is necessary to establish a dialogue between structural conditions and political agency (Hale 1994). The level of mobilization increases through "external influences or new internally generated understandings of oppression" (ibid., 27). In this case the external influence exercised by the Communist Party and the structural changes that led to the agrarian reform increased the level of insurgency of indigenous peasants. However, it was the combination of this influence with the indigenous understanding of oppression and exploitation that established the basis for political action. Even if articulated to the class struggle promoted by the Communist Party on the one hand, and the modernizing policy promoted by the state on the other, indigenous militancy was not necessarily based on the same understanding of oppression. The consequence—at least in this phase of the struggle—was that indigenous peasants did not immediately question the basis of the hacienda regime and its exploitative structure.

Although indigenous mobilization was pivotal in the push toward the promulgation of the agrarian reform laws, other factors also contributed to making the hacienda system obsolete. The agrarian reform was also promoted nationally by a fraction of the landowning sector who demanded radical changes in the agrarian structure in order to respond to market demands (Barsky 1988). In this view, the landowning bourgeoisie was demanding agricultural modernization, that is, the introduction of new technology, formalization of labor relations, and reduction of estate size to maximize production. These demands were formulated within the framework of international forces fostering modernization in Latin America as represented by the Alliance for Progress. Some scholars emphasize the role played by the class struggle between landowners and peasants, both at the national and international level (Guerrero 1983). In the aftermath of the Cuban Revolution, Latin American elites and states had become particularly wary of the consequences of social unrest in their own countries. In order to address the potential revolutionary threat, Ecuadorian national leaders and the ruling elite considered it essential to pacify conflicts in the countryside. Arguing along the same lines as Guerrero, Paola Sylva (1986) emphasizes the management of political power. With the incipient process of industrialization, the highland landowning elites saw their sphere of political control threatened by the diminishing national importance of the agricultural sector. Faced with this loss of power—and not wanting the conflict to intensify—the landowners were forced to make some concessions to peasant communities.

These different interpretations of events are not mutually exclusive. The country's agrarian structure was facing pressures of a different nature. The push toward industrialization was slowly moving the socioeconomic axis from the country to the city, which clearly jeopardized the hegemony of landowners. Attention to the new landowning generation is crucial to understanding the changes taking place in the heart of the agrarian economic structure (Sylva 1986). The children of the *gamonales*, many of whom had studied abroad, were bearers of the policy of agricultural modernization; the large old estates were no longer profitable, and it would be costly to mechanize them. In addition, the pressure exercised by the indigenous peasant community was considered a dangerous source of rebellion that needed to be contained.

The situation in Tixán presents an additional factor: the discontent of local nonindigenous people in rural highlands who were not powerful landowners. According to various testimonies, discontent against the powerful landowners in Tixán began to escalate around the 1950s. Reaffirming the political relevance of ritual events among nonindigenous people, the first clear manifestation of this discontent came especially from families of "medium rank" when they denied Julio Teodoro Salem the role he had played many times in order to impose his prestige: hosting (*priostazgo*) the bullfight for the town festival of San Juan, celebrated in June. According to Don M. L., "Forty years ago, the young people in town did not need the Salem anymore for the bulls; we brought them from Atapo or from Galte. We did not want anything to do with the haciendas anymore, because they used to hold us over a barrel when it came to politics; we had to vote for them, and if they did not win, they did not give us the bulls. We did not want to be their slaves" (1992).

The overt rejection of Salem's power implied that the sale of potatoes no longer took place on the Salem haciendas. For the most part, the sale of potatoes had moved to the hacienda Zula, in the area of Totoras, or sometimes even to Galte, in the western range. Julio Teodoro had thus already begun to lose control of the town's upper- and medium-ranking families. They no longer had any reason to tolerate his disrespectful and arrogant behavior or to silently accept his overwhelming power.

The Agrarian Reform Laws: The Struggle Continues

The 1960s and 1970s were decades of profound socioeconomic and political change in rural Ecuadorian society. State-sponsored modernization policies aimed at fostering national progress and economic growth. The first Agrarian Reform Law was passed in 1964 and the second in 1973 as part of the new national policy directed at modernizing the agrarian structure. The first agrarian reform legislation eliminated the regime of unpaid labor in the haciendas by abolishing the huasipungaje and replacing it with a regime of waged labor.[25] It was decreed that all arrears accrued by the peasants during their years of unpaid labor (and as such difficult to calculate) had to be recognized by the adjudication of the huasipungos to all the workers who had held them over the years. At the same time, the law established wage scales and prohibited all forms of unpaid labor. The Ecuadorian Institute of Agrarian Reform and Colonization (IERAC) was the state agency responsible for applying and enforcing the agrarian legislation.

Although the first law did not directly attack the landowning power structure, the claims for the adjudication of huasipungos meant that the Quichua peasants were indeed demanding not only rights as laborers, but also rights to land. After the first agrarian reform, land rights became the focus of peasant claims, which called into question Ecuador's agrarian structure, especially in the highlands. Land rights also acquired a symbolic significance: they were considered as reparation of an ancestral debt that white society had contracted with indigenous people and that dated back to the Spanish conquest. Elements directly related to the ethnic cause were gradually incorporated into the content of the struggle and, as demonstrated in the indigenous uprising of May 1990, eventually called into question not only the agrarian structure, but also the constitutional basis of the state.

> This is how we made it; in Quito we worked with the FEI, so we worked making demonstrations, as they called them, to claim huasipungos. So we went by train for free. Doctor Carlos Julio Arrosemena was the president [of Ecuador] and he gave us a free train ride to go to Quito to fight, from all over the country. A hard fight. At that time there was hardly anybody fighting with us because we fought for the organizing, we had the strength to fight to get the law for indigenous people to free us so that we could live in peace. And so for this work fighting for the agrarian reform, the military junta of Jorge Lara, he gave us the reforma agraria and so we got the huasipungos. (Taita Pedro Marcatoma, 1992)

The second Agrarian Reform Law attempted to readjust land tenure throughout the country and deeply affected the hacienda power structure. According to the law, sharecropping and all other types of labor relations considered exploitative were abolished. Renting out of land was restricted and subject to approval in situations such as the landowner's illness or disability. The legal right to priority for purchasing land that was granted to legalized indigenous communities (or cooperatives or associations) brought even more profound changes in the agrarian structure.

Should the landowner ignore this right, legalized communities could initiate conveyancing lawsuits (*trámites de afectación*) through the IERAC.[26] Between 1975 and 1979, 55.9 percent of hacienda lands were adjudicated, via lawsuits, by the IERAC in favor of peasant communities, associations, and cooperatives because landowners routinely refused to sell their land to indigenous peasants (Ramón Valarezo 1992). Indigenous communities could initiate legal action also on grounds such as the landowner's violation of the labor rights of workers, the landowner's refusal to hand over huasipungos, demonstrated instances of unproductive land use, or demographic pressures exercised by indigenous populations on adjacent territory. Lands thus assigned to or purchased by indigenous communities were declared inalienable, and the regime of land ownership was declared communal, as opposed to individual.

The second law of agrarian reform became the framework within which ethnic protest was expressed. The mobilization of indigenous peasants on the one hand and the terratenientes' attempt to defend their power on the other became fertile ground for conflicts over land (*conflictos de tierras*). However, the penetration of landowners' power into the state apparatus, including the IERAC, often made legal action ineffective, with lawsuits taking years to be resolved. *Gamonalista* power was so deeply rooted in Chimborazo that the haciendas were scarcely affected by the 1964 law, and the majority of landowners refused to hand over the huasipungos. In this first phase of agrarian reform, the most affected estates generally were the public properties of Asistencia Pública.[27] Between 1964 and 1974, only 21.655 hectares, equivalent to 5.7 percent of the province's farmland, were affected (Ramón Valarezo 1992, 118–25). The Asistencia Pública and the Catholic Church of the cantons of Chunchi and Colta owned 20.9 percent and 39.3 percent of this land, respectively. The fight on these properties was the result of mobilization by the Socialist Party and was later continued by the communists in alliance with peasants on state haciendas.[28]

With the 1973 legislation, the IERAC gradually adopted a conservative policy, supporting landowners to defend their properties. The trámites de afectación initiated by indigenous communities in Chimborazo were often resolved with a declaration of exemption in favor of the landowner. The consolidation of IERAC conservatism had deep repercussions on the Indian-state relationship.[29] The process of mobilization had gradually positioned indigenous protesters as social actors in search of alliances with the government against the landowners. This type of relationship was established during the liberal era, with the issuing of laws and decrees that were supposed to protect the indigenous population (Clark 1992).[30] This process, which coincides with modernization of the state structure, led to the "recognition of higher (and more distant) state authorities, coupled with a questioning of the legitimacy of most local ones" (ibid., 25). Abuses perpetrated by local authorities continued despite the state's attempt at a tutelary regime. Starting in the 1970s, the vision of the state as a tutelary entity of the indigenous population and rights was profoundly redefined. The alliance of IERAC, and therefore of the state, with the landowning elites redirected the indigenous struggle over land against landowners and state, with both perceived as the expression of the same abusive power structure (see Pallares 2002, 40). "The authorities, the IERAC, what did they do for us? Nothing. We poor went to the authorities since we had an agrarian law and they were beating us, 'Indian, rocoto, traitor, communist'—that is how they treated us" (Taita Pedro Marcatoma, 1992). After the promulgation of the laws, the role of the "state-as-provider" clashed with the effects of gamonalista power, motivating indigenous peasants to use extralegal measures to defend their lands. Land conflicts became more acute in Chimborazo Province at the end of the 1970s, when legal action through the IERAC proved to be ineffective.[31]

Despite all odds, agrarian reform took place in Tixán, with the majority of the communities acquiring legal status after the promulgation of the first agrarian reform legislation (table 1). Different communities mobilized at different points in time. The first anejos to organize were, according to Victor Estrada, those under Julio Teodoro's domain, in the Pishillig area, which is today divided into three communities and one farmers' association.[32] The anejos of this area were not huasipungueros, but they took part in the same type of labor claims that led to the first law of agrarian reform. However, the anejos that received Taita Ambrosio's advice were indeed huasipungueros. Although Taita Ambrosio had begun mobilization campaigns on his hacienda in the late 1930s, the other communities of huasipungueros and *partidarios* did not begin to mobilize until the 1960s.[33] Alongside wage claims, their fight focused specifically on land claims with huasipungueros demanding the adjudication of the huasipungos, which they eventually obtained.[34] Lawsuits were associated with complicated cases, especially when hacienda lands were claimed by free communities to whom the landowners had denied access to pasture and water. From IERAC records, it seems that the haciendas that caused more conflicts with

Table 1. Communities in Tixán with legal status

Communities	Resolution No.	Date
Pishillig	150	10 February 1938
Quislag	150	10 February 1938
Sanganao	149	10 February 1938
Chalaguan	4457	22 June 1959
Guaylla Grande	4591	20 July 1965
Guaylla	4591	20 July 1965
Llallanag	0384	15 January 1968
La Merced	2639	16 October 1969
Pachagsí	0676	24 October 1974
La pacífica	0209	13 June 1984
Pishillig Chico	0345	26 June 1984
Pachamama Chico	0371	9 July 1984
Pachamama Grande	107	21 November 1988
Pueblo Viejo	0045	31 January 1990
Quislag Chico	0055	5 February 1990
San Carlos de Chuquira	0118	5 March 1990
Busilchi	0172	5 March 1990
Gusniag	0182	30 March 1990
Cobshe Bajo	003632	26 November 1990
Shishilcon	0156	22 March 1991
Pishillig Urtzuquís	0161	25 March 1991
Aypud	?	?

The data refer to the communities affiliated with Inca Atahualpa.
Source of data: IERAC, Chimborazo.

the indigenous peasants were Moyocancha, under Rosa Matilda Salem de Gallegos, and those under Julio Teodoro. The lawsuit for Moyocancha was initiated through the IERAC in 1974, while the claim against Julio Teodoro had a long history, having started with Pascual Estrada's first lawsuit.

By the end of the 1970s, most of the land conflicts on former Salem haciendas had been resolved, and the lands had been adjudicated to former huasipungueros and workers. By the time the agrarian reform legislation was passed, the five Salem haciendas had been further subdivided, among many inheritors, as if to confirm the national trend to reduce the size of land estates. Starting from the 1950s, tracts of hacienda land had in some cases already been sold to nonindigenous people. The gradual process of land acquisition led to the formation of new communities, some with names that reflect the legacy of the hacienda period. As a general tendency, those who had led the protests served as presidents in their own communities for a few years, by and large trying to build the infrastructure of the new communal settlements.

The patrones timpu had come to an end. The hacienda regime, which had so profoundly marked social relations and informed the way people of different groups related to each other, had been severely affected. According to Pedro Marcatoma, the memory of that struggle is intrinsically intertwined with the struggle that he, as a cabecilla first and as a catechist later, would undertake for the sake of the advancement of indigenous people and future generations. In the fight against injustice, the demands of the past resonate with the demands of the present: "Derecho propio [our own right] is that we asked for our liberation, to hand in the huasipungos, for our needs, so that the patrón would not take them away, as pawns, as they used to say; it is asking to get them back, our own law so that they pay what we earned. Today there are no haciendas, only communities, but we have our rights as indigenous, rightly claiming the way our ancestors lived, how they were mistreated so that we can awaken and seek liberation and our sons can be in peace. So that we no longer live like during the time of the patrones" (Pedro Marcatoma, 1992).

CHAPTER TWO

Tixán Becomes Modern

The self-contained world of the hacienda regime exploded, dispersing all its contents—lands, produce, political power, racism, and inequality. By reincorporating new and old pieces, the people inhabiting that world reconstituted a new one and repositioned themselves as well as they could.

The two decades following agrarian reform brought changes that profoundly impacted the distribution of power and resources in many rural parishes of the Ecuadorian Andes, reconfiguring social relations and imaginaries around race and ethnicity. In Tixán many indigenous and nonindigenous people gained access to resources such as land, labor, services, and local political power. A new white elite emerged from among families that had not been among the prominent, local, "good" families during the hacienda period (mainly those who owned land), and many chagras and Quichuas were rapidly incorporated into the local market economy and political affairs. Notwithstanding this drastic reconfiguration, the new local hierarchies did not question some of the principles on which they were premised. Class and race remained the main criteria for defining privileges and prestige and for allocating resources among Quichuas, chagras, and tixaneños. Yet the process of ethnic mobilization that had led to agrarian struggle did challenge the remapping of discrimination. Counting also on the renewed Catholic Church as an ally, indigenous organizations integrated new demands into their struggle, initiating the phase epitomized by the "despertar de los indios" (the indigenous awakening). In this context the Inca Atahualpa was born.

Figure 1. View of Tixán from the Pan-American Highway. Photo by author.

The New Masters

The process of disintegration of the hacienda regime was underway in Tixán even before the agrarian reform. The onerous costs required to maintain extended landholdings compromised the financial position of many landowners, forcing them to sell their properties.[1] Under agrarian reform, the land market supposedly favored indigenous buyers who had worked on the haciendas as huasipungueros, yanaperos, and sitiajeros.[2] However, some tixaneño families, many of them former piqueros, also bought plots in both sectors of the cordilleras.

The gradual yet profound restructuring of local land tenure that affected the distribution of power and resources fit in with a larger process of socioeconomic change that was taking place at the national level.[3] An emerging entrepreneurial sector increasingly pushed the country's economy toward industrialization. In addition, the oil boom of the 1970s created an atmosphere of optimism that fed dreams of great wealth and progress. The state-led modernizing process reached even the most isolated highland towns, bringing changes that completely redefined the socioeconomic structure and often led to the decline of the rural sector.

In the 1960s the "good" families of Tixán started to leave the town. Subordinated within a landowning regime that was now losing credibility and power, these families responded to the dream of progress by migrating to cities. They sold their land and moved away from Tixán in search of a better life. The wealthiest migrated to the coastal cities, others to Quito, and others made their home in Riobamba. However, they did not cut off their relationships with their hometown and did not sell their houses in Tixán, to which they would return for the San Juan town festival every June.

The completion of the local section of the Pan-American Highway, in the 1970s, diminished the importance of the Quito-Guayaquil railway service in local agricultural and commercial trade with the coast. As testimonies of tixaneños stated, the potato trade ended with the opening of the highway. Lorries now arrived from the capital of Cotapaxi, the highland province north of Chimborazo, to buy the produce directly from the former haciendas. The closure of the railway stations in Alausí and Tixán affected people who had made their living from coastal trade via this railway line and led to the disappearance of important rural figures such as piqueros and piareros, sinking the townsfolk into desperation.[4] The former piquero Don B. B. recalled, "Here in Tixán it became impossible to sell our produce because in the highland markets we all sold the same things, so prices went down. Also now to buy a banana we had to go to Alausí or Riobamaba. So many of us moved to the city" (1993).

These dramatic and rapid changes forced the tixaneños to look for new livelihoods. Whereas the "good" families chose to move away, the "medium" ones, former piqueros, former piareros, and other landless families stayed and took advantage of the new opportunities. According to Doña María, some of them even tried to form an agricultural cooperative, but their dreams foundered because of leadership struggles that ended with some of the cooperative's leaders absconding with the members' money: "We tried to form a co-op, but we were not lucky with our managers, who collected the money and then escaped with everything, leaving us with nothing. People here are not trustworthy" (1993). When land purchases did not succeed, grocery shops and trucks became an alternative source of income. Faced with the closure of their businesses following decrees by the liquor-store council, many chichería owners invested their resources in transportation—becoming modernized piareros, using trucks instead of mules. Grocery shops and small-scale agricultural trade also flourished.

These changes involved also Quichuas and chagras. With land acquisition, both groups encountered new challenges related to maintaining and increasing productivity and to commercialization. Although it coexisted with the traditional subsistence economy, the supposed modernization of farming pushed the indigenous sector toward the market economy. Market profits were the main resource for the cancelation of debts. As commonly occurred in other Andean countries pursuing agrarian reform, the state launched various initiatives with the intention of assisting farmers and developing agriculture (see Postero 2007). One such example was the creation of the Banco Nacional de Fomento (Development National Bank), a state-run entity that gave loans to farmers, providing access to capital for improving production. However, this plan did not serve the indigenous sector, due to high interest rates and a difficult application procedure that discouraged indigenous peasants, many of whom were illiterate.

Since the 1970s, low interest loans offered by the Catholic NGO Ecuadorian Fund Populorum Progressio (FEPP) have been pivotal in opening the land market to indigenous communities at the national level. Taita L. B., who took the lead in the legal recognition of the Pachagsí community, remembered, "I used to go to Quito to talk to Estuardo Valle from FEPP; he was the secretario nacional of FEPP. At that time FEPP helped us a lot. They talked to us, they made sessions in the offices, they talked to ministers and prepared the paperwork, they accompanied us to IERAC; that is how they helped. They said, 'You can win but you need to organize, you can win your communal lands,' so they said" (Taita L. B., 1992). The FEPP was created at the beginning of the 1970s to help peasants with loans for productive activities, while their land-acquisition fund was created in 1991 with money from the Episcopal Conference. The FEPP sponsored the collective use and purchase of land by establishing as the principal qualification for the loan that the land be collectively administrated and not be divided among the purchasing members.

Communal land tenure in this case referred to a group of partners within a given community and not to all community members. The partners worked their land according to the *minga* system of collective labor; most of the profits from the harvest were used to pay off the FEPP loan. According to FEPP officials, it was not uncommon for the owners to divide the collective land among themselves after paying off their debt to the FEPP. Land tenure, therefore, was not necessarily the main basis for community identity, despite the fact that indigenous communal lands were declared by the agrarian laws to be inalienable and indivisible. Yet the productive tasks continued to be performed through mingas, an institution considered pivotal for maintaining community cohesion and identity. L. P., a young activist of the Inca Atahualpa, explained, "The minga is a form of participation that we have inside our communities: if there is something to do, clear paths, clearing of the fields, cleaning the school, building the communal house, we work with mingas all together" (L. P., La Pacífica, 1992).

The changing land tenure and economic opportunities had a significant impact on local interethnic relationships. Gradually the production of communal lands oriented toward larger markets, such as those of Riobamba and Cuenca, while the surplus of household production remained for the local markets of Tixán and Alausí, which became centers for local, small-scale commerce after the closure of the coastal railway line. After losing access to the potato fields of the haciendas, the former piqueros tried to fill the vacuum by buying the produce of indigenous communities. This produce was then resold to locals on a retail basis, or in the Alausí market on a wholesale basis. In both cases, larger profits derived from speculation than from retail sales. The tixaneños took advantage of the commercial inexperience of the indigenous sector, paying indigenous farmers less than the market price for their produce. Moreover, since the crop was typically purchased before harvest, producers became indebted to buyers in times of drought and crop failure.

The precariousness of this economic system for indigenous producers was compensated by an increasing number of interethnic ritual kinships such as compadrazgo and padrinazgos relationships, mostly involving Quichuas and townsfolk. Economic criteria guided the choice of compadres and the acceptance of such proposals. In fact, the immediate obligations of the compadres and *padrinos* (to donate the baptism trousseau for the baby or the wedding attire for the bride and groom) represented only the beginning of the relationship, the signing of a symbolic contract.[5] The ensuing obligations created relations of interdependence, which were generally to the disadvantage of the indigenous or peasant party. While the tixaneño compadres gained easy and secure access to the produce and labor of their indigenous god-family and godchildren (*ahijados*), the indigenous ritual kin gained access to small loans with interest, hospitality in the town during festivities, and a degree of flexibility with late payments on debts in times of crisis. If the socorros given in the haciendas contributed to maintaining a system of symbolic, lifelong indebtedness, the compadrazgo relationship, with its demands for ongoing repayment of loans, made indebtedness a practical reality. Under this system, many indigenous families were forced to mortgage part of their lands in exchange for short-term loans. On some occasions a temporary "loss" due to unpaid loans became an unexpected "inheritance" of land for the white lenders.

A further minor advantage the compadrazgo relationship bequeathed to the tixaneños was the acquisition of loyal customers in their grocery shops, where their indigenous partners could make purchases on credit (*al fiado*). In the rare case in which an ahijado wanted to attend the secondary school in town, the compadres would offer their ahijado board and lodging in exchange for help with tasks and domestic chores. A. L., one of the founders of the Inca Atahualpa, grew up during this period of profound change. Although he had been too young to participate in the agrarian struggle, he was originally from Pishillig Yacupungo, a community that fought intensely against the terrateniente Julio Teodoro Salem. Owning no land, his family was not well positioned and thus resorted to different expediencies to make a living, including interethnic compadrazgo: "I had a *madrina* [godmother], her name was Celia, and she told my father to send me to high school, and so my father told me she had said that, and so he said, 'Let's go to high school," and he sent me to high school here in Tixán. When I attended high school, I used to spend some time at her shop helping out and she fed me" (A. L., 1992).

The post-agrarian reform adjustments led to a growing interdependence between the town and the communities, epitomized by the increasing frequency of interethnic relationships and arrangements. New market demands led to a greater need to incorporate other actors into productive cycles. The arena for interethnic confrontation (exploitation, unequal reciprocity, and racism) moved from the hacienda to the town, thus relocating the dominant power structure and its accompanying forms of abuse. New white "amitos" appeared and multiplied. This shift in the administration of local power and resources was exemplified by the advent of a new generation of parish civil officers. With the dismantling of the trilogy of power of the hacienda regime, the new tenientes políticos were elected from among those "medium" families who had stayed in the town.

Additionally, the position became highly politicized and intertwined with party politics. Don E. P., who was elected as a civil officer three times between 1979 and 1992, changed political affiliation each time in order to win the elections. Belonging to a "medium" family, he was called in town "el indio" for his supposedly mixed racial origins. Summarizing the changes in the local administration of power after the agrarian reform, he stated, "I came in with a different mandate, to look after the people from the countryside. The gamonalismo ended here in 1979, with President Jaime Roldós. I put an end to gamonalismo in 1979, pulling down the armor of the oligarchy. It was then that the people started to govern themselves. Before, there were some powerful families here, who did everything among relatives" (Don E. P., 1992). Yet, despite the demise of the local oligarchy, which Don E. P. praised himself for initiating, Quichuas and poor people continued to suffer from the abuses of elected officials.[6]

This shift in control was also evident in labor relations. Notwithstanding the supposed disappearance of precapitalist forms of labor that were enforced under the hacienda regime, the system of sharecropping (*aparcería* or *al partido*) was widely adopted throughout the Ecuadorian Andes. This system regulated labor relationships both within indigenous communities and in the town, and offered a solution to two different problems: shortage of labor and of land.[7] Tixán urban migration following the agrarian reform caused a labor shortage among the local white landowners, especially during the sowing and harvesting seasons. Sharecropping was an arrangement between the tixaneños, who had come to own the land, and the indigenous (or, less often, chagra) sharecropper (*partidario*), who did the physical labor. Depending on the specific arrangements, if the actual seeds or their cost were shared, the harvest was supposed to be split evenly. Otherwise, the final harvest was divided proportionally according to the contribution of each partner.

Sharecropping soon became a means of establishing social status and redefining local social hierarchies in response to structural changes in the parish. Even when the harvest was divided evenly and the two parties to the unwritten contract were interdependent, the landowner always had a higher status than the person who worked the land. The hierarchical relation had a racial as well as a class dimension: typically the landowners were tixaneños and the workers were Quichuas or chagras. In this context, being white meant having a respectable social status and owning land.[8] Furthermore, the system of sharecropping established differences among workers insofar as the status of a sharecropper was considered higher than that of a waged peasant.

This socioeconomic adjustment was central to redefining the relationship between Quichuas and tixaneños, and it aggravated local interethnic tensions that had until then remained latent. Again A. L. recalled, "At that time, the mishus in the town mistreated us. 'If I met them, I could kill those Indians,' they would say, and many more bad things they said. But to me no, because I was hiding, and sometimes I did not go out of my madrina's house. Only if I had someone else to go back to my community, then I went out" (1992).

However, interactions between tixaneños and chagras remained infrequent. Fewer in number than Quichuas, chagras were not targeted for the economic "development" of the town. For chagras, compadrazgo relationships with the tixaneños were less crucial; everything stayed within the family. Chagras practiced strict endogamy, especially in the communities of the eastern cordillera, and took advantage of the state's modernizing agrarian policy in order to increase their agricultural productivity. Slowly and subtly, chagras freed themselves from the direct dominance of tixaneños and pursued their own social advancement. Loans granted under various agricultural development plans allowed many chagras to invest in their land to improve productivity and buy cattle. Their economic position gradually improved, and some chagra families became wealthier than many tixaneño families. Chagras even came to be the main providers of bulls for the bullfight afternoons of both the San Juan and the harvest festivals, thus increasing their stature in everyone's eyes.[9] However, not all chagras were successful. Some chagras from both cordilleras continued to work under new landlords from the town by selling their labor during the planting and harvest seasons. Some of them moved to neighborhoods on the outskirts of town that tixaneños considered unsuitable for "good" tixaneño families. Their presence was not easily tolerated by the new elites whose members often considered chagra and indigenous local inhabitants guilty of "degenerating" Tixán's good reputation.

Post-agrarian reform changes, therefore, had repercussions, not so much on the relations between chagras and tixaneños, but on the relations among chagras themselves. Internal socioeconomic stratification intensified. Some chagras continued to strengthen their identities and economic positions by becoming independent from the town, their independence leading them to define the symbolic boundaries of their difference with increasing determination. Other chagras, meanwhile, turned to the parish capital; they made Tixán their home and made its residents their bosses and compadres. The latter process has been slower than the former, and became evident in the 1990s.

This intensification of internal stratification also holds true for indigenous comuneros. At the community level, the aparcería was crucial for the household subsistence of landless *comuneros* (usually former arrimados), who could not afford to participate in the purchase of collective lands. They accessed the system of aparcería through either real or ritual kinship. While their subsistence was guaranteed, their social status as landless sharecroppers limited their access to other resources.

No significant change took place in the relations between chagras and Quichuas until the formation of the Inca Atahualpa. Abuses and conflicts in the countryside continued, with the only difference being that as the chagras began to consolidate their economic position, their status both in the town and the countryside was further redefined. In the Pishillig sector for examples, which was originally controlled by Julio Teodoro Salem, both chagras and Quichuas shared the land that remained after the hacienda was dismantled. The abuses perpetrated by chagras against indigenous commoners persisted and increased, and tensions mounted to the extent that four separate communities were formed. A. L. actively participated in this process.

> The chagras then always mistreated us; if some of us had some barley or something else growing here or there, those chagras came on their horses and took it and nobody said anything; if they said something the chagras would beat them up. For example, at Carnival time chagras came on their horses, and always coming on the side of the house, they took some small animal, hens, guinea pigs; they stole something and they entered the house and took other things and nobody said anything because they were scared. But then people in my community, I talk about my community because I don't know about the others, they got fed up, "We can't live like this, we can't always suffer," and so I contacted the MAG [ministry of agriculture] in Alausí, and we coordinated with them, and they tried to help us. And so I told my people that a mishu was going to help us and so they were happy and so we started to work and people split and made their own community, Yacupungo. (A. L., 1992)

Re-imagining Communities

Agrarian reform also had considerable impact on the formation of indigenous communities and identity, a process that is closely intertwined with state policies (Lucero 2003; Pallares 2002; Rappaport 1994; Rappaport

2005). Broadly defined, the *comunidad* (community) is a cornerstone of indigenous identity and political ideology throughout Latin America. Considered fundamental to the indigenous social milieu both in the sierra and the Amazon, the comunidad is constructed as antithetical to Western individualism. It is not only the space where resources are shared collectively, but also the entity that regulates residents' lives. An individual has an identity only by belonging to a community, and the collective or comunidad has priority over the individual (Lucero 2003).

Yet, as a specific space the comunidad is a modern creation. As the case of Tixán illustrates, agrarian reform advanced *comunalizaciòn* (formation of communities) and brought about significant changes in the dynamics of communication and relationships within the Quichua world. Agrarian reform led not only to the restructuring of the hacienda regime, but also to the spatial and social disintegration of the anejo and the constitution of communal space in its place. As legal entities formed to meet the requirements of the agrarian reform, the "comunidades" also became territorial and social units. The Law of Communes and Cooperatives of 1937 did not have the same impact on indigenous settlements. The goal of that law was to incorporate into Ecuadorian national territory every inhabited center such as anejos, *caseríos*, comunidades, and *parcialidades* (rural districts joined to boroughs, hamlets, and communities). None of these units, in fact, had been legally recognized under the Law of Political and Territorial Division of 1897, in which the lowest level administrative unit was the rural parish. Therefore, the 1937 law was intended to give legal status to "peasant communities," even if the basis of this legal recognition was demographic and not territorial. In the context of modernizing the agrarian structure, the legal recognition of the free "comunas" and cooperatives sought to foster the transformation of indigenous peons into modern peasants (Lucero 2003). Territorial units were controlled and legislated by the ministry of social assistance (Ministerio de Previsión Social), which designated the territorial patrimony of communities through ministerial decrees. Their boundaries were based on property titles, if there were any, or on state adjudication of vacant lands (*tierras baldías*).[10] This patrimony was understood as indivisible and inalienable, and therefore could only be transmitted through inheritance; title could not be sold, mortgaged, or transferred to anybody who was not a part of the commune (Costales and de Costales 1962, 67–89). Only three sectors in Tixán were legalized under the 1937 law (see table 1, p. 70). The vast majority of other communities were legalized, during the 1960s and 1970s, following a trend that was apparently widespread throughout the highlands due to the requirements of the agrarian laws (Zamosc 1994).

The legal recognition (*personería jurídica*) that communities obtained through agrarian reform also included a territorial unit. Those communities consisted of private houses scattered around a communal center, which served as the area for public activities, with the school, the meeting room, the chapel, and the communal lands adjudicated or purchased under the agrarian reform laws. Due to the well-defined and limited area of land allotted to the community, the houses were closer to each other than they had been in the anejos. This spatial readjustment implied new internal alliances that were no longer based solely on kinship. Neighbors were no longer necessarily members of the same family. In addition, the intensification of and growing dependency on the market economy also determined the emergence of new social networks. Even those lands that were considered communal were in reality purchased by more or less large groups within the community and not by the community as a whole. Land purchase and acquisition created new social relations and partnerships. Only former huasipungueros were entitled to receive the huasipungos. Former arrimados, former sitiajeros, and former yanaperos were able to acquire lands only through communal purchase. Different opportunities and economic possibilities created new hierarchies and reinforced existing ones, with landless comuneros working as sharecroppers for fellow comuneros who owned land.

In many cases these spatial and structural changes, together with the fact that the hacienda no longer existed to guarantee household subsistence, led to more internal conflict. The level of competition grew, manifesting itself as envy or actual ritualized vendettas. People's comments about their fellow comuneros often sounded to me at odds with the idealized vision of community as the oasis of collective rights and equality. Indeed, some of these comments portrayed communities as veritable hells of black magic and revenge. The family in the Pachagsí community with whom I lived for three weeks had recently suffered a loss: the mother of P. B., the head of the household. M. B., his young wife, spoke openly about her life in Pachagsí. She had grown up in the city and had come to the community after marriage. Her husband was secretary of the Inca Atahualpa at that time, and his comrades often teased him with jokes alluding to M. B.'s beauty and elegance and the chances of someone "stealing" her from him.

However, I noticed that, regardless of the occasion, M. B. would not wear the same elaborated clothing in the community space that she wore when she went to town. In a conversation about her mother-in-law's death, M. B. explained why she clothed herself differently in Pachagsí: "They do this [evil eye] when they see that you now have good clothes or more things, or when they see that you get on well with everyone. They want to see you poor and alone, not talking to anybody, yes, then they're happy. They did the bad [black magic] on P.'s mom until she died, because she fought against some others to buy a piece of land, and those people harmed her for revenge" (1993). Her husband seemed to share this view of the community space. When I greeted him one morning and asked how he was, he replied, "I was so scared last night, compañera. I had to come back from Yacupungo at night alone in the dark. It's dangerous, some enemy might just . . ." (1993).

In the functionalist interpretation, envy in the Andean context is understood as a mechanism that dissolves conflict and promotes solidarity by imposing control over scarce resources and their distribution (Brush 1974, 29). This functionalist emphasis requires a diachronic reappraisal. Dependence on the market economy has been growing in indigenous communities, which increases internal stratification. In communities today, it is inevitable that some people buy more land than others or acquire their own means of transport or other resources. The control mechanism over scarce resources, activated through envy, is impossible to maintain in this new situation. It is no longer simply a matter of scarcity, but rather of profound changes in the economic structure. The case under discussion indicates a clash between cultural and structural dimensions that manifests itself in conflict (Geertz 1990). Envy no longer fulfills its role of control and redistribution, but has become symptomatic of a conflict that may eventually lead to breakdown.

Furthermore, the demands of social life have also changed. More assemblies are necessary because more decisions need to made—for example, those pertaining to school, applications, legal claims, and annual elections for the community council (*cabildo*). There are catechism meetings for Catholics and services for evangelicals. There are collective work responsibilities, such as mingas, on community land. The concentration of geographical space is matched by a corresponding intensification of social responsibilities. This leads to the proliferation of internal, collective micro-identities, which are no longer based purely on patronymics. Kinship identities, in many cases, break out of strictly defined community boundaries to establish alliances beyond the community's "imagined" border. In the former anejos, the alliance among members of the extended family group, the *ayllu*, was the fundamental unit that upheld the socioeconomic structure of each household. Now people resort to cross-community kinship bonds when all other internal alliances have failed, as when a neighbor does not collaborate, when a partner does not provide support, or when close relatives do not help. To go to another community space in search of other, more distant family nuclei seems to have become the last resort. The perception of distance, not only spatial but also social and political, has changed.

This symbolic intracommunity condensation is matched by a corresponding symbolic intercommunity condensation. If, before, the various anejos remembered and reaffirmed alliances and conflicts on ritual occasions, nowadays the communities have a much more concerted field of interaction: assemblies, meetings, and participation in markets. The formation of the Inca Atahualpa, for example, has intensified interactions among its affiliated communities. Moreover, the physical space is also more concentrated; the area of the former anejo of Pishillig accommodates today three communities and one association. This intercommunal neighborhood has made relationships more direct and more frequent. The new context of interactions not only generated new intercommunity micro-identities, but also increased competition for power and resources.

Within the Quichua world, old social identities were redefined and new ones created, the latter being accompanied by new values and social skills that deeply affected the lives of Quichuas in Tixán. The acquisition of land pushed them toward a market economy, which had been marginal to their economic activity during the hacienda era. Credit, loans, interest rates, fair prices, and productivity became major concerns for all community members. Despite interethnic conflicts, the Quichuas had gone from being exploited peons to being modern farmers; this new subject position gradually led to a redefinition of their power relations with the local nonindigenous population, who, as the founder of the Inca Atahualpa asserted, now had to respect them.

Parish Economy and Production

State-sponsored ideas of progress and modernization brought changes that transformed Tixán's economy and its appearance. Houses were no longer made of adobe, but of concrete or brick. State-funded infrastructure also developed in town, including potable water and sanitation systems, street lighting, a health center, and telecommunications.

As a rural parish, Tixán's local economy continued to be based primarily on agricultural production and, to a lesser degree, on raising cattle. Modernization of the agrarian structure nationally, state-led modernization (which included building infrastructure and roads, mechanization, and pursuit of industrialization), and the opening of a new and expanded agrarian market led to new trends in the commercialization of crops and produce. In Tixán, production ceased to focus on barley as the main commercial crop, followed by wheat, potatoes, maize, peas, lentils, large beans, and small quantities of quinoa. Productivity depended on altitude, with potatoes and large beans being the only high-altitude crops. The cold climate at altitudes above 3,600 meters made cultivation difficult, and cattle-raising thus persisted as the main productive activity. The principal crops for markets outside the parish were barley and wheat, while all the other crops were sold in the local markets in Tixán, Guamote, and Alausí. Wheat flour emerged as another important product for the parish economy. Flour had been produced in the town since the hacienda times, when the town's only mill was owned by a white family who charged, in cash or goods, according to its own interests and the perceived ethnicity of the customers; the mill owner openly exploited Quichuas and chagras, who had less favorable terms for milling than did the miller's compadres, relatives, or local allies.

Subsistence and market economies became equally effective for both indigenous and nonindigenous people. Household plots and community lands constituted the two main types of land tenure in the indigenous and chagra communities. Production from household plots was allocated to family subsistence and exchange; surplus production was sometimes sold before the harvest, principally to compadres from the town or at the local markets. Production from community lands was sold in larger markets at Alausí, Riobamba, and Cuenca (capital of the southern highland province of Azuay), and occasionally at the coastal market.

Among tixaneños, land tenure was based on private ownership, and household production was allocated either for family consumption or for the market, primarily the markets in Alausí and Guamote. The town itself represented a retail opportunity for the small-scale production of potatoes, wheat, and barley. Harvests bought in advance from indigenous producers were used for market speculation. Occasional wage labor and sharecropping regulated the labor relations on tixaneños' lands. The increased interdependence between indigenous and nonindigenous farmers brought about by agricultural modernization gradually redefined this form of precapitalist relations of production in a way that disguised its exploitative nature. In some cases sharecropping arrangements became more complex and expanded the network of labor relations and exploitation. In most of the sharecropping cases that I came across in Tixán, the parties involved in the transaction were also compadres. Their ritual kinship functioned as a form of moral obligation, a relationship which both parties could hardly refuse when asked. At the same time, the compadrazgo would guarantee some degree of access to produce and labor.

In the context of the indigenous economy in Tixán, household production from agriculture or raising animals, reciprocity associated with exchange and barter, and seasonal migration combined in different ways to constitute the main sources of household subsistence. Productive activity depended again on the altitude. In higher páramo communities, it was based mainly on cattle-raising, using a system of communal pastures. Surplus household production was used for exchanges that provided access to products of different microclimates. Nonetheless, this model of verticality was not necessarily restricted to extended family ties (Murra 1975). Ritual kinship could be similarly effective.

The practices of minga and *maquita mañachi* (or *ruegue*, as the Quichuas sometimes called it) are local examples of Andean reciprocity, a system of moral economy that is widespread among indigenous populations in Andean countries (Alberti and Mayer 1974). *Minga* refers to the provision of labor for any kind of community work in which at least one member of each household must participate. Literally "lending a hand," *maquita mañachi* refers to an exchange of labor between members of the same extended family or between compadres, especially during planting and harvest seasons.[11] As L. P. explained, "If there is harvest in one's plot, we use ruegue; we go from house to house asking for a hand. If one day someone asked me for a hand, I can some other day ask that same person for a hand" (1992). These two forms of reciprocity regulated access to extra labor when it was needed, while temporary migration to cities or to the coast in search of seasonal work reflected the need for extra income for nonsubsistence expenses.[12] Although many Andean indigenous groups had adopted this expedient since colonial times, the phenomenon became more widespread after agrarian reform due to the increased need for cash for expenses associated with farming (Glave 1989).

In general, members of communities that were closer to the Pan-

American Highway migrated more frequently than those living at a higher altitude and greater distance from the highway. In the context of the politicization of ethnic identity, migration was perceived by indigenous grassroots and national activists to have highly negative impacts on the preservation of indigenous culture. They considered migration responsible for the refusal of migrant male youth to wear traditional clothing and to speak vernacular languages, and for the spread of new diseases and new forms of violence.[13] A. L. commented on the impacts of urbanization on young indigenous men, like himself, who left to find work in the city. He could not remember clearly what had been on his mind when he had moved to the city, but it sounded like he did not want to be singled out as an Indian: "When I left to go work in Quito, I didn't wear poncho and hat. I don't know why I didn't use them; maybe I thought that in the city I had to look like another mishu or maybe not, I don't know what my idea was, but I didn't wear poncho or anything else."

In 1990 the Inca Atahualpa launched a vigorous campaign to control and reduce migration, especially during the planting and harvest seasons, when agricultural activities were intensive and extra labor was needed to increase production and repay debts. Nevertheless, in the context of the market economy, migration remained necessary as a crucial source of cash income for expanding production by acquiring more land or agricultural implements.

Problematizing the Parish

When describing Tixán and the parish in general, indigenous and nonindigenous locals emphasized what they perceived to be major problems: isolation, neglect, and lack of services and infrastructure. For many highland parishes, the decline of the railroad adversely affected local commerce. With the closure of the railroad in the 1960s, Tixán became relatively isolated; the same happened to the cantonal capital of Alausí, which gradually ceased to be an important agricultural trading point, a distinction based on its railroad connection to the coast. The Pan-American Highway is today the only major road connecting Tixán and Alausí with the provincial capital Riobamba and the southern province of Azuay. During the years in which I conducted my fieldwork, access to the communities was problematic due to the terrible condition of the paths, which were often almost impassable, especially during winter rains. Depending on the distance, people and goods traveled to and from the communities in hired trucks, on horseback, and by foot.

From the perspective of community residents, education and health services were particularly neglected and inadequate. Although by the late 1990s most of the indigenous communities had elementary schools, many of which were bilingual, the school dropout rate was high. According to Inca Atahualpa leaders, many people in the parish, especially the indigenous, were illiterate (see Inca Atahualpa 1992). For preschool-age children, the educational needs of the area were covered under a ministerial program called Operation of Children Rescue (ORI), funded and administered by national and international NGOs through the ministry of welfare. Created in 1990, and originally named the Communal Network (Red Comunitaria), the program aimed to provide nursery schools for children under six, with an emphasis on nutrition. The communities that were granted nursery schools selected the people to staff them. The ministry was responsible for providing teacher salaries and training, as well as authorizing their qualifications.[14]

There were no health centers in the communities. According to two nuns who were based in the Pachamama sector and offering assistance to the nearby communities, the high rate of infant mortality was largely due to respiratory problems and measles, particularly in the páramo communities. Another common health problem was parasitism, because water for human consumption was usually acquired from ditches alongside the fields and pastures; few communities had either piped water or potable water. The nearest health center was in Tixán, and it was not equipped for emergencies. Non-official medical attention was also offered by *curanderos/as*, healers who used herbal and natural remedies for common illnesses such as colds, flu, and bacterial infections.

In the area of agricultural production, progressive deforestation and soil erosion were partially responsible for the decreased fertility of the soil and the increased winds. Elders who had lived in the haciendas often pointed out the changes in land productivity. R. L., an elder from Pachagsí, said, "I remember that when we were already old, the wind started and everything got bad, crops dried out and went bad. Here in this community we have very little grain now. Before there was very little wind here, little wind in June, July, and August; August we had a little, but not too much, very little wind here, it was very sheltered. Now there is drought and little grain" (1992). Logging resulted in the almost complete disappearance of native trees, such as quishuar and llillín, which protected crops from night frosts. In many cases, the foreign species used in replanting, especially pine and eucalyptus, did not adapt to the Andean highland climate, showing little resistance to disease. One such example is in the nearby parish of Palmira, close to an area known as "el Desierto de Palmira" (Palmira Desert). This area, whose deforestation is blamed for the strong summer winds that now blow across the whole sector, from Palmira southward, was reforested with pine trees, but they were soon ridden with disease.

Soil erosion and degradation seemed to be linked to modernization and the needs of the market. Farming gradually became semi-mechanized. Yokes were still used for plowing, especially on the steep slopes. Until 1998, the Inca Atahualpa owned the only tractor available to the communities of the parish. Most of the land was not irrigated because of the lack of water. Furthermore, the demands of the market economy pushed some farmers to monoculture, which depletes the soil and reduces productivity. Taita R. L. remembers, "Before we had no tractors, only yokes and hands nothing more. . . . We had no fertilizers then, nothing nothing, only animal manure, sheep dung; we harvested a lot of grain. Now with fertilizers potatoes taste bitter. . . . Before if the soil was enough, we let the land fallow for a year, then we sowed any grain we knew, but we divided, corn on the one side and lentils and lupines on the other side depending on the soil. Now everything together—together all the grain all the time" (1992). According to Alfonso, an agronomy student who worked for many years with NGOs on agricultural production and with the Inca Atahualpa, soil use in Tixán was not guided by its properties, that is, whether it was sand, clay, black, moist, flat, sloping.[15] In addition, the harsh climate and the strong summer winds caused infestations and disease that were combated with chemical pesticides.

The mandate of progress and modernization as understood by the Ecuadorian state and that was premised on the rationalization of land tenure transformed the life of everybody in Tixán. Old lords left, new masters appeared. Relationships of economic interdependence augmented interethnic conflict and reinvigorated ethnic and racial stereotyping among Quichuas, chagras, and tixaneños.[16] Neglect, economic difficulties, droughts, climate change and soil erosion, high commercialization and production costs, and land conflicts gradually affected everybody, Quichuas, chagras and tixaneños alike, hindering their dreams of progress and wealth. In this context, a growing process of politicization of ethnic consciousness led indigenous groups at the local and national levels to increasingly exercise power and gain access to the decision-making process.

The Era of the Inca

This reconfiguration of power relations in post-agrarian reform Tixán had to account for the consolidation of a process of mobilization that gradually transformed indigenous actors into public political subjects, both locally and nationally. Thus began a new political phase, during which indigenous demands expanded beyond the settlement of land conflicts that had lingered since the agrarian reform, toward recognition of their cultural and ethnic diversity. In this phase indigenous activists and commoners could count on a new political ally, one that emerged from the dismantling of the hacienda regime: the Catholic Church. It can be argued that the Catholic Church had maintained an ambivalent attitude toward issues involving the administration of indigenous people since colonial times, allowing for some of the priests and religious orders to support indigenous causes at different historical moments in different ways.[17] This time, however, theological changes from within the religious institution divided the clergy into a conservative segment, which continued to harbor the same ambivalence and often sided with the established regime, and a progressive segment, which under the mandate of liberation theology initiated seminal work to support organizing among indigenous and poor people. In the vision of the progressive element of the church, there would be no more abusive priests in Tixán, but rather supportive Fathers and indigenous catechists who encouraged people to unite and fight for their rights. The creation of the Inca Atahualpa sheds light on this process.

The Bishop of the Indians

The 1960s and 1970s represent a turning point for the Catholic Church in Latin America. The Latin American Episcopal Synod held in Medellín, Colombia, in 1968 expanded on a preoccupation, expressed in 1967 by Pope Paul VI in his *Enciclica Populorum Progressio*, with the role of the Catholic Church in countries where the majority of the population were poor and struggling for survival. Whereas the *Enciclica* only mentioned the need to pay attention to these compelling social issues, the synod in Medellín urged Catholic Church officials and representatives to commit to supporting and assisting the poor in their quotidian struggles against poverty, exploitation, and discrimination. This proposal was later formally deemed liberation theology (*teología de la liberación*) by the Peruvian priest Gustavo Gutiérrez. He emphasized the responsibility of the Catholic Church to help the poor to free themselves from poverty and oppression, a responsibility premised on Christian faith and the teaching of Jesus Christ. Considered a politicized proposal imbued with Marxist ideology, liberation theology was not accepted by the Vatican until the 1990s, and many priests in Latin America who did embrace it were persecuted by repressive regimes during the 1970s. The murder, in El Salvador, of Archbishop Oscar Romero, who was shot in 1980 while celebrating Mass, attracted international attention to political repression and human-rights violations in Central America.

In Ecuador, liberation theology took root in provinces with large proportions of indigenous people and among priests who were in direct contact with indigenous realities. In Chimborazo, Bishop Leonidas Proaño, a leading figure in the diocese of Riobamba, was nicknamed Bishop of the Indians for his lifelong commitment to defending and advocating for indigenous people, who constituted the majority of the poor in the province. His influence extended beyond provincial boundaries, as he urged the Catholic Church in Ecuador to champion indigenous demands with both the government and local authorities. Most priests in his diocese followed this mandate to the extent that they came to be perceived by local agrarian elites as communists and subversive priests. By the end of the 1980s, most of the mobilizing efforts in Chimborazo Province and elsewhere in the country were led by the Catholic Church. The church's leadership reduced the Federación Ecuatoriana de Indios (FEI) to a far more marginal and secondary role in the political process. When I asked Enrique Bazante, founding leader of the FEI in the province, why the federation had lost ground among indigenous actors, he blamed the FEI's internal conflicts and power struggles among its political factions. These frictions, he said, "poisoned the movement; there was no clear leadership any more and people got fed up" (Enrique Bazante, Riobamba, 1993).

However, other factors intervened in the process and allowed the progressive fringe of the Catholic Church to take over the FEI. The first is related to the messages that the church was sending to the poor, which fit with the phase in the peasant movement that followed the agrarian reform struggle. There were pronouncements, often made by Bishop Proaño, which denounced the regime of exploitation and abuse which the indigenous sector and the "poor" continued to suffer.

> The situation of indigenous people, from all points of view, was deplorable. Indians were sunk in total poverty: economically, dispossessed of their lands and exploited; socially, marginalized and scorned; culturally, reduced to ignorance and illiteracy; politically, considered peanuts. . . . From the sociological point of view, they were victims of multiple, destructive complexes, such as ignorance, fear, mistrust, passivity, fatalism. (Bishop Proaño in Enriquez 1989, 14)

> In Latin America we address as poor indigenous people, blacks, peasants, slum dwellers, the unemployed, the under-employed, laborers, and many craftsmen. . . . [T]he poor are those who . . . suffer from all the weight of the dominance of social classes which had been imposed on them. They are the scorned. (Bishop Proaño 1989, 3)

The use of the past tense in the first of the bishop's quotations reflects his view that the "Indians" were finally awakening and starting to assert their right to respect and dignity. These messages alluded to the double condition of exploitation suffered by Indians and blacks in the country, which derived from their class status and their racial status. Their mobilization as peasants, which had occurred under the direction of the FEI during the agrarian reform, was no longer enough to address the problems that they continued to experience, even after becoming legally entitled to land. They had to struggle against prejudices, rooted in colonialism, that were still obstructing their access to resources—land, capital, education, and power—and to equitable treatment.

The second element is related to the organizational structure of the Catholic Church, which made it possible to consolidate and spread messages among the indigenous masses. Its highly decentralized and capillary presence allowed the message of liberation theology to reach even the most remote areas of the countryside. In accordance with this message, the church assumed responsibility for striving for a more just society. "Faced with the tensions which conspire against peace, which go so far as to even insinuate temptation to violence; faced with the Christian concept of peace . . . we believe that the Latin American Catholic clergy cannot exempt itself from assuming truly concrete responsibilities. Because to create a fair social order without peace is an illusion . . . and [it is] is an eminently Christian task" (Bishop Proaño 1991, 13).

In the mid-1970s the progressive arm of the Catholic Church launched consciousness-raising campaigns among indigenous communities. In Chimborazo, as in many other provinces with a large proportion of indigenous people, this new pastoral commitment to the poor also implied the training of indigenous catechists, who would exhort their communities to organize and defend their dignity. These factors functioned as structural elements that favored the formation and consolidation of what came to be called the indigenous movement. Many of the local, provincial, and national federations were born with the active participation of Catholic priests and missionaries.[18] The case of Tixán illustrates this process and illuminates the complex composition of political forces and networks that intervened in the formation of the indigenous movement in Ecuador.

Long Live King Atahualpa

The events that led to the actual birth of the Inca Atahualpa were the result of a longer process of mobilization in which progressive Catholic forces played a pivotal role. The struggle for agrarian reform already had mobilized all of the Tixán communities. Many of the elders I interviewed about that period established a link between that struggle and the mobilization that followed. According to Taita L. B., there was a continuum between the land struggle and the political phase: "This way we fought and organized and we are still organized and we have our own organization, the Inca Atahualpa. And thank God we are united" (1992). This perception, however, underscores a complex political process in which new actors and new circumstances appeared.

This process started in Tixán with the arrival of Father Benito and two Spanish missionaries remembered as the "Cuquis." As Taita Pedro Marcatoma recalled,

> At that time [the 1970s], there was Father Benito. He was born in Spain; then came his comrade Alejandro, and comrade Antonio Cuqui. So when he came, he appointed us as catechists. As catechists we went from community to community, saying that we were going to train catechists in every community in every area. So to make a proper organization of this, Taita Bishop—God bless him—Leonidas Proaño invited us to wake ourselves up to do some missions, and there was everything to be done. Then, thank God, came Father Benito, and when he went, Father Pedrito [Pedro Torres] came and

> we set to work. And thank God, now we have our own thing [Inca organization] to claim our rights. (1992)

Father Pedro Torres, appointed to serve as parish priest between 1985 and 1993, identified Monseñor Proaño as the key figure in the mobilization of the province: "He came with new proposals, promoting housing cooperatives, creating popular radio stations [*radiofónicas*] and so on and so forth. After 1972, after the second agrarian law the Church of Riobamba planned a whole mobilization move for the agrarian struggle in the province and the example of Chimborazo was then replicated in other provinces such as Tungurahua, Bolivar, Cotopaxi, and even Imbabura. At that time they started to organize grassroots organizations and communities to make sure they got the lands they were entitled to. It was different from the unionist model of FEI; this was with the grassroots" (1992).

As affirmed by Father Pedro and by Taita Pedro Marcatoma, those who spread Proaño's messages and proposals at the grassroots level were indigenous catechists, young indigenous men who had been trained by the church in Riobamba. In Tixán in 1982 the local indigenous catechists started to talk of federation to the presidents of their communities, and from 1986 they called the people to large public assemblies (*tandanacui*). The presidents of several communities from Tixán and Achupallas parishes participated in these assemblies. At the outset, attendance at these meetings was good, but then something happened, and the assembly of February 1988 was a total fiasco, with hardly anybody in attendance. Father Pedro Torres attributed this failure to the presence of the FEI in the area. Since 1986 FEI leaders had been campaigning against the idea of forming a federation other than the FEI in the area. P. B., one of the youngest of the Inca Atahualpa's leaders, confirmed and explained the modality of this interference.

> We first had a problem with those from FEI in '86; the communities of Pachagsí, Pacífica, Merced, Cocán, they belonged to FEI, and so one day they were in a meeting with the catechists and they [FEI] came here with a lawyer, Gualle, who was a leader of FEI, and interrupted in the meeting, because he was also candidate for deputy. And so they came and interrupted our meeting with the catechists in order to oppose the formation of a federation, because they said it was not worth it to further divide the organizations since most of the communities were already affiliated with FEI. And so they had to follow with FEI and not with another federation. (1992)

Father Torres, however, offered a more nuanced explanation, remarking that the indigenous locals had had little interest in the idea of a local federation, that they had not known what would be involved, and when faced with a fight between the church and the FEI, chose not to participate.

Other factors, therefore, led to the decision in favor of forming the Inca Atahualpa. In a long collective interview I conducted on the genesis of their organization, M. P., A. L., and P. B., who were among the most active members and leaders of the Inca Atahualpa at the time, and Father Torres tried to reconstruct all the details of what had happened in late 1988. They remembered this as a year marked by intense political activity involving both the páramo and lower communities—commonly referred to as *los de arriba* (those from above) and *los de abajo* (those from below)—of the Alausí canton.[19] This reconstruction proved to be challenging since they were not always in agreement on what exactly had happened first, what assembly, what action, or what day. What came out clearly, though, were their shared motivations and intentions, the memory of which was still vivid for all of them. The account I offer here, therefore, may entail some factual imprecision, but it faithfully portrays the political motivations and purposes expressed by the activists' words.

The páramo area of Zula, Achupallas parish, was known for its marble mines, which were the property of the Ecuadorian state but administered privately on a competitive basis. In 1988 the struggle for adjudication of the mines led to serious confrontations between two nonindigenous families, the Coronels and the Jayas. The Coronels lived in Riobamba, while the Jayas, who were locally based, had been working in the mines for a longer period. The indigenous people of the neighboring communities of Achupallas parish, already organized as the Federación de Comunidades Indígenas de Achupallas, decided to side with neither family, but rather to participate in the dispute as a third party competing for adjudication of the mines on behalf of the indigenous workers. However, another group of indigenous workers, from a sector called Totoras, also wanted to participate in the competition and were forming another federation, which later became the Asociación de Trabajadores Autónomos Minas de Zula Indígenas de Chimborazo (ATAMZICH). In both cases they were seeking allies in order to build a stronger indigenous front. Thus, the support of the communities from the lower lands, los de abajo, of the parish of Tixán became paramount. In May 1988, as M. P. reminisced, a whistleblower from the Santa Lucía community alerted people that *totoreños* had decided to ransack the Tixán communities.[20] "I was president of Yacupungo at that time and I remember my deceased brother-in-law was then president of Santa Lucía and that community was involved in the problem then. So because he was my brother-in-law and had compadres and ahijados in Yacupungo, he came one night as a whistleblower to alert that the attack was coming on that given day at that exact time and so 'you have to unite so that they don't come,' he said. And so we decided to go to Totoras to offer support to avoid the ransacking" (M. P., 1992).

Words and news about the ransackings had already spread, so everybody knew they were real. Totoreños had already pillaged La Dolorosa community, "taking everything, setting houses on fire, eating their animals, they even killed a man and forced a woman to lift him on her shoulders, they said" (M. P., 1992). M. P. clarified, however, that at the beginning each community in the Tixán area individually responded to those threats, offering to help protect Totoras, just as Yacupungo people had done. In their meetings the catechists again suggested unity. Los de abajo decided finally to go together to an assembly that totoreños had called for in Santa Lucía, during which they were supposed to sign legal papers to form the organization, with the minister of agriculture to serve as witness. Forty-eight communities participated in the assembly. But something went wrong. Once there, the people of los de abajo found out that the organization about to be created was to include only eleven communities of mineworkers, rather than all the communities that had offered support. A. L., who was in charge of communication at the assembly, recalled, "I had the microphone, so when I realized we were not included, I said in the microphone, 'No, comrades, since they don't include us, then let's go and have another meeting.' And so from Santa Lucía people came down to Yacupungo, and they started to talk to see if it was worth it to support totoreños, if it was worth it to have another directive [board], and so on and so forth. And here we stayed for hours discussing behind closed doors until ten at night" (1992).

Although the idea of creating an indigenous federation in Tixán had been germinating for a while and was strongly encouraged by the local Catholic priests, the specific circumstances prompted people to decide to create their own federation. The time had come for los de abajo to unite and take action on problems that had long been distressing their communities—cattle thieving and violent robberies—in addition to the new threats. Representatives of the communities at the meeting in Yacupungo unanimously voted in favor of creating an organization initially called Rey Atahualpa (King Atahualpa) and later renamed Inca Atahualpa. M. P., who became the first president and active leader of the organization, remembered this moment with excitement. Invigorated by the newfound unity among its members, Rey Atahualpa members started their march uphill to meet again with los de arriba: "There we were, all of us marching together and shouting, 'Long Live Rey Atahualpa.'" The march was meant not merely to show support to the páramo folks, but rather to display force and determination and to demonstrate that los de abajo were ready to defend themselves from any and all external aggression. Thus, on the same occasion, two organizations were formed, one of los de arriba and one of los de abajo. Inca Atahualpa soon became the most representative among the four indigenous organizations in the canton of Alausí, and it was affiliated with twenty-two of the twenty-nine indigenous communities in Tixán parish.

To reinforce the idea of unity as a foundation for success was a spectacular and successful action that various communities undertook during that same period of intraethnic confrontation in order to put an end to chagra abuses and thievery. Everybody knew who the thieves were, but it was only when the communities came together that they gained the necessary strength to punish the thieves and so finally put an end to a long-term and violent abuse.[21]

Once the Inca Atahualpa was established, Father Torres remained a powerful and central ally of the organization as well as an advocate of indigenous people. He consistently participated in local processes of ethnogenesis and formation of indigenous identity.[22] Father Torres was the first, for example, to suggest that the founders of the new organization reconsider the name King Atahualpa and choose a "more indigenous" version. The final version of the organization's name, Inca Atahualpa, may have more than one origin, however. One may be related to the Messianic myth of Inkarrí, which is well known in Andean indigenous cultures and has inspired rebellions and uprisings in the Andes since the colonial period (Burga 1988; Flores Galindo 1987; Ossio 1973). The most widespread version tells how the Inca Atahualpa, whose body was quartered and buried, will be made whole again and return to earth to restore order.

Although the myth had been recorded mostly in the Peruvian Andes, I was able to trace a variation of it in the Tixán area. In my conversations with Taita Xavier Buñay on "las cositas de Dios" (God's little things), I asked him about the origin of the name Tixán, which local literature attributed to the ethnic group originally populating the area, known as Tiquizambis. Without mentioning the name, he replied that there the *runas* (Quichua for indigenous people) were led by the Inca Atahualpa.

> Atahualpa was runa like me, but fat, so very fat and black, and there was no clothing at that time, only ponchos, but good poncho, and a sheep belt but no clothes. Atahualpa was from Nisag, then he said, "So, ladies and gentlemen, why are you paying attention to Alausí people? I want you to make house here; go to the mountain to make a house." With a handful of stones, with one only stone he killed seven, eight he killed, *carajo*, with one stone he killed the white men, he himself killed the white men who came to make a house. His name was Atahualpa Rumiña Rumiñahui, three words. Atahualpa and Rumiñahui the same person. The white men said, "I order you make house in Alausí," and Atahualpa killed the white men with one stone. . . . There, lower than Alausí, there is a river, the Chanchán River. There, there is a door with key. Atahualpa is in there, in there enclosed, alive, in Nisag. A good bronze key, the mountain Nisag, Atahualpa Rumiñahui, the stone, *rumi*, is, there he is. The mountain has gotten him. . . . There he is, locked in by the bronze key. He is not coming out because the mountain has gotten him because he was fierce. He killed around ten or twenty, so because he contradicted the mountain, the mountain locked him in. . . . Atahualpa, son of God, sent by God, he came to give law, everything, so no government can defeat him. For being rebellious he was locked in, and he will only come out the Day of the Judgment. (Taita Javier Buñay, 1992)

A romantic view might attribute the naming of the organization Inca Atahualpa to an evocative and perhaps unconscious link to this myth, which the elders supposedly still remembered. Without dismissing this possibility, I suggest that the reference to Inca Atahualpa in this case articulates with the official historical narration of nation-state formation and therefore engages with the role that indigenous people have played in that process. Ecuador's official history emphasizes the figure of the Inca Atahualpa as the Ecuadorian contribution to the Incaic empire, the last courageous Inca, who defeated his Peruvian rival impostor, Huascar, and bravely resisted the Spaniards. An emblem of stamina and dignity in the official narrative of the nation, Atahualpa is represented as the contribution of indigenous people to the nation's glorious past. When I asked the founders of the Inca Atahualpa why they chose this name for their organization, they alluded to the historical importance of the Inca Atahualpa in the fight against the Spanish invaders. For M. P., the primary founder of the organization, Atahualpa symbolized strength and perseverance: "Our organization is as courageous and brave as Atahualpa, and we are not going to accept any insults or abuse, even from los de arriba" (1992). The initial choice, which used the word *King*, promptly corrected after the intervention of Father Torres, reflects its usage in official history, which indigenous people learn at school.

This example shed light on the intricate ways in which the process of modernization and national formation is constantly reinterpreted by groups who traditionally have been considered to be operating at the margins of the state (Poole and Das 2004). Formal education has incorporated indigenous groups into the homogenizing cultural policies of the nation-state and transformed the official narrative of the formation of national identity into a site for producing contested meanings and readings of that identity and history. In the case of the organization Inca Atahualpa, the virtues attributed to the historical figure of Atahualpa were considered meaningful for political action in two separate spheres: to reiterate and reaffirm ethnic identities, and to announce the emergence of new political subjects.

The earwitness makes no effort to look, but he hears all the better. He comes, halts, huddles unnoticed in a corner, peers into a book or a display, hears whatever is to be heard, and moves away untouched and absent. One would think he was not there for he is such an expert at vanishing. He is already somewhere else, he is already listening again, he knows all the places where there is something to be heard, stows it nicely away, and forgets nothing.

—Elias Canetti, *Earwitness*

CHAPTER THREE

Invisible Victories

Postreform changes had major implications for the empowerment of the local indigenous population. In this chapter I focus on the quotidian sociality of the conflict involving Quichuas, chagras, and tixaneños in spaces which usually are not regarded as political, for example, marketplaces, grocery shops, and ritual kinship (Alvarez, Escobar, and Dagnino 1998).[1] In these realms the manipulation of verbal and nonverbal communication codes sheds light on the inventive yet coded ways in which people reconfigure daily their position of weakness in a context of racial subordination. My interest here is to examine how indigenous people have processed the changes and responded to the domination imposed on them by new masters. Drawing on previous studies of quotidian politics, I define this space of political action as the space of invisible victories in which the weak manage to temporarily reverse their position of subordination.[2]

The expansion of daily encounters and interactions among Quichuas, chagras, and tixaneños associated with their increased interdependence offered an opportunity to redefine power relations among the three groups. The preexisting state of conflict not only continued, but also expanded, incorporating spaces the groups increasingly came to share in their quotidian routines. Interethnic conflict became ritualized through codes of interethnic behavior more or less established and continuously enacted to challenge or affirm existing hierarchies.

The encoding of these behavioral patterns in Tixán is the result of decades of interethnic friction that produced common semantic fields in which social actors learned to know and understand each others' position and intentions (see Eriksen 1992). These interactions and the semantic fields which they inhabit are imbued with relationships of power, whose frames of reference are the dominant cultural codes and symbolic systems. Such conflict is latent in daily interactions informing the rhythm of what is perceived as the "normality" of the everyday. Its apparent invisibility contrasts with the confrontation displayed in the political performance of the Inca Atahualpa. Rather than being regarded as passive, the politics of everyday life is a form of contestation whose ephemeral nature impedes substantial changes in the power structure (de Certeau 1988; Hale 1994).

In this respect, everyday life belongs to the realm of tactics, of actions that encroach on the other's territory without being able to conquer it completely. Tactics require waiting for opportunities to manipulate events and turn them to one's own advantage. Tactics, thus, depend on timing; they are not planned, but rather take place "blow by blow." In this view, tactics are "the art of the weak" (de Certeau 1988, 37–38). Unlike strategies, which typically are formulated in relation to specific goals, tactics take place as habitus, that is, as historically produced behaviors and actions that are not clearly (or at least openly) aware of their own ends (Bourdieu 1991, 92). The quotidian and reiterated dimension of the conflict has contributed to creating a habitus of resistance and contestation which informs the way different people relate to each other in everyday interactions.

My analysis of daily life tactics in Tixán focuses on areas in which interethnic relations were occurring most frequently. These were the marketplace, economic transactions in shops, compadrazgo (ritual kinship) relations, sports, and relationships of production. According to the parish's power structure, the "weak" were supposedly the Quichuas and the chagras, and the "strong" were the tixaneños. Relationships of dominance were challenged and redefined in everyday interactions, even if the reversal of power relations was only temporary (Scott 1985).

Central to understanding the invisible victories of quotidian politics in Tixán is the process of political mobilization that functioned as a legitimizing force for everyday "apolitical" actions. This symbolic empowerment of quotidian resistance acquired more significance after the formation of the Inca Atahualpa. A synergistic relationship was established between invisible acts of resistance and public displays of empowerment, with these two dimensions of political action constantly nurturing and legitimizing each other.

The Habitus of Resistance

Responses to conditions of interethnic conflict have historical and experiential roots. Previous studies of counterhegemonic indigenous practices in Latin America have taken into account the historical period regarded as relevant by the rebels' collective memory (Hill 1996; Stern 1987b). This historical recollection emphasizes the continuity of racial discrimination against indigenous people since the Spanish conquest. The impact of this historical consciousness on political struggles, however, depends on the specific social and political context of each country. The conservative alignment of the Miskitu against the revolutionary Sandinistas in Nicaragua contrasts with the progressive struggle against economic and social inequality as spearheaded by indigenous movements in Ecuador, Bolivia, and Colombia (Hale 1994). Yet in all those struggles the past acquired meaning in the present as an ideological foundation of their demands vis-à-vis revolutionaries, the state, and civil society.[3]

In the case of Tixán, *ñaupa timpu*, or ancient historical time, is retained in indigenous memory and coincides with the hacienda period.[4] This recollection, which focuses on mistreatment, exploitation, ignorance, and misery, feeds into an "official political discourse" that resonates with the one formulated at the national level by the indigenous movement (Thurner 1993, 45). This selective remembering, furthermore, is not generation specific, since all of the people I interviewed—young, adult, and elderly committed to the political struggle—shared the same image of that period.[5] Although the discourse about exploitation has been promoted by left-wing parties and activists since the beginning of the twentieth century, it has been widely reinterpreted and permeates not only the public and political spheres of indigenous discourse, but also the domestic one, feeding into a structure of feeling according to which even the most apparently "innocent" interactions inspire in the weak a guarded and defensive attitude.

A Manichean reading of past and present sustained by the negative image of the abusive past is the foundation of the concept of an indigenous awakening that informs indigenous political discourse.[6] In the past indigenous people have suffered in a state of servitude, poverty, and abuse. Accordingly, hacienda peons are portrayed as victims of an unjust regime. This self-produced depiction of subdued hacienda serfs as "pre-political victims" is counterposed to the more recent achievements of the "Indians" after they had become organized.[7] These two contrasting images support an interpretation of indigenous politics that often is promoted by social scientists, which places the emergence of indigenous political activism in Latin American at the beginning of the twentieth century, following implementation of state-led modernizing projects (see Thurner 1993, 41–45). However, between the supposed quiescence of the hacienda era and the political activism of more recent modern times is a state of silent contestation that coexists with forms of adaptation to the status quo expressed in daily life (see Stern 1987a). Many studies of indigenous politics in the Andes have underlined the continuity of indigenous insurgent practices reflected in their myths, such as the myth of Inkarrí.[8] Stern describes this structure of indigenous insurgence and rebellion at the Andean level: "a cultural memory nurtured and sustained by Andean peoples during an earlier period of 'resistant adaptation' to colonial rule," a memory that carries the utopia of radical transformations under a neo-Inca flag (1987a, 72).

Studies of the Ecuadorian case also underline this continuity by examining the uprisings against colonial rule organized by indigenous people in the highlands (Segundo Moreno Yánez 1985; Ramón Valarezo 1993). The political discourse produced by "modern" indigenous activists captured this continuity in their notion of "five hundred years of indigenous resistance," which became the motto of indigenous rejection, in 1992, of the celebration of the discovery of the Americas.

Thurner's study on the haciendas of the Zambrano family in the Chimborazo canton of Colta reveals how after the colonial period, aspects of daily life, such as the recurring petty theft of hacienda resources, also provided evidence of culturally defined mechanisms of resistance to abuse and domination (Thurner 1993, 56). In the manner of Brechtian forms of resistance, Quichuas' practice of *chalana* (literally, "gleaning") was used as a weapon against the landowner's power (Scott 1985). The chalana consisted in gathering all the produce left on the field just after harvest. Usually performed by women and children, this practice provided an additional source of produce for household subsistence (Cordero 1989, 25). In the context of the unequal and hierarchical relationship of the hacienda regime, chalana acquired a counterhegemonic symbolic efficacy. Thus, indigenous peasants were not simply gleaning from unfamiliar fields, but symbolically poaching on their master's property and production. It was not the material damage that determined the offense, but rather the impertinence of the challenge—the intention to violate the landowner's property rights by appropriating produce. However, indigenous peasants engaging in chalana (*chaladores*) did not act with the manifest purpose of harming their masters. Chalana belonged to the realm of indigenous economic strategies for defending family subsistence—and it is still used today.[9] It was not accompanied by any additional act overtly directed against the master.

Petty theft is another example of what Scott defines as weapons of the weak. The archive of *tenencia política* in Tixán is replete with reports of animal theft, especially cattle and sheep rustling, allegedly perpetrated both by Quichuas and nonindigenous people since hacienda times. The archival records show two types of theft: the first perpetrated by indigenous peons from haciendas against their own masters, the second perpetrated by Quichuas and poor nonindigenous peasants against wealthy tixaneño families. In such cases legal action was taken and punishment inflicted respectively by the hacienda administrators and the teniente político, who more commonly made the thieves pay for or return the stolen property.

These acts can be interpreted as cases of banditry common in precapitalist societies, where stealing was an endemic form of social protest adopted by the poor to redress abuses perpetrated by the rich (Hobsbawm 1959). Whether or not organized into livestock-rustling gangs as in the highland communities in the sierra of Cuzco, theft of livestock in Tixán had the more evident intention of attacking the hegemonic power of landowners and local white elites (Orlove 1973; Orlove 1990). Cattle rustling on hacienda lands was largely symbolic, because while the theft of one animal rarely caused hardship for the wealthy landowners, it constituted a symbolic act of aggression against their established power. Similarly, when a robbery involved local poor people or Quichuas against a powerful local family, the transgression was less in the damage caused by the theft and more for challenging the codes associated with relationships of domination and submission. The symbolic efficacy of such challenges derived, therefore, from a common language of abuse, which allowed the masters to understand the significance of the unspoken attack. At the same time, these rebellious acts of thievery reinforced and validated the existing system of abuse and exploitation, often violently imposed in order to exercise power and control (Poole 1991). While such acts therefore underscore the limitation of the art of the weak in reversing power relations, they rested their political efficacy in the building of a repertoire and memory of resistance to domination.

Another challenge to the landowners' power recorded in documents in the parish archive involved the silent and almost unperceived occupation of hacienda properties by free indigenous workers who maintained their condition as yanaperos or sitiajeros. Encroachment often consisted of grazing cattle on hacienda land without the landowner's permission. Once again, this was less a matter of material damage and more of symbolic defiance to the power of the mishu masters.

With the demise of the hacienda regime these forms of contestation became obsolete and were replaced by other tactics that responded to the changes in the parish and their effects on its inhabitants. The following examination of the politics of everyday life capitalizes on a process of "historic accumulation" of resistance practices in order to understand how Quichuas, chagras, and tixaneños responded to inequality and structural adjustments after the agrarian reform.[10] I consider the realm of everyday life as an intermediary state of resistance bridging supposed quiescence with active political practice. The examination of everyday practices of resistance, which I define in Bourdieu's terms as the habitus of resistance, establishes a dialogue between structural constraints and agency (Bourdieu 1977). In this case, structural factors—the colonial regime, the formation of modern states, and modernization—produced changing yet persistent conditions of discrimination against indigenous people that continuously nurtured multifaceted forms of resistance (Scott 1992, 45).

The Politics of Space

Economic transactions in Tixán constitute a complex process involving a range of parties. With the push toward a market economy and the completion of major roads in the area, transport became an important factor in the production process. Transportation to and from marketplaces emerged as an early indicator of the interdependence among ethnic groups. Indigenous people needed means of transport to sell their produce at local markets, and many tixaneños had become truck owners, making regular trips to such markets—Alausí on Sundays and Guamote on Thursdays. The truck owners charged for transporting each passenger and for bulk goods.

Familiarity and convenience made people choose trucks over the more impersonal and unreliable public bus service. Everybody in town knew who the truck owners were, and soon their regular trips to the markets became a reliable and useful service. Additionally, it was much easier to transport goods on these trucks than on the buses. Degrees of familiarity were emphasized by the distribution of the space on board. The place one occupied within the truck marked status and defined a symbolic frontier. The first time I traveled on one of these trucks, I was about to board the trailer when Don Pedro, the vehicle's owner and driver, stopped me and said, "No, no, Doña Enmita, you can sit inside; it is much more comfortable and warm." I had not realized until that moment how many people could squeeze into the cab of a truck. There were five of us, including the driver. Aside from the privileged treatment I received for being a gringa, and particularly as a foreign woman, sitting in the cab was my entry into the politics of space. The tixaneños, in this case the owner of the truck, his wife, and two other men from the town, were those who normally enjoyed a privileged place in the truck's cab, seated comfortably and sheltered from rain, cold, dust, and sun. Indigenous passengers always travel behind in the open trailer. Quite commonly young indigenous men straddled the sides of the trailer, while women and older men took a seat or stood on the bed of the trailer. As a pedestrian, I had often seen trucks crammed full of indigenous people. The men's ponchos transformed passing trucks into a choreography of red figures flowing along the parish's major road. These rides were common, and everybody knew their origins and destinations. During that trip to the Alausí market on Don Pedro's truck, the conversation of the men in the cab revolved around prices in the market for crops such as potatoes and barley. However, my unusual presence prompted Don Pedro to explain, pointing with his head at his indigenous travel companions in the back: "They are used to traveling like this. They are páramo people, whereas it is too cold for us out there. Of course, if someone from the town insists on traveling and I have no space left inside, they have to make do traveling in the back with the *indianada* [crowd of Indians]" (1992). I knew by then that the term *indianada* was used pejoratively by white people to lump together an unspecified group of indigenous individuals.

A similar spatial separation occurred in other social contexts. On interprovincial buses, for example, indigenous passengers normally sat in the back, and this also occurred in churches (see Crespi 1981, 486). Such symbolic spatial frontiers transformed certain places in Tixán into spaces, in other words into frequented places in which difference and hierarchies were produced (de Certeau 1988, Massey 1994): there were meeting places for "*los del campo*" (Quichuas and chagras), and others for the tixaneños,

Figure 2. The main street in Tixán. Photo by author.

just as there had been chicherías for Quichuas and liquor stores frequented only by tixaneños. Also, indigenous parishioners attended Sunday Mass at eight in the morning, while tixaneños went at eleven. Even the mapping of the neighborhoods was defined by ethnicity; indigenous inhabitants usually settled at the entrance of the town, while chagras and poor mestizos settled at the periphery beyond the church, on the western slopes.

These forms of spatial boundaries functioned as de facto practices of segregation. For example, when I asked some indigenous people in Tixán why they did not attend the *rocola* (a type of canteen with a jukebox), their answer was always the same.[11] They felt they did not belong there, since the space was culturally and socially defined as nonindigenous. According to A. L., "We don't play cards, we don't listen to that music; that is for mishus." Eventually, I realized that Quichuas would not enter spaces in town that were owned, administered, and run by tixaneños, unless it was necessary.

Exceptions to these coded behaviors usually took place through compadrazgos. Having a compadre in town who owned a truck, for example, enabled one to enjoy certain privileges normally reserved for townsfolk, such as traveling in the truck's cab. In the course of a long conversation with P. B., who at the time was the Inca Atahualpa's vice president, I asked him about having tixaneños as compadres. He recalled one rainy Sunday when he and his wife had gone to Alausí. They had called on their compadre, who owned a truck, and without even asking, P. B. had opened the door of the cab and let his wife inside. With a smile on his face, he said, "It was raining; there is a reason why he is my compadre."

These spatial frontiers were either spontaneously maintained or momentarily questioned without challenging the power structure that produced them. In the case of the rocola, it is clear that the increased interdependence among Quichuas and tixaneños had not redefined dynamics of social distance in other aspects of social life, where economic and other interests were not at stake. Entertainment remained a highly segregated space. However, the presence of the Inca Atahualpa in the town led to the adoption of the same exclusionary politics of space by the subordinated groups in order to redefine their position in daily interactions. Instead of overtly questioning the division of space, Quichuas managed to create new spaces in which de facto spatial segregation excluded tixaneños. The example of the indigenous communal house (*casa comunal*) exemplifies the way these new spaces became sites for contesting power relations. Quickly known in town as the "house of the Indians" (*casa de los indios*), access to the casa comunal was implicitly restricted to Quichuas and to Inca Atahualpa's affiliates, while tixaneños would enter only if summoned for a specific reason by an indigenous person. In this specific case, of the casa comunal, the imposition of spatial exclusion was reinforced by the Inca Atahualpa. The house was built as the Inca's headquarters with funds from a Canadian NGO. Its location was highly strategic, since it was the first house that came into view when entering town from the Pan-American Highway as a way of symbolically marking the territory as indigenous. The presence of the Inca offices further legitimized the use of the house by Quichuas and chagras and the exclusion of tixaneños.

In the case of the casa comunal the process of creation of such spatial frontiers also becomes a site for the redefinition of power relations. Problems related to purchasing the land on which to build the communal house delayed its construction and completion. According to documents, the small plot located at the entrance to town belonged to the community of Pachagsí; it was adjacent to a plot belonging to Doña Celia, a woman

Figure 3. Inca Atahualpa casa comunal. Photo by author.

from the town who was the godmother (*comadre*) of A. L., at the time the Inca Atahualpa secretary. Problems arose because the documents were unclear about the boundaries of Doña Celia's property. She claimed that the Inca had to pay her since the plot they needed included a portion of her land. Doña Celia sought the intervention of her godson (ahijado) to help resolve the problem in her favor, but he did not take her side. Inca Atahualpa leaders arbitrated the dispute: they called witnesses from town to determine the location of the old street that had allegedly separated the two properties. One of the key witnesses supported the organization. However, as a homosexual, he was a marginalized figure in the town, and his testimony was not considered valid; Doña Celia scornfully dismissed him as being a "pobre marica" (poor faggot). From the grocery shop Doña Celia owned, news about the controversy spread. Soon the whole town knew about the dispute, and many townsfolk tried to reassure Doña Celia and to convince her that the "Indians" could never win. After several months of dispute, however, both parties reached an agreement that, to the surprise of the tixaneños, favored the Inca Atahualpa. The dispute's resolution remained the major topic of conversation in Doña Celia's shop for days.

Although she was not satisfied with the portion of land finally assigned to her, at that point nobody wanted to provoke the indianada and risk an uprising. In the view of Doña Celia's husband, Don T. G., "That's how it is today. It is impossible to reason with them [Indians]; otherwise they shout at you or even revolt. Now they also want a communal house just for themselves. I am not going to set foot in it, what for?" (1993). Don T. G.'s anger following the dispute expressed the feeling of many other townsfolk who had no stake in the house itself but felt intimidated by the increasing presence of "Indians" in town.

The politics of space, thus far, underscored the complexities related to the process of indigenous empowerment in the parish. In both the casa comunal and the rocola cases, spatial segregation was the result of an act of voluntary withdrawal by a group who felt its presence was not welcome and generated a feeling of aversion toward those specific places.[12] Observing spatial restrictions functioned as a tactic adopted by the weaker party to avoid overt rejection and confrontation. Exclusion, therefore, was not legally enforced or imposed, but rather relied on shared social codes that enabled social actors to anticipate and expect specific behaviors. On the other end, this form of self-exclusion allowed for symbolic acts of empowerment. In the case of the casa comunal, the absence of those who were normally the powerful made it a space where interethnic domination did not occur (Scott 1992, 122–23). In the context of the town's relationships it represented an instance for the inversion of patterns of domination, whereby the Quichuas managed to exclude tixaneños from a site in their own territory, symbolically placing the powerful in a position of weakness.

The Marketplace and Its Abuses

Specific behavioral codes besides spatial exclusion and boundaries came to reinforce social hierarchies in shared spaces such as markets, public transportation, and economic transactions at large. In the Ecuadorian Andes, marketplaces have been notorious sites for identifying both discrimination and racism. Hugo Burgos's detailed study of the marketplace in Riobamba (1977) emphasizes the persistence of deprecatory and abusive attitudes of nonindigenous buyers toward indigenous sellers. In "colonialist markets" (*los mercados colonialistas*), transactions always began with bargaining and ended with the *arranche* (snatch) (ibid., 262–75). The latter consisted of a nonindigenous person stealing from an indigenous seller by snatching the sack of the product in question and running off with it. Until the 1960s, only indigenous buyers and sellers had to pay a fee to enter the markets.

According to testimonies and hearsay in daily conversation in the markets of Alausí and Guamote, the arranche still occurred, although it was less customary. When talking about this topic, nonindigenous people stressed the change of attitude among indigenous sellers, who apparently no longer passively accepted the abuse. This change of attitude toward abuse refers to a new phase of indigenous politics epitomized by the phrase "indigenous awakening." In Tixán many tixaneños characterized this phase by naturalizing the contemporary Quichuas as being rebellious (*alzamenteros*). M. P., on the other hand, as president of the Inca Atahualpa considered fighting against this type of abuse to be the responsibility of all four cantonal organizations.

> There are still a lot of people who treat us like poor ignorant animals. In Alausí, for example, we know cases of bank clerks who, when Indians go there to cash a check, give us less money because they assume we don't know how to read and so we cannot count money. They do that especially with older people. So one day we came down to the town and went to talk to the manager and now these things do not happen that much. We need to do that. We have to talk to people and let them know that we are organized now. Now we know how to defend ourselves. Even our elders and our youth are learning now. (M. P., 1992)

The process of political organizing has been crucial for raising awareness of the multiple levels on which discrimination occurs and for redressing abusive practices. Such process had empowering effects also on indigenous sellers at the marketplace who felt confident to respond to any attempt of abuse and prevarication, even if it was not always successful. Arranches in Alausí were under control because nonindigenous persons feared that such incidents might cause a major confrontation. Even without resorting to structured political oratory, in everyday confrontations indigenous individual responses came to be aligned with the local process of mobilization. Townspeople in Alausí, for example, started to fear "Indians." Since the 1990 uprising, town dwellers have responded warily and anxiously to marches organized by indigenous organizations in the cantonal capital, such as the annual march for Columbus Day, on 12 October, during which townspeople watched the indigenous crowd through the safety of their windows.[13] This context of mobilization rendered the attempt of an arranche highly improbable, at least at that time, and interethnic market transactions left little space for bargaining.

Public transport is another arena for abuse and tension. Road transport remains the major form of transportation in Ecuador for the vast majority of the population who cannot afford air travel. During my eight years in Ecuador, bus service improved substantially, especially in the capital city and for services on long interprovincial routes. A selective mechanism was introduced based on the differential cost of fares. The best, newest, and most expensive buses provided seats to all passengers and had amenities such as videos and a restroom. However, such improved services were not available on shorter routes linking parishes and cantons within a given province. Intraprovincial service remained more or less the same. In rural areas, small, old, and colorful vehicles, crammed with people, bulk goods, and sometimes animals, transported anyone and anything as long the fare was paid. In these circumstances, strong odors from food, sweat, and animals were not uncommon. Yet nonindigenous passengers considered "Indians" to be solely responsible for the odors and inconvenience. Many times I observed nonindigenous women covering their noses with handkerchiefs when indigenous persons passed by their seats. On one such occasion an indigenous man stood next to a nonindigenous woman in an aisle seat. At first she reached in her purse for a handkerchief and covered her nose. The man looked at her for a split second, but did not move, so she emphasized her discomfort by spraying cologne on the handkerchief, which she held over her nose until the man moved farther back, after a seat became available.

Although regulated by the ministry of transportation, intra- and interprovincial transportation nationwide is operated by small private companies. Given the improvisational and informal nature of the service, the government's attempts to control fares are often ignored. Fares fluctuate at the drivers' discretion, particularly on routes between small rural towns and the provincial capital; fare hikes are typically justified by invoking increased gas prices. Fluctuations in the fare on my trips between Riobamba and Tixán, for example, were the norm and seemed to be related to passenger's perceived ethnic identity and the amount of baggage or freight. The different linguistic registers used in the ticketing transaction seemed to help passengers discern between justified and abusive fare hikes. If the rise was caused by a real increase in fuel prices, it typically showed in the determination of the drivers' voice and attitude and by the fact that the new price was communicated to every passenger. However, when there were abusive attempts to raise prices, the passengers targeted for unjustified fare hikes were generally indigenous.[14]

Normally payment did not involve verbal communication other than a short "a ver" (come on) directed indiscriminately to all passengers when the money was not ready in their hands. In situations of a fare increase, nonindigenous passengers would receive an explanation, even if not solicited. This was even more often the case on the route between Riobamba and Tixán, since the driver and the passengers often knew each other. With indigenous people, it was a different matter, and the likelihood of a dispute due to unjustified overcharge was not uncommon. On one occasion an indigenous male passenger, like other passengers before him, deposited the money for the fare in the driver's hand. After scrupulously counting the coins, the driver gruffly said, "Subió" (it has gone up), without offering any explanation. The indigenous passenger ignored the request and without uttering a word walked toward the back of the bus despite loud protests by the driver, who, nonetheless, did not take any further action against the passenger. In this case attitudes and words, or the lack of words, reproduced a semantics of domination according to which not all of the actors have equal access to different communication fields (Guerrero 1991b; Parking 1982). Silence in response to the attempted abuse and lack of explanation was the indigenous passenger's only available tactic for disengaging from the conflict without submitting to the ruse.

As the examples from the bus show, resisting and rejecting oppression in daily life are concealed beneath multivalent responses that do not necessarily propose an alternative system of meaning (see Hale 1994; Scott 1985). The examples of the handkerchief and the fare increase offer an opportunity to analyze the "art of the weak" (Casagrande 1981; de Certeau 1988; Scott 1985). In Casagrande's words, "These [behaviors] may range from withdrawal or a posture of defensive hostility, through servile deference or feigned ignorance of expected or prescribed behaviour to 'realistic' accommodation to the dominant society and manipulation of its representative" (Casagrande 1981, 262). In both cases above, the weak responded by "feigning ignorance." Faced with what amounted to a lack of communication, the "weak" defended themselves by responding in kind—rejecting communication, in their case by silently ignoring the abusive demand. In the case of the handkerchief, the indigenous man chose simply not to respond to the demand implicit in the woman's gestures. In the case of the fare abuse, the conflict of interest became an occasion to reproduce ethnic confrontation by means of behaviors that left little room for negotiation and dialogue. These interactions took place where there was no familiarity, personal relationship, or closeness between the two parties. By remaining unresponsive in these circumstances, the weak were able to defend themselves without provoking an open conflict.

Chatting and Buying

The small grocery shops that proliferated in Tixán after the agrarian reform presented a completely different scenario of the management of conflict of interest and ethnic discrimination. As "total social spaces," these shops had multiple functions; customers could socialize, shop, and eat. In these circumscribed spaces, economic transactions occurred simultaneously with social and cultural reproduction. Each street in town had at least one or two grocery shops to serve the immediate neighborhood. A shop's clientele therefore was based on proximity. For example, shops at the entrance to town or on its western side had mostly Quichuas and chagra customers, whereas shops in other locations served tixaneños. The shop on the town square had a more diverse clientele, especially on weekends when the local street market and Sunday Mass brought a heterogeneous crowd to this part of town.

Located on the ground floors of the town's adobe houses, these little shops opened their doors to the street. Basic wooden shelving displayed a smattering of canned food, pasta, sodas, trago, a limited selection of fresh produce, notebooks, and other basic school and cleaning supplies. A few of the shops also carried basic household and sewing materials. Daily homemade bread was an important item in these shops. Even the smallest of shops offered customers a bench, where they could sit and savor freshly baked bread and a soda. A door in the back, usually covered by a curtain, marked the boundary between public space and the owner's private residential space.

Economic transactions demanded attentiveness since shopkeepers commonly cheated on prices, a practice widely complained about in Tixán. Prices often increased from one day to the next with no apparent justification. Shop owners tried to maximize their profit from each and every transaction—with Quichuas, chagras, tixaneños, gringos, and even their own relatives. However, unlike the fluctuating bus fares, the shop owner attempts to cheat customers that I witnessed were openly questioned and rejected every time. Any price hike stimulated negotiations in which the shopkeeper and customer exchanged justifications and challenges regarding price changes, with the discussion sometimes even extending to the condition of the national economy. There was more room for bargaining if the transaction involved someone who was socially close to the shopkeeper or a regular customer. In these cases the stakes were high: the shopkeeper might lose a customer, or the customer might lose the convenience of buying on credit (*al fiado*).

Although the shops were public spaces, the range of activities in the shops and their familiarity created an intimate atmosphere in which everybody felt comfortable to sit and talk. With dim bulbs barely dispelling darkness, these shops were the only places besides churches where local women could gather without the usual scrutiny of their husbands. Shops were also the prime locations for producing and spreading news and gossip. People gathered in shops to socialize and drink after chicherías and liquor stores were banned, so the strong scent of sugarcane alcohol pervaded them on weekends.

Quichuas and chagras frequented a given shop on the basis of a compadrazgo or sharecropping relationship with the owners, or because they felt they received better treatment. Don Leo, my next-door neighbor, owned a small shop, where I became a regular customer. Among his customers were his godchildren from the countryside, so it was not uncommon to see indigenous and chagra women in his shop. My shopping at Don Leo's store was never limited to a simple impersonal transaction. We talked about different things: the weather, family matters, the latest gossip, the rise in prices, and important upcoming events involving the town. Those conversations also included other people who happened to be in the store. Indigenous women particularly liked to linger there when traveling in small groups. In addition to purchasing their provisions (e.g., rice, pasta, salt, sugar, and bread), they stole a few minutes from their busy day to drink a soda and chitchat among themselves in Quichua. They quietly talked about family and community matters despite the puzzled stares of a frustrated audience who could not understand them. My indigenous friend Juana explained to me that they did not like to share with tixaneños any information regarding life in the indigenous communities: "These are issues we don't want the mishus to stick their noses in because they are mean and bad gossipers." Linguistic switching was a tactic used by Quichuas to establish distance by excluding tixaneños from conversations while encroaching on their territory. The same politics of language was adopted in the markets, where the use of Quichua was further emphasized in transactions involving indigenous sellers and customers when discussing prices in front of mishu customers.

At the end of the 1980s, one of the first victories of the indigenous movement was to incorporate bilingual education as part of the formal public-education system. The bilingual program consists of primary education taught both in the vernacular language and Spanish by bilingual teachers. The vast majority of indigenous communities nationwide have bilingual schools, both in the highlands and in the Amazon basin. Indigenous activists consider their language to be a principal component of their cultural and ethnic identity. Furthermore, the 2008 constitutional reform recognized the right of indigenous people to be educated according to their language and culture.

In Tixán, where the indigenous group at that time did not claim a specific ethnic name, their vernacular language was the hallmark of their ethnic identity.[15] They called themselves Quichuas and defined the harvest festival they celebrated each August as the festival of the Quichuas (*fiesta de los quichuas*).

Among themselves, in markets, in shops, and on trucks, indigenous people spoke in Quichua, rejecting interethnic communication. The white population of the town, unlike the former hacienda owners and managers, did not speak Quichua, or at most just a few words. Spanish, therefore, functioned as the official language of interethnic interactions. In addition, since Spanish was the language of government, many indigenous leaders spoke in Spanish among themselves and during the Inca Atahualpa's meetings. However, they immediately shifted to Quichua when some indiscreet ear was close by, for example, a non-Quichua speaker who had not been invited or who at a given moment the indigenous speaker wanted to prevent from understanding what was being said.[16]

This defensive linguistic strategy could not be adopted with chagras. Even if chagras considered Spanish their mother tongue, they also spoke Quichua to the extent that their Spanish had many idiomatic expressions derived from Quichua. Among themselves, and with others, they generally spoke in Spanish. However, in the meetings of the Inca Atahualpa, when they needed the attention of the leaders, they resorted to Quichua. Chagras, therefore, considered being bilingual an advantage. Even townsfolk sometimes had to rely on them as translators when they wanted to communicate with indigenous persons, generally elders who did not speak Spanish. The ambiguity and hybridity of chagra ethnic identity was underlined by their linguistic skills. Although chagras spoke the language of the "whites," tixaneños consider their Spanish to be incorrect. To be well-spoken (*bien hablado*)—in other words, to have the gift of eloquence—was considered by "good" townsfolk families to be an ability of the few. Being well-spoken coincided with class. Less wealthy tixaneños supposedly did not speak well, but chagras were considered to be the most poorly spoken among locals who had Spanish as their mother tongue. "Chagras speak like Quichuas," Don T. G. remarked, and this was one of the reasons why they were considered "Indians who think they are white" (*indios que se creen blancos*). Quichua language's syntax and vocabulary influenced the chagras' Spanish. In the national discourse on mestizo identity, a Quichua-inflected way of speaking Spanish is considered as a feature of the chagra identity. Yet despite these differences and tixaneños' low opinion of chagra speech, townsfolk showed no signs of misunderstanding the Spanish spoken by chagras.

The shops were spaces in which power was temporarily deconstructed and redefined. Tixaneños, who had traditionally taken advantage of the Quichuas' poor command of Spanish to cheat them on prices and deceive them in disputes before the local authorities, were put in a position of linguistic disadvantage. This symbolic inversion of power relations was further reinforced by the fact that the disadvantage took place within earshot on their own territory. Perfectly aware of this inversion of their subject position, the tixaneños once again attributed it to the newly rebellious indigenous character. One day I was in Doña Celia's shop, and the wife of one of her indigenous ahijados came in to buy some flour. On her departure, Doña Celia said sadly and disingenuously, "Before, the Indians were more respectful. They entered my shop and greeted me, 'How are you, my milady.' Today they come in, barely greet me—even my godchildren. They ask for what they want and then they cut the conversation short and start talking among themselves. What are they saying?"

Linguistic barriers establish privacy and exclusion. The topics of the conversations inaccessible to townsfolk also contributed to the creation of an exclusionary privacy, regardless of the gender-specific tendencies in topic choices, that is, whether it were the personal, family, or community affairs discussed by women, or the agricultural and political matters discussed by men. Although treated as ordinary conversations, these chats evoked a specific reality: a private world to be defended from intrusion by precluding communication. Private and intimate conversations referred to a world unknown to the outsider and one to which he or she was not invited. Using a form of exclusion that historically had defined their subordinate position, Quichuas were now excluding tixaneños and denying them access to a whole semantic domain.

Defensive attitudes guided interethnic conversations, whose topics ranged from prices and crops to the health of family members. Although the aim of this type of conversation was to establish contact, especially when people had compadrazgo and sharecropping relations, the elusive replies of indigenous interlocutors—vague responses such as "bien" or "ahí nomás" for "OK"—were attempts to minimize the flow of information. The vagueness of responses in these conversations revealed underlying conditions of tension and conflict in interactions that were guarded on both sides. Repetition of such communicative patterns had turned them into a habit, and they acquired an almost feigned spontaneity.

We Are All Compadres

Interethnic ritual kinship became a crucial response to the new needs of the Quichuas and tixaneños in post-hacienda Tixán. Compadrazgo relationships refer to the custom of choosing godfathers and godmothers (padrinos and madrinas) for both baptisms and weddings. For a baptism, the baby is the godchild (ahijado) of his compadres, a relationship between the households of the godchild and the godparents. The heads of these households thenceforth address each other as compadre and comadre (godfather and godmother). In the case of weddings, the obligations of compadrazgo are established between the bride or groom and the godparents.

Commonly, compadrazgo obligations function as a double mechanism: to guarantee support for the well-being of the ahijados and the newlyweds, and to give the two households access to land, labor, bartered goods, and forms of reciprocity such as the minga and maquita mañachi (Bourque 1995, 102–4). This framework is typical of compadrazgo exchanges and obligations when the relationship is established within the same ethnic group. Specific procedures constitute the proper way of initiating such a relationship.

> For baptism, the parents looked for compadres by going to plead [*rogar*] to a family to arrange for their child be baptized. It was not quick to have compadres accept. Sometimes there were discussions among themselves as if the parents were good or not, or if the compadres would be good or not. First they gave the word "OK" and then the parents would bring camari. . . . Once the baby was baptized the madrina would give diapers or something for the baby, and when the child was older he had to go salute his compadres and be respectful, and the compadre would greet him and receive him, giving food and drink. (Taita R. L., 1993)

A similar procedure was followed for weddings, with the exception that the mothers of the bride and the groom would look for the compadres together. Among the obligations of padrinos and madrinas to their young protégées was to advise the new couple on how to live amicably and build a good life together.

During the hacienda period, compadrazgo networks supported the internal socioeconomic structures of each group, the indigenous community on one hand and the town on the other. Although tixaneños sought ahijados among indigenous families in an attempt to gain access to the harvests of both huasipungueros and free workers, the economic dependence of indigenous households on the town was minimal. Interethnic ritual kinship at that time was uncommon and mostly controlled by townsfolk.

The structural changes affecting the town made this separation difficult to maintain. After agrarian reform, Quichuas increasingly looked for compadres among the tixaneños, who could help them with their ritual expenses, which had previously been covered by socorros (subsistence doles). Other advantages included having a place in town to stay overnight if necessary, and assistance with the education of their children. As the new structure of land tenure took shape, the compadrazgo network's increased alignment with the system of sharecropping helped address land and manpower shortages. However, Quichuas with land and access to manpower through kinship used interethnic compadrazgo to gain access to other kinds of services, such as transport, loans, and education.[17]

In all cases, relationships of ritual kinship bound godparents and godchildren to each other through obligations of availability and reciprocity.

The mutual exchange of obligations was accompanied by repeated actions that acquired a ritual character. For example, an invitation (el ruegue) to become compadres was always accompanied by an offering of food and alcohol. Once the relationship was established, both parties were bound by a series of minor obligations, such as providing hospitality and offering food or drink at each meeting in order to continuously invoke and affirm the bond. Quichuas' visits to their tixaneño compadres during Sunday trips to town, for example, usually took place in a shop and were marked by an offering of trago by the host.

Yet, despite their parameters and conventions, interethnic ritual kinship relations were not uncomplicated. According to some elderly indigenous people, the mishu used to take advantage of their ritual kinfolk. They made them work their land and bought crops in advance at a lower price because they were compadres. They agreed to make loans, but demanded substantial collateral, such as land. Moreover, they would ask their indigenous compadres to donate potatoes, guinea pigs, and lambs for the town's annual San Juan festival. Conversely, apart from providing their ritual kinfolk a place to sleep in town, compadres from town gave next to nothing for the indigenous festival of San Pedro. Moreoever, tixaneños, even when compadres, often took advantage of the Quichuas' drunken revelry during that festival to steal their belongings or to increase their perennial indebtedness by selling them alcohol. Although compadrazgo was meant to respond to mutual economic interests, Quichuas remained the disadvantaged and subordinate party.

In the context of the growing politicization of ethnic consciousness, however, Quichuas gradually took control of compadrazgo relations for their own purposes. Although mutual convenience governed the formation of ritual kinship relations, the decision-making process changed significantly. Faced with an increasingly assertive indigenous presence in local politics and productive activities, tixaneños started to feel pressured to accept the compadrazgo commitment when asked by an indigenous party. On the other hand, if they wanted to establish a compadrazgo relationship with an indigenous family, they had to be considered *bien llevados* (on good terms) with indigenous people, a label that served as a sort of mirror image of the alzamentero. The transformation of "Indians" into rebels meant changes, including a radical change in the way local mishus and chagras treated them. As M. P. declared on different occasions, the Inca Atahualpa demanded respect from local people. In most daily interactions, this involved greeting Quichuas and treating them courteously and fairly. Yet such changes were not immediate. Linguistic codes, for example, shifted only gradually. As Father Torres pointed out, the townsfolk's use of the second-person form of *tu*, instead of the respectful *usted*, or of paternalistic phrases such as *mi hijito* (my little son) slowly became less common, especially when tixaneños were addressing an unfamiliar indigenous person. To be considered bien llevados required that one's treatment of indigenous people be impeccably respectful.

Gradually, Quichuas began to control the selection and refusal of potential mishu compadres. At the same time, there emerged among the indigenous an unspoken expectation of equity in reciprocal obligations, which tixaneños felt obliged to fulfill. Both parties in the relationship had to benefit from it. Thus, interethnic compadrazgos not only proliferated, but came to be preferred by many indigenous people. Access to transportation—meaning access to available, reliable, and fairly priced transportation—became pivotal to indigenous farmers who had land. Increasingly, sharecropping arrangements involved a third party in transactions, usually landless Quichuas hired by indigenous farmers to work on their tixaneño compadre's land. The workers received a wage, and the sharecropper who had hired them retained the profits from the sale of his own portion of the harvest. In all these cases ritual duties were crucial; the partidarios had to provide good food and drink to the workers to ensure that they would work for them again. The incorporation of third parties into this labor relation rendered the distinction between landowner and worker far more complex.[18]

From the early 1990s, Father Pedro Torres, a staunch advocate of indigenous cultural survival consistently opposed mixed compadrazgos in Tixán, considering them a serious threat to traditional indigenous customs as well as occasions for abuse of Quichuas. Despite Father Torres's influence among the Quichuas, however, his stance was often disregarded. P. B. was among those who overtly challenged Father Torres's opposition to mixed compadrazgo. At the time of the wedding he and his fiancée decided to choose a truck-owning tixaneño to be padrino. As godfather, the tixaneño had to provide the bride's wedding dress and selected traditional Western wedding attire: there would be no ponchos, no hats, no traditional skirts, no shawls, no necklaces—simply a white lace dress for the bride and a dark suit and tie for the groom. Father Pedro had objected strongly, urging P. B. to insist on indigenous attire for the wedding. At the time, P. B. was campaigning for the vice presidency of the Inca Atahualpa's board of directors, and Father Torres considered it essential that P. B. set a good example by affirming indigenous customs. Once he realized his efforts at persuation had failed, Father Torres threatened to not marry them if they did not wear indigenous dress. Rather than change their plans, the young couple decided to wed in the church of Alausí: the bride wore white and the groom wore a dark suit. Notably, the controversy with Father Torres had no further consequences. Other leaders of the Inca Atahualpa found the quarrel amusing. M. P. and A. L. still laughed when they told this anecdote and did not consider P. B.'s decision a betrayal to indigenous culture. On the contrary, his entrepreneurial qualities and dynamism won him the vice presidency of the Inca Atahualpa.

This episode underscores the complexities of social relations and interactions among racialized groups. The tixaneño used his authority as padrino to disregard indigenous traditions and endorse an assimilation logic predicated on Western values and assumptions of modernity and progress. The bridal couple decided not to defy their padrino's decision, which could have jeopardized the future advantages that the relationship might yield. In this specific case, the significance of the attire seems to have had more relevance for the priest than for the indigenous community, which is accustomed to negotiating the dichotomy between tradition and modernity in numerous and nuanced ways. The episode also underlines the complexity of the process of politicization of ethnic identity. The quest for authenticity is less an indiscriminate notion formulated by indigenous activists than an experiential condition linked to specific circumstances that render the quest meaningful. P. B.'s selection of an interethnic compadrazgo had its rationale in the context of individual economic choices. A successful relationship that could bring benefits—access to transport at reasonable prices or even for free—also implied obligations; acquiescence to a white wedding dress and dark suit was one of them. In the context of the harvest festival, however, the politics of clothing and its ethnic "typification" became pivotal vis-à-vis local indigenous political affirmation. Clothing itself, therefore, is not always a marker of the strength or affirmation of indigenous culture. In everyday politics and decision making, cultural assertion is calculated in relation to strategies such as interethnic compadrazgos and their capacity to contribute favorably to productive activity.

However, in some cases the moral obligations of compadrazgo are not met, as suggested by the dispute between Doña Celia and her godson over the land for the Inca Atahualpa's communal house. When the godson did not take Doña Celia's side in the land dispute, their relationship of compadrazgo was damaged. Thereafter, he could no longer personally ask for her help; his wife had to make the requests instead. This mediation was sufficient to save appearances and also the benefits that ritual kinship might still offer to both sides.

These two examples indicate the impacts of ethnic mobilization on the politics of everyday life. Quichuas could achieve control over everyday life choices as exemplified in the case of interethnic compadrazgos. In the case of the conflict with Doña Celia, political alignments superseded individual interests and interethnic alliances. The process of politicization in the parish led by the Inca Atahualpa functioned as a powerful catalyst for raising consciousness and awareness about exploitation and oppression among indigenous and nonindigenous alike. It has created new and more effective opportunities to reject individual abuse. The image of the *indio alzamentero* (rebellious Indian) refers, therefore, to a new political actor in both politics and daily life who threatens the supremacy and control of the mishus. It represents a new tactical response to abuse and oppression, which has replaced the tactics of submission exemplified by the weapons of the weak (Crespi 1981; Scott 1985). Thus, interethnic compadrazgo is no longer a straightforward expression of an asymmetrical relation (Guerrero Arias 1993, 98). Even Father Torres, who opposed interethnic compadrazgos, acknowledged,

> The axis of interest is shifting; it is no longer on the white side but on the Indian side—"I am interested in choosing this padrino because he has a truck, because he has a shop, because he buys potatoes, or because he puts the seeds, because he does this or the other." It is more for the sake of indigenous interests that they seek and choose compadres in town, not like it was before when it was a family from the town that had its *indiecitos* [little Indians], and sometimes they converted them into Christians, or made them study and so on. (1992)

Despite the ambiguity and contradictions still embedded in interethnic interactions, mixed compadrazgos have acquired a counterhegemonic potential favorable to the indigenous party.

The Tactics of the Eating Houses

To further understand the role of the Inca Atahualpa in the management of interethnic conflict in daily life, it is important to look at two additional sites in the politics of the everyday in Tixán. Just a few years after its formation, the Inca Atahualpa physically consolidated its presence in the town by opening a milling center and a *comedor* (eating house). These spaces became exclusive domains of los del campo (those from the countryside) and were rarely frequented by tixaneños.

The mill represented a conquest for rural indigenous people and for the Inca Atahualpa. It was part of a development project carried out by the Ecuadorian NGO Social Diffusion and Studies Center (CEDIS) and financed by the Canadian NGO Development and Peace. The mill went into operation in 1993. The purpose of the project was to create a center where grains could be purchased, stored, and milled, and where indigenous people could sell their crops at market prices, thereby avoiding the exploitation of advance sales. The profits generated by the milling center's services would provide revenue for the Inca Atahualpa. Furthermore, the center competed with the only other mill in town, owned by a tixaneño, where indigenous customers always felt cheated and exploited. The mill immediately became the gathering place for Quichuas and chagras, particularly on Sundays. As it was one of the few mills in the area, customers arrived from many sectors neighboring the parish. It was at the millhouse that the indigenous community assembled to chat, joke, fight, and even settle misunderstandings with or without the intervention of the Inca Atahualpa's leaders. As a direct predecessor of the communal house built near the Pan-American Highway, the millhouse was where the Inca met, resolved disputes, and conducted public relations.

An eating house, the Ñucanchic Micuna Huasi (literally, "the house of our food") opened in town shortly after the mill opened. Initiated in 1993 as an attempt to create an indigenous women's organization around a productive activity, the comedor served meals on the weekends. The wife of A. L., Juana, who lived in town, ran the comedor with the assistance of two other indigenous women.[19] Word of its delicious meals quickly spread through town, making it popular among the indigenous and chagras. Tixaneños, however, only went there occasionally.

The mishus responded swiftly to this symbolic invasion of town space. This time they used the tactics of encroachment to regain control over their territory. Before the Ñucanchic Micuna Huasi, there had been only one comedor in the town, located in one of the grocery shops owned by a tixaneño woman. As soon as Ñucanchic Micuna Huasi opened, the tixaneños' hunger exploded: from one Sunday to the next, new comedores, or food stalls, had sprung up on the busiest streets, including one just opposite the indigenous eating house. All of these eating establishments were run by tixaneños. From an economic perspective, the creation of comedores responded to a business opportunity based on market demand. Yet the symbolic meaning of the tixaneños' response strictly related to the tensions among the three groups. Townsfolk felt their territory had been invaded and therefore acted to reestablish control. One day I stopped in at one of the new tixaneño comedores. The owner, Don Alejo, was surprised to see me there, since by then I was identified in town as an Inca Atahualpa collaborator, and he asserted, "We in town can prepare good food, too, you know? Now try it and see if it is good or not." The competition did not last long. There were not enough customers in town to support so many comedores, and Quichuas, with few exceptions, preferred the Ñucanchic Micuna Huasi, against which the improvised comedores could not compete.

Only occasionally did tixaneños dare to eat at the Ñucanchic and usually did so on the pretext of trying out its good food and showing fellow townsfolk that they had nothing against the "Indians." The first time this occurred, townsfolk gossiped about it for a week. Don Fausto, the object of this attention, stated, "Why not, if the food is good. I get on well with the runas." Eventually, other tixaneños, the bien llevados—generally the truck owners—overcame their apprehensions, went to eat among los del campo, and were received without any problems. Their presence, after all, meant profits for the business. After a while, tixaneño customers no longer constituted news, but they never became a regular presence.

In the context of local interethnic tension, any site or activity had potential for conflict. In addition to possible internal conflicts, every new initiative, especially if lucrative, was received with suspicion and envy associated with interethnic friction. This constant state of latent confrontation manifested itself in particular attitudes and behaviors in everyday life. The imposed distance and the self-isolation in the case of the mill and the communal house are examples of this tension. The Ñucanchic Micuna Huasi, however, was an exception to such behavioral patterns. The presence of tixaneños at the comedor became plausible, since it was a public space and there were business interests involved. In addition, as expressed by Juana, the presence of tixaneño customers was taken to indicate their recognition of the Quichuas' culinary abilities: "If they come here to eat it is because we cook good food, for everybody and cheap" (1993).

Combat on the Soccer Field

Sports were another realm in which interethnic tensions were affirmed and ritualized. In Tixán this took place on the soccer field, where every match served as a "dramatization of social relations" through the antagonism of direct combat, similar to the ritualization of military combat (Bromberger 1991, 171).

In addition to the harvest festival tournament, in which the competing teams represented various indigenous cantonal organizations, an intercommunity soccer championship was established in the parish 1991.[20] Less important matches were played on improvised community fields, whereas more important ones were played on the town field. The criteria for organizing these championships differed from those applied to national and international events. In Tixán these tournaments were lengthy. My friend Javier, who worked with the Inca Atahualpa on behalf of an Ecuadorian NGO, was perennially puzzled by the workings of the championship. One day we were chatting over a cup of coffee at the convent house, and he commented, "It never ends, it is super long; every team plays every other team in the first round, and then plays them again in the second round, and so it goes on forever." Father Torres promptly rebuked him with a smile: "Don't be ridiculous. After so many years living here, you still don't get it? It is a matter of fairness—to give teams who lost in the first round a chance to win in other matches. Go ask the Pinta brothers if you don't believe me." The two brothers, who were from the La Pacifica community and who always organized the championship, confirmed Father Torres's observation: "We have to be fair with every team, no preferences. Maybe one time, one can have a bad day and play bad and that does not mean the team is weak. The team with the most victories wins the tournament" (L. P., 1992). The bien llevado tixaneño, Don Mario, always acted as referee. The intercommunity tournaments functioned as a mechanism to strengthen community identity beyond the final scores by reinforcing networks of internal alliances. The popularity of soccer in the indigenous world is a result of "the penetration of popular urban characteristics" following modernization (Guillet 1974, 144). Modern activities such as soccer have become a source of prestige for indigenous youths, occasionally replacing the traditional cargo system (ibid., 148). In Tixán, for example, the two brothers who organized the championship were themselves excellent players and gained prestige from it not only at the community level but also inside the organization.

In 1992 the Inca Atahualpa began competing in the tournament with its own team. Their participation expanded the event; all the games were played on the town's field. In 1993 the Tixán town team joined the tournament, increasing its importance and the pressure on participating teams. Gradually, this tournament evolved into a complex event at which multiple identities and rivalries, both intercommunity and interethnic, were disputed via games. The three groups—Quichuas, chagras, and tixaneños—faced each other every Sunday on the field in ritualized conflict, a modern form of *tinku* (an Andean form of ritual battle) (Platt 1986a). "The thing is that the indigenous teams were getting really good," said L. P., then president of the Inca Atahualpa, "so we wanted to measure us with locals who believed they were better than us. We wanted to show them we could play well or even better" (1993). In this case, Quichuas invited the other teams to participate, becoming the hosts on alien ground. The tixaneños accepted the challenge, since it was a question of publicly defending their threatened and invaded space. Victory on the field represented a symbolic reconquest of tixaneño territory and reaffirmation of their superiority. As Don Mario said, "I don't root for anybody in particular, but I am from the town so I am happy if the town team wins so as to defend their honor in their own town" (1993).

Beyond its competitive characteristics, the championship also created an occasion that helped contain undercurrents of conflict among the groups. As part of the sportive celebration, the event continued afterward in the shops, where the losers bought soft drinks and beer for the winners. Among the losers were also those who had lost bets and had to pay their stakes. The web of relations woven through the game at both the individual and collective level led to friendly contact despite a latent vindictiveness related to interethnic tension. Contrary to the battle on the soccer field, where Quichuas and chagras competed to demonstrate their worth vis-à-vis tixaneños and among each other, the post-match drinking functioned as a symbolic recognition of equality, during which time hierarchies were momentarily blurred. In those moments, all drank together as players who had fought together and competed in a game.

Soccer tournaments are another example of the many nuanced ways in which interethnic conflict was handled in ethnically politicized Tixán. In a complex game of open confrontation (even if ritualized), dialogue, exclusion, and self-exclusion, the three groups negotiated their spheres of influence and power in sites and activities of daily life. In Tixán these tactics acquired a counterhegemonic significance when performed in the space of the other, on the territory of the dominant group. The weapons of the weak in this context were not thieving, slander, sabotage, arson, desertion, or gleaning, as they had been in the time of the haciendas. Nor did they lead to direct conflict. In their game of temporary empowerment, the weak adopted the same semantics of domination (exclusion and self-exclusion) in order to reverse their subject position, even if only momentarily. The presence of the Inca Atahualpa provided social pressure to justify and legitimate control over the abuses. The local political empowerment fostered by the organization enabled Quichuas and chagras to exert pressure on tixaneños, often putting them in the defensive position as the weaker party.

The structural conditions of rural modernizing and political mobilization provided an opening for indigenous people to articulate their opposition to the discrimination that they had suffered since colonial times. Their mobilization allowed them to assert their presence on the local political scene. The Inca Atahualpa represented political subjects who always had fought against racial discrimination, but had not always been successful in politically articulating their grievances and pressing for change. The confluence of structural conditions and agency, therefore, was crucial in empowering the indigenous population in Tixán. Quichuas gradually found channels, via the Inca Atahualpa, to articulate their struggle to the ongoing structural changes and thereby redefine the local distribution of resources and power.

The hero-tugger potters around monuments and tugs on the trousers of heroes. They may be of stone or of bronze, but in his hands they come alive. Some get up in the middle of traffic. They had best be left alone. But the ones in the parks are the very ones we need. He sneaks around them or else he lurks in the bushes. When the last visitor has gone away, the hero-tugger jumps out, heaves himself skillfully onto the pedestal, and stands next to the hero. He remains there awhile, mustering his courage. The hero-tugger does not climb any higher, that would be inappropriate. . . . He contents himself with the modest place that is proper for him. He is still clutching folds in the trousers. But if he works hard, never misses a night, and keeps tugging more and more firmly, the day will come, the radiant day, when he will heave himself up with a powerful surge, and in front of the whole world, he will scornfully spit on the hero's head.

—Elias Canetti, *Earwitness*

CHAPTER FOUR

When the Hills Turned Red

The consolidation of ethnic mobilization gradually institutionalized mechanisms for the inversion of power relations or invisible victories that were embedded in daily life. During this process both local and national indigenous organizations led actions to empower and develop their constituencies as well as affirm their own political legitimacy. The forging of ethnic identity, struggles for land, development policies, and enforcement of indigenous justice are arenas in which indigenous organizations such as the Inca Atahualpa intervened in order to consolidate their political legitimacy vis-à-vis their constituents and the state. As part of the Inca Atahualpa's efforts to serve as an agent of political empowerment for the local indigenous population, it engaged in interventions in the conflict ridden arena of land acquisition.

The Power of Land

Struggles over access to and control of land have played a crucial role in constituting indigenous collective memory of resistance. Fundamental for indigenous social and economic reproduction, land is identified in indigenous political discourse as pivotal for defining indigenous identity. With the national consolidation of the indigenous movement after the 1990 uprising, demands related to land acquired a new political dimension for their relevance not only to productivity, but also to quests for political autonomy and self-governance.[1]

The agrarian reform laws provided for state intervention in the expansion, control, and management of the land market via the IERAC. A new phase of mobilization started in response to the difficulties indigenous farmers encountered in acquiring land under the new legal framework. Land conflicts generally emerged over disagreement about the purchasing price, or when, especially in the case of haciendas, landowners did not meet the conditions stated in the agrarian law. In each of these cases, the IERAC had the authority to arbitrate and settle the conflict. Land conflicts had surged by the mid-1980s, particularly in the provinces of Imbabura and Chimborazo, which had the highest concentration of haciendas and indigenous peasants (Dubly and Granda 1991; Rosero Garcés 1991). The interventions of second-grade organizations (SGOs), such as the Inca Atahualpa, were crucial in this second phase of agrarian mobilization.[2]

The 1980s were characterized by a deep recession ensuing from the fall in petroleum prices. The Ecuadorian dream began to falter, the great foreseen industrialization proved unsuccessful, and Ecuador returned to its status as a primarily agrarian country. Agrarian problems, therefore, received full attention. Both public and private sectors attempted to modernize farming by providing political support and credit to small- and medium-size producers.[3] Deeply affected by the recession, indigenous peasants, whose livelihood had become largely dependent on the market, increased their demands for land. Inflation precipitated a decline in the purchasing power of the national currency, the sucre. Consequently, agricultural profits from farming in the highlands decreased, due to the increasing prices of agricultural raw materials and industrial foodstuffs. Additionally, the wages of indigenous temporary migrants were deeply devalued, and the crisis in the industrial sector led to a steep decline in job opportunities for migrant workers (Rosero Garcés 1991, 135).[4] Unemployed workers of rural origin returned to their rural homes and agrarian activities. All of these factors contributed to a general deterioration of the rural economy and standard of living, which refueled agrarian conflicts between indigenous communities and landowners.

Numerous violent confrontations related to cases of land acquisition contributed to agrarian unrest. During his successful presidential campaign, in 1988, the social democrat Rodrigo Borja Cevallos vowed that his administration would "turn its eyes to the countryside" (*volver los ojos al campo*) and pay attention to the problems of Ecuadorian farmers. During Borja's administration (1989–92), legal claims processed by IERAC concerning land disputes increased considerably. This trend was confirmed in a study by the Center for the Study and Social Promotion (CEDIS), which showed a threefold increase in the number of claims registered at the national level in 1990 (899) compared to 1989 (300). Of 899 cases, 239 were decided in favor of the landowner (Rosero Garcés 1991).

Land "Invasions"

Chimborazo acquired a reputation for being a conflict-prone province during the late 1980s, mainly because of land disputes. The forceful voice of the landowning sector and the local media denounced the threat of continuous land conflict that had disturbed Chimborazo farming since the second law of agrarian reform of 1973. At the same time, Bishop Proaño's commitment to the poor led the local Catholic Church to support indigenous peasants and help mediate their conflicts with the landowners. The popular image of the province envisioned it as threatening: communist priests, aggressive and rebellious Indians, and heated land conflict. The tension became so acute that, in 1989, the landowning sector of Chimborazo launched a campaign against certain Catholic priests, including the parish priest of Tixán, Pedro Torres. Father Torres recalled that the landowners had accused the priests of being the brains behind and instigators of indigenous rebellions in their parishes. On 26 February 1991 a paramilitary group linked to the local landowning sector, the Nationalist Ecuadorian Front (FRENAE), detonated a bomb targeting the diocese of Riobamba and leveled threats at the local bishop, Victor Corral (*Punto de Vista*, no. 459, 11 March 1991). During this period, the specter of the Sendero Luminoso (Shining Path) appeared in Chimborazo, with airstrips allegedly built in the páramos of the parish of Tixán for arms-laden planes from Peru. The evangelical churches also participated in spreading these rumors and stories, appealing to potential indigenous converts by alleging that the Catholic Church had links with terrorists. Echoes of this situation reached a larger public via national newspapers and alternative news magazines such as *Punto de Vista* (Point of View), edited by CEDIS, which published several articles about the atmosphere of conflict in Chimborazo and denounced the army's attempts at militarization in some indigenous communities.

Problems escalated to such an extent in Chimborazo that by the early 1990s the media had published reports alleging the existence of paramilitary bands financed by landowners to retaliate against and end the indigenous attempts to take control of land. As reported in *Punto de Vista* on the presence of paramilitary forces in Chimborazo, the then vice president of the Inca Atahualpa was kidnapped by four men, one of whom he later identified as having been seen on different occasions at the IERAC office in Riobamba. He was drugged, brought to Loja, interrogated on the Inca Atahualpa's activities, beaten, and finally released. Claims that indigenous people and activists in the province were being beaten, attacked, or even disappearing abounded in that period (Ortiz, Pablo 1991; Tamayo, 1991, "Hablan paramilitares y Comuneros", 1992). In the meantime, the indigenous uprising of 1990 also foregrounded the process of indigenous political organizing nationwide.

The lengthening delays in the legal process and the influence of landowning interests in the local IERAC contributed to the state of unrest in Chimborazo. Gradually, conflicts involving terratenientes and grassroots organizations began to evolve around more aggressive tactics such as land seizures (*tomas de tierras*), also called land invasions. Indigenous farmers and peasants used the term *land seizures* to emphasize their right to recover their lands. Conversely, landowners used the term *land invasions* to suggest that they were victims of indigenous aggression and violence. M. P. stated this difference with conviction: "They [landowners] said that we were invading their lands, were kidnapping the owners, but it was not like that. They did not pay any attention to us, or sent their armed men to scare us, so we occupied the property we wanted to buy to have them talk to us, at least pay attention to us and try to reach an agreement" (1992). Land seizure or land invasion consisted of occupying the property in dispute—sometimes by introducing herds into the pastures—and stopping productive activities on the property, thereby forcing the owner to sell. In cases where the owner resided on the property under dispute, the occupiers, who typically outnumbered the landowner, did not allow the owner to leave until an agreement had been signed. This specific action provoked owners to allege kidnapping, maltreatment, and torture by the occupiers. Each side voiced its complaints: landowners accused indigenous peasants of obstructing the peaceful development of the country's agricultural economy. In return, indigenous protesters accused landowners of exploitation and aggression and of impeding the application of the agrarian reform law.

Documents and Voices

The canton of Alausí under Father Torres's jurisdiction was considered one of the province's more conflict-prone areas. Although IERAC records reveal that the majority of the land disputes in the canton involved small producers and small landowners, the imaginary of widespread rural violence derived from a few cases of extralegal action, rather than from the number of legal disputes. The dynamics of land conflicts developed in this intertwining of legal formalities and discourses on land claims, allowing strategies to emerge that help to comprehend the complexity and singularity of this type of conflict in Alausí.

For the analysis of the conflicts in the canton's eight parishes, I took into account the records of conveyancing lawsuits (trámites de afectación) filed at the regional department of the IERAC, in Riobamba, Chimborazo, between 1988 and 1991, a timeframe largely corresponding to the administration of President Borja Cevallos. I had access to the records of 59 of the 61 cases filed during this period (see table 2). According to the data, 62.7 percent of the land disputes at the cantonal level were over small properties (up to ten hectares), commonly arising between peasants themselves, and in some cases between relatives. According to a national trend, the number of cases in the Alausí canton increased considerably in 1990. A clear tendency to accelerate the procedure within IERAC began in 1991, after the indigenous uprising in May and June of 1990. During the uprising, one of the demands of indigenous activists, both locally and nationally, focused on the agrarian conflicts and the adjudication of lands to indigenous communities.

The most conflictive parishes were Achupallas and Tixán, where the big haciendas of the past were located (see table 2). The two major problems that exacerbated conflicts were the length of legal process and the defense of the landowning interests.[5] I focus here on three major cases. Two were in Tixán parish and had been resolved by the time of my fieldwork: the Pachamama Chico case, over 360 hectares; and the Shushilcón case, over 45 hectares. The third and most contentious case concerned 10,950 hectares of the hacienda Pomacocho, situated in the Achupallas parish.[6]

In all three cases, the disputes involved indigenous communities whose members had been working on the haciendas and the respective landowners of those haciendas. The disputes arose because the owners refused to sell their land to their former workers, violating their right of priority

Table 2. Total land dispute cases, Alausí Canton, 1988–91

Parish	Small Properties (up to 10 hectares)	Medium Properties (up to 60 hectares)	Large Properties (over 60 hectares)	Total Cases
Alausí	6	1	1	8
Achupallas	4	3	4	11
Cumanda	6	1	0	7
Huigra	1	0	0	1
Multitud	6	1	0	7
Pumallacta	1	0	1	2
Sibambe	7	1	2	10
Tixán	6	3	4	13
Total	37	10	12	59

Source of data: IERAC, Chimborazo.

in the purchase of hacienda land. However, in the Pachamama Chico and Pomacocho cases, indigenous workers also accused the landowners of exploitation (that is, of not paying them for their work). The plaintiffs in the Pachamama case complained that the landowners had exploited their parents and their grandparents, who, unable to understand the Spanish language, had been ignorant of their legal rights. The claim in the Pomacocho case involved more egregious offenses. An IERAC report of 4 September 1990 stated that indigenous peasants who worked on the hacienda as cowhands and field foreman earned 3,000 sucres per year, which was only 5 percent of the legal minimum wage for rural workers.

The Shushilcón case was different. Some community members had worked on the hacienda as sharecroppers until 1972, when they made their first claim against the owner because he did not want to fulfill a verbal promise of sale. Over the years and against different owners (Mr. Hernández, Ms. Fiallo, Mr. Rodas), the plaintiffs kept filing and losing their cases. In 1977 they became salaried workers. Yet sixteen of those who had worked under Mr. Rodas had already initiated a claim because he had broken his promise to sell. This first claim lasted seven years and led to nothing, since the plaintiffs failed to appear at a meeting at IERAC. The situation grew even more tense when Mr. Rodas persisted in not selling the land and when one of his sons did not pay workers for threshing work. This episode provoked a violent protest against the owner's son, which led to insults and physical aggression. Augustín, one of the workers, declared, "Years later we started to fight again because the owner never sold us anything and also because he did not pay us. One day the owner's son, Don Victor Guillermo Rodas, did not want to pay us for the threshing so we try to beat him" (1992). In 1991 Mr. Rodas initiated a claim against twenty-five workers because they had allegedly "invaded" and stopped sowing: "We stopped sowing because the owner did not sell. Our lawyer told us that [it] was the state that had to pay the owner, not us. But it was not true, so we lost the opportunity to buy. So we left the lawyer" (Augustín, 1992). The case was later archived because Mr. Rodas did not appear at the hearing. At this point, the workers sought the intervention of the Inca Atahualpa and the provincial federation Indigenous Movement of Chimborazo (MICH), whose leaders both intervened in the negotiations, and the case was finally settled with a sale.

The claims filed by workers from Pachamama Chico and Pomacocho for violations of labor laws were dismissed: first, because the plaintiffs were considered occasional workers; second, because the landowner declared that he did not recognize the plaintiffs as his workers.[7] Since the labor cases did not proceed, the communities went to the IERAC and filed their cases as matters for land adjudication. Indigenous plaintiffs from Pachamama claimed that their lawyer delayed the proceedings by not submitting necessary documentation to keep the case open.

In all these cases, obstacles in the legal proceedings pushed the plaintiffs to extralegal action that influenced each case and its outcome. One tactic involved pressuring the landowners through land seizure. With no authorization, members of the communities occupied the disputed properties to halt work and productive activity, and they closed the roads and paths leading to the properties. In the Pomacocho case workers challenged the 1989 IERAC resolution that declared the property unencumbered because it was part of a natural reserve. In 1991 the owner, Borja, signed an agreement for the sale of property for eighty million sucres. Various organizations were present at that meeting, among which were representatives of the ATAMZICH and of the Achupallas federation. However, that agreement was not honored. Indigenous plaintiffs therefore occupied the property. The land seizure lasted for more than five years because the negotiations for the sale were at a standstill. The relationship with the owner became extremely tense. Attempting to pressure him to an agreement, hacienda workers forced him to remain on the property, so he filed charges of kidnapping against them. It was not until 1998 that an agreement was reached.

The Pachamama case was different. The relationship between the workers, a mix of former huasipungueros and waged peons, and the owner, Ligia Guerrero, had been peaceful and mutually respectful. However, reacting to the owner's refusal to sell, a few community members decided to organize to persuade the owner to sell. S. P., a comunero from Pachamama, remembered that at the beginning, only a few workers participated: "We got together eight or ten of us, and we went to talk to the others, that our fathers and grandfathers had been cheated by the terratenientes because they only spoke Quichua and they did not know about the agrarian reform, and about their rights. Now we had the law and the owner didn't want to sell, so we got the support of other comrades" (1992). They initiated a lawsuit at the IERAC, but nothing happened. Finally, they occupied part of the property's pastures and other land of the hacienda with their animals: "We had to occupy the whole property to have her pay attention to us. Every family controlled a piece" (S. P., 1992).[8] This land seizure lasted approximately one year, until the parties signed the first sales agreement, in October 1990.

According to records of these cases, land seizures became significant political actions involving people from other indigenous communities in the area. Summoned by the cantonal indigenous organizations, impressive numbers of indigenous peasants met on the seized properties to support and encourage their comrades at different stages of the struggle. With a vivid and evocative image invoking how the hills took on the color of the indigenous ponchos worn by the gathering peasants, my next-door neighbor Alma reminisced about the struggle between Quichuas and the hacienda owners: "When the hills turned red, not even the policemen dared to intervene" (1992). These massive convocations occurred especially during encounters with the landowner. According to S. P., because of the fear of these gatherings, the landowner, Mrs. Guerrero, never appeared at them: "She didn't show up the day we told her, but later and never alone; she brought the teniente político or members of the *junta parroquial* and some policemen with her because she was scared of us" (1992).

The intervention of the Ecuadorian Funds Populorum Progressio (FEPP) in sales negotiations appears as a pivotal element in reaching a final agreement. After the indigenous uprising of 1990, FEPP started to administer funds obtained from the conversion of part of Ecuador's external debt. The funds were allotted by the Episcopal Conference for purchasing land on behalf of peasant organizations that did not have access to sufficient funds. Loans from the FEPP had low interest rates, typically 18 percent, instead of 45 percent or 53 percent, as charged by banks. The fundamental requirements for these loans was that the beneficiaries agree to not divide the purchased lands, to protect the land from deforestation, and to retain the mortgage with the FEPP until the loan was paid off. The FEPP loans enabled the communities of Pachamama, Shushilcón, and Pomacocho to purchase the land, with the Inca Atahualpa acting as guarantor of the loans and Father Torres as mediator in the negotiations.

As the case studies show, collective action and mobilization helped to catalyze settlement of these land disputes. The legal proceedings filed through the IERAC, whether involving the land and labor disputes or verdicts of reversion, expropriation, or exemption, functioned merely as legal support in sales negotiations and agreements. Indigenous collective action forced the state, embodied by IERAC and the landowning sector, to redefine the hegemonic alliance that had permitted landowners to maintain control over the land.

The Inca Atahualpa and the Land

These collective actions present a line of continuity with the isolated insurgent activity of the past and with Brechtian forms of class struggle in the area, especially minor cattle thievery and momentary land occupations (Scott 1985, 29). Yet the scale of the protest had changed. The process of mobilization spurred by the pre-reform agrarian struggles legitimized those forms of resistance as unmistakable political actions led by consolidated political actors. The numerous cantonal, provincial, regional, and national federations gradually born in modernity gave shape to a political movement that has maintained a state of permanent mobilization. The Inca Atahualpa emerged as a powerful ally and mediator of indigenous communities involved in land disputes with landowners.

This passage from individual or isolated protest to permanent collective mobilization underlines two major steps in the formation of local political actors. The first relates to the empowerment of indigenous communities as political subjects emerging simultaneously with the agrarian reform. The fleeting and almost feigned occupations simulated by indigenous peons when trespassing with their animals on hacienda pastures became land seizure organized by communities in open protest against landowners as a tactic by which to force sale of the land. The second step underscores the process of institutionalization of indigenous power that transformed land occupation into massive collective action. The expansion of the protest to people and communities not directly involved in the conflict contributed to the politicization of ethnic consciousness. Second-grade organizations such as the Inca Atahualpa and ATAMZICH disseminated and amplified the insurgent message among their constituencies. Using their networks and alliances, they made "the hills turn red" by summoning crowds of Quichuas in support of communities in conflict. The first president of the Inca Atahualpa, M. P., explained the procedure and the organization's role: "The comrades from the community in struggle usually came to see one of us [Inca Atahualpa board members] or Father Torres asking for our support. So we passed the voice to the presidents of other communities, and usually on the day of the meeting with the landowner we showed up, hundreds of us, to help the comrades negotiate. They felt strong like that" (1992). For the three cases analyzed here, the intervention of SGOs was pivotal for the final resolution of the conflict. In the case of Shushilcón the Inca Atahualpa also helped negotiate the price: "Nina Pacari told us about FEPP that gave us the money, but the comrades of the Inca [Atahualpa] helped to lower the price, as they said to the owner that they didn't agree with what he was asking, and he got scared and lowered" (Augustín, 1992). As in the case of Pomacocho, interorganizational rivalry did not impede the capacity of SGOs to collaborate on behalf of their affiliates and in the name of a generalized principle of reciprocity that activated a more abstract sense of ethnic solidarity.[9]

In this local process of ethnic mobilization, land seizures became a rite of passage underscoring the birth of new political subjects. Following Max Gluckman's critique of Arnold van Gennep's conceptualization of rites of passage, I analyze land seizures as rites of passage that aim at questioning rather than ratifying social relations (Gluckman and Forde 1962). They present all three major stages in passing from one social condition to another (van Gennep 1960). The ritualization in this context is given by the repetitive and codified dynamics of the acts. The initial stage of spatial separation is rendered by the concentration of community members at a given site, the disputed property, away from their own social environment. This site becomes the locus for the transition stage, the spatiotemporal liminal state in which the codified order is suspended and chaos reigns, reversing social norms and principles. The third stage, of reincorporation, corresponds to the final resolution of the conflict. The two parties to the conflict are reincorporated into their normal lives, yet in different roles: the owners are no longer the masters, and the former workers are no longer subordinates.

As rites of passage, land seizures epitomize the process of local empowerment of indigenous actors. However, being political rites, land seizures sanctioned not only the passage but also the transformation of social roles and hierarchies according to which they reversed the subordinate role to which indigenous peasants were relegated. The stage of reincorporation, therefore, also marks the beginning of a new social order. Indigenous organizations served as a constitutive part of this redefined social order, for they acted, as the case of the Inca Atahualpa shows, as promoters and guarantors of the new local power structure.

Beyond their numbers, frequency, and real or perceived violent confrontations, land disputes initiated by indigenous peasants between the end of the 1980s and the end of the 1990s became notorious because they challenged the power structure that aimed at reinforcing and reinstating the control that white elites had over power and resources. In Tixán, supported by a preexisting process of mobilization, indigenous peasants and their organizations were often successful in gaining control over their land.

Toward a New Leadership

The dynamics of post-agrarian reform struggles also brought significant changes in the chain of leadership within the indigenous social structure. Structural and ideological changes associated with modernization have led to changes in the mechanisms and discourses of indigenous insurgence. Collective forms of leadership, such as communities and organizations, have gradually replaced the figure of the cabecilla. Communities with boards of directors (cabildos) as legally recognized entities took the place of the caciques and cabecilla as leaders of political action. The communalization process that followed the agrarian reform empowered communities, rather than specific leaders (such as Ambrosio Laso in the past), as the referent for political collective action. As spatial and legal entities, indigenous communities became "imagined communities" that could demand their right to autonomy and self-governance. According to Leon Zamosc (1993), three fundamental factors contributed to the growth of the organic capacity of indigenous communities after the agrarian reform. First, the dissolution of the gamonalista establishment led to the redistribution of local power and the emergence of grassroots indigenous organizations. Second, this redistribution led to a redefinition of ethnic conflict at the parish and the national levels. Third, the massive movement that established public schools during the administration of Jaime Roldós Aguilera and Osvaldo Hurtado (1979–84) led to the formation of a new, educated indigenous leadership that was pivotal in the mobilization process both at the community and SGO levels. Furthermore, external forces such as the FEI, the progressive Catholic Church, and national and international development agencies also had an integral role in this process. The combination of these elements transformed indigenous communities into potential agents of development and empowerment on behalf of their members (Zamosc 1993, 290–94).

However, the complexity of communal consolidation also prevented communities from assuming the cohesive role that the rebel leaders of the past had had in spreading insurgent messages beyond community boundaries. The proliferation of communities increased competition over local resources and control, making it more difficult for a single community to lead a transcommunal insurgent action. Leadership was assumed instead by cantonal, provincial, or regional second-grade organizations (SGOs), which represented the interests of various communities vis-à-vis the state, local elites, and development agents. For example, the Inca Atahualpa's involvement and mediation in land conflicts in Tixán enabled the actions initiated by the single communities to grow in scale and political significance. By promoting demonstrations and gatherings of large numbers of people, SGOs such as the Inca Atahualpa challenged the alliances between the state and landowners, forcing them to obey the law. In this context, indigenous organizations rather than single communities became the state's antagonists (León 1991, 410).

Two external factors are important in this process. Firstly, NGOs and other development agents were crucial in strengthening the political legitimacy of SGOs. In the 1980s, for example, most funds for development projects on behalf of indigenous people were negotiated and administered directly by indigenous communities. Even an organization like FEPP distributed its loans to communities. This trend started to change toward the end of the 1980s, due to maladministration of funds by persons elected as community representatives for the projects.[10] As a result of these problems, NGOs and development agents introduced a new funding requirement: the involvement of an SGO to administer and manage a development project, the assumption being that SGO leaders would be more capable of successfully performing these tasks.

The second factor is linked to the racial prejudice informing social hierarchy in Ecuador. As antagonists of the state and elites, single communities had little opportunity for success. The dynamics of land conflict made it difficult for communities to file claims with IERAC and to negotiate with individual landowners. The power to effectively negotiate required a level of political legitimacy beyond that of community politics. The ability of SGOs to mobilize large, multicommunity gatherings conferred on them the legitimacy to be heard and to exert pressure on state representatives and local elites. This process gradually transformed indigenous organizations—from second-grade level to the national level—into bodies with power and authority and, therefore, in Foucault's terms, able to produce knowledge. As such, the SGO discourse of power and truth not only spoke of a state of discrimination that was destined to end, but also sought to reproduce its own institutional legitimacy. Thus it was that an SGO like the Inca Atahualpa could become the vehicle of empowerment for the entire indigenous sector of the parish, legitimizing its existence and its actions vis-à-vis the state and the dominant society as well as its own constituencies.

This organizational consolidation and the context in which SGOs were operating led to the formation of a new leadership, which in some cases created tensions within communities and organizations. New indigenous political cadres gradually coalesced during the twentieth century. They were constituted by individuals, mainly indigenous men, who had not only some formal education and competence in the Spanish language, but also some experience of the surrounding nonindigenous world. Educational campaigns led by progressive political forces and indigenous activists since the early decades of the 1900s contributed to this process. By the late 1960s, indigenous mobilization had a significant number of formally educated activists who later initiated the long campaign to create a bilingual education program within the public-school system. Bilingual education was one of the most prominent political campaigns sustained by CONAIE in the 1980s. Furthermore, the involvement of many indigenous communities and organizations in development policies, whether or not promoted by the state or exclusively by NGOs, has made Spanish literacy a requirement of any indigenous candidate for a position of leadership both at the community and organizational level.

This new leadership profile was incorporated within existing cargo systems, altering some of the traditional requirements for leadership. The use of ritual obligations and responsibilities for political purposes known as the cargo system is widespread in the Andes.[11] The system of host obligations, priostazgo, also a mechanism for the redistribution of goods at the communal level, is the foundation for building social prestige (Botero 1991a; Eulalia Carrasco 1982; Rueda 1982). This system of responsibilities and ritual obligations was maintained during the hacienda era. The elders I interviewed in Tixán on this topic spoke about its importance. Taita A. V., who had been a hacienda mayoral, explained how to build a political career: "To become well known one had to *pasar fiesta* [sponsor a ceremony] and be a good *prioste*; then people would know he would be a good regidor [authority responsible for community festivals]. It was all about being known as someone who gives and is responsible. Only like that one could then become a leader, like an alcalde [mayor of a community]."[12]

This system largely survived the agrarian reform and merged with the formal authority system identified by the state at the community level called cabildo.[13] However, the criteria for leadership became more complex. The obligation of generosity implicit in the cargo system had to be accompanied by other skills, with Spanish literacy as a prerequisite. "Modern" leaders had to be able to negotiate with nonindigenous authorities, state representatives, and NGOs—all of whom moved in a world of written words and numbers. Gradually, Spanish literacy and formal education replaced other skills such as eloquence, which had been essential attributes of leadership and prestige in the past. With the process of postreform structural adjustment, land ownership became a further prerequisite for leadership. The agrarian reform struggles and the adjudications of huasipungos favored former huasipungueros in the building of their political leadership, often as presidents of their newly formed communities.

The combination of these two elements opened leadership positions to younger men accelerating their political careers. The selection of the Inca Atahualpa's leaders exemplifies this process. While its first two presidents were well-respected and established community leaders, those who followed were younger but had more experience in political and economic negotiations with the mishu world. This trend was reinforced after the presidency of Taita E. V., the Inca Atahualpa's second president. Taita E. V. was an elderly and highly respected leader from Pachamama, a sector that indigenous people in Tixán considered as home to traditions of leadership.[14] Taita E. V.'s experience in the agrarian reform struggle provided symbolic capital for establishing his leadership first within his community and later within the Inca Atahualpa. Yet his prestige did not last. As president of the Inca Atahualpa, Taita E. V. often found himself in embarrassing situations because he was illiterate and had to delegate the writing of memos and reports (*oficios*) to the secretary. P. B., the vice president at the time, a young indigenous man from the lower sector of Pachagsí, took advantage of Taita E. V.'s illiteracy to boycott his leadership by constantly remarking on his inability to write. It was not uncommon to hear P. B. make polemic remarks against Taita E. V., especially in the context of Inca Atahualpa meetings, where he often complained that the president "could not even write a report" (*no puede ni escribir un oficio*). P. B.'s campaign against Taita E. V. aimed at advancing his own standing within the organization. Although Taita E. V. responded by repeatedly proposing his own resignation, the other board members thought that the president's resignation would weaken the organization and set a negative precedent. Accordingly, they reprimanded P. B. and tried to manage the tension in order to gain time until the next election.

The case of another activist within the Inca Atahualpa, however, exemplifies the limitations of this process. A. L., a young native of Yacupungo, served several terms as secretary of the Inca Atahualpa. He and M. P. were the two historical founders of the organization. Despite having amply demonstrated over the years his dedication and his competency, and despite being the first indigenous man of the parish to obtain a bachelor's degree, A. L. knew well that his political career within the organization had no future. His wife, Juana, lamented one day, "A. L. will never become president only because he has no land. But for all the rest he knows much more than all those who are sitting in there [the Inca Atahualpa's leaders]." Although Juana felt her husband did not receive the appreciation and respect that he deserved, A. L. accepted his fate with resignation, knowing that any attempt to fight the requirements would be doomed. Land ownership was a key factor in social stratification within indigenous communities, with landless Quichuas often placed at the bottom of the pyramid. In the words of a comunero from Pachamama Chico, landless comuneros in his community "are here just like arrimados."[15] Indigenous men without land or livestock did not have social prestige and were not eligible for political positions. Despite possession of modern skills such as formal education, fluency in Spanish, and experience with the white-mestizo society the lack of property was detrimental to one's political career. A. L. never became president or even vice president of the Inca Atahualpa. Although he maintained his contacts with the organization, he eventually decided to leave the board of directors.[16]

This examination of land conflict demonstrates the extent to which land ownership was a crucial element in indigenous political struggle in the Andes. Land ownership was not only a means to defend and ensure cultural and material survival, but also the space from which Quichuas have struggled against hegemonic power since the hacienda regime and where they have produced identities, social and political relations, and hierarchies (Massey 1994). With the politicization of ethnic identity, it became evident that land, as much as culture, could not be regarded as a mere "building block" of ethnicity, but as enmeshed with the formation and consolidation of new political subjects.[17]

The political relevance of land ownership in indigenous struggles was confirmed by another important national uprising, one led by CONAIE in 1994. In 1992 a powerful group of landowners in Quito created an NGO, the Institute of Agrarian Studies (IDEA), to conduct scientific research on land tenure. Based on its studies, the landowners concluded that "Indians" in the highlands preferred individual land tenure to communal ownership. Therefore, they argued, indigenous communities founded on the basis of communal settlement of land tenure did not actually exist. They used this argument to generate a proposal for a new agrarian law in which indigenous land would no longer be considered inalienable and would be transformed into individual property, which would thus allow each individual to sell his or her plot. This proposal was presented to congress in May 1994 and approved by the government as the Law of Agrarian Development. However, national indigenous leaders called for an uprising to protest the new law, considering it to be an attempt to destroy indigenous culture and establish a new modern hacienda system. The government nominated a special commission in which indigenous activists took part through their national representatives. This commission reexamined the new agrarian law until all the parties reached an agreement. The amended version established that indigenous communal lands could be sold only when at least 60 percent of the community voted in favor of the sale. Although the law remained a menace to indigenous lands and communal values, this second uprising demonstrated once again that indigenous people were ready to fight against threats to their culture and integrity and to their legal rights in land ownership.

Shuc Yuyailla! Shuc Shungulla! Shuc Maquila!

On 28 May 1990, a group of about two hundred indigenous peasants occupied the Santo Domingo church in Quito.[18] A sign hanging from the church wall read, "Five hundred years of resistance, not even one hacienda in 1992" (*500 años de resistencia, ni una hacienda más en el '92*). This action was considered to mark the beginning of a massive indigenous uprising which lasted until 6 June of the same year. The 1990 uprising made evident the magnitude and relevance of this second phase of agrarian unrest for the affirmation of the indigenous movement locally and nationally. The events of late May and early June 1990 have become part of Ecuador's official history. This massive indigenous uprising in all of the highland provinces deeply shook the nation. Commentary on the uprising notes its historical importance. "Earthquake" and "revolution" were terms used to emphasize the uprising's explosive effect on national consciousness.[19] The local Latacunga newspaper *El Día* reported it as an "earthquake" produced by hidden "ghosts," namely indigenous people who suddenly "were roused from their deep lethargy and burst onto the political scene" (quoted in V. José Almeida 1993, 7).[20] Various indigenous leaders and scholars defined it as a historic event (*hecho histórico*) that convulsed and surprised the entire country.[21]

The media played a crucial role in determining the relevance of the uprising since they became spokespersons for hegemonic social groups in the country: the military, landowners, politicians, and religious leaders. Despite the existence of different points of view, the interpretation proposed by the first three groups had a common element: indigenous protesters were perceived as victims of manipulation by specific forces (subversive Catholic priests, communists, and pro–Sendero Luminoso guerillas) that had pushed them to take these drastic measures. By denying the agency of the insurgents, such voices considered their claims to be the fruit of a subversion that threatened and destabilized the country.[22]

The way the uprising originated and developed is emblematic of the widespread malcontent among indigenous peasants and farmers. Those who occupied the Santo Domingo church in the capital, Quito, wanted to protest the IERAC's poor performance in handling land conflicts. The IERAC was accused of repeatedly favoring the landowning sector with declarations of exemption. The protesters also demanded improvement in the marketing of agricultural products. The protest had a historical precedent: in December 1961 indigenous huasipungueros occupied the same church during a demonstration encouraged by the FEI and demanded agrarian reform. The seizure of that church in 1990 was encouraged by the Coordinadora Popular, a group formed by a coalition of leftist and progressive Catholic forces, whose objective was to represent and coordinate the agrarian claims of the indigenous grassroots. Gradually, representatives of the Catholic Church and major indigenous organizations such as the ECUARUNARI also joined the protesters. At first, Ecuadorian society did not take this event seriously. The Borja government refused to engage in dialogue, severely condemning the invasion of the church. Nobody anticipated that the seizure was a prelude to a major mobilization.

Nonetheless, the uprising did not come as a complete surprise. About a month earlier, on 25 April, at CONAIE's fifth national meeting in Pujilí, Cotopaxi Province, several representatives of indigenous organizations had pushed CONAIE's leadership to promote an indigenous uprising. It was considered necessary to protest against the agrarian situation in the country and to demand that the government take action on agricultural policies promoted during the electoral campaign, that is, to resolve conflicts, to institute a fair credit policy, and to control the prices of agricultural raw materials. During that meeting, participating organizations openly expressed their discontent. The representatives of the Inca Atahualpa, for example, reported that in July 1989 they had presented to the executive director of the IERAC-Chimborazo, Dr. Luis Luna Tobar, a document with their demands concerning land. The IERAC never responded to their claims.

Faced with the initiative of the Coordinadora Popular, the CONAIE finally responded by calling for an indigenous uprising for 4 June. At the beginning, not even indigenous activists themselves foresaw the action's scope and magnitude. Between 4 June and 8 June, interprovincial roads in the highland region were closed. Local and urban markets were not provided with the necessary agricultural products. In addition, indigenous insurgents "invaded" cities, cantons, and parishes, and halted economic and productive activity as well as the circulation of agricultural produce to and from local markets. Day and night, teams of indigenous men and women maintained control over assigned areas, including main roads, streets, and marketplaces. Gradually, all highland provinces joined the uprising, and by 5 June, the whole sierra region was paralyzed. The provinces of Cotopaxi, Tungurahua, Bolivar, and Chimborazo were particularly hard hit. In the latter, two protesters were killed during skirmishes with the army as it tried to suppress the uprising.

Provincial radio broadcasting was pivotal in gathering people together and propagating the insurgency. As a product of the renewed and progressive Catholic Church, the creation of local radio stations since the 1960s aimed at broadcasting both educational and indigenous-language programs. The first radio station to open in the sierra was Radio ERPE (Popular Ecuadorian Radio Broadcasting), in Riobamba. Other provincial stations sharing the same principles—such as Radio Latacunga, in Cotopaxi—subsequently appeared. By 1990, radio broadcasting was already well established, reaching most of the indigenous communities of the sierra. In Chimborazo, organizations and communities communicated with each other and maintained contact through Radio ERPE.

Many communities found out about the uprising through the radio: it was as if radio broadcasting was disseminating the insurgency to indigenous communities throughout the mountains, overcoming their isolation. The multiplying effect of the broadcast took the insurgents by surprise. The testimonies compiled by Jorge León often expressed a sense of awe at the scale of participation: "It was like a dream, all together, we were strong, everybody with ponchos and hats, reeeeed!"; "I never thought we were that many runas" (1994, 34). As León indicates, these mechanisms were central to defining a collective consciousness. In certain circumstances, physical contact—the feeling of belonging to a like-minded group epitomized by a crowd—is necessary for acquiring confidence and power (Canetti 1984). The uprising was one such moment, and the image and reality of the crowd had a multiplying effect that encouraged more people to join the insurgency.

Along with the collective action, the CONAIE presented a document to the government: *Mandato por la defensa de la vida y los derechos de las nacionalidades indígenas* (Mandate for the Defense of Life and the Rights of the Indigenous Nationalities). Its sixteen points or demands constituted the basis for negotiations. Some of these points were directly related to the uprising and to the structural causes leading to it.

The combination of the depression of the 1980s, which was associated with the end of the petroleum boom, and the return to democracy operated as a structural opening for the recognition of diversity and had a significant impact on the formation of new political actors. In his electoral campaign, Rodrigo Borja promised to restore democracy after the repressive and conservative government of Febres Cordero (1985–89). His campaign promoted a social policy that would resolve the nation's most serious problems, including agrarian issues. According to some commentators, the crisis itself would not have precipitated the 1990 uprising had it not been accompanied by the democratization of Ecuadorian politics, which favored indigenous mobilization and opened a space for negotiation (León 1994; Rosero Garcés 1991). The *Mandato*, therefore, was a response to such crisis and political promises.

The *Mandato*'s sixteen points addressed three different sets of claims: concrete demands concerning the conditions of the peasant population, those concerning the popular sectors, and those of a constitutional character more directly concerning ethnic issues (Moreno Yánez and Figueroa 1992, 94–95). However, even the points that refer to agricultural policies or infrastructural demands are almost always framed to underline their ethnic specificity. Only three of the demands that refer to the country's agrarian problems do not mention the indigenous population explicitly (points 2, 3, and 9). Even the request for cancelation of the debt acquired with FODERUMA, FEPP, IERAC, and the Banco de Fomento (point 6) is specifically formulated in relation to the situation of indigenous peasants.

All of the other demands concern improving the living conditions of the indigenous populations and their rights to autonomy and self-determination. The *Mandato* calls for a declaration of the Ecuadorian state as plurinational by recognizing its ethnic and cultural diversity (point 1). This recognition includes indigenous traditional authorities, languages, and cultural practices, such as traditional medicine. Point 15 addresses the responsibility of the state to make this recognition viable by sustaining indigenous traditional medicine and bilingual education with the same level of financial support that it gives to the "Western" medical system and formal education.

Provincial and cantonal organizations from Cotopaxi, Chimborazo, Tungurahua, and Bolivar presented their own list of claims to provincial authorities. The acceptance of such demands was presented as the only possible solution to the state of insurgency. The demands of the provincial mandates were no different from the measures requested in the national mandate presented by the CONAIE: an end to all abuses and discrimination; infrastructure projects; measures to control prices of gasoline, raw agricultural products, and other commodities; and the resolution of land disputes. Most provincial demands, however, were understood as crucial for improving conditions among the rural population more generally. The platform presented by the Coordinadora Provincial del Levantamiento Indígena y Campesino de Chimborazo is a case in point. This Coordinadora was created to coordinate the uprising in the province and gathered many SGOs not affiliated with CONAIE. Strongly influenced by the Maoist-inspired discourse of the left-wing party Movimiento Popular Democrático MPD, the Coordinadora called for measures that would benefit not only indigenous but also nonindigenous peasants and farmers.

An analysis of indigenous demands during the uprising underscores both the strengths and limitations of the politicization of ethnic identity. The apparent divergence in the way the *Mandato* and provincial demands address class and ethnicity relates to the specific power structure of which any organization and their constituencies were part. Provincial and cantonal organizations were representing the interests of their grassroots vis-à-vis local authorities, and, as in the case of the Inca Atahualpa, their grassroots were not limited to indigenous people. National confederations like CONAIE presented their demands to the government on behalf of the entire indigenous sector, becoming the main producer of ethnic political discourse vis-à-vis the state. The multiplicity of positions and perspectives in the insurgency discourse during the uprising strengthened the political legitimacy of the entire organizational structure of the indigenous movement, with CONAIE becoming the uncontested head of both the movement and its grassroots.[23] The massive turnout consolidated the collective political consciousness of participants by assembling a body of testimonial documents, the various mandates' points, with which numerous indigenous organizations acquired visibility vis-à-vis the local and national authorities.

On the other end, the quest for recognition and autonomy as formulated in the *Mandato* is also informed by the legacy of exceptionalism enforced during the colonial era to "protect" the native populations. In point 11, for example, the call to exempt indigenous merchants and craftsmen affiliated with the CONAIE from import and export taxes is premised on a notion of a tutelary regime that constituted the ideological basis for extracting *tributos* (head tax) from indigenous people during the colonial era. This type of contradiction underlines the ambiguities and tensions inherent in the politicization of ethnic identity and is linked to the way in which class and ethnic demands are articulated in the indigenous struggle.[24] It poses the question of how ethnic political agency can produce change at the level of hegemonic power and cultural values, and what this change might entail. As peasants and as a marginalized sector, indigenous people, along with other marginalized sectors of society, fight for a more inclusive economic policy and a fairer distribution of national resources, and against state corruption. They struggle to redefine power relations vis-à-vis the state and society. In pursuit of this goal, the indigenous movement uses the discourse of modernity (equal rights, social justice, economic development) in order to break those mechanisms that excluded indigenous citizens from political participation. Although their quest for the recognition of diversity challenged the homogenizing policy of the nation-state and the liberal notion of individualized citizenship, their use of images such as the "poor Indian" reinforces state narratives of backwardness and the "Indianization" of poverty, which have impeded the exercise of full and equal citizenship for the indigenous population.

Despite their inherent ambiguity, the body of demands presented by the indigenous movement during the uprising represented the first organic and unified political platform that questioned the constitutional bases of the Ecuadorian state both locally and nationally (see ILDIS 1991; CEDIME 1993; León 1994; Moreno Yánez an Figueroa 1992). The political significance of the uprising went beyond questioning state economic policy by showing the profound implications of such policy on the indigenous population. It openly denounced the contradictions and tensions related to a society that despite being multicultural was still deeply pervaded by racial and ethnic prejudices. Articulated for the first time simultaneously at national and local levels, the quest for recognition therefore represented a challenge to the supposed homogeneity of the Ecuadorian nation-state, since it implied a redefinition of its constitutional premises. The 1990 uprising and the political process that ensued demonstrated that the recognition of diversity in modernity—that is, the political dimension of multiculturalism—is a highly contested terrain. Whether or not inherent in liberal concepts of equality and citizenship, the contradictions related to this process open a space for political action that involves both states and political actors from minority groups who have been historically marginalized and subordinated (Benhabib 2002; Kymlicka 1995; Taylor 1994). The opportunity for political change in modern multicultural democracies, therefore, is intrinsically related to political agency and not structurally generated or readily granted by governments and elites. Demands for recognition of ethnic diversity are formulated within the framework of modern principles that includes universal human rights, collective rights, and the right to participate in modern economic and political processes. Yet the Ecuadorian indigenous movement shows that the quest for recognition of ethnic diversity also implies acknowledgment of ethnic and territorial distinctiveness, which challenges the univocal idea of state and national sovereignty. Demands for self-determination and self-governance—for example, an ethnic administration of justice—pose the question of jurisdiction and territoriality, which addresses the integrity of national sovereignty in multicultural societies.

These complexities are exemplified in the document that the Organización de Pueblos Indígenas del Pastaza (OPIP) presented to the government in August 1990, following the May–June uprising, as the proposal of the lowland indigenous peoples. This document not only addressed indigenous peoples in terms of *nacionalidades* (nationalities), but also called for the recognition of the territoriality of the lowlands indigenous groups. They demanded their share of the profits from the petroleum industry, since the extraction of oil took place in and affected their territories. The government reacted strongly to the terms *territoriality* and *nationality* by immediately cutting off dialogue and accusing "Indians" of wanting to create a new state within the state.[25] The CONFENIAE's document along with CONAIE's *Mandato* opened a debate on the constitutionality of indigenous demands and the challenges facing the Ecuadorian state's official recognition of diversity. This debate led to the declaration, in the 1998 constitution, of Ecuador as a pluricultural and multiethnic country. According to this new definition, the 1998 constitution recognizes cultural and ethnic diversity, though it only vaguely recommends the presence of indigenous and Afro-Ecuadorian citizens in the state apparatus. The 1998 constitution also notes the obligation of the state to guarantee the continuity and quality of bilingual education, and recognizes the validity of traditional medicine. Furthermore, it opens a space for the recognition of ethnic autonomy by highlighting the necessity of involving traditional ethnic authorities in decision making at the local level.

The 1990 uprising acquires even more significance in the context of the changes introduced by the 1998 constitution. Beyond the immediate results of the negotiations, the uprising strengthened the indigenous movement and its presence in the national political scene. Indigenous "subjects" gained legitimacy as new political actors able to mediate and negotiate with the state for their recognition. The media may have portrayed them as victims of dirty manipulation by subversive forces, but nobody could deny the impact of their collective action. They gathered in numbers to paralyze roads and markets and to demand their rights as citizens and peoples. For the first time it was not a "ventriloquial" discourse speaking for them (Guerrero 1993, 1994); it was their own voices that reached the ears of nonindigenous society and the ruling classes.

To the state, the uprising meant pressure toward change. According to Andrés Guerrero (1993), with the affirmation of the modern nation-state in Ecuador, the "Indians" became "*sujetos indios*" (Indian subjects) instead of "*indios tributarios*" (tributary Indians) as they had been during the colonial and the republican age. This shift meant a feigning of ignorance on the part of the state with regard to a population that was in an ambiguous category. Indigenous people were halfway between the ethnically different subject excluded from the exercise of sovereignty and power—they could not vote—and the Ecuadorian citizen. In the absence of specific legislation on ethnic issues, the administration of the indigenous population was delegated to the local sphere of power—the tripartite powers of the hacienda regime—subject to conflicts negotiated in everyday life "without entering into the political stage" (ibid., 102).

The disintegration of this type of administration began with modern struggles through mediating organisms like the FEI, which engaged in "*ventriloquía política*" by indirectly bringing the indigenous sector into the national political scene (Guerrero 1993). With the levantamiento of 1990, this process of disintegration was complete: indigenous organizations at the national and local levels became political actors who eliminated mediating organisms and established, for the first time, direct dialogue among indigenous citizenry, the state, and civil society. Therefore, the challenge the indigenous movement presented to the state with the uprising relates to the substitution of "ethnic administration" with a political practice in which indigenous subjects claim citizenship rights, participation in the exercise of sovereignty and power, and recognition of their diversity. This shift implied the movement away from an individualized and homogenous concept of citizenship to one that respects difference and collective rights. With the uprising, the indigenous population ceased being Indian-subjects and became "different citizens" (León 1994). It consolidated indigenous people as political actors and "diverse" citizens claiming their role in the shaping of the modern society and state.[26]

Tixán Also Rebels

As a member of the Coordinadora Popular, Inca Atahualpa leadership participated in the seizure of the Santo Domingo church, then returned to Tixán, bringing the uprising to their parish. "Some of us," A. L. declared, "went to Quito to join the protest against the IERAC. Then the comrades from ECUARUNARI also participated and started a hunger strike. And then the CONAIE called for the uprising so we came back here and told the communities we had to join the protest for our lands and for our rights as indigenous people and everybody agreed" (1992). Insurgent Quichuas from communities affiliated with the Inca seized the town center and forbade all productive activity in the area. Juana was also among those very active in the local uprising: "All of us men and women, we blocked the road to access the town and did not let anybody go out, not even to feed the animals. Nobody could go to work or sell at the market or do anything. We took turns, day and night at the blockade on the panamericana and other comrades would bring food and water. We also had to make sure they didn't work in the communities, that all the compañeros joined the protest but the organization controlled that. Only the evangelicals didn't support." The unrest sowed terror: one tixaneño lost his cow for daring to defy the prohibition. Nobody risked provoking the "Indians"—there were too many. With a very serious expression on her face, Doña Celia answered my question about that experience: "All of them came down to the town, men and women, they even brought the kids. And they were furious, you had seen them. And it was all over the town and the roads" (1993). Neither the inhabitants nor the authorities could do anything about the situation.

The nonprofit CEDIS reported on the uprising in different provinces of the highlands by letting the protagonists collect their own voices and testimonies. Such voices were published in a special issue of *Punto de Vista* (no. 421, 11 June 1990). I reproduce here an excerpt of a speech released by an unspecified protester in Tixán during an assembly in the town square. The speech exemplifies many of the claims raised during the uprising. It is an excellent example of the political discourse produced by many indigenous SGOs at that time.

> Compañeros, do not believe what they say in Alausí that the brutish Indians don't know what they are doing. Even if we aren't lawyers, even if we aren't educated, we do feel what we do. Why are we here? To advance, to claim our rights. We aren't here so that people from the town make fun of us. It is not that we want to go against the town, it is not that we want to favor our race. We want to unify, see the people of the town together with the indigenous people. They all have to collaborate. They all have to participate. It is not that because they have money they believe they are better. We are not going to allow this! This is why we have rebelled.
>
> Compañeros, comuneros from different organizations, in this fight

> we have to be one fist, one only union. Let's have no doubts! Let's have no fear! We aren't doing anything wrong. We are claiming our rights! (The crowd agreed) We live eating soil, swallowing dust in order to feed our animals; in order to produce a quintal of potatoes. How much sacrifice! . . .
>
> Compañeros, let's have no fear. Some scare us, they come with helicopters to kill Indians. "Indians you will die like dogs! Indians you will die like sheep!" No, compañeros, it is not true. . . . The government knows what we demand, it knows who we are compañeros. We also are Ecuadorians. We will keep fighting for our organization, for our advancement. The government will accept. If tomorrow or after tomorrow we will need to fight we will keep fighting, compañeros! Have no doubts! ("Somos Ecuatorianos" 1990, 8)

The chagras also joined the uprising, both as members of the Inca Atahualpa and as peasants affected by the agrarian crisis. Their affiliation to the organization became an element of differentiation from the tixaneños. Their participation in the fight emphasized their "exploited" condition, which they shared with the indigenous sector and was the basis for their solidarity. Like other provincial and cantonal organizations, the Inca Atahualpa presented its list of demands to the local authorities. As also claimed in the speech, the Inca Atahualpa's platform was not exclusively for indigenous people but included points pertaining to nonindigenous peasants. None of the activists in the cantons of Chimborazo Province called off the protest until provincial authorities signed an agreement to act on all of the demands presented by the indigenous insurgents.[27] As Taita L. B. put it, "We alone couldn't have gotten all we got. We fought and thanks to our organization we got the authorities to accept our demands" (1992).

The uprising functioned as another building block in the consolidation of the political strength and legitimacy of SGOs. They not only represented their grassroots vis-à-vis the state and provincial authorities, but also unified the insurgents and coordinated the protest against the local nonindigenous population of the parishes. The disintegration of the ethnic administration began with the agrarian struggles and led to a progressive redefinition of the structure of local power (Hernán Carrasco 1993). The rebellion of 1990 represents the apex of this disintegration. During the uprising in Tixán, the Quichuas' demonstration of strength led to substantial changes in interethnic relations: everybody started to acknowledge everybody else with greetings. As M. P. eloquently declared, remembering the uprising, "The era of the amitos and patroncitos has ended; we the indigenous people no longer have to salute the mishus with reverence and kiss their hands. Now everybody salutes everybody, even if they don't like it" (1992). The uprising was celebrated as a victory both for the Quichuas and for the Inca Atahualpa, which affirmed its legitimacy at the parish level as a powerful entity.

This consolidation of SGO political legitimacy was also fostered by external factors, one of which was the intervention of NGOs in matters of "development" among indigenous communities.[28] The economic crisis of the 1980s and the gradual enforcement of structural adjustments throughout the 1990s across Latin America led to a significant increase in development projects as antidotes to poverty and responses to the immediate needs of indigenous people. These were also the decades in which the cause of indigenous peoples and the discourses of human rights gained attention at the international level (Brysk 2000; Postero 2007). Development and indigenous-rights discourses converged in the policies adopted by many local NGOs and agents of international cooperation, which oriented their interventions especially toward minority groups. I have explained, for example, the pivotal role that FEPP played in the realm of land acquisitions. In this context, SGOs such as the Inca Atahualpa served as vehicles for the "development" of their affiliated communities. In the understanding of M. P., development is not merely an economic strategy, but a cultural one.

> We have here a storage center and we are thinking of organizing workshops for handicraft, so that with these workshops I think we can rescue our own culture and language, such as for example the earthworms that is our tradition for cultivating the land. Also for textiles because we have here wool, we have sheep, while there is a lot of people here that wear ponchos made of cotton or nylon, so we forget our culture. If we run workshops for textiles, then we can wear our own ponchos worked by our own hands, made by us with our own material so we don't forget our own culture. (1992)

With the consolidation of the Inca Atahualpa, all development projects on behalf of the Quichua population in Tixán, ranging from productive activities to cultural rescue, came to be managed by the organization. Since international aid organizations preferred to finance projects which involved SGOs rather than single communities, SGOs became indispensable for the development of grassroots communities (Ramón Valarezo

1992). Demands, complaints, conflicts, FEPP loans, development projects, all had to be channeled through the Inca in order to have any chance of success. All development projects in Tixán funded by international agencies—the milling house, the comedor, and community irrigation channels—were promoted and negotiated by the Inca Atahualpa on behalf of its affiliates. Although communities maintained their fundamental role in controlling internal redistribution, with the politicization of ethnicity which peaked with the 1990 uprising, they lost their representative role vis-à-vis the state. In their place, SGOs became the crucial entities for the empowerment of indigenous people. Consolidation of the Inca Atahualpa's political legitimacy, therefore, also meant the imposition of its control over the affiliated communities, which generated tensions between community members and leaders and the Inca Atahualpa. Yet, despite internal contradictions and tensions, through affiliation to an SGO such as the Inca Atahualpa, local indigenous communities and the Quichuas at large established a basis for shared interests and collective action that defined their social identity both as a group and as political actors.

CHAPTER FIVE

Words and Scars

The dynamics that led to the formation of the Inca Atahualpa as well as the arenas through which the organization consolidated its political legitimacy resonate with the overall lived perception of a life of injustices that Quichuas' resilience managed to reverse. The rejection of los de arriba's vexations, the struggles against the *cuatreros* (cattle thieves) and against terratenientes were all understood to be actions that the organization had undertaken in order to correct different forms of injustice and to affirm their people's right to justice and fair treatment. Being committed to this cause, therefore, the Inca Atahualpa engaged in the administration of justice as one of its major interventions. The authority that the Inca Atahualpa acquired for resolving all types of domestic and community disputes and crimes gradually led the organization to become the town's leading administrator of justice for both indigenous and non-elite tixaneños, expanding notions of indigenous justice, or derecho propio, as defined by the Inca Atahualpa's leaders, beyond ethnic boundaries.

The examination of indigenous justice in Tixán presents several elements that highlight the complexities of legal pluralism in a postcolonial society. Unlike in the former colonies in Africa, different corpuses of law and order, usually defined as customary law, have not been sanctioned in Latin America by indirect colonial rule (see Obarrio 2010). It was only in the 1990s that indigenous justice systems were recognized by constitutional reforms.[1] Therefore, the practice of customary law has only recently gained visibility in the discussion about indigenous rights to ethnic diversity.[2] This discussion has both produced and questioned a compartmentalized view of indigenous justice as separate from positivist or national law, as a body of practices that coexist and have the right to coexist, but is different from national law. Drawing on Boaventura de Sousa Santos's definition of interlegality (1995), the case I analyze here shows instead the extent to which such systems are in fact both highly porous and interconnected. As discussed also in other studies of indigenous justice in the Andean region, the very notion of derecho propio (literally, "our own rights") participates in heterogeneous juridical utterances and practices and cannot be separated from sociopolitical practices and histories that are at once local, national, and transnational.[3] The analytical focus on porosity and interconnections challenges reified notions of indigenous justice and underscores their dynamism and their potential for social change. At the same time, the notion that "justice" in a multicultural context is made in dialogue with different juridical traditions, rather than in isolation from them, is important when examining practices, such as corporal punishment, often considered as peculiar to indigenous justice systems and questioned because they "offend Western sensibilities" (Van Cott 2000, 222).

The other element that speaks of the complexity of interlegality relates to the specific conditions and fields of force in which social actors operate. In the realm of interethnic conflict in Tixán, the affirmation of derecho propio beyond ethnic boundaries challenged local elitist power networks and the authority of local state representatives. At the same time, the preexisting state of interorganizational rivalry transformed the making of indigenous justice into a highly contested terrain that defied the authority of the Inca Atahualpa and also conflicted with some of the principles on which indigenous rights are predicated nationally. However, in the absence of conditions that capitalized on these internal divisions in order to delegitimize indigenous political practice, confrontation among the local indigenous organizations did not jeopardize local indigenous empowerment at large. The case under discussion, therefore, highlights aspects of the complex relationship between political distinctiveness and democratic change.

The Long-standing Problem of Thieves

The affirmation of the Inca Atahualpa's legitimacy as an administrator of justice started with the victory over *cuatrerismo* (cattle rustling). Cases of animal thieving on tixaneños' properties and on haciendas are well recorded in the parish civil office archive. However, chagra cattle rustling against Quichuas did not appear in the records, emerging instead in my interviews with indigenous elders on the patrones timpu. The lack of official records makes it difficult to establish the magnitude of the problem. Yet the memory of the abuse was kept alive and vivid in those who directly or indirectly had been victims of that violence. With the dismantling of the hacienda regime, sporadic thefts became systematic cattle-rustling operations organized by chagra gangs. The perpetrators would arrive at night, ambush people in their sleep, assault them, steal their animals, and disappear into the darkness.

> If a thief goes in around Cherlo, nobody else should go to the rescue; with gunshot they used to come back and give orders. That happened because they were thieves. They stole cattle, sheep, anything. They said they'd kill us. "Kill them, kill them," they said. A thief came in; we were fast asleep in the bedroom, and he knocked the door down and came in and grabbed us from the bed, killed and made off with the animals. They came well wrapped up, well masked, who's going to recognize them? One comes in and the other's outside already taking the animals, and then they escape into the field. (Oral testimony, Gusniag community, 1992)

Many of the robberies were carried out by chagras from Pishillig and Cherlo sectors, and increased after many communities in those areas had formed. Some Quichua inhabitants of those localities remarked on the long-standing problem of chagras' abuses and insults. These confrontations led to the partition of Pishillig into four separate communities.[4] This case of banditry was not a counterhegemonic social protest directed against the master, but the endorsement of a new form of hegemonic power derived from the structural changes brought about by modernization. The state of ethnic conflict and racial discrimination is pivotal to understanding this phenomenon. In the context of post-agrarian reform changes, some chagras expanded their dominance and control over Quichuas by capitalizing on the preexisting culture of abusive power and banditry.

The awareness campaign launched locally by the progressive wing of the Catholic Church addressed all forms of racist abuse and discrimination. The memory of the old forms of abuse, together with the experience of the more recent gang attacks, became a political patrimony for the younger generations, who responded to Father Torres's call for unity by mobilizing against cattle rustling. Many people said that almost everyone knew, or at least suspected, who the thieves were, but nobody dared to take action, fearing retaliation. M. P. and A. L., from the community of Yacupungo and future leaders of the Inca Atahualpa, decided to mobilize people against the thieves. Their campaign offered the possibility of transforming ineffective individual attempts at defense into powerful collective action against the rustlers, thereby eliminating or reducing risk of retaliation. People from the communities felt comfortable telling the future Inca Atahualpa founders the names of the rustlers. They said that cooperation and solidarity finally led to the victory over the thieves. In a joint effort of people from Pishillig and Cherlo, the thieves were captured and severely punished in early October 1988.

Father Torres remembered the fear of the chagras that time: "The first action was against the robberies. It was only one, in Tolatuza and Cherlo. I remember it was a Friday in October because I was celebrating Mass in Pishillig San Francisco and since they have gained fame for being *ladrones*, then that day they started to tremble, they started to cry, they begged me for protection because from everywhere they had heard the news that the hunting beat was coming" (1992). M. P. described the operation: "We got together, we were about a thousand people. We organized beats, that is, we entered in the houses of those who we knew had stolen, and we recognized the stolen things, at times they acknowledged they had stolen them. We did the same with the stolen animals. We made them confess and then we took them for punishment. We were many, they could do nothing" (1992). M. P. continued, recounting how the thieves were taken to the community of Yacupungo, stripped naked, and bombarded with questions by the leaders of the affected communities. After they had made their confessions, they were beaten with nettles (*hortigar*) and finally buried up to their necks for one entire day. After enduring such punishment, the culprits were reintegrated into their communities and resumed their normal daily activities alongside the rest of the comuneros.

Following this exemplary campaign of *castigo* (punishment), the robberies declined. The disciplining of the thieves was a key factor in the imminent formation of the Inca Atahualpa and for its future leadership. Interethnic tension and discrimination between Quichuas and chagras combined directly with the preexisting process of mobilization undertaken by indigenous catechists and became a powerful catalyst for collective action. People began to realize that unity was essential for the success of actions that could benefit their communities. The punishment inflicted on the thieves was a Quichua act of *revancha* (revenge) against the chagras, and its exemplarity taught the chagras a lesson.

Although at the time of the victory over the cattle thieves the organization was not yet officially formed, the action was a watershed moment in the local process of politicizing ethnic consciousness and was celebrated by the Inca Atahualpa leaders as the organization's first success. The Inca Atahualpa came to embody a political subject that no longer fought silently against racial discrimination; it had successfully transformed malcontent and protest into a political process capable of effecting change. Some chagra communities even became affiliated with the organization.

Between Cabildos and Tenientes

The multicultural constitutional reforms of 1998 (and the most recent one, of 2008) regarding indigenous rights have officially given legal recognition to practices that had de facto existed since precolonial times, even if experiencing processes of major changes. One such realm of de facto practices involves the body of principles and measures that in the constitution and in anthropological discourse have been identified as indigenous justice systems. Yet such systems cannot be understood as separate from other juridical systems with which indigenous authorities have been interacting or forced to interact for over five hundred years. As corroborated by Tristan Platt's study in the Andean region (1982), indigenous actors incorporated the discourse of "law" and legality very early in colonial history. In Bolivia, for example, indigenous chiefs used to address the Spanish Crown with legal property titles as instruments with which to defend their lands from dispossession at the hand of *encomenderos*. This type of interaction and contact, therefore, has deep historical roots and has functioned as an unspoken indirect rule according to which indigenous people produced and administered their own systems of law and justice with varying degrees of autonomy.

The habitus of asymmetrical interactions generated an exercise of legality that falls appropriately under what de Sousa Santos defines as interlegality, a realm of "different legal spaces superimposed, interpenetrated and mixed in our minds, as much as in our actions, either on occasions of qualitative leaps or sweeping crises in our life trajectories, or in the dull routine of eventless everyday life" (1995, 473). The discourse of legality therefore served as a discursive framework which gained legitimacy in many other realms of social life, a characteristic that Mark Goodale (2006a) deems peculiar to the Latin American region. The construction of indigenous identity, for example, is tied to a space that could be defined as indigenous by law. The variation in degrees of autonomy for indigenous justice systems depended, in fact, on how colonial authorities first and the modern state later imagined and defined the space that indigenous subjects should occupy, both physically and sociopolitically, within the space of the colony and of the modern nation. The administration of indigenous justice in Tixán underscores this intricate set of relationships and their spatial dimension. It is exactly in this spatial dimension that the Inca Atahualpa intervened in order to subvert the distribution of power in the parish.

Before agrarian reform, the tenientes políticos managed to interpose themselves between the ethnic authorities and the indigenous masses because of the ambiguous legal status of native chiefs, whose authority was neither recognized nor delimited (Guerrero 1989, 21). As explained earlier, agrarian reform had a profound impact on the shaping of indigenous space. In the highlands, communities became the indigenous space par excellence. Additionally, the reform also redefined the distribution of power and resources that impacted on what Andrés Guerrero has called the ethnic administration. Starting from agrarian reform changes, the cabildos were recognized by the state as community authorities in charge of community affairs, while parish civil officers and the civil registry were the main state representatives at the parish level. For the administration of justice, though, the only juridical system recognized as legitimate was the one enforced by the state. Locally, it was the parish civil officer, teniente político, who as state representative performed as a justice of peace, responsible for resolving disputes and making the final resolution. For major crimes, such as murder or robbery, the parish civil officer was only the first link in the legal chain. He was in charge of apprehending the culprit, interrogating him or her in order to establish the facts, and then turning him or her over to the police. The case then would come before the cantonal judge. However, even if not officially recognized, the management of justice at the community level was performed by the cabildo. In some communities, despite the cabildo, more traditional authorities such as the regidores, or governors, retained influence in the communal administration of justice.[5] Disputes at this level would not normally exceed community boundaries and therefore would not come under the jurisdiction of the state authority. The de facto autonomy of cabildos meant that unless a dispute or a crime was brought to the attention of the parish civil officer, the communal administration of justice did not take place in the public domain, and nonindigenous people learned about indigenous ways of administering justice mostly by word of mouth. This also meant that the teniente político could feign ignorance and not intervene even in major cases handled at the community level.

However, the lack of official recognition of such customary systems of authority and justice kept them in a liminal position, suspended between legality and illegality, which Deborah Poole relates to the peculiar nature of Latin American jurisprudence, which was nurtured by both Anglo-Saxon and Roman legal philosophies. If for the former customary justice derives its normative character from its ancestral nature, the latter considers its normativity at risk because of its oral character, which exposes customary juridical practice to the risk of becoming illicit (Poole 2006, 13). Decisions made under customary procedures were therefore both licit and illicit, meaning that they could be overruled or challenged at any moment, even by comuneros who were dissatisfied with how their cases had been handled by their community authorities; in such instances, the case would be taken to the teniente politico, who would then handle it according to the "law." Customary indigenous justice, therefore, had the ambiguous role of providing autonomy to indigenous authorities and at the same time depending on state law for binding decisions, especially in those cases in which the cabildo or other figures were unable to resolve a dispute. In such cases, the teniente político was the first figure in the legal state chain with the necessary authority to adjudicate a case.

The arbitrariness of power exercised by the teniente político occurred in these cracks within ethnic administration. The parish civil office was the space in which both the "sanctity of law" and the legitimacy of the state revealed their fallacious face and transformed the "promise of a guarantee" into a threat (Poole and Das 2004, 36). This very ambivalence forced indigenous people to fluctuate between the various systems, often unable to avoid the abusive power of the parish civil officer.

Both state instances of local administration—the public registry office (*registro civil*) and the parish civil office—are remembered by Quichuas of older and younger generations as historical sites for exploitation, abuse, and mistreatment of indigenous people. The practice of giving camari (eggs, chickens, or some other animal) that many Quichuas referred to in the interviews as "dar camari para que hagan caso" (giving camari to make the officers pay attention) was an attempt to contain the effects of discrimination in the realm of the administration of justice.[6] The authorities had a strong tendency "to not pay attention" to Quichuas, especially when they came empty-handed. According to testimony, in quarrels that involved only Quichuas and chagras, the party who arrived first or who gave the best camari won. In mixed disputes involving whites, it was up to the parish civil officer to decide if there was a case or not. Often when Quichuas brought claims against white locals, the civil officer would explain, paternalistically, that there had been no crime and would dismiss the case without further discussion. "We have heard so many times of Quichuas who were tricked by the teniente político," A. L. declared. "When a person from the town complained to the teniente politico, they did not send any communication to the comunero, so the Quichua did not appear at the tenencia, and he [the teniente] closed the case in favor of the mishu. This was common practice" (1992). The changes that came with the dismantling of the gamonalista regime and the advent of a new generation of parish civil officers did not end abuses within the tenencia política. Even though the tenientes políticos exalted public works built during their administration as a proof of their contribution to modernization and the development of the communities, Quichuas and poor local townsfolk were still subject to mistreatment.

Not many people came to the tenencia política during the weeks I spent working in the the archives. The office space bore little trace of the state: just a small flag adding color on the officer's desk and an image of the president hanging on the wall. When he was attending to someone, the teniente and his secretary sat behind the desk, while the plaintiff or defendant, or both, stood in front of them explaining and arguing their case. After the officer orally dictated the sentence, the secretary transcribed it for the archive. One day a woman whose raggedy appearance suggested she was poor came in carrying a baby on her back. The teniente político ordered her to sit on a bench next to the desk, then listened to her complaints, which involved the father of her baby having left her without support. She was originally from a chagra community, but had moved to town with her mother. The baby had been born out of wedlock. While listening, the teniente político turned to his secretary every once in a while, whispering comments that would provoke them to laughter. A prolonged silence followed the conclusion of the woman's complaints. The teniente político looked over some papers, then passed them to the secretary. At first I thought they were addressing the case in some way. Instead, after a few minutes of glancing at various papers, he turned to the woman and told her that he could do nothing for her. Using the second-person form, he said, "What do you want me to do, go out chasing the guy in the fields? Only God knows where he is hiding. Better you forget about it." The woman remained silent on the bench for few more minutes, then got up, thanked the officer, and quietly left, with her head down. This episode speaks clearly of the persistence of discriminatory judicial practices that disregard the rights of certain citizens based on their perceived racial (and gender in this case) identity. In 1990 the parish civil officers were still elected from among the new local elites and were therefore representative of the new white power structure. But a third party appeared as a de facto justice administrator in the parish: the Inca Atahualpa.

The Inca Atahualpa and the Making of Justice

Shortly after its formation, the organization established a local service for conflict resolution in the heart of town. Every Sunday morning, the board of the Inca Atahualpa met with people to discuss and resolve their quarrels: recognition of illegitimate children, marital disputes, accusations of robbery, quarrels about land boundaries, and many other problems. Soon, the Inca Atahualpa's justice sessions were incorporated into the busy agenda of activities that many indigenous people from the area carried out in Tixán on Sundays. Since the sessions were open to the public, many attended just out of curiosity.

The sessions' procedure was the same for all cases. Once the complaint was received, the board sent citations to all parties in the dispute, summoning them to appear on a specified date to resolve the case. On the scheduled Sunday, the leaders met with those convened, listening to and conversing with both sides in order to reach an agreement that would satisfy everyone. The Inca Atahualpa's board performed both as mediators and as adjudicators. When their mediation did not result in an agreement, the leaders themselves made a decision, which had to be respected by both parties in the dispute. Once a resolution was reached, the arrangements were formalized by signing a written agreement. Disputants would be punished if they failed to fulfill their obligations and to abide by the terms of the agreement.

Fines and castigo were the most common sanctions; their degree depended on the type of infraction. A recurrent form of punishment was the *baño* (bath)—throwing the wrongdoers into a pit of cold, filthy water in the middle of the night. In cases of adultery, the wrongful lovers and often their parents received their bath and were shamed further by being made to walk around the community soaked and sometimes naked. Another punishment, applied in cases of minor theft, was *hortigada* (nettling), which consisted of hitting the guilty party with stinging nettle branches.[7] More serious cases, such as robbery and murder, were punished with *latigazos* (whippings) or *garrotazos* (blows by wooden clubs called *garrotes*).

When they started, in 1990, the sessions took place in the priest's residence, where the organization had a room for its office, with a desk, typewriter, and filing cabinet. Due to the larger crowds on Sundays, the leaders occupied a bigger room that normally was used for catechism instruction. The sessions were public, with attendees silently seated on the floor. In 1992 the sessions moved to the millhouse.[8] The procedure remained the same, with no variation and no possibility of less formal alternatives: the same day, the same hour, and the same format. The paperwork—that is, the summons and the final agreement—further imbued the proceedings with formality.

As the case of the chagra woman who sought the help of the civil officer in her domestic dispute showed, the same ritualized formality of justice proceedings took place within the tenencia política. Yet the attention paid to the disputants was very different. I witnessed the Inca Atahualpa deal with a similar case of domestic dispute, which involved two families from two different communities. On the day of the meeting, members of both families came before the Inca Atahualpa's leaders to defend their positions. The room was crowded. People from both communities came to show their support. The plaintiff claimed that a man from another community was the father of her baby, while the man, who was married to another woman, denied it. After the first round of talks, the exchanges between the two parties became heated. The president of the organization then took control of the situation. He listened to the parties again and again, asking questions and noting contradictions in pursuit of a confession which could lead to a final resolution of the dispute. After almost an hour of heated debate, the man finally acknowledged paternity and asked that custody of his son be given to his family. This claim provoked further turmoil. The Inca Atahualpa's board decided to make a final ruling: the man was ordered to pay a fine and child support to the mother of the child;

custody was given to the mother; and both the man, the woman, and their parents were to be punished with a "bath" in their community for the adultery.

This episode highlights several elements that indigenous people in Tixán attribute to derecho propio. One of the most deeply rooted criteria about justice in the handling of a crime or a misdemeanor was what I define as a kaleidoscopic notion of shared guilt. Similar to the *tardecer* discussed by Joanne Rappaport (2005) in the case of Nasa indigenous justice in Colombia, in Tixán responsibility for a wrongful act falls on the multiple individuals who directly or indirectly were responsible for putting their fellow commoner or relative—the main culprit—in the condition to commit a fault. According to this, it was not the wrongdoers alone who were to be punished: their parents, for example, could be punished for not having properly educated their children. In cases of major crimes, such as robbery or murder, even community authorities could be held accountable for having failed to prevent the crime by providing alternative opportunities to their fellow commoners.

Another common principle in the practice of derecho propio was the idea of the redemptive power of corporal punishment. Derived from its public nature, its exemplarity was meant to be an instrument by which the authorities and the whole community taught a lesson to the wrongdoers and to the crowd of spectators. The castigo functions as the cathartic moment in the making of justice, after which order can be restored by reintegrating the wrongdoers into the life of the community. This same principle seems to be rather widespread across indigenous justice systems in Latin America and framed in the ideal of harmony, which Laura Nader (1991) recognizes as a subaltern's strategy to deal with conflict in postcolonial societies. In the discourse of indigenous intellectuals in the Andes, the idea of harmony in justice making is linked to the intrinsic value of community life (Fernández Osco 2000; Rappaport 2005). In Tixán indigenous authorities understood the ideal of harmonic balance in communal life in terms of building of consensus, emphasizing the need to codify the appropriateness of the procedures followed to make justice. According to M. P.,

> It is necessary to punish so as people learn what is wrong, but we do it the way it has always been done because each fault has its deserved castigo. Castigos teach a lesson so that people remember and can be part of the normal life again. At the Inca we made *estatutos* [codes] and we discussed them with the community presidents and we ap-

> proved them, so now if they complain that we punished badly, we have the estatutos so we can say, "We have estatutos, you said yes." What is in the estatutos is what cabildos also apply in the communities, but sometimes they don't punish that way, this is decision of the cabildo. (1992)

M. P.'s words underscore the intricate relationship of derecho propio with tradition, power, and autonomy. In the realm of general principles that regulate punishments, there is a process of negotiation that constantly redefines those principles and at the same time establishes a sphere of action according to which punishments can and cannot be applied authoritatively. A discrepancy appears when one analyzes derecho propio under the rubric of "customary," for the very notion of customary underscores a tension between its supposed fixity, as derived from its ancestral nature, and its volatility, as caused by its customary and often oral principles. Derecho propio is not an approximate and frozen-in-time system of justice, but rather a codified yet dynamic body of legal principles and practices that maintains a highly fluid relationship with both "ancestral" and culturally "foreign" practices. This fluidity is particularly patent in the performative dimension of legal practice.

From the Brutish to the Brave Indian

In Tixán the administration of justice became vital to the restructuring of local power relations and called into question Indian-state relations. Indigenous activists at the time did not aim at becoming tenientes políticos, a position that is obtained through political elections; yet they undermined the civil officers' authority by interfering in their jurisdiction. The service the Inca Atahualpa offered in town resolved the ambiguous position occupied by community authorities in the realm of justice making. The organization broke the imposed "racial-spatial order" of law by bringing derecho propio into the heart of town, therefore expanding the space of community justice and indigenous authorities' jurisdiction beyond community boundaries (Rahier 1998). An examination of the procedural elements followed by the Inca Atahualpa in their justice sessions highlights features of subaltern political strategies by underscoring the extent to which the fluidity of derecho propio connects with social and political change.

The maturation in the 1980s of the process of mobilization that started with agrarian reform struggles and the birth of the Inca Atahualpa, in 1988, led to the redistribution of power in the parish. As M. P. declared, gaining the respect of tixaneños was not easy. Actions such as the fight against cattle rustlers and land conflicts were important for making tixaneños show respect. Quichuas deserved to be greeted, acknowledged, and treated courteously in everyday interactions. The second goal was to be able to exercise power in the parish; the affirmation of indigenous authorities was crucial to achieving this goal. M. P. led the organization during this process, since he believed that ending the abuse of power was paramount to effecting a substantive change in power relations: "Tenientes políticos always abused us, we had to give them camari or some other thing in order to be taken into account. Yet, with the Inca this is over, now we ourselves make our own justice" (1992). For the Inca Atahualpa, the making of indigenous justice was understood in relation to nonindigenous justice and had a profound moral dimension, where derecho propio became the legitimate form to correct of the history of injustice suffered by indigenous people. The organization succeeded where the teniente político had failed: to offer the "sanctity of law" and the "promise of a guarantee" (Poole and Das 2004, 36).

The point of departure in the constitution of the Inca Atahualpa's legal excellence with dispute resolution, which was the jurisdiction of the teniente politico, was its emphasis on efficacy, as opposed to the lengthy and often abusive legal quagmire of the state justice system. This meant the ability to offer a rapid, binding, and final solution to a dispute. One element, for example, that helped to speed up the procedure was the use of physical force in response to a person's failure to appear at a hearing, a situation which had historically been used to resolve cases against indigenous people. When a party failed to appear, a delegate of the organization was assigned to bring the absent contender before the "judges."

However, even if indigenous justice was practiced, it was still not officially "recognized" as legitimate by the state. The Inca Atahualpa built its legitimacy in the parish by capitalizing on the solemnity of its performance. "Solemnity," here, is the space in which interlegality becomes manifest. Beyond classificatory political definitions (derecho propio vs. nonindigenous law), many elements in the Inca Atahualpa's legal performance cannot be easily attributed to a distinct and discernible body of knowledge and values. A genealogy of legal performance suggests a history of overlapping practices and incorporations that created a common universe of reference easily recognizable to individuals and groups of different backgrounds. Ritualization of the procedure, use of physical force, orality, and literacy were all elements which belonged to this common universe.

The Inca Atahualpa justice sessions followed a formal and codified structure uncommon in sessions held by cabildos at the community level, which usually took place in a less formal environment, such as at the house of one of the parties or cabildo members. Some community leaders told me that only in more complicated cases were the meetings held in the communal house or in a communal space so that everyone (typically men) could participate in the discussion. With the Inca Atahualpa, the scenario was always the same: as in the tenencia política, the leaders were seated behind a table, listening to the parties who stood in front of them—"docile bodies" with their hats in their hands as a sign of respect. This standardized and ritualized procedure ensured the right to fair treatment for each person. The physical placement of people, the solemnity of the oath, and the codified procedure are also trial elements in the Western justice system and represent the perceived neutrality and superior character of justice. The performative power of these elements conferred on the Inca Atahualpa's board members the same superior character conferred on judges in a Western court of justice.

The oral dimension of justice proceedings was another element that allowed the Inca Atahualpa to "take over" the civil officer's jurisdiction. Oral proceedings are a primary feature of indigenous customary practices. As many indigenous elders affirmed, good authorities had to be able to speak effectively and appease conflict with words. The primary goal was to find a solution to the dispute. A good president, like a good regidor of the past, was someone who knew how to make people come to an agreement. Oral arrangements privilege agreements over sanctions and the discovery of the truth. Interestingly, oral justice was, and still is, practiced in local state administrations (local municipalities), since the civil officer's position is comparable to that of a justice of peace. The verbal justice of parish judges had three main characteristics in common with indigenous justice: its orality, its immediacy, and its personalized character (Guerrero 1989, 23).

In the past the same oral format in parish civil proceedings was used to disadvantage indigenous contenders. Quichuas' poor command of Spanish worked against them whenever they had the opportunity to orally defend their interests before the authorities: "Our elders could not speak Spanish well, they only spoke Quichua," A. L. commented. "When they went to the tenencia política for a quarrel, they could not understand what the authorities were saying and they would take advantage of that to close the case in favor of the mishus" (1992). A former officer of the pre-reform period interpreted this type of interaction as proof that "Indians" were "brutos e ignorantes" (brutish and ignorant), an image that has long informed white racial imagery of indigenous people in Ecuador.[9] In the Inca Atahualpa's justice sessions, the oral component legitimized in both justice systems has worked as common ground on which Quichuas could negotiate an effective administration of justice.

A new element was incorporated as a formal procedure of indigenous justice: written documents in Spanish (the summons and resolution agreement) that gave additional significance to decisions made by its authorities.[10] As an element of the dominant culture, the written document symbolically functioned as proof that "Indians" were well situated in modernity. Education was pivotal in one's ability to conform to conventions of modern society and national identity. It became a prerequisite for the exercise of full citizenship. Only educated citizens could exercise fully the right to participate in modern national projects. The right to education was among the claims indigenous activists formulated in order for indigenous people to be considered equal citizens and to fight against the racialization of backwardness. Indeed, access to formal education was a primary claim in the first indigenous struggles, in the 1930s. Bilingual education, for which the indigenous movement had begun to fight in the late 1960s, was the instrument through which indigenous citizens could both become part of the modern state and defend their cultural diversity. For educational purposes, vernacular languages were codified and adapted to writing. In a hegemonic context, where the legitimacy of social and political action is guaranteed in writing, indigenous leaders used written documents as a symbolic and practical tool with which to fight domination (Ramón Valarezo 1993; Wogan 2001).[11] However, in the realm of redefining the racist imaginary, it is the document written in Spanish, not in the vernacular language, that has the most symbolic value as the new seal of power of modern indigenous authorities. There is no longer a need for the *tinterillo* (improvised attorney) to write on behalf of indigenous people, since they can write themselves.[12] By transforming the image of the brutish and ignorant Indian into a modern one, Quichuas managed to challenge the network of local dominant politics built on patron-client relationships.

These and other elements foreign to the indigenous cultural context were integrated also into indigenous social and political practice, such as in meetings and assemblies, whether at the community or the organizational level. Examples include the formal greetings of the leaders and the president, the naming of a secretary, and the written agenda for the meeting, which was common for meetings with NGOs or with nonindigenous authorities.

By 1992, these characteristics of the Inca Atahualpa's justice sessions had resulted in its affirmation beyond ethnic and parish boundaries, with several mishu farmers bringing their property disputes before the organization. These mishus were not only tixaneños, but also from nearby parishes. The most common cases brought by mishus involved neighbors or relatives who did not respect property boundaries, problems concerning distribution of inherited land, and disputes about the utilization of irrigation systems. There were also cases involving mishu and Quichua disagreements stemming from their relationship as sharecroppers. The Inca Atahualpa succeeded in resolving most of these conflicts. Neither of the other cantonal organizations had succeeded in exercising the same level of power and authority in cases such as these. The credibility the Inca Atahualpa gained with nonindigenous farmers also derived from the consolidation of its power in the parish, especially from its role in mediating land conflicts. With the solemnity of their sessions, the organization demonstrated to whites that Quichuas took things seriously and that their authorities deserved respect since they knew how to resolve conflict fairly and quickly. This perception was confirmed by some tixaneños who consulted Inca Atahualpa's leaders about disputes. As Don Mario asserted, "With them [the Indians] it is much faster and they always manage to find a solution for all" (1992). At the level of the imaginary, the 1990 uprising had confirmed to the mishus that "Indians" had become alzamenteros and brave. In the case of the Inca Atahualpa's trials, the influence of this new perception about indigenous nature promoted speedy and definite resolutions to the conflicts.

However, negotiation on principles and resolutions was inevitable. For example, nonindigenous people did not agree on the principles leading to corporal punishment: "I know this is how they make justice in their communities," Don Mario affirmed, "but for those who are not Indians this is not acceptable" (1992). Accordingly, cases brought by nonindigenous people to the Inca Atahualpa justice sessions were usually resolved with monetary fines and agreements, even though castigos were never fully ruled out and worked as a potential threat to those who would not abide by the stipulated agreements.

The case of the administration of indigenous justice discussed here underscores the extent to which cultural distinctiveness is not inherently exclusionary and is not built on a dichotomous notion of cultural authenticity, but rather on a constant process of cultural negotiation. The expansion of the legitimacy of derecho propio beyond parish and ethnic boundaries offered the opportunity to receive fair treatment and to be heard equally to chagras and nonindigenous persons who were not members of the local elite and who traditionally had denigrated and even abused Quichuas. Customary law in this case "cannot be studied as an ancient lifeways," but as a space that indigenous people use to both affirm their identity and at the same time produce change (Rappaport 2005, 230). It is an example of the many possibilities of interlegality, one in which two systems and its related actors can coexist in order to guarantee a more democratic exercise of power. Derecho propio, therefore, works as a criticism to state law comparable to other cases of vigilantism in the Andean region (Harris 1996, 8; Starn 1999). Yet, unlike the *rondas campesinas* (peasants rounds) in Peru that functioned as the alternative to the state, indigenous justice in Tixán emerged as a complex network of systems articulating community authorities, organizational authorities, and the parish civil office, which the Inca Atahualpa never formally replaced. Overtly linked to indigenous claims of self-determination, the practice of derecho propio in Tixán did not propose customary law as a form of "countermodernity," but as an alternative way of thinking about justice making and of articulating discourses of state sovereignty and cultural distinctiveness (Rappaport 2005, 230). Thus, the application of derecho propio and the creation of a juridical practice independent from state authorities consistently challenge the construction of territorial boundaries in modern states even though they do not attempt to create a new state within the nation-state (see Falk 2001, 49).

The Return of the Thieves

In November 1992, cattle were stolen from the community of La Merced. Gossip reported that somebody from the community itself might have been involved in the robbery, so the Inca Atahualpa took up the case. Nevertheless, due to tension among the leaders of the organization at the time, the case did not receive much attention.[13] In early April 1993, an extraordinary event was given priority during the Inca Atahualpa's board meeting discussion. The secretary reported that on 4 April a tractor was stolen from the hacienda of San Carlos adjacent to the Pachamama Grande community, a hacienda owned by a white farmer. During the course of the discussion, the tractor's disappearance acquired an important implication for the Inca Atahualpa's leaders: they all agreed that the robbery could not have happened without the help of someone from the nearby community. According to M. P. (then president of the Inca Atahualpa), it would have taken at least two persons with considerable knowledge of the area to move the tractor from the hacienda to somewhere beyond the immediate vicinity. In view of that, the Inca Atahualpa's authorities decided to form an ad hoc security committee and immediately start to work on the case.

All normal everyday activities involving the Inca Atahualpa's leaders—administration, agricultural tasks, and planning meetings—were disrupted by the event, which became the major topic of conversation inside and outside the organization. The specter of past violence and thievery in the area came back to haunt people's memories: "Let's hope thieves are not back, compañera," Juana told me, very worried. "They harmed and attacked so many people" (1993). Everybody speculated on the identity of the thieves and whether or not they were from the area, offering opinions about the potential outcome of the investigation. Yet many were confident that the Inca Atahualpa's leaders would be successful in identifying the perpetrators and in resolving the case.

After preliminary findings, the security committee established that the tractor was no longer in the area. But the investigation proceeded without much successs, so M. P. asked the equipo técnico at the time to accompany and support them during the process.[14] On 26 April, someone reported to the Inca Atahualpa that a comunero from an affiliated community had, during the course of an altercation with his cousin (who was at the time the treasurer of the Inca Atahualpa), implicated both himself and his cousin in the robbery. The accuser and his relative were soon detained and brought to the community of Pachagsí for interrogation. Meanwhile, following another lead, the ad hoc security committee went to Riobamba in search of other accomplices, including a nonindigenous man from the nearby parish of Licto. In the subsequent twenty-four hours, all the suspects were brought to Pachagsí for interrogation. Since the nonindigenous alleged thief had fled, his mother, his younger brother, and one of his cousins were taken in his place.

The Pachagsí community center was occupied for the event. The school was used as a detention center and the communal house for the trial. The interrogations started immediately, were held at night, and were videotaped. All the questioning was conducted in Quichua, at a rapid and sustained pace. The same question was asked at different moments to trap the suspects and disclose lies through contradictions and inconsistencies. This pressure and tension was conducive to obtaining a confession. After several suspects confessed, the theft was reconstructed: a gang of thieves who were based in the capital, Quito, and who had hideouts all over the country had commissioned the crime, but they were never found. The man from the parish of Licto acted as an intermediary, making the contacts and organizing the robbery, while four community members from two different communities actually stole the tractor from the hacienda, brought it to the Pan-American Highway, and handed it over to the thieves. Some of the peripheral figures were interrogated and released, while others were found guilty of minor offenses such as concealment, including the Inca Atahualpa treasurer, who was a relative of one of the thieves. Ironically, the four thieves themselves had been swindled, since they had been paid with counterfeit dollars and checks with insufficient funds.

The second day after the arrest, the tractor's owner arrived in Pachagsí, accompanied by two policemen, to demand that the thieves be handed over to the authorities. The Inca Atahualpa's leaders refused and M. P. commented that they would make justice according to their customs and culture that they had learned from their ancestors. He reassured the police that once the facts were established and the guilty identified, they would be turned over to the Investigations and Offenses Bureau (OID).

The interrogations and related punishment lasted a week. Having confessed, the accused were punished according to the gravity of the crime. In addition to the four primary culprits, the mother, the brother, and the cousin of the nonindigenous man from Licto were also punished, because they had not properly educated and controlled the delinquent youth. The punishment, consisting of hanging the guilty by wrists tied behind their backs and then hitting them with a garrote, varied only in the intensity of the blows and the length of the beating.

During these events, the tractor case was the principal concern of the Inca Atahualpa'sauthorities. Confessions and accurate documentation of the procedure was the basis of a written report for the organization's archives. Everybody worked hard, sometimes even until late at night, to prepare the report and deal with the prisoners. Meanwhile, the news had spread, even to other cantonal organizations. The authorities of the Inca Atahualpa then decided to summon every second-grade organization of the canton to an assembly, including the representatives of the local Catholic pastoral and evangelical churches.[15] Building on their consolidated experience in controlling local thievery, the leaders felt that such a grave act called for public disclosure and clarification. Their motivation was twofold. On the one hand, given the disruption the case had caused, the Inca Atahualpa's leaders wanted to restore local tranquility by showing that the thieves had been caught and properly punished. On the other hand, as the vice president put it, they wanted to show that they could control the thieves and knew how to apply derecho propio. The day before the assembly meeting, the Inca Atahualpa's authorities decided to reschedule it, since their report was not ready. More important, they were still undecided about what to do with the four principal culprits. Needing more time to make this important decision, they instructed the Inca Atahualpa's secretary to immediately send a written communication with the new date for the meeting.

On the day originally scheduled for the assembly, the leaders of the Inca met instead in Pachamama Chico to establish the final details and gather the last of the testimonies. They also discussed the procedure to follow with the principal wrongdoers—whether to reintegrate them into the community, keep them under arrest, or hand them over to the police. The major preoccupation was fairness. All of the organization's board members agreed that the four indigenous thieves had received the punishment that they deserved, but at the same time they wanted to ensure that the thieves would not repeat their actions. After a couple of hours discussing and modifying the report, the Inca Atahualpa's leaders decided to release the family members of the man from Licto, but to keep the four indigenous perpetrators in custody until the day of the assembly meeting. On that occasion, the guilty would be exposed to public shame and then released. However, the meeting was interrupted when someone arrived from Pachagsí with the alarming news that ATAMZICH members had seized the community center and were demanding justice. The leaders of ATAMZICH claimed that they had not received the written communiqué about the rescheduled meeting and that they did not intend to return to their communities empty-handed. They wanted justice to be served again—in front of them and by them.

By the time the leaders of the Inca Atahualpa arrived at Pachagsí, it was too late to clarify the misunderstanding. The community center had been taken over by los de arriba. About five hundred men, women, and children of all ages were occupying the square opposite to the house where the prisoners were being held. As the experience of land conflicts had shown, massive concentrations of people symbolize the imposition of power. The leaders of both organizations talked briefly. A few minutes later the person in charge of the prisoners conducted the four indigenous thieves to the square, where the leaders of the ATAMZICH—their faces covered by hoods—interrogated and punished them in public. The punishment was the same, the only difference being that this time the confession was immediately followed by the beating. After their punishment, the thieves were returned to their prison, and the crowd eventually dispersed.

On the day rescheduled for the assembly, all those summoned attended. People started arriving early at the designated place in La Pacífica, and by early morning it was already crowded with adults and children from the affiliated communities. When the meeting began and the report was released, the Inca Atahualpa representatives moderating the event were unable to maintain order. They interrupted each other and were interrupted by people yelling from the crowd. Everyone spoke at the same time, demanding more punishment—specifically harsh corporal punishment—for the four thieves. Someone from the crowd even proposed cutting off the thieves' ears or a finger. After several hours of discussion, the assembly reached an agreement: each organization would take one of the four thieves and continue the interrogations and punishment for one week. The outcome of the assembly overtook the Inca Atahualpa's leaders' purposes and expectations. Although they did not agree with the further measures, they were unable to impose their will on the assembly; they momentarily had lost control of the situation.

A week later, the prisoners were handed back to the Inca Atahualpa, who decided to hand them over to the police. The town square was packed on the day the OID came to Tixán for the prisoners. Hundreds of spectators—Quichuas, chagras, and people from Tixán—watched the event. The prisoners were brought into the square by the Inca Atahualpa authorities and publicly handed over to the police inspectors, together with a written report of the case. A few weeks later the Inca Atahualpa's board was notified that the indigenous thieves had been sentenced to three years in jail.

The local press covered this event. The Riobamba newspaper dedicated a whole page to the case (*El Espectador*, 20 May 1993). In the past *El Espectador* had published articles on land seizures and conflicts involving landowners and indigenous communities in which Catholic priests were labeled as "agitators" and Quichuas as "kidnappers" (*El Espectador*, 4 August 1992). In contrast the tractor case was treated with more detachment, and the comments were limited to describing the facts. This difference is significant in the context of class and interethnic conflict at the local level. The events this time did not involve members of the landowning sector or important families with power at the provincial level. It only involved "Indians" and poor mestizos, and the case was therefore treated as an internal settling of accounts.

Once the situation settled down and everyday life resumed its rhythm, elderly Quichuas who had had experience as leaders in past land struggles communicated personally their remarks to the Inca Atahualpa's leaders as a way of evaluating the case for future reference. In their view, the case had not been handled properly. One of the elderly commentators, Taita Pedro Marcatoma, with whom I talked about the case, insisted that a good leader needed to be able to talk to and convince the wrongdoers about the gravity of their actions; he needed to understand the reasons that had led to their wrongful acts. If someone stole, it was because the president of his community and the cabildo had not been able to provide his people with the means they needed to improve their life. Guilt was always shared, which meant that the responsibility for a criminal act never belonged only to the perpetrators. In his opinion, the cabildo members should have been punished, too. After a short pause, he continued: "When they get released, they will want revenge" (1993). I was not quite sure I had grasped the reasons that Taita Pedro believed would motivate a desire for revenge in the thieves. "Too many beatings," he promptly added. With that remark, which resonated with that of other elders, he commented not only on the excessiveness of the punishment, but also on the expected consequences of unjust treatment.

Interestingly, these discrepant views did not lead to a debate within the organization. Self-criticism by Inca Atahualpa leaders was limited to the final decision that they felt forced to make: they questioned only the efficacy of handing the prisoners over to the OID, considering it a demonstration of weakness in front of white people and the state authorities.

Justice and Power

The confirmation of the Inca Atahualpa as a superior body of justice in the parish highlights some of the contradictions of the process of institutionalization of subaltern politics, as exemplified by the tractor case. On that occasion, the application of derecho propio was a demonstration not only of power exercised by society on its transgressive members, but also of a power struggle that involved the second-grade organizations from the canton of Alausí.

Although an age-old rivalry was pivotal in the final formation of the Inca Atahualpa, it is difficult to determine exactly the mapping of ethnic alliances in contemporary times.[16] Colonial administration and later state policies informed the administrative division of the territory and its people. Ethnic identities have been shaped and reshaped along these processes. Modernization accompanying agrarian reform further impacted the formation of local communities and ethnic identities. The distinction between los de arriba and los de abajo crosses parish boundaries, and páramo communities are split between the two parishes of Achupallas and Tixán. Yet their affiliation to any organization was determined not so much by parish boundaries or ethnic affinity, but rather by economic interests. Some communities from arriba, such as Pachamama Chico, became part of the Inca Atahualpa instead of the ATAMZICH, since it had no interests in the marble mines. In the same parish of Achupallas, some communities joined the Federation of Achupallas instead of the ATAMZICH for similar reasons. In many cases, the current communities do not reflect their kinship groups (ayllu) even if they still maintain their kinship bonds through reciprocity.

Interorganizational rivalry typically responds to factors, such as the reproduction of ethnic identity and the forging of economic and political interests, that bring the four organizations into competition for power and control over local resources. The tensions created by this internal rivalry had not been underestimated. Aware of the potential risks of factionalism, back in 1991 the leaders of all the organizations in the canton created a coordinating institution, the Coordinadora de Alausí, comprising two delegates from each of the four cantonal federations. The main goals of the Coordinadora were to coordinate efforts and maintain common leadership criteria so as to enhance the efficacy of their political actions at the cantonal level. It also had to manage the power of any single organization. However, the Coordinadora never gained sufficient legitimacy to effectively control rivalry among organizations. First, it was perceived that disagreements and errors could have fatal consequences for all: M. P. who had been very committed to the idea of the Coordinadora affirmed, "Afterwards, if there is a problem, not only one, but all the organizations pay" (1993). Second, ATAMZICH and the Inca Atahualpa had acquired far more experience in handling conflict and obtaining resources for the affiliated communities. Their weight and influence within the Coordinadora was overwhelming. The Inca Atahualpa in particular inspired jealousy, since it had the largest number of affiliated communities and the most experience handling land conflicts: "When there were problems that they could not resolve," M. P. recounted, "we went, we brought out people, we tried to move arrangements forward. . . . This is the confidence the rest of the organizations have" (1993). The Inca Atahualpa served both as an example from which to learn, but also as a competitor to defeat.

The tractor case provided an opportunity for the other organizations to symbolically take revenge on the Inca Atahualpa and undermine its prestige. By seizing the community center where the prisoners were held and punishing the thieves with their own hands, the ATAMZICH questioned the validity of the Inca Atahualpa's decision and punishments. This challenge was further reinforced when the other organizations in the assembly decided also to punish the thieves themselves, for a third time. The organizational power struggle in the tractor case, therefore, had two major impacts: first, it motivated the Inca Atahualpa to publicly affirm its authority as the superior administrator of justice; second, it led to redundant displays of corporal punishment.

Contrary to the other cases of oral justice I described earlier, in which agreements counted more than established facts (or "truth"), in this case establishing the actual culpability of the accused was instrumental to the affirmation of the Inca Atahualpa's capacity to achieve justice.[17] Due to lack of material evidence, confessions were used to determine the guilt of the accused, to the extent that the interrogation decided the case. Contradiction being the key element by which guilt was determined, it was necessary to interrogate the accused several times, the rapidity of the interrogation giving the accused no time to think between one question and the next. Although this procedure was quite common in the local proceedings of indigenous justice, both at the community and organizational levels, the perceived gravity of the tractor case increased the pressure and made confession unavoidable for the accused.

In this case, the relevance of the "truth of the facts" was reinforced by adding to the procedure other formal elements—the filming of the interrogations and the preparation of a written report—that were intended as evidence of the Inca Atahualpa's legitimacy as a superior judicial entity. However, the dispensing of punishment introduced controversy into the application of customary rights. Physical punishment is an element of derecho propio, of supposed Incaic origins. Under the Incaic kingdom, theft was classified along with major crimes such as enmity, adultery, treachery, witchcraft, pride, and conspiracy against the Inca (Guamán Poma de Ayala 1988).[18] The punishment for these major crimes was usually death. The guilty were thrown into a deep hole infested with ferocious animals that were ready to devour them (ibid., 276). In the case of kidnapping and rape, the guilty were hung by their hair until they died (ibid., 283). Torture—including torment by rope, lash, or stones—was also a common tool for obtaining confessions (ibid., 277). The tractor case did not involve the death penalty. However, some traditional elements were applied, such as corporal punishment and holding the prisoner in a hole for days, the latter being precisely the punishment that the other organizations inflicted on the thieves after the resolution of the assembly.[19]

Other punishments, such as hanging perpetrators by the wrists and beating them with garrotes, may also relate to other practices, although it is difficult, perhaps impossible, to determine the exact historical and cultural roots of such practices: "With European conquest and colonization, these spaces of death blend into a common pool of key signifiers binding the transforming culture of the conqueror with that of the conquered" (Taussig 1987, 5). In any context the use of violence and the politics of terror function as instruments of power. In this case violence is not simply related to the cultural dynamics of power and control internal to indigenous societies. There is a history of violent interactions in which indigenous people more commonly have been the victims (Poole 1994; Starn 1999). Physical abuse and corporal punishment were common practices, to discipline disobedient workers during the hacienda period as well as in the realm of local official justice. In the 1970s a ferocious murder, wherein a man was brutally stabbed thirty times, was committed in Tixán. According to townsfolk, the motive was a fight over a woman. The murderer, a tixaneño, was denounced by his own brother and held prisoner in the parish civil office. His arrival in town on his release, in 1992, triggered memories and fear among tixaneños. People who were young at the time of the murder remembered peeping through the windows of the tenencia política and seeing two policemen hanging the criminal by his wrists and beating him with a club until he confessed. After his confession, the man was sent to prison in the provincial capital.

In all of these accounts, the body is the object of the application of violence. Scars become the evidence of what happened; they are the permanent reminders of the norms and rules that society inflicts on the bodies of its members (see Clastres 1980; Foucault 1976). The body becomes the locus for punishment and for disseminating the truth. Corporal punishment, therefore, is an instrument by which to punish and to inform. Its public character is a demonstration of power before the masses, of a power that is capable of making the guilty the creator of his or her own condemnation (Foucault 1976).

In the tractor case, indigenous justice incorporated the symbolic efficacy of forms of violence and justice that historically had been legitimated by dominant structures of power. The incorporation of derecho propio in this case is built on the historical process of asymmetrical exchange of legal criteria and practices. Obtaining the truth through physical coercion in the tractor case represented the triumph of the power of the persecutors—first the Inca Atahualpa and later its rival organizations.[20] The politicization of ethnic rivalries led to redundant punishment. The thieves were punished three times, each time more severely. Each round of punishment was inflicted by a different entity. The excess of physical violence, underscored by the victim's bodily suffering, is the deepest manifestation of the strength of justice (Foucault 1976). In addition to this, the Inca Atahualpa handed the prisoners over to the OID in order to regain control of the situation. Therefore, the prisoners were judged not only by the indigenous justice system, but also by official law.

Physical punishment is useful for the economy of power, but, when unjustified (according to the elders' perceptions), runs the risk of compromising the principles on which justice is based, the derecho propio in this case, and so becomes "illicit." The balance that a fair punishment is supposed to restore and the reintegration of the wrongdoer that it is supposed to allow were thwarted by the excess and, therefore, castigo became a potential threat. Additionally, the different punishing entities imposed their will without a process of consensus building.

Despite the elder's criticisms, the case generated a different type of debate. The Inca Atahualpa's leaders perceived the unfolding of events and their loss of control as a demonstration that the realm of justice was a contested terrain in which they had to intervene forcefully to defend their legitimacy. In 1998 I had a long conversation in Quito with A. L. about derecho propio. He told me that since the tractor case, local organizations had been discussing different strategies for controlling the threat of theft in the area. The four organizations were apparently disagreeing about what would constitute an exemplary punishment. From A. L.'s words, it appeared that the more extreme the proposed corporal measure, the greater perceived competence of the organization in matters of justice: "We know how to punish them; if you strike them with electricity they won't do it again" (A. L., personal communication, 1998). I asked A. L. if he thought those types of corporal punishment contradicted principles of human rights. His answer highlighted the complex relationship of human rights and justice as manifested in different juridical systems: "You put someone in prison and the person gets marked for life, while for us we punish harshly but then that person is reintegrated into the life of the community like everybody else." A. L. added that once they were out of jail, even the thieves in the tractor case had been reincorporated into the community, and people had forgotten about it. Incidentally, when A. C., member of the Inca Atahualpa, was kidnapped in 1991, allegedly by the military, he declared in an interview with *Punto de Vista* that he had been robbed and beaten while he was captive: "They kicked me, they beat me, they made me bleed, they stepped on me, *they applied electricity to my hand* while they were asking me a million questions" (*Punto de Vista*, no. 459, 11 March 1991, emphasis added). Once again, as in the case of the hanging and beating associated with the tractor case, there are grounds for a discourse on power, control, and the body that indigenous and nonindigenous justice systems share, which becomes commonly sanctioned for their efficacy. In this case the porosity, the ubiquity of these practices, and the coded messages they contain blur the boundaries of legality and illegality, of inside and outside the law, and underscore the extent to which indigenous and nonindigenous systems of justice and control are bound by a common yet asymmetrical history of violence, abuse, and mutual contamination.[21]

The complexities highlighted by the tractor case exemplify the tensions and potential risks of factionalism and rivalries within the indigenous movement. In this specific case internal competition over power and resources led to an extraordinary reinterpretation of the derecho propio. However, neither the potential contradiction of principles nor the interorganizational tensions per se were perceived as problematic or ultimately disempowering by the indigenous leadership, but rather as manifestations of weakness vis-à-vis state powers. This perception is pivotal for understanding elements that can or cannot jeopardize the legitimacy of the indigenous movement. In the realm of indigenous politics the potential disempowering danger of internal factionalism needs to be measured against the changes indigenous movements and organizations have been able to promote both locally and nationally. In the tractor case the perceived weakness displayed by the handing of the prisoners to the OID had no consequences, since local authorities (namely the parish civil officer) did not use the momentary challenge to the Inca Atahualpa's political legitimacy to regain control over the administration of justice.

Derecho Propio

The examination of the Inca Atahualpa's performance in the administration of justice needs to be contextualized within the wider body of demands formulated by the indigenous movement at the national level. The tension between equality and diversity as a contradiction inherent to the liberal definition of citizenship in multicultural societies has led many Latin American states throughout the 1990s to revise their constitutions in order to incorporate indigenous demands for self-determination (Taylor 1994). According to Ecuadorian indigenous activists, recognition of diversity implied the capacity of indigenous nationalities to "choose and freely exercise their own political system and model of socioeconomic and scientific-cultural development, on grounds completely defined within the framework of the New Plurinational Nation" (CONAIE 1993, 4).

A pivotal area in the recognition of the indigenous right to self-determination is the legitimization of indigenous traditional authorities and of derecho propio. This definition refers to the set of norms and practices on which the indigenous nationalities base their justice system. Recognition of legal pluralism is an important step toward recognition of multicultural citizenship. The 1998 Ecuadorian constitution officially recognized, for the first time, the legitimacy of indigenous traditional authorities and the right of indigenous peoples to administer justice according to their own principles and values. Nonetheless, the debate on what constitutes derecho propio, as well as its constitutional recognition (reaffirmed in 2008), establishes a set of dichotomies and hierarchies that underscores the ambiguities of multicultural recognition.

Many constitutional reforms in Latin America that have recognized indigenous rights to self-determination have regarded indigenous customary rights as legitimate for the resolution of internal conflicts (Van Cott 2000; Yrigoyen 2004). Although they have recognized the existence of legal pluralism, these reforms have established a hierarchy that privileges the national legal system. The 1998 and 2008 Ecuadorian constitutions validated indigenous traditional justice systems and authorities, but delimited their jurisdiction to indigenous territories. While the 1998 Political Constitution of the Republic of Ecuador restricted the application of indigenous justice by allowing it as long as it did not violate or contradict the national legal system, the 2008 Constitution of Ecuador seems to expand such application, allowing its sphere of action as long as it does not violate the "constitution and the human rights recognized by international declarations" (title Four, chap. Four, art. 171). However, the dichotomy established in the 1998 constitutional reform is maintained, since in the 2008 Constitution of Ecuador, in the section titled "Juridical Function and Indigenous Justice," the latter is ruled under a separate article (art. 171) and differentiated from what is defined as ordinary justice, which is the system that regulates justice nationally, therefore outside indigenous territories and for all Ecuadorian citizens.[22] Even if, relative to the 1998 reform, the 2008 constitution has incorporated indigenous rights more horizontally throughout its body of articles and dispositions, it nevertheless does not treat derecho propio as a valid system beyond ethnic boundaries. This separation of juridical systems draws on ethnocentric definitions of customary rights that reinforce patterns of inequality. As discussed earlier in legal and social-science discourses, derecho propio has been defined as "custom" or customary right (*derecho consuetudinario*) (see Poole 2006; Stavenhagen 1990). Indigenous activists have often reiterated this same distinction when referring to their justice systems in terms of *usos y costumbres* (uses and customs). Some definitions of consuetudinary rights have presented them as a "vague set of norms that we recognize as customary rights" (Iturralde 1993, 137).

Merging together different legal philosophies, the Anglo-Saxon and the Roman, these definitions imply a dichotomy between "law" and custom, usually constructed around the distinction between written law of Western juridical systems and oral principles as constitutive of customary practices. The vagueness suggested by Diego Iturralde refers to the supposed impermanence of nonwritten legal principles as opposed to the permanence of written law. This type of interpretation leads to false dichotomies. First, the fact that normativity in "law" comes from its written nature does not mean that laws and their meaning are not subject to change: decrees, amendments, and repeals are tools to modify the use and meaning of a law. Whether oral or written, every norm or set of norms articulates with diverse political, historical, and cultural spheres in society and is, therefore, bound to change. Confining written and oral legislation within the constraints of specific sets of characteristics runs the risk of reifying and essentializing them. Second, the reference to custom may lead to the assumption that customs are a default mechanism that operates in the absence of a codified system of justice.

As the Inca Atahualpa case shows, every society possesses its own distinctive set of norms that contribute to internal social control. It is not a question of "synthesizing, within the wide spectrum of culture, those customs that could be considered legal" (Iturralde 1993, 131). This image confers on customary rights an improvisational quality. To the contrary, customary rights have, for the society that applies them, the same normative effect and value attributed to the "law."

Thus, the problem pertains not so much to the theoretical definition of the difference between two or more justice systems, but to their application and articulation (Fernando García 2002; García and Chavez 2004). As Goodale discusses, justice systems and laws are systems of representation "that mediate the production of other social meanings" (2006a, 216). The administration of justice is pivotal in the reaffirmation of hegemonic values and social hierarchies. In the multicultural constitutions of Latin American countries, different legal systems are stratified according to their supposed level of complexity and reliability. Treated as unsuitable for application to all citizens, indigenous justice is considered valid only when it is based on and restricted to members of the ethnic group that applies it. The sovereignty of the national legal system becomes a sort of antidote against legal chaos, and its superiority and ascendancy remain unquestioned. If two or more justice systems are presented as mutually exclusive, therefore, their coexistence inevitably leads to clashes that reflect and reinforce patterns of exclusion. However, the Tixán example shows the extent to which the administration of justice can become emblematic of local indigenous empowerment by "invading" and to a certain degree invalidating the juridical functions of the local state representative without excluding or replacing it.

More important, the emphasis on sharp distinctions obscures both similarities and interactions between two or more juridical systems. The case of Tixán shows, as do other cases in the Andean region, that the incompatibility of indigenous and nonindigenous justice is a product of competing spheres of power rather than of preestablished incommensurable differences between the two (Goodale 2006a; Poole and Das 2004; Rappaport 2005). Differences are negotiated and codified in political practice. In the practice of justice making, the specificities of each system's normative principles can be accepted or rejected based on their efficacy in offering viable solutions to conflict. In Tixán, for example, some chagras and townsfolk found the indigenous process of conflict resolution more effective than the one offered by the teniente político.

However, the examination of the Inca Atahualpa's application of derecho propio both in the realm of interorganizational rivalry and interethnic conflict also highlights the ambiguities inherent in the administration of justice in multicultural contexts. The validity of both systems of norms and their applied dimension is a contested terrain in which both past and present practices mesh and interact. In this light, elements such as violence, corporal punishment, and the hierarchical dichotomy of oral and written documents do not appear as essentialized characteristics differentiating indigenous and nonindigenous justice. Each of those elements pertained, and still pertains, to both systems. Yet their application acquires a specific meaning and use according to the context. In the context of ethnic discrimination, the application of derecho propio can produce contradictory discourses on culture, justice, and indigenous rights which respond to the specific challenges that such discourses are meant to address. In the national context of indigenous political demands, for example, the legality and legitimacy of indigenous people's right to live according to their culture and tradition have often been framed by indigenous activists within a larger body of rights connected to the International Human Rights declaration and the International Labor Organization (ILO) Convention 169 on indigenous rights. Accordingly, practices considered expressions of indigenous culture, such as corporal punishment and the adoption of forceful measures in the justice sessions of the Inca Atahualpa, could be considered human-rights abuses. In the context of local power dynamics, contradictory reinterpretations of indigenous justice relate to the specific structure of power and conditions that indigenous actors are trying to redefine and the related challenges.

With the purpose of creating a counter-elitist and antiracist administration of justice in the parish, the codification of indigenous justice in Tixán led to the formulation of ambiguous principles and practices. The debate among the four local organizations on corporal punishment addresses some of these contradictions. Whether "traditional" or acquired, the types of corporal punishment incorporated as expressions of derecho propio articulate with a wider history of violence and physical abuse in which physical punishment has been a strategy of the dominating power to impose class and ethnic hierarchies. The debate on the use of increasingly harsh physical punishment acquired its significance within the local economy and history of power relations. Even in the context of indigenous justice, such practices recall and recognize that physical violence is a valid instrument for the imposition of power and authority. In Tixán corporal punishment became a vehicle for the affirmation of indigenous power at large, as well as a vehicle by which the competing organizations could exercise power over each other. Yet its harsh and redundant application draws on principles derived from the same abusive structure of power that the affirmation of indigenous justice is attempting to invalidate.

The principles and practices of indigenous consuetudinary rights, therefore, are not formulated on fixed cultural notions of what constitutes justice in indigenous societies. The corpus of both legal and extralegal practices that historically has sanctioned the subordination of indigenous people and relegated them to the margins of dominant society included common indigenous people and indigenous authorities. The contemporary process of negotiation and resignification of indigenous justice and its meanings articulate with this complex history of asymmetrical exchange with the dominating culture and justice system (Poole and Das 2004; Rappaport 2005; Starn 1999). In political terms, the tensions between human rights and cultural rights and the inconsistencies they can lead to could serve the state and elites as potential justification for delegitimatizing indigenous authorities and justice systems—a risk that is known to indigenous activists (de la Peña 2002).

Conclusion

The proceedings of the administration of justice in Tixán illustrate the extent of the changes in the parish since the 1970s. The remapping of the local structure of power affected the way Quichuas, chagras, and tixaneños lived, as well as their perceptions of each other. It would once have been inconceivable that an "Indian" could be considered a more capable justice administrator than a parish civil officer. The long-standing racist stereotype of the subdued and ignorant "Indian" is, however, no longer commonplace.

The different dimensions according to which justice became the major arena of such resignification in Tixán shed light on two major points of discussion in my introduction. First, although treated as one of the major implications of the politicization of cultural distinctiveness, the tendency to factionalism has not proved to be necessarily disempowering. To be sure, interorganizational rivalry is certainly problematic. The Inca Atahualpa was momentarily placed in a position of weakness and forced to make unpopular decisions. However, this episode alone did not delegitimize the organization's pivotal role in empowering the local indigenous population. After the tractor case, all other justice sessions, which had been temporarily suspended, resumed as normal, without any apparent major consequences—and the expected and feared revenge of the released convicts never occurred.

The rivalry did not have a disempowering effect in part because local parish authorities made no attempt to capitalize on the Inca Atahualpa's temporary debacle in order to reaffirm the legitimacy of their jurisdiction. In an attempt to defend their own authority, parish civil officers did complain about "Indians" acting as judges, but their complaints never prompted any specific response. Another reason for the lack of repercussions is related to the importance of grassroots organizations such as the Inca Atahualpa in advancing an overall sense of well-being and progress among indigenous people in enclaves traditionally dominated by whites. In my visits to communities to interview elders, leaders, or members of different cabildos, both adult men and women acknowledged that the quality of their lives had improved significantly since the Inca Atahualpa had come into being. Theft and abuse were under control, conflicts were being resolved, and on the whole the communities' needs were being addressed. As a comunero from La Merced put it, "Problems, you always have some, but now we do not feel alone anymore. In my community we feel that now with the organization we can get help to resolve the problems and move ahead" (1993). Many SGOs like the Inca Atahualpa became vehicles for the empowerment and development of indigenous communities. Their cacique-like role in the distribution of all the resources associated with development allowed these grassroots organizations to become agents of regional development (Ramón Valarezo 1993). The disempowering effects of internal factionalism can thus be traced to a more generalized strategy of disempowerment adopted by the ruling classes and to any specific organization's or entity's lack of legitimacy within the movement.

The second major point of my discussion relates to understanding the changes that indigenous movements promote. In the context of ethnic mobilization in which cultural distinctiveness is used as an ideological foundation for political struggle, derecho propio acquires an emancipatory function. In sociopolitical terms, derecho propio in Tixán became not only a means for social control within indigenous societies, but also an instrument with which to reverse the subordination of indigenous subjects to the state and ruling classes. Moreover, it served other subordinate citizens such as chagras and poor nonindigenous people. The Inca Atahualpa undoubtedly opened a space for a more democratic and just exercise of power.

However, the emancipatory function of derecho propio is also tied to a process of codification and formulation of indigenous justice, whose meanings are often contradictory and ambiguous, as the discussion on corporal punishment highlights. In indigenous politics, therefore, neither justice nor democratic change can be interpreted as univocal and formulaic; they are contested and often contradictory terrains whose meanings are constantly negotiated to transform specific circumstances into conditions for indigenous empowerment.

Even if indigenous justice and its principles continued to be a contested terrain for all the local organizations and in relation to the local nonindigenous population and to authorities, their affirmation was conducive to the next step in the process of consolidation of indigenous power locally: to seek participation within the state structure. In 1992, the organization decided to participate in national elections with a candidate for presidency of the cantonal council. Quichuas from four other organizations also presented candidates for counselors, all of them representatives of the Frente Amplio de Izquierda (FADI). The quest for local representation this time went beyond the parish civil office, to include the cantonal council, a political body one level higher in the national political hierarchy. In spite of CONAIE's campaign against electoral participation in 1992, many provincial and cantonal organizations decided to run candidates in the election. Although all indigenous candidates lost in the 1992 local elections in Tixán, the temporary break with CONAIE's political strategies made sense in the context of micropolitics, where indigenous activists were trying to consolidate their presence in local power niches. In the 2004 administrative elections, María Lluilema, the indigenous candidate in the Pachakutik list for the cantonal council, was indeed elected to the council, thus becoming the first indigenous person—and a woman, no less—to represent Tixán parish in the cantonal council.

CHAPTER SIX

Celebrating Diversity

The process that transformed the summer harvest celebration in Tixán into the "festival of the Quichuas" exemplifies the intertwining of culture and politics. During this event, the Tixán public square becomes the site for the ritualization of conflict involving Quichuas, chagras, and tixaneños. A relatively recent creation in historical and ethnographic terms, the harvest festival politicizes indigenous identity, history, and culture by transforming them into ideological foundations of the indigenous struggle. The harvest celebration is now a public spectacle celebrating indigenous identity through "authentic" indigenous dances, music, and clothing that folklorize local Quichua culture. As with indigenous justice, the discourse on indigenous cultural identity selectively incorporates different cultural and religious matrixes, all of which relate to Quichuas' lived experience and historical memory. By drawing on complementary notions of resistance and tradition, as well as on ritual practices, the festival highlights the extent to which Quichuas define their ethnic identity as a political consequence of their everyday life as "indios" in a white-dominated environment, as well as in relation to "traditions" of Indianness. The harvest festival is inscribed, therefore, within an Andean history of celebrations involving indigenous communities which ritualize existing power relations and conflicts.[1]

The Festival of the Quichuas

My analysis of the harvest festival and its process of creation is linked to the context of local interethnic conflict and of political mobilization. The intervention of the Inca Atahualpa in the planning and staging of the festival offers an opportunity to explore the intricate processes through which indigenous politics are institutionalized. The apparent simplification by grassroots leaders in their rendering of indigenous cultural forms can be understood by examining the leaders' collective memory, the specific interlocutors they want to reach, and the network of power relations in their milieu. The folklorization and typification of indigenous culture displayed in the festival, therefore, also relates to the consolidation of the Inca Atahualpa's political legitimacy, whereby the festival became a space for affirming both indigenous identity and the Inca Atahualpa's authority. The combination of these two dimensions reveals aspects of political action that are not easily articulated in ideological and political terms. In other words, the festival shows the extent to which in grassroots politics the politics of everyday life are inextricable from the sphere of political action in which formal and visible political entities such as the Inca Atahualpa actively lead and make plans. To paraphrase Richard Gabriel Fox and Orin Starn (1997), the harvest celebration offers an example of the extent to which revolution is not separate from the quotidian state of silent contestation.

The Preparation

As in previous years, the 1992 harvest festival took place in the town square, over the course of the second Saturday and Sunday of August, right in the middle of the harvest season.[2] The preparation, however, had begun three months earlier, when the Inca Atahualpa included the planning of the festival on its meeting agenda. Although festival responsibilities had been broadly distributed among the affiliated communities the previous year, the Inca Atahualpa meeting was pivotal for shaping the festival and assigning specific duties to the communities and supporters alike. For example, Father Torres's proposal to include in the Sunday Mass a choir of indigenous children singing an indigenous chant (*jahuay*) and carrying crosses of wheat and barley on their backs received enthusiastic approval, and its preparation was entrusted to indigenous catechists in coordination with Father Torres.

The Inca Atahualpa's board of directors, which constituted the organizational committee (*comité organizativo*), then proceeded to assign tasks and responsibilities to the affiliated communities who were represented at the meeting by their community presidents. The comité formed commissions of two or three communities, and to each commission it assigned a distinct set of activities related to the festival. These included the organizing of the intercommunity soccer tournament, the preparation of the arena for bullfighting, and the preparation of the luncheon to be served on the second day of the festival in the *convento* (parish priest house), for which special food was expected (such as potatoes and rice, as well as lamb, which was usually prepared for marriages, baptisms, and other special occasions).

The organizing of cultural activities, such as the dance and the music contests, was left to members of the Inca Atahualpa's board. At the meeting Father Torres proposed that the 1992 festival also introduce an accordion competition: "Many of you play accordion very well, so why don't we nurture our talent [*cultivar nuestro talento*]?" Organizing these competitions was usually time-consuming since it involved finding individuals to serve as judges or prize donors and making sure that competing communities' artists took their rehearsals seriously.[3] Another important item discussed at the meeting was the nomination of *priostes* (festival hosts). The system of *priostazgo*, or host obligations, has colonial origins and is widespread throughout Andean countries (see Abercrombie 1991b). In the hacienda era, priostazgo was a mechanism that secured the system of patron-client relations; landowners chose priostes from among their indigenous laborers, who then, in order to finance their ritual obligations, became indebted to the same terratenientes (see Guerrero 1991b; Guerrero Arias 1993). The contemporary priostazgo system maintains its primary function as a mechanism by which to distribute ritual obligations and responsibilities according to social status and prestige in a community.

Although communal authorities at the meeting reconfirmed their priostazgo commitments, they also pointed out that such obligations had become increasingly onerous and hence difficult to secure. The organization assumed responsibility for finding festival priostes from among people who were not indigenous. Interestingly, the priostazgo of bulls for the bullfighting (*tauromaquia*) had become the prerogative of chagra families, whose real or perceived expertise with cattle provided better access to bulls. Yet more items were needed for the afternoon of tauromaquia: some indigenous individuals offered to provide the *colchas*; the compañeros of the equipo técnico were asked to provide the *alcancía*; and the Inca Atahualpa's leaders committed to providing chicha (corn beer), *canelazos* (sugarcane alcohol drink), and homemade bread for distribution during the festival.[4] The higher the price of the provision, the higher the prestige the priostazgo would confer on its host. At the meeting, the father of the Inca Atahualpa's vice president offered to cover one of the most costly provisions: the brass band, whose music would accompany the festival from start to finish. The session was adjourned with the general understanding, too, that unexpected hosts would come forward later.

The Harvest

After the first planning meeting, at the end of April, preparations for the harvest festival were momentarily put aside. Everybody returned to their normal activities to make sure they were ready for the harvest season, in June. Cabildo members had to organize the mingas (collective harvesting work) for the harvest of the communal lands and make sure all comuneros received their assignments. A special season, the harvest evoked both anxiety and excitement. As some people said, the harvest was "el momento de la verdad" (the moment of truth), the moment when people would know if their sweat and hard work had borne good fruit. Gradually the landscape transformed, as the wheat and corn crops in the communities immediately surrounding the town ripened, painting the view golden and green. It was also the beginning of the dry season, when strong winds covered everything in dust and permeated the air with the scents of soil and crops. After winter's fog and gray, blue skies finally appeared, and the bright sun brought a ruddy glow to everybody's complexion. During one of my long walks to the communities engaged in the harvest preparations, I heard a chant coming from several different directions all at once—a captivating echo. It sounded as if the chant's sharp cries were bouncing from one mountainside to the other, trapped between the two cordilleras. Javier explained to me that the Quichuas harvesters were singing the jahuay, an ancestral harvest chant. According to many local testimonies, this ancient chant always accompanied the harvesting of barley and wheat on community and individual lands. The Quichua word *jahuay*, which means "to rise," formerly referred to the war cry of the Puruhaes, an ethnic group in the northern part of Chimborazo Province (Guerrero Arias 1994, 31). Today, the jahuay accompanies the cutting of the crops in the harvesting mingas.

The activities of the harvesting mingas on community lands that I participated in were highly ritualized. Each worker had a defined role: the men cut the crops (a task considered too physically challenging for women); the women collected the felled crops and helped to form *gavillas* (bales); and community leaders directed the work.[5] The president offered workers the chicha that had been prepared for the occasion and exhorted the people to keep working. Men chanted the jahuay while cutting the crops. One of the cutters, usually chosen from among the elders, performed as *paqui*, the leader of the chanting.[6] He would utter the first sharp cry, and the other cutters would echo him.[7]

The captivating power of the jahuay struck me during my first harvesting minga in Pachagsí. After the initial sequence of sharp, repeated cries, the paqui intoned the twelve verses that comprise the chant, followed by the shouts of the other cutters. During the hacienda era, the lyrics were directed at landowners, exhorting them to offer chicha and bread, and expressed gratitude to God for the harvest (Thurner 1993). The jahuay that I heard typically directed the exhortations at the harvest sponsors, usually the community presidents, although some versions still exhorted the patrón, the landowner. The paqui I interviewed considered the initial cry of the chant to be the performance's pivotal moment. With that cry, the cutters pledge to complete the harvest: "They pledge to the *cerros* [mountains]," he explained, "and ask them to repeat the chant so that all of the communities would know that the harvest season had begun: *Chimborazo, Carihuairazo, uyarispa, taquirishpa* [Chimborazo, Carihuairazo, listen and sing], we sing" (1992).[8] The paqui continued, "The mountains give us the energy and the strength we need for the harvest." In this context, jahuay indicates a call for the sound of the chant to ascend to the mountaintops and to suffuse the skies.

In the barley harvest minga I attended in La Pacífica, groups of cutters competed to be the first to complete their portion of the harvest labor (Thurner 1993). The loaders (*aparijcuna*) proceeded with their task, generally helped by women who were in charge of bale making. One loader kept the lead, the *punta purij*, and did not allow anyone to overtake him.[9] He was responsible for rousing the energy, the spirit, and the effort of the other loaders. Many coveted this important task. The *chaladores*, mostly children, followed behind, collecting the gleanings to bring home. The animals completed the work by grazing and clearing the harvested field.

Participants enjoyed an abundance of food, drink, and music on all of these occasions. The trumpet, flute, and panpipes (*rondín* and the *rondador*) were the most common musical instruments played during the moments of rest. For young single men and women, these were also occasions for engaging in coquettish exchanges. Despite the compulsory nature of agricultural activities, their ritualization and festivity converted most harvesting mingas into popular and highly anticipated celebrations.

The Unfolding of the Festival

The effervescence that accompanied festival preparations started three weeks before the event, when the first leaflets with the schedule of events announced the imminent celebration. From that moment on, the harvest festival became the prevailing topic of conversation for everyone connected to the Inca Atahualpa. The leaflet's front page identified the festival organizers: the Inca Atahualpa, the Pastoral Indígena (a group of local indigenous catechists), and Father Pedro Torres. An opening and closing quote from Deuteronomy specified the purpose of the celebration: to thank God for the harvest. Official invitations were sent to all guests, especially to the other cantonal organizations, authorities, potential priostes, and prize donors.

Saturday

At last, the first day of the festival arrived. People arrived in town early to finalize logistics. By ten in the morning all the local shops were open, selling soda and bread to the incoming crowd. Tixán's main streets were quickly packed with people from the surrounding communities, who were dressed up for the occasion. Most indigenous people wore strictly non-Western clothing that was different from their usual attire. Many men wore round woolen hats and ponchos, some of them white, while the women's clothing was a festival of vivid colors: shawls and red woolen *polleras* (multilayered skirts)—hand-woven and preferably old—fastened by hand-woven sashes with colorful designs. Young girls adorned their necks with beautiful long necklaces and their round hats with brightly colored ribbons, which were an indication of their status as single women. This clothing, people said, was reserved for special occasions. Variations in the color and shape of ponchos, hats, and polleras were associated with a specific locality. When I admired Juana's exquisite hand-woven pollera, she replied, "Yes, compañerita, this is the dress that makes our culture [*hace nuestra cultura*]."

Later that morning, a soccer tournament with teams representing affiliated communities inaugurated the festival on an improvised field in the town square. By early afternoon, the celebration had gained momentum, with the music competition taking place in the same square in front of a thick crowd. The competing music groups represented different communities in the Tixán sector. In all of them, women sang while men accompanied on string instruments (guitars and *charangos*) and drums. Most of the songs, all in Quichua, praised the achievements of the Inca Atahualpa and thanked its leaders and Father Pedro Torres for making the festival a reality. After several hours of music, the judges declared the winners, who were awarded coveted monetary prizes or trophies.

The festival continued through the night in the town's taverns and in the streets that led to the Pan-American Highway, where most of the indigenous people who lived in the town resided. Families and compadres celebrated in the street until dawn. Although the festival was an indigenous celebration, the town dwellers also participated in the festive atmosphere by joining other townsfolk in the *chupe*, a Spanish word used in Ecuador to refer to an act of socializing that is accompanied by heavy drinking.

The ritual space of the festival also created a new opportunity to renew the ties of compadrazgo. In the small shops around the town square, indigenous and nonindigenous individuals, primarily men, were taking advantage of the festive chupe to reinforce their ties of friendship, of compadrazgo, or other types of agreements. The offering of trago, no matter the specific occasion, was understood as an act of reciprocity that usually involved men and implied an obligation to accept it. The host normally acquired the prestige, even if momentarily, by showing generosity and exercising power by inducing his guest to drink heavily. This ritualized game, in fact, often ended with the guest becoming intoxicated, but the power imbalance was typically minimized by the fact that both parties participated in the spree. In the context of the festival, interethnic relations of compadrazgo were reinforced with chupe sessions, in which the host was commonly a tixaneño.

Sunday

An outdoor Mass in the square opened the celebrations, and a choir of indigenous catechists and one of tixaneño women involved in the administration of the convent sang in Quichua and Spanish. The Mass was the only festival activity in which the town dwellers participated openly. It culminated with the priest blessing offerings of wheat and barley tied in the shape of crosses, which indigenous children carried on their backs. Following the Mass, a choir of indigenous children chanting the jahuay led a procession in honor of St. Francis of Assisi, the town's patron saint. A large crowd, including the indigenous and chagra dance groups slated to compete in the afternoon, followed the statue of St. Francis throughout the town. The children's choir brought the sonorous echo of the chant into town, and even townsfolk watching the procession from the windows and the doors of their houses showed signs of admiration for the jahuay's evocative sound. After passing along the two main streets, the procession slowly returned to the square and dissolved.

The afternoon program started after the community luncheon was served in the convento courtyard to all guests and active participants. The same brass band that had been performing incessantly in the streets during the festival accompanied the dance contest. During the competition, the band played familiar tunes that were often used by folk-dance groups in the province. The eight competing dance groups, including two chagra groups, represented eight of the affiliated communities. The dance contest was the main event of the festival in which chagras were clearly visible as a collectivity distinct from the Quichuas. Although the chagras had been present and mingling with the rest of the multicolored public for the whole festival, in the dance contest they were distinguished by their dress. Whereas the indigenous dance attire for the most part consisted of ponchos, *zamarros* (sheepskin over pants), and trousers for men, and polleras and shawls for women, in the chagra dance groups the men wore black trousers and white shirts, and the women wore black, pleated skirts and embroidered white blouses.[10] That year the San Francisco chagra community won first prize. When interviewed, one of the dancers triumphantly described his group's artistic performance as "our own chagra dances" (*estas son nuestras danzas chagras*). He explained that the music, the choreography, and the overall ensemble were the elements that made chagra dance different from the Quichua dance. The chagra's dance steps were quicker and jumpier (*mas saltos y menos pisoteadas*). He also emphasized that his community took the contest very seriously and that the final result was the reward for the many hours of rehearsal.

The day's most anticipated event was the afternoon bullfight. An arena had been built in the middle of the square, surrounded by a multitude of people waiting for the bullfight to start. Some tixaneños gathered on the balconies of their houses, ready to watch. This type of bullfight is widespread in Andean rural highlands among both indigenous and nonindigenous people. Known as *toros de pueblo* (town bulls), these fights do not involve well-groomed bulls and professional bullfighters. All the men who wish to challenge the bulls enter the arena at the same time and start running in front of them, hoping to provoke an attack. Although not formally trained for bullfighting, these local longhorns can be extremely aggressive. The fiercer the bulls, the more thrilling and entertaining the bullfight is for the spectators. In the novel *Yawar Fiesta*, the Peruvian writer José María Arguedas describes how town bullfights arouse feelings that range from fright to excitement, which can even turn into morbid satisfaction in the event of an accident. The bullfighting can last for several hours, during which time various bulls are brought into the arena. During the harvest festival of 1992, the bulls belonged to a chagra family, who were native to the Sanganao community and residing in Riobamba.

Different events constituted the ceremonial bullfight. The first was the offering of alcancías. The members of the equipo técnico mounted the old jeep of the Canadian volunteers and, as priostes of alcancías, started the rounds from within the arena by throwing oranges to the audience. Many people jumped the fences and flocked toward the car, trying to catch an orange or grab them from the back of the jeep; we were quickly surrounded by grasping hands, and fifty pounds of oranges vanished in the blink of an eye. The event proceeded with the presentation of the colchas. Followed by his family and the band, and greeted by the spectator's enthusiastic applause, the prioste of the first colcha circled the arena, displaying its colorful composition. The colcha was then tied to the back of the bull and the fight officially started. The other two colchas followed, one at a time, later in the afternoon, with the bravest bullfighters seizing them off the backs of the charging bulls. The afternoon was a display and celebration of strength, bravery, and virility. When two less fortunate fighters were flung into the air by the horns of a charging bull, a sudden silence subdued the excitement. The audience, stunned, watched as members of the security committee transported the wounded to the local medical post.

Proceedings in the arena lasted until dusk, which marked the finale of the harvest celebration's public events. Gradually, the crowd dispersed, the wind subsided, and quiet pervaded the streets as a cold and star-filled night enveloped the town.

Toward an *Evangelización Inculturada*

Two elements are central to understanding what the harvest festival has come to represent: the change in policy of the Catholic Church; and the ceremonial components of the harvests among the Quichuas of Tixán. Father Torres explained.

> To the Israelites, to the people of Israel, God promised a land and He rescued them from slavery in Egypt, and took them to this land of milk and honey. Also in the Levite He orders them: *when you harvest the grains of your land, do not harvest to the edge of your field, nor gather the remains of your grains; leave them for the poor and the forest dweller*. This is for the chaladores, for the poor. It is sharing; each one should give from what he has received and should take a portion to share with everyone. This is what we are trying to do: rescue a very ancient tradition of the indigenous world, with its color, its joy, and its festivals. In which we can all be happy and in which we try to share what God gave us. Live it from faith and as a reminder of the liberation that God has made for his people. The harvest festival is a popular festival in which everyone takes part, where everyone collaborates, where there is food and drink for all, and where everyone with the same faith comes together to thank God for what he has given us. (1992, emphasis added)

These words exemplify the use of a biblical framework to reinterpret indigenous harvest practices such as that of the *chaladores*.[11] One of the debates that originated during the 1968 synod of the Latin American bishops in Medellín concerned the religion of indigenous peasants. The discussion focused on the need to understand indigenous cults as more than religious syncretism. The progressive Catholic view posited that syncretism would confer on indigenous religion the status of a mere cult—deriving from both Catholic and indigenous roots—or would result in the juxtaposition of different religious elements (see Wachtel 1976). The alternative proposal was to interpret indigenous religion as "popular religiosity," a phrase that addressed a specific manifestation of popular religious feeling, where "popular" referred to marginalized and poor social strata. The indigenous cults and reinterpretations of Catholicism were thus considered an expression of this popular religiosity.

In the context of this debate, evangelism came to be viewed as a potential instrument of liberation insofar as it would promote and defend popular religiosity. This perspective was later defined as *evangelización inculturada* (Andrew Orta [2004] translates it as "theology of inculturation"), which chronologically followed the debate on the theology of liberation. The 1979 Latin American bishops' synod in Puebla de los Angeles (Mexico) recognized the value of popular religiosity as a constitutive element of peasants' historical identity (Marzal 1988, 38). However, as Paulo Suess (1993, 8) argued, the synod of Puebla still spoke of the peasantry in a generic sense, without taking into account its ethnic component. According to Suess, due to the growth of Latin American indigenous movements, it was important to focus on the process of evangelization and speak of an evangelizing practice, evangelización inculturada, that no longer wished to impose "foreign" cults. According to this reinterpretation, the rescue of cultural expressions and ancestral religions became a priority. The process of inculturación to which Suess referred also involved the evangelizers. They had to learn the codes, the signs, and the values of the indigenous culture in order to be able to reinforce and defend their popular religiosity. It was the missionary who had to be "incultured": "The more the missionary is 'inculturated' in the life of these people, the more he is questioned and asked and the more the Indians want to know about his world. . . . The missionary's silent presence inevitably provokes dialogue and sooner or later gives him the opportunity to fulfill his hopes" (Suess 1993, 40).

From the perspective of Father Torres, therefore, the harvest festival in Tixán was an expression of both the Quichuas' popular religiosity, bringing together Christian and indigenous traditions, and of the evangelización inculturada. It fulfilled two simultaneous objectives: to rescue founding elements (myths and rituals) of the indigenous "cosmovisión" and to reassert the validity of an evangelical practice that respected the indigenous culture and, therefore, did not result in aberrant and destructive practices.

Although inscribed in the complex and ambiguous history of church-Indian relationships, the case of the harvest festival in Tixán problematizes evangelización inculturada as a theological practice that was born out of a debate that questioned power relations (see Orta 2002). Its application and interpretation, therefore, cannot be considered univocal and clear. Father Torres, a strong believer in the theology of liberation, understood that the attention paid to indigenous popular religiosity was above all an attempt to rescue indigenous culture from denigration. His effort to equate Catholic with indigenous religious practices and values went beyond the intention of evangelizing indigenous parishioners by translating Catholicism into Quichua religiosity. His interpretation of the chalana, for example, was his way of publicly legitimizing Quichua cultural forms in a context in which Quichua religiosity was equated by local nonindigenous parishioners with superstition. His commitment, however, was not based in a vacuum; it was in dialogue with the local process of ethnic politicization according to which Quichuas negotiated their own understanding of religiosity and faith. Quichuas and the Inca Atahualpa thus appropriated the space of the festival beyond its religious meaning.

The Creation of the Festival and the Indigenous Ancestor

The first harvest festival took place in the town of Tixán in 1982, on the initiative of two Spanish missionaries, Antonio and María del Carmen. Better known as the Cuquis, the missionaries decided to involve the whole population of the parish—indigenous and nonindigenous—in an act of thanksgiving to God for the harvest. While respecting indigenous cults, the major objective of the celebration was to establish a more equal and just act of thanksgiving. Immediately prior to the emergence of this celebration, Monseñor Leonidas Proaño, bishop of Riobamba, had abolished the practice of collecting *primicias* (first fruits) and *diezmos* (tithes), in an effort to end an abusive practice that had become customary under the hacienda "trilogy of power"; in that context, the demonstration of faith and thanksgiving to God that the Bible teaches had turned into a mechanism for exploiting indigenous peasants and expropriating indigenous agricultural production.

In Tixán, the abusive nature of the collection rooted in the hacienda regime survived the dismantling of that power structure. Typically, the priest selected a tixaneño who enjoyed his good graces to be the *primiciero* (first-fruit collector). During the harvest season, the fruit collector was responsible for collecting the quantities "offered" by those from the country (los del campo). However, these quantities were inevitably determined by the greed of the primiciero. According to a former sacristan, the collection was distributed among the parish, anejos, and schools. Nonetheless, he continued, "how it was distributed was a question that we [sacristans] could not answer" (1992). Moreover, indigenous parishioners were doubly exploited. Many priests distributed these products unfairly and in most cases, nothing reached the neediest. Many non-elites in Tixán, not only Quichuas, reminisced about abuses perpetrated by the priests, such as misuse of alms, solicitation of offerings and camari, and even sexual abuse.

With the message of Christian faith and the elimination of the primicias, the Cuquis felt the harvest required a celebration as a symbolic act of gratitude to God. The first harvest celebration they organized consisted of a special Mass on a Sunday in August, in which the entire local population participated, and offerings were gathered and distributed among the neediest. This public act of thanksgiving created by the Cuquis gradually evolved into the harvest festival.

The harvest festival cannot be considered merely an invention of the local priests. As Father Torres affirmed, "The indigenous ancestor is part of this celebration, with its own traditions and customs and the expression of faith, gratitude, and acknowledgment of God for the grain that He allows them [the Indians] to collect" (1992). The indigenous ancestral component in this case is the *buluay*, a Quichua term meaning "termination" or "culmination." Buluay is the culminating moment of the harvest; it is also the festive moment and the joy that accompanies the completion of the harvest, the last minga. It is meant to demonstrate gratitude for the entire harvest. Several testimonies indicated that this celebration existed "desde siempre," since time immemorial, and therefore predated the emergence of the hacienda system. On the day of the buluay, the ritualization of the activities performed during each harvesting minga acquired special emphasis. With this culminating harvest, the last golden patches of barley and wheat coloring the summer hills disappeared. On this day of abundance, the supply of food, chicha, and trago seemed endless.

The minga, the jahuay, and the buluay are considered by indigenous people to be ancestral practices that, even as they express gratitude to *ashpamama*—the local Quichua word for Mother Earth—for the harvest, also reinforce social norms such as collective participation, cohesion, and unity. As one paqui said, "The harvest for us means giving a hand, it is unity. We must learn because through the chant we know that they are harvesting in other communities, so we have to follow and harvest too. As they sing in other parts, we have to follow in order to follow custom; so it is that unity is made" (1992).

Another ancestral element traceable in the harvest festival addresses the pan-Andean celebration of the Inti Raymi, the name—meaning, literally, "the sun festival"—adopted by the Incas for their summer solstice celebration (Guaman Poma de Ayala 1988). During the Incaic Inti Raymi, all members of the powerful empire remembered the Inca. Under Catholic evangelization, the festival was made to coincide with the celebrations of Saints John and Peter, and often acquired those same names. These festivals are celebrated at the end of June and strongly emphasize the fertility of the land. Many other festivals take place throughout the Ecuadorian highlands in June and July, all relating to the fertility of the land and serving as propitiatory rites for the coming harvests (Thurner 1993).

The Displaced Festival

The harvest festival has changed considerably since its inception. Many changes started with the arrival, in 1986, of Father Torres, who entrusted the organization of the festival to the indigenous catechists. New events were introduced almost every year: contests for dance groups and music groups, bullfighting, soccer tournaments. Beginning in 1989, the festival was slated to last for two days, the second Saturday and Sunday of August, a date that falls in the middle of the harvest season, which runs from June to September.

The evolution and expansion of the festival under Father Torres's guidance also led to the gradual appropriation of the festival space by the Quichuas. According to a former sacristan, the introduction of the community luncheon meant that donations were not sufficient to feed everyone; therefore, the town dwellers began to participate less. Another key element in the gradual withdrawal of the tixaneños was the appearance of the Inca Atahualpa, in 1988, and the role the organization played in the control of local abuses. As the former secretary of the organization A. L. remembered, "During the festival, many town people, above all the youths, would take the microphone and make fun of us. Besides they speak Spanish and we speak Quichua, but they do not respect that. So we decided that the harvest festival had to be the festival of the Quichuas" (1992). In 1988, the Inca Atahualpa took control of festival planning, displacing even the *pastoral indígena* and leaving it with responsibility only for the organization of the Mass. That year the tixaneños gave up their last prerogative: the preparation of the bread. Over time, the two-day festival came to be viewed by many (indigenous, nonindigenous, and chagras) as the occasion when the "Indians" took over the town.

However, an additional element contributed to transforming the harvest festival into the "festival of the Quichuas." People from indigenous communities of the Tixán and Palmira parishes used to celebrate the summer solstice on San Pedro (St. Peter's) Day, 29 June, in Tixán's town square, but that celebration was eventually displaced to a community. I was unable to establish the exact period when such fiestas started to take place in the town; whether or not that might have occurred during hacienda times, most of the testimony I collected mentioned the participation of the parish civil officer as the most important nonindigenous person at the event.

According to these testimonies, the San Pedro celebration was spectacular. Taita A. L., a senior from Yacupungo community, told me that people from all of the communities, including Galte, used to participate in the San Pedro fiestas. "The fiesta started very early in the morning," he recounted, "when men dressed as captains and soldiers [popular characters representing hacienda administrators] arrived in the town square wearing very brightly colored clothes and riding fine horses all decorated with mirrors. It was quite a sight! The first one to arrive won the square for his anejo" (1992). The winner would then ride around the square, offering drinks to all and celebrating the victory, and everyone in the square would dance to the band. Lasting two days, the celebration was filled with drinking, eating, dancing, and, of course, toros. Everyone I interviewed—Quichuas and tixaneños alike—remembered a character who had regularly participated in the festival, Anacleto, as if he were a mythical figure. An indigenous man from Pueblo Viejo, Anacleto always distinguished himself as a brave and courageous bullfighter. Mimicking the gestures of this famous torero, Taita A. L. described the scene: "He always arrived all dressed in white, and armed with a lance ready to kill a bull. And he always did: he knelt in the middle of the arena holding his lance forward and with great bravery waited for the bull to charge him so he could plunge his lance into the animal's chest. And so he killed the bull" (1992). Once the bull was dead, its parts were distributed: a leg, the chest, and the *shungu* (Quichua for "heart" and "holder of thoughts") belonged to the matador, and the other leg was presented to the parish civil officer who had donated the fences for the construction of the arena.

By and large, the fiesta of San Pedro was an occasion for ritualizing intercommunity rivalry, which also included the communities of the Palmira parish. The contest to win the town square was a ritualized expression of such rivalry. Ritual battles are widespread among the indigenous cultures of the Andes, appearing, for example, in Inti Raymi celebrations that take place throughout the highland regions of Ecuador. The San Pedro festival in Alausí, too, used to begin with the seizure of the square by the indigenous people from different local communities. Cristóbal de Molina (1989) mentions ritual battles between the *hanan* and *urin* halves of the Inca empire. In Quichua, these rituals are called *pugllay*, meaning "to play."[12] The ludic dimension conferred by their ritualized character does not, however, prevent them from being actual battles. The confrontations in the Inti Raymi festivals have been explained as propitiatory rites connected to the fertility of the earth, the spilling of human blood being considered necessary to ensure a good harvest (Hopkins 1982, 176). Tristan Platt (1986a) offers a more complex explanation. In the case of Macha of Bolivia, the ritual battles (*tinkui* in Aymara) respond to a logic of complementary opposites that divides Aymara political and social space. By means of ritual battles, the moieties simultaneously reaffirm their identity, their difference, and their complementarity. In the seizure of the Tixán town square during the San Pedro celebration, two opposing sectors confronted each other: Galte and Tixán, which formed part of two of the biggest haciendas in the area, Moyocancha in Tixán and Galte-Tipín in Palmira. However, this conflict never escalated to violence.

Splendor aside, the overall context of the fiesta posed challenges to the Quichua participants. The teniente político on duty charged a fee to enter the square: ten sucres for captains on foot, twenty sucres for those on horseback, amounts that in the post-agrarian reform were equivalent to the monthly salary of a participant. A generous teniente would provide musicians (a brass band) as a donation. The tixaneños took advantage of the festival to overcharge for drinks and accommodations, and to request highly valued belongings (even land) as collateral from indigenous *fiesteros* who had no more cash to pay for their drinks. The conflict displayed in the San Pedro festival in Tixán, therefore, also had an interethnic dimension. All ritual obligations were framed by the context of unequal reciprocity in which the teniente político faced the indigenous captains in a symbolic confrontation, opposing the town authority against the indigenous ritual authorities. The town authority represented the power of the mishus and of the state, serving, himself, as the symbolic site of the ethnic conflict, while the town served as the symbolic setting for a conflict of a different nature, an intercommunity one.

This ritualization of domination, which Andrés Guerrero (1991a) defines as a semantics of domination in the hacienda regime, is well documented also in the San Juan festivals in Imbabura, in the northern Sierra, and in Cañar Province, in the southern Sierra (see Crain 1989; Crespi 1981; Guerrero 1991b). The relationships of subordination within the local structure of authority and power were reaffirmed and reinforced through a form of ritual reciprocity. The abusive practices characterizing the festival led Father Torres to convince the indigenous people to move the celebration of San Pedro from the town to the communities. Although it is difficult to establish with certainty the year in which the San Pedro festival first took place in the communities, the Inca Atahualpa's first president claimed that the festival's disappearance from Tixán coincided with the birth of the organization, in 1988. He apparently considered the change to be a successful measure taken by the Inca Atahualpa against the abuses of the mishus. A former parish civil officer during that time, a representative of Tixán's prestigious white elites, instead connected the change to Father Torres's arrival. The officer, who did not support what he defined as "la actitud pro-indígena" (the pro-indigenous attitude) of the priest, spoke of the San Pedro festival with much nostalgia, lamenting the loss of income that its displacement represented for many tixaneños and the economy of the town in general: "The San Pedro festival was grand, all those customs and the toros. Also it was important for the townsfolk since their sales would increase because there was a lot of activity in the town during the days of the fiestas. Then Father Pedro decided to move it, and I think it is a bad decision also for the Indians because they don't have that grand of a celebration anymore" (B. B., 1993).

Despite the uncertainty about dates, there is a clear correlation between the displacement of the San Pedro festival from the town and the growing participation of the indigenous people in the harvest festival, which helped transform the harvest thanksgiving Mass into the "festival of the Quichuas." Devotion to San Pedro, the patron saint of rain, remains strong, but his festival's splendor is but a fond memory; its grandeur now depends on the initiative of each community that decides to celebrate. Most commonly, the celebration takes place in a community and is limited to Mass, bullfights, and ritual sharing of food and drink—all acts open to members of the host community and a few special guests. One festival has gradually replaced the other, and with the displacement the intra- and interethnic conflicts expressed in them have acquired other meanings.

Los del Campo Take the Square

In order to understand the meanings that the harvest festival acquired in the local context of ethnic mobilization, it is pivotal to frame its analysis in the context of the politics of identity by focusing on the performative rendering of indigenous culture and its apparent reification.

The Dress That Makes the Culture

The harvest festival came to constitute the space in which the quotidian dimension of interethnic conflict and its subtle, ephemeral nature became visible. Quichuas, chagras, and tixaneños were all at the festival, whether participating or only observing. As the former secretary of the Inca Atahualpa put it, after the harvest festival of 1988 it was clear that the event had turned into "the festival of the Quichuas." This transformation turned the town into the setting for a ritualization of ethnic conflict during which the Quichuas "won" the square. During the festival, Tixán was not simply the place that defined the identity of a specific group of people—the white town dwellers referred to as tixaneños/as—but became a site of contention (Massey 1994). During the festival, the town belonged to the Quichuas. Although the idea to celebrate the harvest festival in the town square was not their own, all indigenous participants seemed to have responded purposefully to it. According to the former cabecilla Pedro Marcatoma, "Father Pedro began this way, and we have not wanted to change. We think that this way we are going to demonstrate to the town what our organization is like, how the indigenous people work, what our culture is like" (1992).

This symbolic "seizure" of the town began with festival preparations: all the planning and activities were carried out by indigenous people. In addition, every festival event served as a public display of Quichua culture and its vitality. Commonly performed at weddings, baptisms, and carnivals, music and song represented in the festival context elements that "made" the culture and, therefore, reinforced, delimited, and affirmed indigenous identity. As one of the participants in the accordion contest affirmed, "The songs we sing are about man's work, about our culture and the work we are doing in the communities. If we see a small hill, we also write songs for it or for young married people in order to have pretty songs. Music is very important because *we all have the capacity to produce music for our culture and our race*" (1992, emphasis added).

The festival space transformed the abstract notion of indigenous culture into its lived experience. Through dress, dance, song, and music, indigenous culture is performed in front of and for everybody. The white ponchos, hats, hand-woven skirts, for example, normally used only on festive occasions such as weddings or baptisms, acquired a different meaning in the context of the harvest festival. The aesthetics and taste as well as the cultural codes embedded in the clothing became vehicles for the public affirmation and revalorization of ethnic identity: they were "the dress that *makes* the culture." The language of clothing in this context was for the Quichuas a way of reaffirming the validity of their cultural life and at the same time served as a tactic for insinuating themselves into the space of others, making the others become spectators in their own space (de Certeau 1988).

In both the discourse of the state on national culture and in the discourse of indigenous people and activists, clothing constitutes a major marker of ethnic identity. Its political significance, however, is often related to the sphere of action in which indigenous people operate. For many urbanized indigenous people, for example, clothing became a less prominent feature of their ethnic identity. For Manuela, a Quichua activist from Chimborazo living in the provincial capital, the use of "traditional" indigenous clothing had a specific context and purpose.

> I was born in an indigenous community just outside the city and went to school here. When I was in high school, for example, I used to wear jeans and pants and all kind of nonindigenous clothing, but I did not feel I was less indigenous. It was only recently, when I started to work with grassroots indigenous women organizations and that I became involved in politics with the Pachakutik movement, that I started to feel that using the *anaco* [a type of indigenous skirt] made more sense to me and to the people I worked with. And now I use it all the time. Now I feel I can choose. I thought about it and maybe when I was younger I did not feel comfortable to be spotted out by my clothing, while now I am certainly proud of being who I am. (2007)

Manuela works with CEDIS on different projects on indigenous women's rights and gender equality, and also entered politics as a candidate in the list of Pachakutik for both the 2006 national election and the 2007 election for the constitutional assembly (only coming close to victory). When Manuela and I talked about the issue of clothing with our common friend

Javier, from CEDIS, he told me that, during her campaign, Manuela had wanted to wear also a hat, an item worn by most highland indigenous women in the countryside. "No, I told her as campaign advisor," Javier explained, "you don't have to look like a woman from the countryside, you are not, you are an educated, indigenous woman and you have to communicate that if you want a chance to win" (2007). They compromised; Manuela wore the anaco, braided her long dark hair, and wore what she defined as "ethnic earrings" instead of the iconic hat.

This episode exemplifies the extent to which clothing has come to reify indigenous culture. Even with all the complicated intertwining of narratives on race, class, gender, place, and modernity that intersect in contemporary discourses on what it means to be indigenous in Ecuador, in the public domain clothing, more than phenotype, remains as the visible marker of indigenous identity. Even if contested, as the case of Manuela's hat highlights, clothing "makes the culture." Yet the claim of "authenticity" deriving from the public dimension of its display is based less on an essentialist understanding of identity than on a dialectical relationship with modernity and the indigenous historical past. At the harvest festival, white ponchos, round woolen hats, hand-woven skirts and sashes, and embroidered blouses are imbued with historical significance. They are old, handmade, material evidence of a past that is still meaningful and that the Quichuas of Tixán do not want to forget. In my conversation with Juana about the "dress that makes the culture," she clearly addressed its affective dimension, explaining that the dresses were precious because people did not make them anymore: "Nowadays we use those cheap skirts made of nylon that people sell at markets. They are easy to wash and good to go to work in the fields, but they are not beautiful, there is no work in it. What I like about the old polleras I wear sometimes is that I know they belonged to my mother and maybe even to her mother before her. For us this clothing has a history, the history of our families, of our communities" (1992).

Juana's words underline a complex understanding of modernity and history, one which is not built on facile assumptions about the values of work and production. Industrial goods such as mass-produced nylon skirts are associated with labor and the productive sphere, in which indigenous farmers participate as hard workers and which is an integral part of their lives. Like Manuela, in other spheres of her life Juana felt compelled to wear other types of clothing, even pants: "Many times when I go to Quito I wear pants because they are more practical for longer trips. My husband wears mishu clothing almost every time he goes to the city, even Riobamba. They are more practical and also people in the city think you are more modern dressed like that" (1992). Yet that work, that modernity, does not produce beautiful or meaningful objects that contain information about who people are and where they come from both as individuals and as collectivities. This second dimension cannot simplistically be reduced to the formula of "invented tradition," nor can it easily be encapsulated into ideological formulations and constructions of the political meaning that the past may acquire in the present. Walter Benjamin cogently grasped the role of the past beyond its more manifest sociological, political, and ideological significance: "To articulate the past historically does not mean to recognize it 'the way it really was.' It means to seize hold of a memory as it flashes up at the moment of danger. . . . The danger affects both the content of the tradition and its receivers" (1969, 255).

As receivers of tradition in different contexts, Juana and her mother probably attached different meanings to the same pollera. Yet for both of them the pollera was associated with their family history and therefore with personal memory. As suggested by Benjamin, a key element here is danger, not just in its temporal dimension, but as a condition that constitutes a defining feature of the life of the dominated and becomes an important element of their structure of feeling. In such a context, the danger—that is, the real and perceived state of constant assault to the integrity of a people victimized by racism—makes material objects such as traditional festive clothing pivotal. Clothing in this context has the capacity to convey a sense of familiarity, reassurance, and protection, and more specifically is associated with one's family history. In the conditions of political mobilization in which Juana lives, the old pollera acquires a manifest political meaning that it probably did not have for her mother. However, it does not lose its more personal and intimate meaning for those who wear it. It is not simply ideological coherence that makes clothing meaningful for political action in this case, but rather, to paraphrase Victor Turner (1970), the condensation of multiple levels of meaning that are at once ideological, political, and existential. The dress "re-presents" on this occasion a symbolic link with a historical and personal memory that serves to justify the Quichuas' current struggle to others and to themselves: they are celebrating their diversity in the square not only to be seen, but also to recognize themselves.

A similar symbolic contestation is carried out by chagras through their dance competition. Their affiliation to the Inca Atahualpa as members of the countryside made the emancipatory discourse of the festival available to them. They rescued their hybrid identity from the devalued and scornful meaning attached to it, both locally and nationally.[13] Their allegedly unrefined, provincial, and backward manners are contradicted by the accuracy of their dances and choreographies, while the sobriety and exclusiveness of the black-and-white attire of their dance group members affirm and underline their distinctive identity as chagras.

The Rivalry and the Contests

The harvest festival reproduced and ritualized ethnic and interethnic tensions in its various competitions and in the intercommunity soccer tournament that expanded beyond the festive occasion with matches organized throughout the year. The music, the dance, and the songs demonstrated to the townspeople the existence and validity of Quichua and chagra cultural life. Simultaneously, the competitions reaffirmed intraethnic rivalries. As one such competitor stated, "We are from Pachamama, those from Pachamama are brave so we sing and greet the communities."[14] The "Indians" won the square from the mishus, yet they competed with their neighbors or chagras for the prizes.

An important aspect of the San Pedro festival was the ritualized confrontation with the local white authorities. In the harvest festival, this confrontation was not lost, but the terms of the relationship of subordination were profoundly questioned and redefined. The public state authority was no longer the major opposing party in the confrontation. The teniente político was excluded from any form of participation in the festival. The unequal pact of reciprocity was rejected, and the parish civil officer was no longer indispensable to planning or staging the festival. However, as with other tixaneños, Quichuas wished to oblige the parish civil officer with one of the contest prizes, because this obligation would force him to implicitly acknowledge the festival and its importance. In the context of the harvest celebration, the power of the state symbolized by local authority lost its legitimacy and was assimilated, together with the rest of the local population, into a more generic category of whiteness.

The harvest festival, therefore, reflects the implications of gradual changes in the local exercise of power according to which the Quichuas were gaining a greater degree of autonomy and self-determination. A significant shift occurred in the emphasis given to the different levels of confrontation traditionally expressed in indigenous festivals in the Andean region. The emancipatory festive narrative that aims at affirming indigenous identity and political power vis-à-vis the local nonindigenous people and the state representative gained more visibility than the intraethnic confrontation expressed in the ritual battles.

Breaking the Balance

In a context of ethnic and racial conflict, quotidian interactions and relationships can be considered ritualized insofar as they are based on the repetition of historically rooted patterns of behavior that allow social actors to anticipate consciously or unconsciously others' responses, defend themselves, or communicate without provoking an open conflict. However, this ritualized dynamic, which is usually disseminated, scattered, and fragmented in multiple locales and simultaneous occurrences, becomes concentrated and condensed in the context of the harvest festival by the spatial and temporal coherence of the celebration. Although cloaked in the seeming harmony of a joyful occasion, festival participants shared the same purpose: to celebrate and to reaffirm their own political and human dignity. The familiar dynamics of exclusion—both imposed by others and through voluntary withdrawal—marked out territories, defined spaces, and established balance throughout the celebration. Faced with the invasion of los del campo, the townsfolk began to withdraw from the festival. The predictability of this behavior contributed to the transformation of the festival into an indigenous celebration. Self-exclusion acts as a sheltering mechanism by which to avoid defeat and transform the potential loss of control into a voluntary act or a demonstration of rejection by those who would otherwise be rejected or dominated. This is the hidden face of conflict, the tension that arises from suppressing forms of direct confrontation that might disrupt the flow of everyday life if conflict were to overtly manifest itself.

However, these ritualized moments and dynamics are subject to outbursts and explosions. In such moments the conflict is no longer masked or disguised, and the contradictory face of oppression and domination appears. The ghostly memory of danger, as Benjamin evoked it, returns like a flash illuminating the conflict and disrupting a tense balance. One such moment occurred during the 1993 festival, when some indigenous people remained in the arena to guard the truck used for hauling the bulls, which was still parked in the square. A group of town youths, allegedly drunk, entered the patrolled area and, supposedly still charged with enthusiasm from the day's bullfighting, pretended to be fighting an imaginary bull. In response to this perceived intrusion, an indigenous guard grabbed his baton and hit one of the youths. According to various sources, these were the basic facts. Competing explanations and justifications, however, spread through the town the following day, acquiring different overtones depending on the group to which the narrator belonged. Indigenous commentators justified the act by saying that the indigenous guard had been frightened and provoked, that, fearing robbery or physical attack, he had reacted in "legitimate defense." Tixaneño commentators, on the other end, attributed the incident to the savage nature of the "Indians," dismissing all accusations of provocation. They maintained that none of the youth had the intention of attacking or stealing and interpreted their actions as an innocent game of imaginary bullfighting, whereas "the brutish Indian attacked them just for the hell of it" (*el indio bruto les atacó de gana*).

This incident exemplifies the structure of feeling that operates in the context of racial discrimination and domination. Suspicion, mistrust, expectation of denigration, and the constant fear of being threatened and attacked seem to determine and limit the possibility of buoyancy and the sense of security, feelings that otherwise appear as the exclusive privilege of the dominating party. In such a context, real and perceived provocations can trigger open confrontation that momentarily breaks the precarious balance created by the quotidian experience of resistance to domination. The aggression in this case was provoked not by anonymous circumstances but by the perceived identity of the other, which aroused suspicion and fear. And as is common in systems founded on a racist imaginary, it allowed no space for individual agency by members of the perceived inferior group. The behavior of one individual—in this case, of one indigenous man—was interpreted as a defining ethnic feature that negatively characterized his whole group.

This episode also illustrates that the reproduction of racist imaginary is not necessarily associated with control in contexts of political mobilization, and highlights the possible disjuncture of dominant ideologies and structures of power in processes of political change. Despite the tension created by the incident, the aggressor was neither punished nor formally charged and convicted. In this case the racist imaginary of the violent

"Indians" functioned as a double-edged sword: it reinforced stereotypes and convictions about the savagery of the perceived inferior race, but at the same time instilled fear in and prompted acquiescence by the dominant group. Violence in this case not only defined the subjectivity of a race, but also came to characterize organized political actors who imposed their control and defended their rights both locally and nationwide. Random outbursts of violence stereotypically attributed to the lack of civilization had become organized rebelliousness. This perceived shift in indigenous behavior (encapsulated in the epithet *alzamenteros*) instilled fear in tixañeños and prevented a violent response to the incident.

The Inca Atahualpa Takes the Town

As the jahuay echoing through the mountains announced the arrival of harvest time, the words of the leaders of the Inca Atahualpa echoed through the old buildings of the square to announce that the moment to act had arrived. This time it was not a chant, but the amplified voice of another winner of the square: the Inca Atahualpa.

The Strategies vis-à-vis the Others

The Quichuas won the square thanks to the pivotal role of the Inca Atahualpa in the festival preparation and organization. Many of the songs performed in the music contests acknowledged this role: "We sing to them [Inca Atahualpa's leaders] to thank them; the organization has come out very well, with twenty-two communities," stated one of the singers. The production of this political discourse and practice is the result of both the resistance embedded in the politics of everyday life and of political mobilization. However, the intervention of the Inca Atahualpa in this process allows for the unconscious habitus of resistance (that generates and feeds the practical sense of subordinate people) to manifest and reveal its generating principles (Bourdieu 1991). In the context of political mobilization, actors acquire consciousness of their actions. Ritualized in the harvest festival, the politicization of ethnic identity produced ethnic consciousness among indigenous festival participants. Their emancipatory message publicly displayed before the mishus and their authorities not only reached the "others," but was also amplified by the voices of the Inca Atahualpa's leaders and reverberated in the ears of the Quichuas, who assimilated it and returned it as a boomerang to the senders. In the interviews I conducted, indigenous leaders of the Inca Atahualpa, indigenous catechists, and festival participants all spoke of their awareness of their identity as Quichuas and chagras vis-à-vis the town mishus, of their understanding of Indianness (and "chagraness") as resulting from historical and political processes. In this case, the production of cultural and ethnic identities is related to culture, to social relations, and to the formation of new political actors.

Yet the reaffirmation of Quichuas' identity is also linked to the reaffirmation of the Inca Atahualpa's power and authority, which is built on traditional mechanisms such as priostazgo and a modern version of the cargo system. Priostazgo in the festival became a site for affirming also the prestige of individual Inca Atahualpa leaders. Since the 1992 festival, for example, the Inca Atahualpa's president has been a generous prioste of colchas, bulls, or the band. This trend has been maintained and reinforced throughout the years. In 1994 the election of new leadership of the organization was scheduled for August, just after the harvest festival. One of the presidential candidates, the former president and founder of the Inca Atahualpa, from Yacupungo, was nominated president of the festival planning committee, a position that had until then been associated only with the organization of tixaneños' festivals. The other candidate was the bullfight's prioste. In the framework of the cargo system, both candidates used the festival as a springboard for their candidacy.

The Inca Atahualpa also subtly capitalized on its influence and power through its ability to solicit and obtain priostes and generous donors. Because of their connections with the Inca Atahualpa, the representatives of NGOs such as FEPP and CEDIS, the manager of Banco Nacional de Fomento, and the associates of Radio ERPE participated in the festival by giving prizes. Their participation, which often aroused jealousy among the tixaneños, was pivotal in publicly consolidating the organization's role as an agent of development on behalf of its affiliates.[15] The participation of outsiders and foreigners also facilitated the involvement of some tixaneños as priostes. Some townsfolk had managed to establish a friendly relationship with both the Inca Atahualpa leaders and Father Torres.[16] They considered the invitation to participate as priostes as an indication of attention and a convenient way of establishing a potentially beneficial relationship: "We must say it, M. P. and the others [Inca Atahualpa's leaders] have done a lot for their communities. It would be good to live all in peace"

(Don Mario, 1992). All these forms of invited participation had their logic within the system of reciprocal obligations. To refuse an invitation to donate prizes could imply an unspoken refusal to maintain good relationships. The invitation to give implies an obligation to accept. The invitation to participate in the festival indirectly conferred prestige and power on festival organizers. Even the Quichuas' eternal foes—the tixaneños and the public authorities, remembered for their never-ending abuses—were invited and thus obligated to participate in the harvest festival. In 1993 two tixaneños donated the band, the parish civil officer gave the trophy for the soccer tournament, and the president of the cantonal council awarded the prize for the best bullfighter.

However, this festival was not like the festival of San Pedro, in which Quichuas' subaltern position was expressed in the abusive relationships of asymmetric reciprocity controlled by the parish civil officer. In the harvest festival, the participation of the local authorities, foreigners, and tixaneños as donors and judges became a means for gaining prestige vis-à-vis the whites, the Quichuas, and the chagras.

The affirmation of the Inca Atahualpa's prestige and strength was also directed toward the representatives of other cantonal indigenous organizations. Interorganizational rivalry was expressed in the festival by the soccer tournament. In 1993 the intercommunal tournament included teams from other indigenous organizations of the canton: General Rumiñahui and ATAMZICH. The word *intercommunal* did not refer in that case to the communities, but instead to federations representing diverse indigenous sectors of the canton.

The Inca Atahualpa as an "institution of will and power" intervened also in the realm of cultural politics to both empower its affiliates as well as to promote its own legitimacy.

Territorializing Identity

When the Inca Atahualpa intervened in the realm of cultural politics by "clothing the difference," local Quichua identity underwent an additional process of reification (Hendrickson 1996). The attire displayed on the stage by the organization's band members established a "cultural model" that typified the sector's traditional indigenous dress. All of the Inca Atahualpa's musicians wore distinctive items of old clothing, such as white ponchos and white round woolen hats. When I asked about their clothing,

A. L., one of the musicians and secretary of the organization at the time, responded that those were "*typical* dress of the sector, ponchos and hats that our fathers and grandfathers used to wear" (1994, emphasis added). In this context, the differences among the various indigenous groups in the area were ignored. At first glance, this "typification" could be interpreted as a process of homogenization of indigenous culture strictly related to the process of institutionalization of the politics of indigenous identity. As an institutionalized agent of local Quichua power and cultural politics, the Inca Atahualpa adopted a strategy of cultural homogenization that could be compared to state-sponsored politics of folklore. In the rhetoric of the ideology of mestizaje, the culturally and ethnically mixed Ecuadorian identity was to be found in the various manifestations of folkloric dances, typical dresses, and souvenirs, both celebrating and supposedly resolving the heterogeneity and idiosyncrasy of the national populations and cultures. Similarly, in the attempt to forge a local Quichua identity, the Inca Atahualpa embodied in its own representatives a simplified rendering of Quichua culture. Not only did dress in its multiple versions "make the culture" because of its familiar link to the past, but it also in its typified version became the marker of a homogenized local indigenous culture.

A closer examination of the manipulation of dress codes problematizes such cultural operations, in this case the intertwining of culture and politics. The clothing that prevailed as "typical" of the local indigenous population at large was originally specific to the area of Yacupungo, the home sector of the Inca Atahualpa's founders. This choice exemplifies the politicization of internal distinctions among the different indigenous sectors of Tixán parish, namely the higher communities located in the Yacupungo sector (Pachamama, Curuquingue, Santa Cecilia, etc.) and the lower ones in the Pachagsí area (Pachagsí, La Pacífica, La Merced).[17] In reproducing a homogenizing cultural policy, the typification responded to the same logic of confrontation that was ritualized in the toma de la plaza in the San Pedro festival when opposing the two sectors of Tixán and Galte. The process of formation of the Inca Atahualpa underscored the extent to which new political affiliations and alliances revolved around preexisting rivalries and confrontations among different indigenous sectors even beyond parish limits.

Accordingly, the forging of alliances in defense of specific interests (for example mine exploitation or the fight against cattle thieving) accompanied other criteria defining affiliation. Local intraethnic rivalries took shape and were manifested in different ways and moments: in the formation of the Inca Atahualpa, in the administration of justice, and in the harvest festival via the soccer tournament. The one expressed in the manipulation of clothing brought about another level of rivalry—this time internal to the same organization. This rivalry involved páramo and valley communities of Tixán, but it was limited to those that were affiliated to the organization. Such communities considered themselves, in terms of origins and ethnic identity, to belong to different groups. P. B. was the first leader from the Pachagsí sector to ascend to the presidency of the organization, which until then, in 1996, had remained in the hands of leaders who were natives of communities in the sector of the Inca Atahualpa's founders. Territorialization was, therefore, a significant element in the forging of political alliances within the organization; it intertwined with multiple layers, where place not only articulated with different socioeconomic arrangements (pastoralism or agriculture, more frequent urban migration, etc.), but also highlighted specific processes of formation of a given ethnic identity. "Typical," in A. L.'s words, is to be understood as typical of his sector, Yacupungo, and linked to his sector's ancestors. The appearance of the Inca Atahualpa's music group dressed in this style epitomized the identity of the organization as remarkably close to the higher communities of the Tixán parish. As a matter of fact, white ponchos and round hats were never adopted as the typical clothing of the local Quichua population, nor did they become the typical dress of the festival.

The Changes

In February 1993, Father Pedro Torres was transferred from Tixán to São Paulo, Brazil. He did not leave of his own accord. Due to his commitment to the indigenous sector and his direct interventions to mediate land conflicts in the Tixán communities, he acquired a reputation as a subversive priest among the landowners and provincial authorities. In 1989 the Chamber of Agriculture in Riobamba instigated a furious press campaign against Father Torres, accusing him of inciting "Indians" to revolt. On that occasion, both the religious sector and the international NGOs active in the area staunchly supported him. For several years after that incident, however, a military intelligence agent followed the priest's every move in the town and reported his supposedly subversive activities to the armed forces. After the 1992 electoral victory of the conservative Republican Unity Party (PUR), Father Torres was sent to Brazil to study the pastoral activities of the Catholic Church on a more theoretical level.

Father Torres's departure brought about changes above all in the activity of the Inca Atahualpa, which had found him to be an important ally. The impact of his absence on the harvest festival was most pronounced in the festival's programming, with the incorporation of events not considered "typically" Quichua and that increased the participation of nonindigenous people in the festival. Since 1993, the festival has included not one, but two bullfighting afternoons, sponsored by the Inca Atahualpa's leaders, and a three-way competition of Ecua-volley (Ecuadorian volleyball), in which teams from two communities and the town participated. The main events took place on a new stage constructed in the square since the Tixán festival of San Juan in June of 1993. In the same year a group of musicians from the Inca Atahualpa won the music contest, but offered the prize to the second-place group. The accordion contest was abandoned. Furthermore, for the first time in the harvest festival, a popular *verbena* (public dance party) was held, at the town hall.[18] Two indigenous musicians from La Pacífica community performed, and two women from the town offered the canelazos for the party. The Sunday Mass was scheduled to coincide with the soccer tournament, making attendance at Mass and the procession noticeably sparse.

In 1994, the harvest festival lasted from Saturday to Monday. That year the list of guests and priostes was longer: the leaders of the Inca Atahualpa, the Canadian volunteers, indigenous organizations from other cantons, NGOs, chagras, tixaneños, the Bishop of Riobamba, the president of the Casa de la Cultura Ecuatoriana of Riobamba, and a representative from the CONAIE. These guests donated prizes, trophies, or colchas, or served as judges in the contests. The organizers predicted that many of these donors would not attend the festival, but felt it was important that their names nevertheless appear in the program. That year there were two verbenas, and the Inca Atahualpa was the prioste of the first one. Both verbenas were successfully popular. Participation in the soccer tournament reached as far as the provincial capital and included two teams from outside the parish, one representing an indigenous group from the canton of Guamote and the other representing a neighborhood organization in Riobamba. Mass was again sparsely attended. The moment of the blessing passed almost unnoticed, and the children with the wheat crosses on their backs were only a pleasant memory. Except for the chagras, even the dance contest had few participants.

All these changes attested to the fact that the harvest festival had become the festival of the Inca Atahualpa. The festival's religious features, such as the Mass and the parade, did not receive the same emphasis as they had when Father Torres was involved. Conversely, the events that could acquire a political relevance received particular attention. In the realm of intraethnic confrontations, the Inca Atahualpa reinforced its prestige vis-à-vis other cantonal organizations by extending its networks beyond the cantonal limits. The expansion of political ties and networking was fostered through sporting events such as the soccer and volleyball tournaments, which included teams from Riobamba and Guamote, and the building of prestige derived from the priostazgo of events that reached out to a wider audience (the bullfights and the verbenas). These elements foregrounded the major role that the Inca Atahualpa came to play in the planning and development of the festival. The organization took the reins of the event and transformed it into its masterpiece, the symbolic representation of its power and authority.

From the Square to the Dance Hall

The politicization of indigenous identity as manifested through the harvest festival in Tixán highlights the complex relationships among indigenous grassroots activists and other actors who converged in forging a political practice centered on the recognition of indigenous rights. Despite different understandings of the terms and forms for shaping a multicultural society, the rescue of indigenous cultures became a vital part of the discourse of missionaries, social scientists, artists, and indigenous leaders at the national level. The Catholic Church played a pivotal role in indigenous mobilization. Represented by the Cuquis and Father Torres, the Catholic Church was crucial to the evolution of the harvest celebration into the festival of the Quichuas. The "pro-indigenous attitude" (actitud pro indígena) of Father Torres surfaced even in his sermons, during which he often spoke openly against the abuses and prevarication suffered by the "Indians" since time immemorial.

This dialogic process of assimilation, transformation, and utterance of different voices in political practice underscores the fluidity and richness of subaltern politics. The case of Tixán shows the difficulties in differentiating and isolating spheres of political action, as well as the shortcomings of separating the politics of daily life from organized political action. Although different in scope, these two dimensions are profoundly intertwined and constantly nurture each other. Thus, a political and institutionalized power such as the Inca Atahualpa may operate in grey areas in which goals and the strategies to achieve them are not clearly and openly articulated. In other words, following de Certeau's distinction between tactics and strategies (1988), tactics do not belong exclusively to the realm of the everyday life politics.

Following the departure of Father Torres, the attention that active participants and the public showed for the festival's cultural events shifted toward popular verbenas, in which the tixaneños participated by offering canelazos. Even certain elements, such as the extended length of the festival and the position of president of the planning committee, were incorporated from the tixaneño festival. Father Torres had always been a strong supporter of forging an indigenous cultural authenticity built on a clear separation of what was or not indigenous. Did the Quichuas of Tixán start "mestizising" after he left? The ritual confrontation with the tixaneños in the public square, together with the "everyday" assimilation of certain cultural characteristics of the other, allowed the Quichuas to conquer symbolic niches of power previously denied to them. The town hall belonged to the town and, therefore, also to the Quichuas, who exercised their rights by holding their dances in the place designated for such activities: "If they [tixaneños] use this space for San Juan, we are now using it for the *cosecha* celebration" (M. P., 1994). The organization of verbenas demonstrated that Quichuas were as capable of holding dance parties as were the mishus. The space of the town hall allowed them to expand their public cultural display from the square to the dance hall.

As with other festival activities, the Inca Atahualpa planned and carried out the verbenas, encroaching on the realm of the other "by poaching in countless ways on the . . . dominant cultural economy in order to adapt it to their own interests and their own rules," all elements that de Certeau attributes to everyday life politics (de Certeau 1988, xiii). These mechanisms in everyday life interactions were retrieved and ritualized on the occasion of the festival, a form of poaching that enabled the Inca Atahualpa to assimilate the local nonindigenous culture (the dominant cultural economy), as well as the emancipatory discourse of actors such as Father Torres, and transform them for its own ends. Throughout the festival, therefore, the Inca Atahualpa both affirmed and denied claims of authenticity. It is not possible to speak, at least in this context, of a process of mestizaje, but instead of diverse ways of exercising power and authority by adopting models otherwise imposed by the dominant other (Sánchez Parga 1985, 107). Yet these adoptions are to be understood as tactics of consumption, which transform both cultural systems of reference.

The wile-catcher looks around corners and will not be deceived. He knows what is hidden behind innocent masks, he knows, as if lightning had struck him, what someone wants from him; and before the mask falls of its own accord, he makes a quick decision and tears it off.

He walks softly in order not to frighten masks prematurely. If he has to say something, it sounds gentle, he speaks slowly as though it were difficult for him. . . . He thereby lulls the enemy into false security. . . . The wile-catcher takes his leave, gives the scoundrel his hand, shakes heartily, says ingenuously “I’ll think it over,” and starts off for home in order to arrange and systematize the wiles, of which none has eluded him.

—Elias Canetti, *Earwitness*

CHAPTER SEVEN

Beyond Recognition

My examination of the Inca Atahualpa's political practice has delineated the different arenas in which access to power and resources is disputed by grassroots organizations, and has contextualized the local case within the larger process of political empowerment of indigenous people at the national level. I now focus on the national level in order to examine the reach and limitations of such political empowerment.[1] The Inca Atahualpa case and its successes offer an opportunity to analyze the distinction between local and national politics, and the different predicaments related to these separate yet interrelated spheres of political action.

Latin American Multiculturalism

The 1990s and the first decade of the new millennium are characterized by remarkable and rapid changes in the relationships between the indigenous movement, the state, and civil society. I analyze the challenges facing the indigenous movement in Ecuador by examining the major events in indigenous politics since the 1990 uprising, which led to the "postrecognition phase," officially initiated with the recognition of ethnic diversity in the revised constitution of 1998 (Cervone 2003). By "post-recognition phase," I point not to a moment on a linear temporal line leading toward a predefined end, but to a spatiotemporal convergence of conditions that affected the indigenous movement and its relationships with the Ecuadorian state. Accordingly, the postrecognition phase is characterized by a major shift in terminology and political practice defining Indian-state relationships, summarized by the term *multiculturalism*, which is understood as a political paradigm that encapsulates the transition from a supposed homogeneity of national identity to the recognition of ethnic and cultural diversity. In the case of Latin America this political paradigm encompasses both the struggle for the recognition of ethnic and cultural diversity promoted by indigenous movements and the actions taken by different states toward official recognition of such diversity and its supposed incorporation into state politics. These two aspects defining the politics of multiculturalism are inextricably interrelated. Multicultural recognition thus signifies a point of departure—and not of arrival—for the creation of a new and more inclusive society.

Defining Multiculturalism

The term *multiculturalism* appeared in the United States in the late 1980s as an academic and political definition of cultural and ethnic diversity in a given nation-state (Goldberg 1995). However, as scholars have highlighted, in different contexts and epochs the apparently self-explanatory meaning of the term *multiculturalism* contains far more ambivalence and ambiguity than might be supposed.[2] An idealistic and utopian vision of multicultural societies would assume that ethnically and culturally diverse groups are equally positioned and recognized by the state. Yet such an uncomplicated view does not account for the multiple and diverse forms in which power differentials and hierarchies among groups are generated historically, socially, and politically, often framing such distinctions with the language of race and ethnicity. Elazar Barkan's (2001) analysis of multiculturalism and pluralistic models of society historically positions the emergence of those notions as contemporary imaginings promoted by "guilty" nations in order to readdress, among other things, the oppression of native peoples since colonialism. Multiculturalism, therefore, is not simply a descriptive term indicating cultural hybridity or diversity. Whether demanded by social movements or sponsored by states, multiculturalism is a political act of recognition of ethnic and cultural rights that seeks to address historical inequalities and oppression. As such, the politics of recognition produces different and often divergent understandings of the meaning and scope of these rights.

Philosophers such as Charles Taylor (1994) and Will Kymlicka (1995), who have theorized multiculturalism within the framework of liberal political philosophy, consider the issue of ethnocultural diversity and its recognition as an inherent tension of the liberal and universalist notion of rights. Taylor (1994) argues, for example, that the recognition of human rights as universal values implicitly recognizes the right of every individual to his or her own human and cultural integrity. Multicultural recognition, therefore, is the logical consequence of this inherent contradiction. However, the recognition of a diversity of cultures also inherently implies the existence of a number of distinctive collectivities as the beneficiaries of cultural rights—all equally "worthy" of respect. Such a universal principle inevitably creates a tension between the liberal notion of rights, which is fundamentally individual, and a collective notion of citizenship and rights (Kymlicka 1995; Taylor 1994). To this Kymlicka responds by proposing a typology of "diverse" groups and their specific rights. The different subject position of such groups, whether native communities incorporated in the nation-state as a result of colonization or ethnocultural communities born out of immigration processes, also determines different demands (respectively, self-determination vs. integration) and, therefore, different policies of inclusion in the wider "national" community, whose sovereignty is never questioned. As Kymlicka argues, "Multinational states cannot survive unless the various national groups have an allegiance to the larger political community they cohabit" (1995, 13).

In addition to the problems that such typologies present by aggregating socially, economically, and culturally heterogeneous groups, this understanding of cultural rights does not explain the impact of multicultural recognition on national sovereignty and citizen-state relations at large. Nor does it indicate the premises on which "allegiance to the larger political community" is predicated, especially for groups granted self-determination. This perspective, adopted by multicultural states purportedly to include so-called minorities, often leads to conflicting expectations among groups seeking recognition, state apparatus, and civil society. These conflicting expectations generate a highly contested and shifting terrain for multicultural politics and demands. Official acts of recognition of diversity, such as those celebrated in Latin America with constitutional reforms, have generated different and often divergent sets of expectations around the subject position of diverse groups in multicultural societies, especially where racial prejudices remain rampant.

Analyses of indigenous and Afro-descendant movements in Latin America show that the moral mandate of multicultural state recognition as a means of redressing social inequality often has been limited to the acknowledgment of culturally diverse societies, while issues of redistribution of resources and power among groups are disregarded. Scholars, including Nancy Fraser (1997), have argued that culturalist notions of social equality that ignore the economic and political roots of inequality reproduce patterns of exclusion. In Ecuador, for example, official multicultural recognition by the state has not eliminated racial and gender discrimination and other forms of inequality. As in many multicultural societies in the region, despite the adoption of the multicultural paradigm, social hierarchies maintain race and ethnicity as markers that define differential access to power and resources.[3]

As a highly contested terrain, recognition of diversity under multiculturalism creates the promise for the political and social reshaping of a nation and, therefore, the premise for new political demands.

Multicultural States in Latin America

Studies of multiculturalism in the Latin American context generally have focused on Indian-state relations as they have been redefined under neoliberal regimes since the 1990s.[4] Ideally, the multicultural paradigm should have marked the passage from the social protest and mobilization of marginalized indigenous and Afro-descent subjects to their political participation and inclusion. During the 1990s, many Latin American countries opted for constitutional reforms that recognized ethnic and cultural diversity. Yet the multicultural postrecognition phase is fraught with contradictions and tensions. Although supposedly responding to the quest for recognition of indigenous movements throughout the region, constitutional reforms also accompanied neoliberal economic and political measures related to market expansion and curtailment of state and governmental functions, measures that negatively impacted precarious and marginalized social sectors and limited indigenous political participation.[5] Since 1989, under the Washington Consensus, the World Bank and the International Monetary Fund (IMF) have pressured Latin American governments to restrict and gradually eliminate their social responsibilities, thereby redefining the participation of the state in national economies. In practice, this has meant eliminating subsidized services such as water, domestic gas, electricity, and transportation, as well as deregulating and decentralizing operations, which is meant to transfer political and fiscal responsibility to local administrations. In Ecuador this has also meant the adoption of the U.S. dollar as the national currency, which has fueled massive speculation and pushed prices sky high. The economic crisis ensuing from such measures has prompted social protest and unrest that has in turn led to the downfall of governments in Ecuador and Bolivia.[6] It has also led to an increase of street violence and criminality, raising widespread concerns about urban security (*seguridad ciudadana*) (Goldstein 2004).

The worsening of social, political, and economic conditions has clearly foregrounded the limitations and ambiguities of ethnic recognition. Indigenous demands have always implied and addressed the need for economic change. Protests in Ecuador and Bolivia against the privatization of gas, water, social security—and in the spring of 2006 against free-trade agreements—underscore the centrality of economic policy and demands in indigenous political action.[7] On the other hand, the recognition of indigenous rights under neoliberal multiculturalism was limited to a culturalist view of ethnicity, according to which matters of resource redistribution were ignored. Despite the official recognition of ethnic rights, the material concerns of indigenous people were not addressed.[8] Concomitantly, indigenous activists in countries such as Ecuador and Bolivia won seats in the parliament and in local municipalities. Although decentralization policies and electoral participation expanded the opportunities for indigenous activists to be included in the decision-making processes of local and national governments, at the same time they rejected the national economic policies. This is an example of "contested engagements with neoliberal multiculturalism" (Postero 2007, 6). If multicultural reforms expanded the rubric of citizenship rights, neoliberal economics functioned as ground for new political demands.

Economic neoliberalism, however, is not the only challenge indigenous activists faced. As the case of Ecuador shows, the indigenous movement promptly responded to this dilemma by seeking alliances with other sectors of Ecuadorian society and by embracing a political campaign that emphasized economic issues. The renewed yet strong role of the state in national multicultural politics—defined as "Big Government" by Michael Hardt and Antonio Negri (2004)—delimited the legitimacy of indigenous cultural rights and restricted indigenous activists' participation in the decision-making process by defining specific spheres and modalities in which indigenous actors and cultures were "permitted" (Hale 2005; Speed 2005; Walsh 2002). The 1998 constitutional recognition of multicultural Ecuador established a hierarchy of systems of knowledge, all subordinated to the national systems (legal, educational, and medical), which are in turn the only legitimate ones for a disembodied, "non-ethnic" Ecuadorian citizen. The regulatory role of the state is, therefore, meant to define imagined boundaries to ethnocultural diversity in order to defend the territorial as well as cultural sovereignty of the Ecuadorian nation. Despite the expansion of indigenous political participation both locally and nationally, neoliberal multiculturalism restricts and delimits the exercise of indigenous cultural and social practices to pockets where ethnic power is allowed. My analysis of the 1998 constitutional reforms and of the relationship of the indigenous movement under Lucio Gutiérrez's mandate (2002–2005) in Ecuador highlights such inconsistencies.

The Path to Multiculturalism: From Contention Politics to Political Participation

The 1990 uprising represented the beginning of a new political era for the Ecuadorian indigenous movement, when indigenous activists began to negotiate directly with the state around issues of cultural recognition and political participation. Other political actions and measures following the 1990 uprising reinforced and affirmed this new role of the indigenous movement in the national political arena.

With the March of the Yumbos in April 1992 and the uprising against the first proposal of the new Law of Agrarian Development in the spring of 1994, indigenous activists proclaimed their right to political and cultural recognition in the form of sovereignty and self-determination, both formulated in terms of recognition of territoriality and ethnic jurisdiction.

> Self-determination is the right of the nationalities to freely choose and exercise their own political system and model of socioeconomic development in a territory fully defined in the context of the new multinational nation. (CONAIE 1993, 2)

> Sovereignty is the power, decision, and political will of the indigenous peoples and nationalities that will be exercised through the new multinational nation and its respective governmental organs and institutions. (CONAIE 1993, 2)

As a result of this process of politicization of ethnic identity, the colonial category of "indio"—with all of its cultural meanings, semiotics, and symbology reproduced in indigenous collective memory and state policy—

became a symbol of political empowerment. It came to function in contemporary Ecuador as a sign of the indigenous right to difference. During this phase, which I characterize as the recognition phase, the ethnic component of indigenous struggle prevailed over the class dimension at the level of political rhetoric as well as of political strategy. Consequently, ethnic identity politics were foregrounded, and indigenous groups rarely attempted to form coalitions with other social movements.

During this process indigenous politics followed the path of democratic struggle by seeking participation within the state structure. Since 1995 indigenous activists from the Confederation of Indigenous Nationalities of the Ecuadorian Amazon (CONFENIAE) had been working toward the formation of a political party, which was called the Pachakutik Political Movement (Sawyer 2004; Van Cott 2005). In 1996 a political electoral alliance emerged between Pachakutik and Nuevo País, a new antineoliberal movement founded by progressive intellectuals and social forces.[9] Launched in 1996 by the journalist and ecologist Fredy Elhers, the Pachakutik-Nuevo País was conceived as an umbrella political movement gathering diverse progressive forces, from ecologists and human-rights activists to indigenous leaders. This new popular progressive party, Pachakutik-Nuevo País, functioned as the ideal political conjuncture for indigenous activists to reinforce their presence in local and national administrations. Many of the indigenous candidates in the 1996 national elections who were supported by this movement were elected to positions in local administrations and as national deputies. Since then, indigenous leaders have taken advantage of the lack of a clear political platform and of the internal fragmentation within Pachakutik-Nuevo País to gain control of the party. The indigenous political presence within the state apparatus was further reinforced, in 1996, by the creation of the National Council of Planning and Development of Indians and Blacks (CONPLADEIN). The council was meant to be the instrument through which indigenous and Afro-Ecuadorian citizens would design their own development policy and administrate funds accordingly.[10]

By and large, despite ambiguities and contradictions, since 1996 indigenous activists have consolidated their presence in national politics by adopting two supposedly irreconcilable strategies that have strengthened their political power—namely, party politics and social mobilization. During this process, CONAIE, which was consecrated by the 1990 uprising as the most representative indigenous federation at the national level, maintained its role as promoter of mobilization and political actions that required large-scale indigenous grassroots participation throughout the country. Its affiliated organizations outnumbered those of other national federations, such as the Federation of Peasant and Indigenous and Black Organizations (FENOCIN) and the Evangelical Indigenous Federation (FEINE), making CONAIE unquestionably the spearhead of the "movimiento indígena" (indigenous movement). On the other hand, many indigenous activists pursued participation within the state structure both nationally and locally through elections and party politics with Pachakutik. In Tixán, for example, indigenous activists of the Inca Atahualpa managed to have their representative elected to the cantonal council for the first time with Pachakutik in 2004. The combination of these two political strategies was summarized in the comments that frequently appeared in Ecuadorian media, which labeled Pachakutik as CONAIE's political party.

The 1990s, or the "won decade" (la década ganada), were therefore key for the recognition and institutionalization of indigenous rights (León 1994). A key victory came in 1998, when the new Ecuadorian constitution formally recognized the population's ethnic and cultural diversity. The 1998 constitution declared Ecuador a multicultural and pluriethnic country, and acknowledged the right of indigenous people to live according to their own norms, values, religions, and languages. This signaled a change at the level of the state in the recognition of the presence, role, and forces of indigenous social mobilization. As Deborah Yashar (1998) suggests also for the case of Mexico and Bolivia, these constitutional amendments are "important symbolic victories for indigenous peoples that have worked to change myths of national unity" and are at the same time important steps Latin American states have taken toward democratization (1998, 31).

The Ecuadorian case, however, demonstrates the extent to which this recognition bears ambiguities and contradictions that highlight the tensions of subaltern-state relations in multiethnic societies. The intertwining of constitutional reforms, decentralizing projects, and neoliberal economic measures has worked both in favor of and against indigenous political empowerment, especially because the neoliberal project has not resolved preexisting issues of economic inequality and racial prejudice.

Multicultural Constitutional Ambiguities

During the 1990s, many countries—including Colombia, Peru, Bolivia, Paraguay, Guatemala, Venezuela, and Ecuador—reformed their constitutions, recognizing indigenous cultural rights and thus inaugurating the multicultural era throughout Latin America. Amid a more general framework of recognition of cultural rights, constitutional reforms define specific spheres in which indigenous and Afro-descent practices are legitimized (see Yrigoyen 2004). For the Ecuadorian case, these spheres are justice, medicine, and education.

Article 191 of the 1998 constitution legitimizes indigenous authorities and legal systems. In the administration of justice, indigenous systems are legitimized only when they do not contradict principles established by national law: "Authorities of indigenous peoples will exercise their justice functions by applying norms and proceedings of their own in order to resolve *internal conflicts* in accordance with their own customs or consuetudinary rights always when they *are not contrary to the Constitution and to the laws*. The Law will make these functions compatible with the national justice system."[11] This constitutional recognition contains two major limitations. The first concerns its spatial dimension, with "internal conflicts" meaning conflicts that arise within and among indigenous spaces and people. The second refers to the subordination of indigenous justice to principles and norms, or laws, that were in force before the recognition of legal pluralism. The application of such principles and norms has not been revised in multicultural terms. In practice this means that although the recognition of traditional authorities and justice systems has potential for political empowerment, the sphere of action of indigenous authorities is limited to communal politics, noticeably separating the space of indigenous community politics from larger political spaces. As the case of Tixán showed, indigenous justice was being applied within those boundaries even before its official recognition. Thus, the 1998 multicultural reform in matters of justice was limited to legitimizing the status quo, namely the separation of juridical functions and systems in a hierarchical order.

Such separation is maintained also in the fields of education and medicine, where bilingual education and traditional medicine apply only to indigenous individuals and collectivities. In the case of the former, Quichua and other indigenous languages, for example, have not been incorporated into the national education system, since they are not meant to be taught to nonindigenous students. The issue of language is more complex than it may at first appear; one must take into consideration the fact that bilingual education is not limited to linguistic competence, but incorporates expression of indigenous cultures and arts. Despite an official multicultural rhetoric that considers as Ecuador's richness its cultural, ethnic, and biological diversity, there is no official interest in expanding the cultural horizons of nonindigenous citizens, in this case students, by teaching them more about other cultural expressions in their country. In this regard, official multiculturalism has failed to move beyond a folkloric and folklorized conception of "indigeousness" and "Afro-Ecuadorianness." Unlike in mestizaje ideology, according to which the diverse cultural worlds of the Ecuadorian nation all supposedly melted to give birth to one national culture, in the multicultural imagination such diverse worlds are conceived as discrete worlds and considered to be the "properties" of specific groups. According to this mosaic of different cultures, the nonindigenous, non-Afro-Ecuadorian cultural world, still sometimes referred to as mestizo culture, became one such separate world of its own—with one significant distinction: it remained the main and official referent for Ecuador's "national" culture, law, or medicine.

The case of traditional medicine is even more complex, since it entails matters of validation of medicinal efficacy. Despite its constitutional recognition, indigenous medicine, which is usually practiced outside of the national, Westernized medical systems, has not been officially incorporated into the latter and is meant only for treating indigenous patients. For example, the 1998 reform in Tixán has led to the creation of communal centers of traditional medicine, where indigenous people receive treatment. Funded by a German NGO, these centers are meant to serve people from the communities. The local health center in town also used by tixaneños has not officially incorporated practices of traditional medicine, even though nonindigenous healers in the area have long been treating local nonindigenous people. A first question to ask, then, is whether the constitutional recognition of traditional medicine was based on the assumption that such a body of knowledge was indeed valid and effective in general and not only for treating indigenous citizens. The fact that it has not been officially incorporated into the national health system suggests, as in the case of justice, that recognition was limited to the acknowledgment of what was already practiced. This line of argument begs the question of who should be in charge of validating such bodies of knowledge. A third question, referring to the spatial dimension of such recognition, also arises. If traditional medicine is meant to be available to indigenous patients, what about indigenous citizens who live in urban areas and lack access to traditional medicine if it is not made available in urban health centers and hospitals?

These questions underline the complexity of multicultural recognition and its limitations. They address issues of legitimacy and hierarchies in processes of knowledge validation and public policy making. The hierarchical and vertical order of "knowledges" brings to the fore another forgotten, or perhaps ignored, issue, that of racial prejudices. Such prejudices become even more blatant in the field of traditional medicine, especially with the lack of a validating mechanism (such as, for example, its incorporation into the national health system). In social practice, this exclusion rests on a widespread set of prejudices that consider traditional medicine to be primitive, backward, nonscientific, and even based on superstition. These old and refashioned prejudices clearly maintain a hierarchy of bodies of knowledge and practices among which the mainstream, "national" ones are still considered the most effective and advanced.

While states under the predicaments of mestizaje ideologies assimilated and therefore obfuscated diversity, multicultural states have responded to heterogeneity not by incorporating diversity in their different functions, but by regulating it. This regulatory approach defines specific boundaries and jurisdictions in which each and every diverse system may or may not operate. Multicultural recognition, therefore, does not necessarily imply equality, nor does it eliminate discrimination and prejudice against indigenous and Afro-descent populations. The highly selective spaces in which diverse practices are legitimized have institutionalized such prejudices as founding principles, which justify a hierarchy of "diverse" systems. It is not a coincidence that the term *interculturalidad* (literally, "interculturality"), as opposed to *multiculturalismo*, gained momentum among indigenous activists after the constitutional reforms. As Nina Pacari, one of the most prominent leaders of CONAIE, explained, "Interculturalidad implies a more egalitarian process of exchange between cultures. It is a mutual act of acknowledgment and respect, whereas multiculturalismo is the general framework for addressing diversity" (personal communication, 2007).[12] Constitutional recognition of diversity is a premise, a highly general framework. It is just a point of departure. The potential for transforming diversity into a political practice and an opportunity for empowerment and inclusion rests in the hands of indigenous activists.

Decentralizing the State: Opening Doors and Closing Exits

It can be argued that indigenous activists produced their own recipe for disaster by establishing ethnic boundaries for such practices and their validity. Such critical remarks may point at the ambiguities inherent in the politics of cultural distinctiveness. However, it is also important to contextualize political strategies and discourses within the specific set of challenges indigenous activists have faced since the initial stages of their political mobilization.[13] Studies of indigenous politics, for example, have provided ample evidence of the ongoing tension between class and ethnicity informing different phases of indigenous struggles.[14] Indigenous activism in Chimborazo provides a good example of the shift from class-based claims during agrarian reform struggle to the ethnic-based ones that led to the uprising of 1990. The uprising was the result of decades of political mobilization, dating to the beginning of the twentieth century, when the indigenous movement fought against ethnic and racial discrimination in order to assert its rights. During this political process, indigenous activists articulated their political demands in ethnic and class terms (*pobres*, *indios*, and *campesinos*). Their demands pushed toward the redefinition of the liberal concept of citizenship by redefining their position as citizens within ethnic communities, and not as isolated, individual subjects, therefore merging a communalist understanding of rights with liberal individualism: "We, the indigenous nationalities and peoples, have built a solidly structured national political organization with a clear ideology on our own historical and cultural activities and we propose to construct the New Multinational Nation" (CONAIE 1993, 1).

Thus, the main political goal of the indigenous movement during this phase was the redefinition of Indian-state relations on the basis of indigenous citizens' right to equality and ethnic diversity, dimensions that Taylor (1994) considers an expression of the tension inherent in the liberal concept of citizenship.[15] Indigenous demand for recognition of ethnic diversity is thus based on the premise that indigenous citizens belong to the Ecuadorian nation as diverse but equal citizens (as expressed in the indigenous motto "Igualdad en la diversidad," literally "equality in diversity"). On the basis of this claim, indigenous activists succeeded in gaining legitimacy as new political actors and in entering the sphere of direct mediation and negotiation with the state for recognition. They demonstrated vis-à-vis the state and civil society that indigenous peoples could be "protagonists of change, subjects not objects," as the indigenous leader Miguel Lluco declared in reference to the uprising.

The combination of grassroots and party politics after 1996 enabled indigenous activists to initiate local processes for incorporating diversity in public policies and institutions even before official constitutional recognition. The indigenous economist and activist Auqui Tituaña was one of the few indigenous candidates to be elected mayor, winning the 1996 mayoral election in Cotacachi canton, in the northern highland province of Imbabura. As a candidate on the Pachakutik slate, Auqui Tituaña owed his victory and subsequent reelection to the fact that indigenous voters were an overwhelming majority in the canton. During his eight years as mayor, Tituaña worked to integrate all local forces into projects for improving the lives of local citizens, both indigenous and nonindigenous. When I met and interviewed Auqui Tituaña after his first year as mayor, he discussed the difficulties and the positive factors impacting his administration. Areas in which he wanted his administration to intervene included education, health, the environment, and the patron-client political culture affecting the municipality. A convinced supporter of interculturalidad, he asserted that real equality could be reached only by fostering horizontal and equal processes of cultural exchange between people of different backgrounds.

He brought up health policy as an area that was showing positive results in intercultural terms. He remarked that his mandate started by promoting the incorporation of indigenous practices in the canton's major clinic in the cantonal capital. He considered this as one of his most successful policy interventions, noting that he had encountered positive responses from nurses, doctors, and indigenous healers (*curanderos*). His idea was not simply to introduce indigenous practices within the center and make them available to indigenous patients, but to have nurses and doctors validate such practices and incorporate them into their own sets of medical practices, especially in relation to the use of medicinal plants, which was widespread among indigenous people. Auqui Tituaña found that the most striking achievement of this process was that such validation had led nonindigenous local people to acknowledge and accept such practices, in some cases coming to consider them even more effective than Western remedies: "I have heard of people here, mestizo people, saying that finally they can find someone in the *consultorio* [health center] who knows about medicinal plants, which are more effective, less toxic, and cheaper than normal medicines. The funny thing is that even mestizos have been using those remedies for a long time but that practice had never been validated as a contribution of indigenous medicinal knowledge. Now my administration is offering that opportunity" (Cotacachi, 1997). Tituaña's efforts and dedication were rewarded internationally when under his administration Cotacachi won the Dubai 2000 award for the Best Practice of Government and was recognized by the UNESCO Cities for Peace program in 2002. In 2003 the health ministry recognized all the health initiatives promoted by the *alcaldía* with the signing of a *convenio* (agreement) within the parameters of the Law of Decentralization and Social Participation (Ley de Descentralización y Participación Social), which gives autonomy to local administrations (see Ortiz 2004, 144).

The Cotacachi case is an example of successful "participatory democracy," which took shape in the context of the decentralizing project run by the Ecuadorian state, another measure within the neoliberal project of reducing the state's size and scope of activities. During the Sixto Durán Ballen mandate (1992–96), decentralization and the modernization of the state structure became the main concerns in national policy making, and were accompanied by the state's antiwelfare discourse, according to which its subsidiary functions posed a threat to the nation's economic growth.

The creation of the National Council of Modernization (CONAM), in 1994, and the promulgation of the Law of Decentralization and Social Participation, in 1997, provided two powerful tools for the application of neoliberal policies of reduction of public resources.[16] According to the Law of Decentralization and Social Participation, mayors are required to promote the creation of local development committees formed by local political actors—for example, women's associations, workers federations, indigenous organizations—which are in charge of the design of "sustainable" development strategies and projects. "Sustainable" here means self-sufficient, since the state plans to gradually withdraw resources for local projects. This operation, together with the consolidation of the indigenous presence in the electoral process through the party system, granted the indigenous movement greater representation in local governments. Indigenous activists have been elected since 1996 as cantonal and parish council authorities and mayors, especially in districts where most of the population is indigenous. This context favored and enabled the indigenous claim for self-government and autonomy, as expressed in the 1990 Mandate for Life and in the lowland indigenous Defense for the Territory demands of 1992. Yet how is multiculturalism understood and practiced by local administrations?

The success of Cotacachi should not obfuscate the ambiguities and weaknesses inherent in decentralizing projects (see North and Cameron 2003). Despite offering indigenous activists the opportunity to exercise their right to self-administration locally, decentralization neither is conceived nor functions as a mechanism to empower indigenous authorities within the state structure. One of its weaknesses in Ecuador concerns the electoral process itself. The election of indigenous candidates as mayors resulted from the fact that indigenous voters were in the majority and voted en bloc for the indigenous candidates in their cantons. After this electoral affirmation, the Ecuadorian state and other actors, such as the Inter-American Development Bank, coined the term "indigenous municipalities" (*alcaldías indígenas*) as a new category to deploy in the decentralizing project.

However, a clear legal definition of alcaldía indígena was never formulated. The term seems to be based on electoral results, rather than specifying a new, formal sociopolitical entity, which means if indigenous candidates were to lose a cantonal election, there would no longer be an alcaldía indígena in the canton. The project of decentralization was included in the 1998 constitution as a mechanism to promote participatory democracy by involving local social forces in the definition of their own development. Yet the constitution did not specify the mechanisms that would coordinate the recognition of indigenous authorities with such committees of local development in areas where most of the population is indigenous and where local forces do not necessarily match or represent such ethnic composition. In other words, this problem demonstrates the limitations of neoliberal multiculturalism, specifically with regard to its failure to address inequality among groups. Less successful experiences than that in Cotacachi, in fact, highlight the difficulties that indigenous mayors face even in cantons where most of the population is indigenous but where networks of local power are controlled by nonindigenous people and social forces.

The case of Suscal, a canton in the southern highland province of Cañar, provides an example of the difficulties facing an indigenous mayor in managing local administration.[17] The 1996 electoral opening to indigenous activists with Pachakutik resulted in the election of an indigenous female candidate as mayor of Suscal, where the majority of the overall cantonal electorate are indigenous. However, in the cantonal capital itself, the population is primarily nonindigenous, a factor which created formidable challenges to the new mayor's leadership and exercise of authority once in office. Most of her projects and interventions were boycotted by the local nonindigenous population. In the municipal council meetings she was openly challenged by the white male council members. Local interethnic tensions and conflict combined with the dominant gender ideology, which ascribes the space of politics to men, to weaken her authority and leadership to the extent that she became dependent on her husband's interventions for containing the opposition within the municipality. The mayor's political experience within grassroots indigenous organizations and communities was not enough to gain her legitimacy in office or to redefine the local distribution of power, which had traditionally advantaged local nonindigenous elites.

Another example of this dynamic is provided by the case of Huamboya, a canton in the Amazonian province of Morona Santiago. Interethnic conflicts in the lowlands are different in nature and mostly involve issues of land control and exploitation of natural resources. Additionally, they mostly arose with the agrarian reform, during which land in the Amazon basin was considered empty (tierras baldías) and was offered to white colonists in order to foster economic development in that region. Colonization of this area produced intense conflicts between colonists and indigenous groups, who felt that the colonists were invading their territory and usurping their land. In 1996 the indigenous activist Miguel Puwainchir was elected mayor. However, his leadership was persistently boycotted by local forces representing nonindigenous colonists, who historically had opposed indigenous groups in fights over land rights. Puwainchir considered this his primary challenge: "Even if I could count on the vote of the vast majority of the local indigenous population for my election, that doesn't guarantee I have the support I need for implementing policies that can help the indigenous sector. At the level of the local committee of development, all the proposals regarding indigenous concerns are always put in second or third place by the colonists. While we want to prevent deforestation, they want to keep cutting for their pastures, and this is a never ending struggle" (1997). In this respect the Huamboya and Suscal cases are not dissimilar from other cases in Latin America in which decentralizing operations have left intact local power structures and racial prejudices that favor the interests of local nonindigenous elites (Gustafson and Pattnayak 2003; North and Cameron 2003; Postero 2007; Van Cott 2002). On the contrary, as Nancy Grey Postero analyzes in the case of lowland Bolivia (2007), decentralization (associated with the law of popular participation of 1993) and the creation of local territorial grassroots organizations (OTBs) reinforced the control local elites already had over resources and power.

Another limitation for indigenous activism in decentralizing policy relates to the potential restriction of political participation at the national level. Local administrations have the potential to become enclaves of indigenous power and autonomy. They answer the demand for self-determination put forward by the indigenous movement, thereby fulfilling the mandate of the 1998 constitution to create indigenous political autonomy through decentralization. Yet these cases of empowerment of local indigenous authorities are isolated and distinct from the participation of indigenous activists in the national process of decision making. Even if decentralization has offered the opportunity to increase the indigenous political presence in local administrations, obstacles such as patron-client relationships, racial and gender-based prejudices, and the lack of training in the "new technology of knowledge management" imposed by decentralization have often worked against the empowerment of indigenous authorities (Postero 2007, 143). The success of local indigenous mayors in accessing resources on behalf of the indigenous population and in response to their needs has mostly been due to their ability to master the language of rationalization of expenditures and their capacity to generate financial resources for local development. Not even the experience that many indigenous leaders and organizations had gained since the 1980s, through working with NGOs and international development agencies to fund their projects, has proven sufficient for overcoming local patron-client power networks and racial prejudices. Of all the indigenous elected officials mentioned, only Auqui Tituaña had received proper training. From the very beginning of his mandate, he focused on "racionalizar" (rationalizing) municipal expenses, often by eliminating unnecessary positions, a measure that frequently generated internal conflicts.

How, then, to gauge the potential for empowerment? Decentralization policies and political practice are another example of "critical engagements with neoliberal multiculturalism" according to which indigenous activists and social forces opted for working within the constraints of neoliberal political and administrative measures. With all of the ambiguities and contradictions of the neoliberal multicultural project and practice, indigenous activists in Ecuador paved the way to a new political phase, in which they aimed to fully exercise their right to participate in the design and definition of national politics. Beyond the examples of alcaldías indígenas and the complications facing indigenous mayors in their exercise of power, the postrecognition phase offered an opportunity for indigenous activists to reaffirm their influence and pressure, as well as enhance their access to local resources, especially in cantons which capitalized on a preexisting process of mobilization. As the case of Tixán highlights, a combination of electoral empowerment and the redefinition of local power structures under decentralization gradually led indigenous activists in the parish to attain powerful positions, usually monopolized by nonindigenous persons. Since 2000, activists of the Inca Atahualpa have been elected to the local assembly, the junta parroquial.[18] This change has allowed indigenous people to participate more directly in the decision-making process. For example, based on their experience with public childcare services in their communities, indigenous members of the junta overcame tixaneños' reluctance about childcare centers—which the tixaneños usually considered a service for the poor—and opened a center that both indigenous and nonindigenous children could attend. This case underscores the extent to which decentralizing and constitutional reforms worked as a structural opening for indigenous activism. Inca Atahualpa's leaders could capitalize on their wide trajectory of political struggle in order to take advantage of the new opportunities.[19]

Los Indios al Poder

The beginning of the new millennium marked the beginning of the postrecognition phase, in which indigenous activists managed to be elected to national governments in Ecuador and Bolivia. This phase posed new challenges while also reviving old prejudices which multiculturalism had not managed to fully disguise. In Ecuador the first element characterizing this phase is the return of contention politics linked to an expansion of political demands by the indigenous movement and to the formulation of a political platform that incorporated other social sectors around economic concerns. Such an opening allowed indigenous activists to partake in the process that led them to government.

The postrecognition phase exemplifies the indigenous activists' motto "Nothing only for the Indians" (*Nada sólo para los indios*), which highlights the political responsibility that the movement assumed in Ecuador after the decade of the 1990s by spearheading larger social movements (Saltos Galarza 2001). During a 1998 workshop that I organized on behalf of UNICEF, some indigenous leaders began exchanging views about new political strategies that would reinforce their political presence. One of them made a point on which everybody agreed: "We the Indians are not the only poor people in the country; we need to reach out to other sectors of the population who share our same hardships and are victims of many years of unjust and antisocial economic policy."

This shift became evident on 21 January 2000, when a coalition of popular social forces represented by the indigenous movement and a cadre of young Ecuadorian military officers and troops responded to the acute economic and political crisis that had destabilized Ecuador, with the overthrow of the recently elected president, Jamil Mahuad. The implementation of neoliberal economic measures since 1999—privatization, conversion of the national currency to the U.S. dollar, increases in fuel prices, and the gradual elimination of subsidies on liquefied petroleum gas—aggravated inflation and further impoverished the laboring classes, providing fertile ground for social protest. The new self-proclaimed government was composed of a civilian and military triumvirate formed by the general of the armed forces, CONAIE's president, and the former president of the Supreme Court of Justice. The *junta civil*, however, was short lived. The general of the armed forces withdrew from the civilian junta a mere three hours after the attempted coup in order to "avoid bloodshed." The vice president of the toppled government, Gustavo Noboa, was then declared president, and the cabinet was restored.

Unlike other collective actions organized by the indigenous movement in the 1990s, which were widely supported by public opinion, this attempted coup polarized Ecuadorian society along ethnic and class lines. The insurgents were mostly representative of poor indigenous and nonindigenous sectors and of lower ranking military who felt they had been treated as second-class citizens during years of political corruption and economic policies that benefited a privileged few. A wave of fear of being ruled by "Indians" spread among the nonindigenous middle class. Indigenous activists were accused by officials and in local newspaper editorials of destabilizing the country and blocking the already difficult path leading to economic and political national recovery. Nonindigenous Ecuadorian intellectuals also expressed reservations about the movement's political maturity and savvy. In some cases the movement's critics held indigenous leaders responsible for the widespread political crisis and the poverty afflicting Ecuadorians, among whom were many Indians (see Santana 2004). These critical remarks hint at predicaments and challenges facing the indigenous movements vis-à-vis the impacts of neoliberalism, the global economy, and unresolved conditions of internal colonialism in their own countries. The debate that took place after the attempted coup in Ecuador demonstrates that the legitimization of an indigenous political presence at the national level remained incomplete. Nonindigenous politicians and civil society placed most of the blame for the events of January 2000 on indigenous insurgents.

Exactly one year after the attempted coup, indigenous forces again mobilized against the next round of economic measures adopted by the government, specifically, a 75 percent rise in transport fares and increases in taxes and gasoline prices. The protest started as a peaceful demonstration in Quito and in several provinces, but soon escalated into a violent confrontation between protesters and the military, which was deployed swiftly by President Noboa to stop the protests. After two weeks of violent clashes the president signed an agreement in which he agreed to rescind the new economic measures and release everyone who had been arrested during the protest.

During this phase, the indigenous movement was fighting on behalf of "poor people" who, together with indigenous citizens, had been adversely affected by neoliberal economic measures and political corruption. As the former CONAIE president Antonio Vargas stated after the attempted coup, "This is not just an Indian struggle but everybody's struggle." This statement and the events to which it refers suggest that with the attempted coup of 2000 and the protests of 2001, the indigenous movement entered a new political phase, one in which the ethnic dimension of the struggle articulates with more general political concerns that emphasize class dimensions, addressing the socioeconomic vulnerability of the majority of the Ecuadorian population and a new notion of citizenship rights. This articulation is clearly expressed in the Agreements and Resolutions (Acuerdos y Resoluciones) produced by the ECUARUNARI assembly in Otavalo in April 2002. Together with claims that address the indigenous population more specifically (the promulgation of laws that legitimize the indigenous peoples and their justice system), the resolutions expressed not only rejection of the economic measures of Noboa's cabinet, such as privatization of the state energy company, tax increases, and payment of the external debt, but also solidarity with ecologists involved in the campaign against the construction of a new oil pipeline in the Amazon region.[20]

As consolidated and recognized political actors, indigenous leaders are responding to new challenges and resisting attempts to limit their political reach by defining their constituency solely on ethnicity. This new phase, therefore, has required different political strategies and alliances with other sectors of Ecuadorian society.[21]

In the realm of national politics, the gradual consolidation of indigenous presence within the state structure that started in the mid-1990s has not meant the institutionalization and bureaucratization of the movement in the postrecognition phase. Neoliberal multiculturalism functioned as a premise of new political demands, which in 2000 and 2001 led to the radicalization of Indian-state relationships. The attempts of the government in turn to co-opt indigenous leadership within public entities such as CODENPE led during this period to the expulsion from indigenous federations of indigenous leaders declared by ECUARUNARI and CONAIE to be unwelcome ("personas no gratas") because they had collaborated with the Noboa cabinet, ignoring CONAIE's opposition to it: "We sanction all of the comrades who have committed political mistakes and caused division within the indigenous movement, without respecting the CONAIE's political project" (ECUARUNARI 2002, 2).

It is clear that CONAIE, its affiliated organizations, and Pachakutik constituted the most representative coalition within the movement, disenfranchising all those leaders and positions that were contrary to them. Not only did CONAIE remain as the main referent for political actions and mobilizations for the whole indigenous sector, but it also remained the major referent for the state in negotiations. It was with CONAIE that the state negotiated the creation of the three major indigenous public institutions: the Council for the Development of Peoples and Nationalities of Ecuador (CODENPE, formerly CONPLADEIN), the National Council of Intercultural Health, and the Fund for the Development of Indigenous Peoples (FODEPI).

Official recognition, therefore, did not overcome divisions among indigenous political actors, the state, and civil society. Nor did it signify the conclusion of a more acute phase of political mobilization in which state actors were constantly monitored and expected to defer to the political desires and will of social forces. Despite the widespread condemnation of the attempted coup of 2000, the moment was mature for a significant change in Ecuadorian politics, with a growing sector of civil society becoming increasingly disenfranchised from traditional parties, which were often associated with crisis and corruption. Such feelings were embodied by Lucio Gutiérrez, one of the colonels who led the military faction that joined the coup, who later won the 2002 presidential elections with the active support of the indigenous movement.

The Demise of a "Historical" Indigenous Victory

The elections of 2002 led "Indians" to power. Indigenous activists saluted such results as a historical victory since for the first time in the political history of the country indigenous forces obtained seats within the government. The key question for the indigenous activists during this phase was no longer whether they would be recognized by the state and integrated into the decision-making process, but rather what to do from there. During this phase, both the indigenous movement and the state were beset by the tensions arising from the contradictory and problematic nature of the official recognition of indigenous rights in multicultural societies. The political events that led to the rupture of the political alliance between Gutiérrez and the indigenous movement exemplify this disjuncture.

During his electoral campaign Gutiérrez presented himself as a new political force arising from the grassroots and free from long-standing connections to the political oligarchies that had been ruling the country since independence. Echoing the political slogans of the attempted coup of 2000, Gutiérrez's political agenda focused on the fight against corruption and against unpopular neoliberal economic policies. The support of the indigenous movement was key to Gutiérrez's electoral victory. However, as the alliance was not based on a clear political and ideological agreement, it soon revealed itself to be purely opportunistic. From the moment Gutiérrez assumed office, the indigenous leaders of Pachakutik and CONAIE had to struggle to hold him to his pre-election promises, until finally three of their leaders were appointed as ministers, of agriculture, foreign affairs, and tourism. These appointments were celebrated by the indigenous movement as the fruit of almost a century of struggle. Yet the alliance was as tortuous as it was short-lived. Gutiérrez's political ambivalence and ambiguity soon manifested themselves with the signing of neoliberal economic measures: pressured by the IMF, he signed an agreement that included, among other things, the payment of the external debt and a new legislative proposal aimed at further reducing state bureaucracy. Additionally, he did not take decisive steps to reject Ecuador's participation in the Free Trade Area Agreement (ALCA), against which the indigenous movement and many social forces both nationally and internationally had mounted sustained protest. He also entered a phase of political dialogue with the conservative Partido Social Cristiano, a leading proponent of neoliberalism in Ecuador.

However, what determined the definitive rupture, in August 2003, with the resignation of the three indigenous ministers, was Gutiérrez's strategy aiming at breaking and debilitating the indigenous movement from within. He allegedly started by visiting indigenous communities, offering them agricultural tools in exchange for their support in a context in which regional federations were pressuring both CONAIE and Pachakutik to fight within the government against gas price increase (see Tamayo and Serrano 2005). The heaviest blow against the movement was delivered in 2004, when Gutiérrez issued a decree giving the presidency full control over the election of the executive director of the CODENPE.[22] This officer previously had been appointed by the executive board of CODENPE, a body of representatives from each of the nationalities and peoples represented in the council. Taking advantage of the power conferred on him by this decree, Gutiérrez handed control of CODENPE to the leadership of the FEINE (Evangelical Indigenous Federation).

It is important to contextualize Gutiérrez's maneuver within the framework of the redefinition of Indian-state relations at that time. In December 2002 the exiting cabinet of Noboa released the first draft of the Law of Indigenous Nationalities, which would have officially recognized sixteen indigenous nationalities and legitimized CODENPE as the entity in charge of the regularization and enactment of the new legislation. In order to support major changes in CODENPE's organic structure, CONAIE had advocated this legislation. Taking as a point of departure the 1998 constitutional recognition, and despite the fact that at the time the assembly did not approve the definition of *plurinational* proposed by CONAIE for inclusion in the constitution's language, CONAIE continued to pursue the recognition of indigenous peoples in terms of nationalities. Accordingly, it pushed to modify CODENPE's internal structure and have its internal council reconfigured. The council members of CODENPE would no longer be elected by the various grassroots and provincial federations, but by the different indigenous nationalities via their grassroots organizations. This can be considered a strategic political move which aimed at neutralizing the influence of CONAIE's historical antagonists: FEINE and FENOCIN.[23] As a matter of fact, CONAIE's leaders had figured that since the number of affiliated grassroots organizations in each nationality was higher than that of the other two federations, those who would be elected by the different nationalities would highly likely come from within CONAIE's sphere of political influence.[24] By becoming the uncontested representative of all indigenous nationalities, CONAIE would have had influence and control in designating the authorities of CODENPE, of the National Council of Intercultural Health, and of FODEPI. These were the three major bodies responsible for assigning funds and defining policies on behalf of indigenous peoples. The concerns that FEINE and FENOCIN had about CONAIE's hegemonic control over national resources were, therefore, well founded.

Gutiérrez's measure took advantage of this internal power struggle to debilitate the movement and the authority of CONAIE. At the same time, in subordinating the designation of CODENPE authorities to his control, he misrecognized the path undertaken by Noboa for the redefinition of Indians-state relationships, according to which indigenous actors, regardless of their political affiliation, finally would be able to exercise their right to self-determination in the national political sphere.

Internal tension and conflicts had always existed within the indigenous movement, especially due to different ideological matrixes and political strategies. Nevertheless, it had managed to maintain a united front whenever the case required it. Gutiérrez's policy used such internal divisions instead to control ethnic protest and restrict indigenous political participation. His government adopted a three-pronged strategy: delegitimize indigenous nationalities; heighten tensions within the movement; and weaken the role that CONAIE had played in the national political arena since the 1990 uprising (Zibechi 2006). As a matter of fact, FEINE and FENOCIN applauded Gutiérrez's measure, which they saw as a means to gain more control over CONAIE. As the president of FEINE, Marco Murillo, declared, "This change will allow for the CONAIE to lose the hegemonic control it has always had within CODENPE."[25] This strategy definitively ruptured the political alliance between Gutiérrez and the broad indigenous electorate that had brought him to power.

As a consequence of Gutiérrez's ethnic policy, the deepening of internal fissures and disagreements within the indigenous movement, and the weakening of CONAIE's control had negative impacts, especially on indigenous political mobilization. For example, indigenous participation in the popular movement known as the La Rebelión de los Forajidos (literally, "wrongdoers," from Gutiérrez's own scornful comments of the insurgents), which demanded Gutiérrez's resignation on account of political corruption in April 2005, was not as decisive and influential as it had been in previous mobilizations, such as those against President Abdalá Bucaran, in 1997, and against President Mahuad, in 2000. The protestors against Gutiérrez were mainly people from the popular and middle classes in the capital who had been utterly disappointed by the president's neoliberal turn and his alliance with the Christian Democrats, considered to embody economic injustice and corruption (see Burbano 2005).

The nationwide agitation started in February 2005 and peaked with Gutiérrez's forced resignation, on 20 April 2005, amid an escalation of violence that led to the death of the independent journalist Julio García. Precipitating the April protest was the return of Abdalá Bucaram from Panama, where he had fled to avoid corruption charges after the overthrow of his government. Nina Pacari considered the CONAIE's nonparticipation in the protest a tactical error: "Leaders of CONAIE at the time considered the protest as another power struggle between oligarchic forces. They came out too disappointed by Gutiérrez's change of face so they missed the fact that the insurgency against him was a popular protest and not just from his political opponents" (personal communication, 2007). After the *forajidos* protest forced Gutiérrez to resign, Alfredo Palacio became interim president and continued with the same neoliberal economic measures that Gutiérrez had initiated.

Fighting for Economic Justice

These events highlighted the emerging tensions in the strategy of a movement that simultaneously sustained political mobilization and participated within the state structure. The destabilizing policy adopted by Gutiérrez also caused friction between the leaderships of CONAIE and Pachakutik, making apparent the tension between traditional party politics, whose main goal is winning elections to public office, and mobilization, which usually monitors government policies from an oppositional position. Such tensions led CONAIE to the strategic error identified by Pacari: the missed opportunity to forge a strong political alliance with a growing sector of the Ecuadorian population that was ready for substantive social change in the country.

While declaring its intent to remain in the opposition and to monitor Palacio's social and economic policies, the leaderships of CONAIE and Pachakutik took time to discuss their differences in an attempt to reestablish common political ground. This opportunity was offered by negotiations with the United States on a bilateral free trade agreement (TLC), which intensified under Palacio in the spring of 2006.[26] Indigenous activists responded by initiating a series of protests and marches demanding suspension of the negotiations and implementation of an economic policy that would protect the national economy and small producers; they declared an "estado de levantamiento permanente" (permanent state of uprising) in March 2006.[27] This political action gave CONAIE and Pachakutik an opportunity to work together again as political allies. It also reinstituted relationships between CONAIE, FEINE, and FENOCIN, since the latter also had decided to join and support the protest.

The mobilization against free-trade agreements was a key moment, a prelude to the changes in Ecuadorian politics that brought about the electoral victory of the antineoliberal president Rafael Correa, in 2006. Such mobilization involved other sectors of Ecuadorian society and progressive intellectuals in the ongoing debate about global economics and the future of the national economy. Small producers felt threatened by this type of agreement, predicting that they would be unable to compete with the prices of large-scale production that would be injected into the country from the United States. The anti-free-trade-agreement movement, which is transnational in scope, provoked a heated debate in the country around issues of economic justice and national economic growth for which Palacio's neoliberal regime had no answer other than pursuing bilateral negotiations.[28] After the first attempt to contain the protest and dialogue, especially with the indigenous leadership, Palacio was unequivocal that he would neither suspend negotiations nor tolerate indefinite political unrest.

Palacio's response underscores the extent to which neoliberal regimes also present inherent contradictions that pose challenges to the state. Decentralization, even if with mixed results and many ambiguities, represented an opportunity for indigenous actors to increase their political participation at the local level and initiate a local process of negotiation between indigenous and nonindigenous forces. Additionally, despite its ambiguities, decentralization potentially impacted local political culture and practice and the way local authorities related and formulated their demands to the state also in cases of nonindigenous administrations. By means of local development committees, decentralizing projects promoted a new exercise of citizenship by offering to traditionally excluded sectors of civil society the opportunity to actively participate in the definition of social and economic policies.

The case of the U.S.-based oil company Occidental (Oxy) underscores this process. Throughout 2006, intense mobilizations of workers of the national oil company Petroecuador along with local authorities and social forces from the Sucumbios, Napo, Orellana, Zamora, and Morona Santiago Provinces demanded the revocation of the contract with Oxy for oil exploitation.[29] Indigenous activists from Limoncocha participated in the mobilization as local social forces; representatives of CONAIE and Pachakutik also joined the protesters after arriving in Quito in May 2006. Such measures were taken because of allegations that Oxy had violated conditions of its contract. The alleged violations included negative environmental impact and the undisclosed sale of 405 of its shares to EnCana, a Canadian company.[30] In April 2006 President Palacio revoked the contract, a measure that was also made possible by the approval of the Hydrocarbons Law, on 29 March 2006, which granted the Ecuadorian state a more forceful role in stipulating conditions in oil-exploitation contracts with foreign companies, including a higher profit-sharing, of 50 percent, between the state and any foreign oil company. Revocation of the Oxy contract provoked a diplomatic impasse between Ecuador and the United States when the Bush administration intervened to defend Oxy, protesting the revocation of the contract. This impasse caused the United States to suspend TLC negotiations.[31]

The Oxy case is a good example of the mobilizing power acquired by local administrations in forcing the state to intervene in their defense in matters that threatened to negatively impact larger political and economic processes—here, the TLC negotiation. Local administrations in this case forced the state to redefine what was in the national interest. The creation of local development committees by the decentralization law may help to expand the definition of citizenship rights, in that it provides a venue for incorporating the perspectives and proposals of the different social sectors represented in the committees. At least ideally, this model can facilitate a more participatory political practice with the potential to overcome outdated political forms of patron-client relationships and forms of authoritarianism such as *caudillismo*.

Another interesting aspect highlighted in the Oxy case concerns the role of the state in economic policy under neoliberalism. Despite the rhetoric of economic liberalism that leaves economic policies to be defined by the free market, the Oxy case suggests that neoliberal states actively maintain a protectionist role on behalf of corporate economic interests. The intervention of the U.S. government in support of Oxy is indicative of this trend. Despite its neoliberal economic doctrine, the Ecuadorian central government was caught between the pressure exercised by local administrations and that exercised by foreign governments and global corporations, and it opted to oppose the interests of corporate capital. The postrecognition phase, therefore, foregrounded a complex moment, ripe for significant political change across Ecuadorian society. Two factors—the mobilizing force of the indigenous movement and the decentralizing structural opening—empowered sectors of Ecuadorian civil society that historically had been excluded from decision-making processes. Time and circumstances conjoined for a drastic shift in political culture and practice. How did the indigenous movement respond to this new political landscape?

Time of Crisis

Despite its numerous ambiguities, the constitutional recognition of 1998 clearly was a point of departure that offered opportunities for social transformation. However, the implications of such ambiguities become more complex when one analyzes the political process of the indigenous movement in light of the changes taking place in the new millennium. Indigenous political empowerment is not the result of constitutional recognition, but of decades of political struggle during which the movement succeeded in taking advantage of structural openings in order to gain power and visibility in the national political scene. The multicultural moment therefore consists of two major components: the incorporation of indigenous political presence in the web of state and party politics; and the official multicultural recognition formulated concomitantly with neoliberal economic policies. The confluence of these two paths led the indigenous movement to a phase that has been characterized as the "Indians in power" (Ponce 2000). Nevertheless, despite the rapprochement of CONAIE, Pachakutik, and FENOCIN, the indigenous movement appeared not to have survived the "gutierrazo."

The scant participation of indigenous constituencies in the forajidos protests and the results of the 2006 elections are symptomatic of a moment of crisis facing the movement both in the realm of mobilization and in party politics. The most revealing moment in the strategic rapprochement of CONAIE and Pachakutik came in 2006, when the leadership of both decided to nominate the president of CONAIE, Luis Macas, as the presidential candidate for Pachakutik for the October 2006 elections. Initially reluctant to adopt a strategy embracing presidential party politics, CONAIE and Pachakutik later decided to contest the election with their own candidate, rather than support the independent nominee, Rafael Correa. Based on the experience of the alliance with Gutiérrez, the Pachakutik legislator Jorge Guamán advised his party to think twice before forming an alliance with an independent candidate.[32] The results of the elections were disastrous, with Macas receiving 2 percent of the vote. The indigenous voters largely supported Correa. This election strategy was another important mistake by the CONAIE and Pachakutik leaderships, since it precluded them from participating in the promise of profound change in Ecuadorian politics and economics represented by Correa's antineoliberal doctrine.

A combination of structural and conjunctural factors led to this political impasse. First and most obvious, the delegitimizing ethnic policy of Gutiérrez's government further divided the movement and weakened CONAIE's leadership and indigenous institutions. Second, the protagonist role that the indigenous movement acquired in the fight against neoliberal economics radicalized social conflict in the country around regionalist and class-based responses that reconfigured racist imaginary about the "Indians." Yet the most complex and crucial element in this crisis was the disarticulation between the movement's leadership and the indigenous grassroots, of which the 2006 electoral result is a clear indication, with one explanation clearly related to the power struggle confronting leaders of CONAIE, Pachakutik, FEINE, and FENOCIN. Macas's candidacy as a partial antidote to such confrontation ignored the voice coming from the grassroots, which evidently saw in Correa's antineoliberal promises a more convincing opportunity.

At the same time, the implementation of a state-corporate ethnic policy to respond to indigenous demands for self-government coopted indigenous leadership by shaping what Hale (2004) has defined as the "indio permitido," that is, a category that is both accepted and acceptable under a neoliberal regime. The creation of CONPLADEIN, later CODENPE, for example, was an instrument by which to corporatize the indigenous movement in a way that was new in Indian-state relationships in the country. Unlike Bolivia's 1952 revolution, according to which the Bolivian state corporatized indigenous social forces, in Ecuador indigenous mobilization and organizing resulted from contentious politics that saw the influence of leftist parties and later of the progressive Catholic Church, and not from the intervention of the state. During this period "Indians" were characterized as alzamenteros. The redefinition of Indian-state relationships under multiculturalism aimed at transforming "Indians" from alzamenteros into "permitted" by coopting indigenous leadership into public ethnic institutions. "Permitted Indians" are those who work to implement public policies for the indigenous sector and embody the modern, rational indigenous citizen who participates in the economic development of the nation as opposed to the unruly "indio alzamentero" of street protests (see Bretón 2000; Hale 2004).

Despite the fact that such incorporation can also be considered a form of empowerment, since it allows indigenous nationalities a protagonist role in defining their own public policies, the beneficial impacts should be gauged by the ethnographic data. When I returned to Tixán in 2007, after ten years away, I was struck by the sweep of the changes: the Inca Atahualpa is still there, but it is disconnected from other provincial federations and organizations. In the administration of justice, constitutional recognition of multiculturalism has empowered communal authorities who since 1998 have increased their legitimacy vis-à-vis both local nonindigenous authorities and the Inca Atahualpa. Local authorities in the parish and canton respect the cabildo's decisions; neither they nor the Inca Atahualpa interfere with its decisions. Although still meeting with people on Sundays, the Inca Atahualpa's leaders arbitrate few cases and tend to limit their intervention to advice. As the Inca Atahualpa's former activist A. L. declared, "People pay attention and respect the cabildos better these days" (personal communication, 2006).

When one compares the weight of the organization and its influence on the definition of strategies for the development of local indigenous affiliates, it seems that ten years later the Inca Atahualpa's role is limited to that of *tramitador* (i.e., one who prepares paperwork for any application that affiliated communities may need help with) and to looking for funds to sustain productive activities on its own farm. A. L. explained to me that the situation has changed and that it has become difficult to obtain funds: "Now we need to be a specific people in order to access CODENPE's funds. The generic name of Quichuas is not enough" (personal communication, 2006).

A profound disarticulation between the challenges people face in their communities and the realm of national public indigenous policies embodied by "indios permitidos" has pushed indigenous grassroots away from indigenous leadership nationally and even locally. Nina Pacari acknowledged the crisis of leadership, which in her view is both moral and structural. "Unfortunately today we have leaders who lost perspective, blinded by the prospect of power and by seating in the government; others who found in institutions such as CODENPE trampolines for their individual power forgetting about their role to be of service to their people, and finally leaders from grassroots who were not prepared to deal with public policy in public office and therefore did not perform at the best of their responsibilities. We need new young and prepared leaders," Pacari declared, "who can put in practice a new intercultural society founded on mutual respect and justice" (personal communication, 2007).

Silence Is Not Death

This account of the process of ethnic mobilization in contemporary Ecuador highlights the political contours of Indian-state dynamics and the advances and limitations of indigenous mobilization. According to elements that more broadly are described as the economic and political project of neoliberalism, the specifics of the postrecognition phase include the following three features. First, indigenous movements expanded their demands beyond ethnic boundaries by renewing the quest for economic justice on behalf of all sectors of the poor within their society. Second, they adopted different political strategies that aimed at building a broader constituency by combining mobilization and party politics. And third, despite the limitations that I highlighted, indigenous activists increased their level of political participation, especially at the local level.

However, the Ecuadorian case also shows that the postrecognition phase is fraught with contradictions. The weakening of the indigenous movement occurred at exactly the same time as indigenous cultural rights were being recognized by the state. The next set of challenges facing the indigenous movement relates to the ambiguities of multicultural practices. Recognition of multiple social identities is not synonymous with equality of status among groups. The Ecuadorian case suggests that official recognition of indigenous rights refers to a disembodied Indian subject that is isolated from the state structure and confined within the boundaries of local ethnic administrations.

In this respect, it seems that official neoliberal multiculturalism serves as a strategy to contain ethnic demands. This type of ethnic administration is not new, given the colonial ethnic administration under which "Indians" were ruled by separate legislation, La República de los Indios, which recognized indigenous authorities in order to gain access to labor and resources of indigenous populations. As eloquently explained by Andrés Guerrero (1993), with the formation of the modern nation-state—even if each and every Ecuadorian were declared a citizen of the new republic—de facto ethnic administration passed to the hands of local micropowers, for example, the trilogy of power of hacienda regimes. This process endured until the agrarian reform, after which the relationship was redefined as between the state and peasants, and later as between the state and indigenous citizens.

The question of administering ethnic and cultural diversity is, therefore, connected to colonization and to its reorganization in processes of postcolonization. I compare neoliberal multiculturalism to other forms of ethnic administration such as the indirect rule adopted by the British colonial regime in India and in African colonies as a strategy to contain the risk of rebellion and reduce the cost of colonial bureaucracy. In her analysis of indirect rule in Nigeria, Karen Fields writes, "In all aspects consistent with colonial law and order and not repugnant to British law and customs the old life style and native laws and customs would continue with the blessing of the regime. The indirect rule was a conservative strategy designed to maintain native chiefs and their subjects in their place. It aimed at keeping the colonial hamlets peaceful while the colonial economy revolutionarized them" (1985, 30).

Certain premises of colonial indirect rule resonate with the neoliberal multicultural paradigm. In the Ecuadorian case the transition from the rhetoric of mestizaje to that of official multiculturalism is continuous in regard to the cooptation of indigenous political demands by the state and elites, an example of *etnofagia* as proposed by Héctor Díaz-Polanco (2006). However, an important difference must be highlighted. Although indirect rule or similar legislation with colonial roots was adopted as a preventive measure, neoliberal multiculturalism generated from and is subject to a complex process in which international conventions defending ethnic rights and a constant process of political mobilization converged with a hegemonic project of economic change and capitalist expropriation. A historical parallel comes to mind when one analyzes these conditions. The agrarian reforms in Latin America between the 1950s and 1970s were the result of a complex process in which the interests of different social sectors converged but did not merge. Prompted by transnational forces represented by the Organization of American States and locally sponsored by new generations of landowners, agrarian reforms were meant to foster modernization and economic progress in the entire region, as well as calm social unrest associated with masses of poor peasants and indigenous peons who were highly exploited under the hacienda system. Many studies in the Andean region demonstrate that even if indigenous people in the highlands managed to recover control over their lands, they were not the ultimate beneficiaries of these reforms because the large landowning interests retained economic power in the agrarian sector. However, many indigenous people in the highlands did acquire land, and that acquisition transformed their life in significant ways.[33]

Similarly, neoliberal multiculturalism is constantly redefined, reinterpreted, and even engaged by social movements. In the case of Bolivia, for example, neoliberal multiculturalism and decentralization worked in favor of the formation of a new popular movement that gathered diverse popular forces to exercise a new form of citizenship rights that Postero defines as postmulticultural citizenship. By using the language of citizenship, indigenous political actors were able to channel their demands as indigenous citizens in the redefinition of a new model of state and of society that had to be built from below. Social protests provided the opportunity to create a broad-spectrum popular movement, Movement to Socialism, which led to the electoral victory, in 2005, of Evo Morales, the first indigenous president in Latin America, who officially ended the neoliberal era in Bolivia.

In Ecuador, however, even if the indigenous movement followed the paths of combining protests and party politics and of creating a network of social support to expand its constituency, its presidential candidate, Macas, was trounced. Racism played a role in defining a weaker network of support for the Ecuadorian indigenous movement. Nonindigenous voters do not seem to be ready for an indigenous president. Anti-indigenous prejudices remain rampant in nonindigenous sectors of Ecuadorian society. In such a context, the smaller proportion of the indigenous electorate in Ecuador relative to that in Bolivia (where the indigenous population is more than 60 percent of the national population) can play a significant role in electoral results. However, this factor does not explain Macas's electoral debacle. The difference in Boliva's and Ecuador's electoral results is due less to the different language used to formulate proposals for a new society and nation, and more to the lack of such a proposal in the Ecuadorian case. Despite the creation of a broad-spectrum popular movement and the formulation of a political proposal with the language of citizenship, the weight of culturally informed promises in Morales's electoral campaign was key in gaining the support of the indigenous electorate (Postero 2007, 227). The Ecuadorian indigenous movement, instead, was seriously weakened when it arrived at the moment ripe for political change lacerated by internal conflict and unable to capitalize on its political potential in order to generate a proposal of society that could persuade even its own grassroots.

The activist Luis Maldonado self-critically acknowledged the political impasse that emerged with the gutierrazo and the lack of a clear political proposal.[34] Nina Pacari considered this phase as one of "repliegue activo," or active retreat, where indigenous leaders needed to rethink and reformulate their political proposals and organics: "This is not the 90s anymore. A movement cannot always be on the cusp. Also the demands are not the same as the 90s even if questions of lands and education are still on the agenda. We need to redefine our political strategies to make our intercultural project viable. We need to train our leaders, young people and prepare them to the challenges they have to face in office. This is a moment for reflection. Silence is not the same as death" (personal communication, 2007).

Conclusion

I return now to a question formulated at the beginning of this volume: how do we approach and interpret the specificity of indigenous politics? And, more specifically, how do we understand the interplay of cultural and political distinctiveness in relation to larger processes of change in geopolitics and transnational economics? How have the many changes in Ecuador's political culture that have taken place since I concluded my initial period of fieldwork in 1998 impacted circumstances in Tixán? The political processes I have examined account for the period that led to the multicultural turn and the moment in which second-grade organizations such as the Inca Atahualpa came to play a crucial role in redefining local power relations. But what has happened in the intervening years? How have the Inca Atahualpa and the Quichuas in Tixán been navigating the complexities of the postrecognition phase? I have argued that the multiplication of subject positions arising from the politicization of ethnic identity is not inherently disempowering for indigenous movements. Nonetheless, what are the consequences of the politics of ethnic recognition for indigenous people in Tixán?

In addition to having maintained contact with people from Tixán during these intervening years, I returned to Tixán in October 2007. According to what I saw and to what A. L. recounted, the changes in Tixán are consistent with trends described in this book. Like many other towns in the Ecuadorian highlands, Tixán has become "more indigenous," meaning that more indigenous people have moved to the town. Concomitantly, many tixaneños, especially the wealthier families, kept migrating to cities or abroad, leaving behind their elders and their houses and returning for the town's fiestas in June. This change has particularly affected the small grocery shops, which now are run primarily by elders. Features of the harvest festival celebration since 2000 confirm the more culturally and ethnically mixed trends discussed in chapter 6. The participation of tixaneños increased especially with canelazos for the ballroom-dancing nights and alcancías for the bullfighting afternoon. As A. L. pointed out, the economic situation since 2005 has shortened the celebration to two days. In the same year the Inca Atahualpa board reinstated the celebration of the jahuay after the festival's Sunday Mass. The music contest has become more prominent since the creation of the local radio station, Zota Urco, in 2002. A. L., as radio director and musician, provided leadership for enhancing the musical contest and thereby celebrating Quichua artists. The soccer championship grew to such an extent that festival organizers made it a separate event, introducing two tournaments—one at the cantonal level, for teams representing organizations, and another at the parish level, for teams representing local communities.

The Inca Atahualpa endures, although it struggles to sustain its projects.[1] Its weavers' project, initiated in 1998 with funds from the Dutch NGO Esquel, ended unsuccessfully due to problems related to the commercialization of wool.[2] One of the childcare centers, opened in town after decentralization led to the election of indigenous representatives to the local junta, operates in the Inca Atahualpa–owned millhouse. The organization also endorsed the creation of the Zota Urco radio station, supported by funds from the Canadian NGO Development and Peace (Desarrollo y Paz). The radio station emerged as the most active indigenous cultural producer, fostering all of the cultural performances that were reinstated in the harvest festival. The organization also facilitated the creation of two health centers, in the communities of Yacupungo and Pachamama, where only traditional indigenous medicine is practiced.

The most interesting developments, however, are linked to the processes of decentralization and constitutional recognition. Both factors have reshaped the role in local politics of grassroots organizations such as the Inca Atahualpa. Since 1998 the Inca Atahualpa has been gaining local power in Tixán and in the cantonal council. According to the decentralization legislation, parish civil officers and parish assembly members are elected by popular vote and no longer are appointed on the basis of party politics. Since the late 1990s this political restructuring has offered the Inca Atahualpa's leaders an opportunity to be elected as parish civil officers. In 1998, P. B. was the first indigenous person in Tixán to be elected as a civil officer. The creation of Pachakutik also gave opportunities to other indigenous candidates to be elected to municipal offices.[3] For example, the election of A. L.'s wife, Juana, as cantonal council member (*consejala*) in the administrative elections of 2004, is an example of this political affirmation, since it was the first time an indigenous candidate affiliated to the Inca Atahualpa was elected to this office.

Constitutional recognition also has reshaped the way organizations such as the Inca Atahualpa are linked to regional and national federations, specifically with CONAIE: "The new constitution recognizes us as pueblos with our distinctive identity. Now we have rights not just as Indians or Quichuas but each group has rights" (A. L., personal communication, 2006). When asked what he thought those rights were within the movement, A. L. mentioned access to the resources that are administered by CODENPE and its related program, the Indigenous and Afro-Ecuadorian Peoples Development Project (PRODEPINE), a project funded by the World Bank. "With the Inca," he continued, "we are working on finding out where we come from, what was the name of our ancestors. We always just defined ourselves here as Quichuas but now it is not enough. Each indigenous group has a different name, a different identity and that is how resources are distributed. We know that the original pueblo here was the Tiquizambis but we want to find out more about them." This local process of ethnogenesis is symbolized by the name the Inca Atahualpa board chose for the radio station. Zota Urco is believed to have been a powerful chief of the Tiquizambis (Velasco 1979).[4] "This is not about what we learn in the history books at school on the Incas and the Inca Atahualpa. Zota Urco was our ancestor; this is why it is important" (A. L., 2006). In fact, Zota Urco and the Tiquizambis have always been mentioned in the local official history of the canton (Castillo n.d.; Heredia 1985; Liebre Ilustrada 1988). However, the history of the Tiquizambis became relevant to local indigenous activists only with the reorganization of indigenous affiliations by nationality as sponsored by CONAIE. Highland cantonal and provincial federations affiliated with or supportive of CONAIE have been modifying their language by abandoning generic terms such as *indigenous*, *Indian*, or even broader ethnic definitions such as *Quichua*, replacing them with specific ethnic definitions, which they refer to as *nationalities* and *pueblos*. In a press release that the Chimborazo Indigenous Movement (MICH) released on 5 August 2004 to reject the decree of Gutiérrez's cabinet regarding CODENPE (Decree 1833-A), the MICH president Pedro Janeta spoke on behalf of the twenty-six pueblos comprising the indigenous nationality of the province, announcing each of their names.[5]

Inca Atahualpa's activists recognized the implications of this process of ethnogenesis. In order to evaluate their political position within the movement, in 1998 they decided to become independent and unaffiliated with any major federation. Nonetheless, they participated in all major actions organized by CONAIE, including the attempted coup of 2001. Accordingly, they have endorsed the politics of recognition of each nationality: "In 2005 we started to dialogue with CODENPE about resources and we did it as Tiquizambis because otherwise we will not have any representative anywhere" (A. L., personal communication, 2006).

The case of the Inca Atahualpa shows the extent to which internal differences, whether ideological or strategic, were not inherently debilitating. Despite popular myths about social movements being cohesive, monolithic, and coherent, in reality most social movements risk fragmentation.[6] In the case of the Ecuadorian indigenous movement, the most recent redefinition of ethnic identities within the movement suggests a search for a more equitable redistribution of resources, as well as an attempt to consolidate the power of the movement around the most representative of the national federations. This strategy can also be seen as an attempt to avoid excessive fragmentation at the national level. Yet the enforcement of "Big Government" epitomized by Gutiérrez's authoritarian intervention misrecognized the indigenous right to self-government and to political participation, and exacerbated internal differences.

However, the changes I found in Tixán in 2007 also account for a new trend in local ethnic politics that seems to have pushed grassroots organizations like the Inca Atahualpa to a marginal position. Communal authorities gained more legitimacy as a result of constitutional recognition. The administration of justice, which had become one of the strongholds of the Inca Atahualpa's power locally, gradually returned to communal authorities. Moreover, participation in local politics did not necessarily capitalize on the organization's force, but rather followed decentralization and electoral strategies.

Furthermore, consensus and leadership within the organization became particularly problematic. In our informal conversation in 2006 A. L. told me that people from the communities started to complain about the organization's excessive attention to itself and its internal conflicts, usually provoked by the struggle over the presidency.[7] Younger activists such as P. B. used the Inca Atahualpa to launch political careers in local administration—with mixed results. Personalized power struggles pushed some activists, including A. L. himself, to abandon the organization. Although still collaborating with the Inca Atahualpa on cultural activities, A. L. no longer holds a leadership position. Instead he devotes his energy to the Zota Urco radio station, which operates from the millhouse and broadcasts programs in Quichua, ranging from national and local news to music and distance education. A. L. proudly proclaims the success of the radio station and that everybody in the communities listens to it. The station supplanted the organization as a more effective tool for political mobilization in the spring of 2006, when the indigenous movement organized national protests against free-trade agreements. The broadcasts led to mobilization, and a massive gathering of Quichuas in Alausí participated in the protest.[8]

In the competitive arena of development policies and projects, ethnic affiliations more than organizations became paramount for obtaining funds from CODENPE. This change in distribution of resources has affected second-grade organizations, which saw their influence on development strategies for their affiliated communities reduced to that of "tramitador" and had to look for funds to support activities that would keep the organizations viable. Meanwhile, migration to the United States, which in the 1990s was the prerogative of nonindigenous townsfolk, became widespread in the local indigenous communities. Indigenous people increasingly started to migrate "north" to Europe, the United States, and Canada, often with tragic consequences. According to the Inca Atahualpa's leaders, of those who attempt to leave the country each year at least two local indigenous people are reported missing. As of 2008, four local indigenous men had been reported dead in "transit" accidents, three on boats crossing the Pacific toward Mexico, and one at the hand of *coyoteros*. Those who succeed in traveling abroad for work send money home. These funds are often invested in tractors, equipment that can be rented by other community members for sowing and harvesting.[9] Migration has had other economic impacts on communities, making them increasingly deserted and creating shortages of labor and resources. While back in the 1990s the Inca Atahualpa launched an aggressive campaign against urban migration, now many of its leaders have relatives in the United States.

How are these changes and new trends in local politics to be understood? They seem to indicate that indigenous people continue to mobilize beyond and despite their political organizations. What happened in Tixán with the Inca Atahualpa relates to larger trends at the national level, according to which the indigenous movement as a whole seems to have reached an impasse. This political crisis is less related to inherent fragmentation within the movement than to the ambiguities of the multicultural phase. The impasse, therefore, extends more generally to future political mobilization and its struggle for economic justice and equitable redistribution of resources framed in the language of recognition of cultural and ethnic rights.

Scholars debate the issue of whether or not indigenous movements in Latin America have shifted to more class-based claims or whether they have always incorporated this dimension, albeit with different emphases.[10] I consider the postrecognition phase as key for defining the limitations of the class-ethnic divide. The intertwining of official multicultural recognition, which potentially opened the door for indigenous political participation, and the adoption of neoliberal economic policy, which further impoverished the already precarious ranks of the Ecuadorian population, has forced both the state and the indigenous movement to move beyond the politicization of ethnicity. However, the dynamics of this political and historical conjuncture also refute the belief that ethnic, racial, and economic demands can be separated or treated independently. Addressing this tension is the principal challenge facing social movements that are fighting for racial, ethnic, and economic justice.

The following incident clarifies this point. For a panel on multiculturalism I organized in February 2006, in the context of the Abriendo Brechass III Conference at the University of Texas at Austin, I invited two activists, one representing the Afro-Brazilian movement and the other the Aymara movement in Bolivia. Although both speakers addressed the roots of racial and ethnic discrimination in their respective societies and reiterated the need for social justice, their interventions entailed dramatically different political discourses and strategies. The Afro-Brazilian activist vehemently rejected culturalist claims and identified structural conditions of racial discrimination—differential access to resources such as education and the labor market—as the crux of the Afro-Brazilian struggle. In contrast, the Aymara activist rejected any association of Evo Morales's electoral victory with left-wing ideologies and epitomized it as the symbolic return to the ayllu, the sociocultural foundation of Andean indigenous cultures.

Although these contrasting political views cannot be generalized as the only ones formulated within those movements, they are indicative of different perspectives that have their roots in the specificity of Indian-state relations in Bolivia and relations between Afro-descendents and the state in Brazil. Afro-descent cultures in countries like Brazil have been folklorized and exoticized by the state in order to keep blacks at the margins of society while building on the illusion of a racial democracy. Indigenous cultures in countries like Bolivia have been rejected by the state and intellectuals for allegedly being an insurmountable obstacle to modernization and progress. It can be argued that these distinctions have their origins in the different types of discourses and processes produced by colonial administrations concerning the colonized groups under their control, with an emphasis on racial inferiority in the case of black slaves and on sociocultural immaturity in the case of indigenous people. The rejection of a culture-based struggle in Afro-Brazil, then, becomes a strategy by which to unmask the fiction of racial democracy, while in Bolivia the return of the ayllu is a strategy by which indigenous activists can assert their dignity and claim a legitimate space in modernity. Yet both of these movements demand social justice and more equitable distribution of resources.

What are the implications of these apparently divergent political discourses? The postrecognition phase has made it impossible to postulate the separation of ethnic, racial, and class struggle. In other words, indigenous movements must address the challenge of building on a political discourse and strategy that does not alienate their constituencies while at the same time reaching out to other social actors who do not identify themselves as indigenous. In this respect indigenous movements share similar challenges with other transnational umbrella movements, for example, the anti–World Trade Organization movement, whose member groups share high-level objectives yet are profoundly heterogeneous. Michael Hardt and Antonio Negri (2004) argue that the hope for social change today resides in large scale movements that build on the commonalities shared by myriad singularities brought together via globalization, which they define as "multitude" (2004, 128–31). Drawing on this reading of progressive politics, I see the context of indigenous movements in Latin America as having the potential of building on commonalities and of producing mass movements with emergent strategies for political mobilization. The example of Morales's electoral victory may be an indication of such potential.

However, it is too early to predict the results of this process. The Ecuadorian case shows that these heterogeneous movements are not oriented toward a predetermined direction and intentionality. The moment of political impasse for the indigenous movement in Ecuador highlights instead the difficulty of forging a complex new imagining of an all-inclusive society. The postrecognition moment also has affected grassroots organizations such as the Inca Atahualpa, whose role in local politics has been drastically redefined. As Nina Pacari suggests (2007), this is a new phase for the indigenous movement, both at the national and local levels, during which all organizations and leaders are being forced to rethink their role and projects. In this phase, most of the political strategies of the movement have been based on rejection of neoliberal economics. Supposedly the government of the progressive independent president Rafael Correa has put an end to neoliberalism by embodying the kinds of change in Ecuadorian politics and economics that a large non-elite sector of the population had been demanding since the presidency of Gutiérrez. Defining himself as a left-wing Christian and promising a civil revolution (*revolución ciudadana*), during his 2006 campaign Correa presented himself as the candidate who would bring about social and economic justice. Correa enjoyed the support of the indigenous electorate, who did not support his indigenous opponent, Luis Macas. Key to gaining this support was his campaign promise—fulfilled when he came to office—of significant increases in income supports to poor people and single mothers, which he called the "dignity bonus" (instead of the "poverty bonus," which it had been called before). Once in power, Correa strongly opposed free-trade agreements and privatization; he also started to implement a social policy in support of underserved sectors of the population, resuming some of the state responsibilities rejected by neoliberal regimes. He also led the country to a new constitution, which was ratified in February 2008.

Correa's government seemed to offer a favorable conjuncture for the indigenous political agenda in terms of support for its potential intercultural project of society. The questions for the movement, therefore, addressed not only its larger social and political project, but also the kinds of political strategies and alliances that could be forged in this post-neoliberal phase. However, more recent frictions and conflicts between the indigenous movement and Correa's government seem to confirm a trend according to which official multiculturalism, combined with real or perceived authoritarian management in Correa's government, has apparently rendered ethnic demands obsolete. At the beginning of his mandate, Correa's administration endorsed the project of building an intercultural society. The 2008 constitution incorporated diversity in a more transversal and open fashion. The application of indigenous justice, for example, is no longer restricted in terms of being in contradiction with national laws, but in reference to violation of the constitution and its principles of human rights. On a national political platform, the constitutions of 1998 and 2008 and subsequent laws supposedly have moved formally beyond ethnic demands by their legal recognition of the multicultural composition of the Ecuadorian nation. On 11 September 2007, nearly ten years after the first multicultural recognition, Correa's government approved the Ley Orgánica de las Instituciones Públicas de Pueblos Indígenas del Ecuador que se Autodefinen como Nacionalidades que se Autodefinen como Nacionalidades de Raíces Ancestrales (Organic Law of Public Institutions of Indigenous People of Ecuador Who Define Themselves as Nationalities with Ancestral Roots). This law provides for the legal recognition of the public bodies responsible for ethnic administration, such as the National Secretary of Intercultural Health, CODENPE, and FODEPI. These bodies have the authority to define the modalities for the incorporation of ethnic and cultural diversity and to refine strategies for the development of indigenous peoples. This was the first law to establish the legal and operational parameters for multicultural recognition since the 1998 constitution.[11]

Yet, after the ratification of the 2008 constitution, Correa's administration shifted to what Rene Baez, an activist with the Center for Alternative Thought of the Central University of Quito, defined as "a statist model of development that allows for no real popular participation. His actions are a violation of the new constitution" (in Burbach 2010). The seeds of such a shift were already inherent in his campaign promises. In the economic policies at the beginning of his mandate Correa addressed the ethnic problem within the general framework of the fight against poverty (e.g., the dignity bonus). This was consistent with the approach promoted by multilateral agencies such as the World Bank since the 1970s, and therefore maintained the same neoliberal emphasis on temporary measures for poverty reduction that precludes implementing structural changes to reduce socioeconomic inequality. At first, such measures paradoxically won the support of the indigenous electorate. Grassroots leaders in Chimborazo told me that people in the communities were asking for concrete measures to address their problems, particularly the lack of economic resources. One of the leaders, who heads a local nonprofit, spoke sympathetically: "They [indigenous people from communities] pay little attention these days to the ethnic discourse of the national leaders" (2007). He provided an example related to indigenous medicine: "How are they going to support those leaders who talk of indigenous medicine and shamans and curanderos and traditional stuff and then when they are sick go to the private hospital to get treated? They say they want to go to the private hospital, too." The disarticulation between the grassroots and their leadership appears profound and underscores a major problem. The policy of the "indio permitido" related to neoliberal multiculturalism created a real or perceived socioeconomic gap between the figure of the national leader in charge of designing policies on behalf of the indigenous sector and the figure of rural indigenous commoners afflicted by poverty and a paucity of resources and services. Accordingly, national leaders are perceived as betraying the very same culture they are claiming to revitalize and defend.

However, the ambiguity of Correa's position on the ethnic question and his shift to a "statist model" became evident in 2009 with a series of measures that profoundly alienated the indigenous sectors and social movements in the country. A series of unpopular measures led to a major uprising in September of the same year. A new mining law was passed, in 2009, that many activists and ecologists in Ecuador considered to have been "written in the neoliberal model" by favoring the privatization of natural resources extraction and ignoring environmental concerns. The protests that the law generated were dismissed by Correa as "Left and ecological infantilism" but led to the resignation of the then energy minister Alberto Acosta, who had been a staunch supporter of Correa (Burbach 2010). In January 2009 Correa closed many of the programs and projects run by CODENPE and eliminated its secretary, claiming that the council was malfunctioning and insolvent. In March 2009 the government issued Executive Decree 1585, which created the Subsecretary of Education for Intercultural Dialogue to replace the National Board of Bilingual Education (DINEIB), which had been created in 1992, after almost a decade of demands and claims by the indigenous movement. In a move similar to Gutiérrez's disempowering policy, Executive Decree 1585 placed bilingual education under the umbrella of education policies as promoted and controlled by the ministry, reducing if not eliminating the participation of indigenous linguists and administrators.[12] The decree generated debate about the solvency and qualifications of indigenous administrators who had governed the DINEIB in the past and those appointed by Correa to positions within the new subsecretary. In June 2009 the government issued Executive Decree 1780, which assigned to Catholic missions in the Amazon, the Galapagos, and the northern coastal province of Esmeraldas (where Afro-Ecuadorians are the majority) the task of "strengthening the culture and evangelization as well as promoting the integration into the socioeconomic life of the country of all the human groups that inhabit those territorial jurisdictions" (Decree 1780, Art. 1).[13] It also established that the designated missions, with the state's financial support, take charge of the creation of missionary schools for primary, bilingual, technological, and professional education in those same jurisdictions. These decrees were issued also in the context of other proposed reforms that addressed the adjudication and control of the water supply (and oil and mineral exploitation in indigenous territories), which were highly contested by large sectors of the Ecuadorian population, including but not limited to indigenous ones. The combination of such measures impaired the rapport between Correa and the indigenous movement, the latter providing a unified front in the rejection of all these measures and decrees. It organized an uprising in September 2009 and made the following demands: reinstitution of the DINEIB and CODENPE; suppression of Decree 1780, which was considered to be facilitating the recolonization of indigenous groups by the Catholic Church; and revision of the drafts of laws that regulated access to water, oil, and minerals. The uprising forced the government to initiate a dialogue with the indigenous movement, although relationships continued to be tense and confrontational.

According to these conflicting perceptions, the post-neoliberal moment forces both the state and the indigenous movement to rethink the significance of the politicization of ethnicity. Thus, the specificity of indigenous demands and the movement's political project remain as unclear as the ethnic policy adopted by the post-neoliberal state. In other words, the examination of indigenous politics highlights the question of whether and to what extent "diversity" in the postrecognition and post-neoliberal phase has the same potential for political and social change that it had until the 1990s. Problems of representativity, leadership, and the distance between movement leadership and indigenous populations have not been solved. Yet the friction and tension between Correa and the indigenous movement seems to have helped indigenous activists become more unified, with a renewed sense of purpose. In my interview with Nina Pacari in 2007 I mentioned a comment that I had heard, in the context of the fiftieth anniversary of the constitution of the Latin American Faculty of Social Sciences chapter in Ecuador (FLACSO-Ecuador), about "the ethnic not being in fashion anymore" (*lo étnico ya no está de moda*). Pacari looked at me and smiled, then said "If they really believe that, we will see. If they challenge us, we will be there." The uprising of September 2009 and the resolution taken in the extraordinary CONAIE summit on 26 February 2010, to call for a plurinational uprising against all the mentioned decrees and policies, confirmed her remark. Research will continue to illuminate how and the extent to which social movements made of myriad "singularities"—including indigenous movements—are successful in redefining citizen-state relationships in their efforts to build more just and equitable societies.

Appendix

Ecuadorian Official Laws and Documents

1990, August 23, Official Communiqué of the Presidency of the Republic ("Documento de la CONAIE es inacceptable pues busca crear un estado paraleleo")
1994 Law of Agrarian Development (Ley de Desarrollo Agrario)
1997 Law of Decentralization and Social Participation (Ley de Descentralización y Participación Social)
1998 Political Constitution of the Ecuadorian Republic
2001 VI Ecuador Poblational Census
2001 Organic Law of Municipal Regimes (Ley Orgánica de Regímenes Municipales)
2007 Organic Law of Public Institutions of Ecuadorian Indigenous Peoples which define themselves as Nationalities with Ancestral Roots (*Ley Orgánica de las Instituciones Públicas de Pueblos Indígenas del Ecuador que se Autodefinen como Nacionalidades de Raíces ancestrales*)
2008 Political Constitution of the Ecuadorian Republic
2009 March, Executive Decree 1585
2009 June, Executive Decree 1780
2009 Draft of Law of Water Supplies (Proyecto de Ley de Recursos Hídricos)

Primary Sources

IERAC Registry, Chimborazo Branch

Title Deeds N. 712
1989–1991 Land Claims, Canton of Alausí

Tixán Parish Civil Office

Archival records (not classified by date and not indexed)

Indigenous Documents

Inca Atahualpa

1992 Unión de Organizaciones Populares "Inca Atahualpa" (mimeo)
n.d. Proyecto de convenio de funcionamiento de los centros de cuidado diario infantil en las comunidades rurales de la matriz de Alausí y Tixan (mimeo)

Coordinadora Provincial del Levantamiento Indígena y Campesino de Chimborazo

1990 Demandas Organizaciones Indígenas y Campesinas de Chimborazo

CONAIE

1990 Mandato por la Defensa de la Vida y los Derechos de las Nacionalidades Indígenas
1992 Proyecto Político de la CONAIE
2010, 26 February Extraordinary Assembly Communiqué

MICH

1984 Movimiento Indígena de Chimborazo (mimeo)

OPIP

1990, August 5, Acuerdo sobre el derecho territorial de los pueblos Quichua, Shiwar y Achuar de la provincia de Pastaza a suscribirse con el estado Ecuatoriano (mimeo)
1990 Conferencia Continental "50 Años de Resistencia India Territorio y Recursos Naturales. Una Ponencia del Encuentro Continental Indígena en Ecuador"

Additionally, this book refers to internal documents by the Inca Atahualpa.

Newspapers

El Comercio

Política, "OXY: Palacio no irá a Miami por declaraciones de Jewell," 26 May 2006

Política, "Manifestantes piden para sus provincias UDS 1 por barril de crudo; Serrano recibió a los dirigentes," 9 May 2006

Política, "Pachakutik teme otro fracaso," 3 April 2006

Política, "El TLC, OXY y la asamblea hacen el milagro de resuscitar a la Conaie," 18 November 2005

Política, "Los Indígenas se pelean el CODENPE," 10 October 2003

Política, "Los Mestizos no estamos de acuerdo con que paralicen la ciudad," Enrique Proaño, 6 April 2006

Política, "Los Indígenas se pelean el CODENPE," 20 October 2003

El Espectador, 20 May 1993

El Hoy, *Política*, "CONAIE coincide en tildar de fracaso diálogo con Gobierno," 26 February 2010

Punto de Vista, n. 421, 11 June 1990; n. 459, 11 March 1991; n. 519, 18 May 1992; n. 520, 25 May 1992

Online

Llacta, http://www.llacta.org

Glossary

alcalde	Traditional Indian authority in hacienda times.
alzamentero	Quarrelsome, rebellious.
anejo	Old name for an indigenous settlement.
arranche	The stealing of a product, typically in a marketplace (i.e., a sack full of something). When the seller and the buyer do not reach an agreement on the price, the latter diverts the attention of the former and runs away with the product.
arrimado	Fig., "stuck on." It refers to members of huasipunguero households in hacienda times.
cabildo	Community council.
camari	A gift given by an inferior to his or her superior (Quichua).
comadre	Godmother.
compadre	Godfather.
chicha	Corn beer.
cholos	Indians who leave their community to live in a city.
gamonal	Very powerful, conservative, and repressive landlord.
gamonalismo	A political regime in which power is exercised by the local gamonal.
huasicama	Housekeeper who worked for the landlord during hacienda times (Quichua).
huasipungo	Vegetable plot assigned to indigenous peons working in the hacienda.
huasipunguero	Huasipungo holder.

jahuay	Traditional chant sung by Quichua farmers during the harvest.
mayoral	Indigenous leadsman.
mayordomo	Field foreman.
minga	Communal work that would benefit a group of people or the whole community (Quichua).
mishu	White people (Quichua). A scornful term.
mita	System of forced labor imposed on the indigenous population during the colonial and republican eras.
páramo	Moorland situated between 3,600 and 4,200 meters above sea level.
piareros	People in Tixán who rented their animals to carry hacienda products from the mountains to the railway station.
piqueros	People in Tixán who bought potato beds from the landowners and sold the products in the market.
primicias	Offers in products given by peasants to the local priest to thank God for the harvest.
priostazgo	Host obligations in a festival.
prioste	Host of a festival.
regidor	Staff holder. Traditional indigenous authority in charge of justice in hacienda times.
runa	People (Quichua). "Indians" use it to refer to themselves. It is used by white mestizos scornfully.
sitiajeros	"Indians" living outside the hacienda who used hacienda pasture for their own animals. In exchange they had to work for the landowner. This system of obligations was called *sitiaje*.
socorros	Subsistence doles.
taita	Father (Quichua). Used also to show respect.
tandanacui	Public meetings (Quichua).
terrateniente	Powerful owner of a big land estate.
yanaperos	"Indians" living outside the hacienda who used hacienda water and wood supplies and in exchange worked for the landowner (Quichua).

Acronyms

ATAMZICH	Association of Indigenous Workers of Indigenous Zula Mines in Chimborazo
CECI	Centre for International Studies and Cooperation (Canadian NGO)
CEDIS	Center of Social Studies and Diffusion (Ecuadorian NGO)
CONAIE	Confederation of Indigenous Nationalities of Ecuador
ECUARUNARI	Awakening of the Ecuadorian Indian
ERPE	Popular Radio Station of Ecuador
FEI	Ecuadorian Federation of Indians
FEINE	National Federation of Evangelical Indians
FENOCIN	National Federation of Indigenous and Black Peasant Organizations
FEPP	Ecuadorian Federation Populorum Progressio (Catholic NGO)
FODEPI	Fund for the Development of Indigenous Peoples
ID	Democratic Left
IERAC	Ecuadorian Institute of Agrarian Reform and Colonization
INEC	National Institute of Statistics and Census
INHERI	National Institute of Energy and Hydraulic Resources
MAG	Ministry of Agriculture and Cattle
MPD	Democratic Popular Movement
OPIP	Indigenous People from Pastaza Organization
SGO	second-grade organization

Notes

Introduction

1 Ecuador is divided administratively into regions (sierra, coast, and jungle) and provinces. Provinces are divided into *cantones* (cantons), which are subdivided into *parroquias* (parishes), the smallest administrative unit at the state level. In this context, parishes do not correspond to ecclesiastical units.

2 See Gustafson 2009; Postero 2007; Rappaport 2005; Speed 2008a.

3 Abercrombie 1991a; Abercrombie 1991b; Barre 1983; Botasso-Gnerre 1989; Maria Elena García 2005; Gustafson 2009; Mattiace 2003; Pallares 2002; Postero 2007; Rappaport 1994, 2005; Sawyer 2004; and Warren 1998, among others.

4 Colloredo-Mansfeld 1999; Kearney 1996; Lagos 1994; Meisch 2002; Orlove 2002; Weismantel 1988.

5 By modernization, I refer to state-led interventions that sought to foster national economic progress through infrastructural projects such as road construction and expansion of telecommunication and sanitation systems, as well as industrialization and agricultural mechanization.

6 Albó 1989; Pallares 2002; Postero 2007; Rappaport 1994; Sawyer 2004; Seligman 1995; Urban and Sherzer 1991; Kay Warren 1998; Yashar 2005.

7 For a more comprehensive discussion of the Ecuadorian case, see Whitten 2003.

8 See the discussion in Kay Warren 1998, 8–9.

9 Escobar and Alvarez 1992; Hale 1997; Melucci and Diani 1992.

10 Cervone 2002; Kearney 1996; Mattiace 2003; Pallares 2002; Postero 2007; Zamosc 2004.

11 Albó 2002; Gustafson 2002; Hale 2002; Hill and Santos-Granero 2002; June Nash 2001; Rappaport and Gow 2002; Rappaport 2007; Pallares 2002; Warren J. 2001; Warren and Jackson 2002; Kay Warren 1998; Postero and Zamosc 2004.

12 *Páramo* refers to moorland situated between 3,600 and 4,200 meters above sea level, while lower land communities range from 2,800 to mid-3,000 meters.

13 For other examples of this type of complexity in the Andean region and Mesoamerica, see Albó 2002, de la Peña 2002, Rappaport and Gow 2002.

14 The most representative national indigenous federation is CONAIE. The Federación de Indígenas Evangélicos (FEIN) and Federación Nacional de Organizaciones Campesinas Indígenas y Negras (FENOCIN) are two of the main national rivals of CONAIE. Although multiethnic, they are less representative than CONAIE. In 1996, the state created CODENPE (originally called COMPLADEIN), an agency dedicated to designing development policies for indigenous nationalities and the Afro-Ecuadorian population. It is administered by indigenous activists and intellectuals.

15 This operation interested mainly highland Quichua groups, since Amazonian groups have always been organized by their ethnicities (Shuar, Achuar, Quichua-Canelos, Huaorani, etc.).

16 See, for example, Salomon 1981a.

17 See Mattiace 2003; June Nash 2001; Pallares 2002; Kay Warren 1998. Jonathan Hill (1996) highlights this tendency to factionalism as distinctive of indigenous struggle to access dominant sources of power and wealth even in colonial times.

18 Coups with active indigenous participation took place in Ecuador in January 2000 and in Bolivia in February 2003. This type of contradiction can become highly problematic in the context of political violence, as was the case in Peru's dirty war of the 1980s, which involved the Shining Path (Sendero Luminoso) guerrilla movement and the counterinsurgency forces. As Orin Starn (1999) points out, the supposed beneficiaries of revolutionary change paradoxically became the principal victims of revolutionary violence.

19 Assies, van der Haar, and Hoekema 1999; Cervone 2003, 2007; Gustafson 2002; Dietz 2004; Mattiace 2003; Postero 2007; Zamosc 2004.

20 See discussion in Zamosc 2004, 132.

21 Nicola Foote (2006), among others, highlights that such dominant notions applied differently to highland and lowland indigenous cultures, according to which the latter were associated with wildness and savagery, rather than with tradition.

22 See, among others, Anderson 2009; Bigenho 2002; Cervone 2002; Fernando García 2002; Gustafson 2009; Martinez Novo 2005; Murray Li 2000; Povinelli 2002; Rappaport 2005; Speed 2008b; Warren and Jackson 2002.

23 See, among others, de la Cadena 2000; Greene 2009; Warren and Jackson 2005.

24 I do not depict politics as an arena of simple joyfulness and optimism. As Canetti (1984) evocatively describes, affective responses can also lead to destructive and damaging individual and collective reactions. Additionally, the values of everyday life also play a major role in contexts of acute political violence. In his poignant analysis of the impacts of the Shining Path's violence on indigenous communities in Ayacucho, Horacio Ponciano del Pino (1998) highlights the relevance that values rooted in everyday life, such as affective family

bonds and networks, have had in defining the disaffiliation of many indigenous peasants from the guerrilla movement's struggle. This disengagement had fatal consequences for many indigenous communities that were caught between two foes and decimated by counterinsurgency forces or by *senderistas*.

25 *Cabecilla* is a Spanish term for addressing de facto leaders.

26 INEC VI 2001. The census in Ecuador divides the population according to the area (urban or rural) and gender, and the percentages refer to the provinces, cantons, and parishes.

27 Five of the twenty-nine communities are situated in the western cordillera. Yuyaute Bajo and Llallanag are inhabited by the chagras or nonindigenous peasants. Sanganao is mixed with both chagras and Indians. The last two, Yuyaute Alto and San Juan de Tipín, are inhabited solely by Indians. All other communities and associations are situated in the eastern cordillera and are inhabited by Indians, except the chagra community of Pishillig San Francisco. Yanayacu is a chagra association, and Urtzuquís is a mixed community. The term *community* primarily refers to a settlement with houses and a community center, which includes at least a church, a school, and a small square. When they did not use the term *community*, indigenous people used *anejo* to refer to their settlements during the hacienda period, which were primarily defined by kinship and ethnicity. The term *comuna*, community, was established by the 1937 Law of Communes and Cooperatives and entered the local vocabulary in the 1960s, in the context of the agrarian reform struggles.

28 The overthrow of the elected president Abdalá Bucaram, in 1996, in which Indians and diverse social sectors actively participated, did not generate the same negative response.

29 See Cervone 2007; Gustafson 2009; Hale 2001, 2008a; Rappaport 2005; Smith 1991; Speed 2008b.

30 I conducted fieldwork from November 1991 to December 1993. During my subsequent residence in Ecuador, which lasted until December 1998, I visited Tixán in the summer of 1994 and the spring of 1997. I thus lived in Ecuador from 1991 to 1998.

31 *Gringo/a* is a pejorative term used in Ecuador to identify foreigners; the diminutive *gringuito/a* attempts to soften the negative and hostile connotations.

32 Gabriela Vargas-Cetina asks, "Are we to support notions of authenticity while we analyze the arbitrary basis on which it is established?" (2003, 11). Yet, as the analyses of indigenous politics by Rappaport (2005) and Speed (2008a) show, it is a matter of questioning the anthropological framework of analysis to better understand the process under examination and build knowledge in collaboration.

Chapter 1: The Time of the Lords

1 *Taita* is a Quichua word for *father* and is used to show respect to elders.

2 All quotes from interviews I conducted will be noted in this manner hereafter. Some of them were recorded while some others have been taken from my field-notes.

3 *Anejo* is the word that was used previously, according to the Law of Territorial Political Division of the Republic, issued in 1897 to define a rural demographic unit made up of separate *chozas* (huts) joined by paths and by a small square and a chapel. Another word was *caserio*, which differs from the anejo by not having paths or a square. The territorial aspect is implied in the word *parcialidad*, which referred to a minimum extension of cultivable land. It could include several anejos or caserios (see Costales and de Costales 1962, 71–73).

4 The Quichua word *yanapero* means a person who helps in work, yet connotes subordination. In the Inca empire, the yanaperos were separated from their families to work as servants for the Inca and other noble families (see Murra 1989, 238–44).

5 For example, this is the case of the highland hacienda Guachalá, bought by a German named Klinger in 1840, and the coastal property of Tinalandia, given in 1935 to the Russian Platonoff family by president Frederico Páez. The latter was 2,000 hectares taken from a territory occupied by Tsachilas, an indigenous nationality commonly known as Colorados.

6 In record no. 712, held in the archives of the Chimborazo branch of the former Ecuadorian Institute of Agrarian Reform and Colonization (IERAC).

7 Of the communities of the eastern range today, almost all were included in the perimeter of Moyocancha, with the exception of the sector of Pishillig and the anejos Gusniag, Chalahuán, Pueblo Viejo, and what is now known as Pachamama Chico. In record no. 712 (IERAC archives, Chimborazo), Pachamama Chico appears as part of a separate hacienda of the Salem family assigned to Julio Teodoro, and not as part of Moyocancha.

8 The inhabitants of Pachamama Chico assert that they have nothing to do with those of Pachamama Grande: "Ellos son otra gente" (They are other people).

9 For information on vertical control of different ecological niches, see Murra 1975.

10 Although the laws punishing debtors with imprisonment were formally abolished in 1918, the concertaje system continued until the agrarian reform of the 1960s.

11 Guachalá became a tourist resort, as did many other former haciendas throughout the highlands. Diego Bonifaz became the mayor of the canton Cayambe, where Guachalá is located, and is an active supporter of the indigenous movement.

12 Many landowning families throughout the highlands fit into this description,

for example, the former president of Ecuador Galo Plaza, of the Plaza-Laso owners of the hacienda Zuleta in Otavalo, and the former president of Ecuador Neptalí Bonifaz, of the Ascazubi-Bonifaz owners of Guachalá.

13 Hornado is a kind of roast pork that is popular in the highlands and especially in Riobamba.

14 The Misión Andina was a project designed by the United Nations in 1952 and run by states of the Andean region since the late 1950s to integrate indigenous peasants in the market economy.

15 I visited Don A. H. in his house in Riobamba in 1993. I was not authorized to use the tape recorder during this interview, so I took notes. The testimony presented here is rendered as accurately as possible.

16 The name *gamonal* is derived from *gamon* (asphodel), a parasitic plant that grows in rocky soil. The term was first used in Peru around 1860.

17 The name *piarero* derived from *piara*, which refers to a group of four donkeys.

18 Mestizaje as an ideological formation of hybridity has been adopted by the state in order to attempt to forge a homogenous image of the national population. Since I consider the term *mestizaje* and the correlated mestizo identities to be ideological labels rather than analytical categories, in this text I use the more neutral *nonindigenous* as a general descriptive term to identify those who do not consider themselves and are not considered by others to be indigenous.

19 The Quichua word *camari* refers to a gift made in the context of asymmetric reciprocity by an inferior to a superior or by someone who is in the position of disadvantage with respect to the one who receives it. The equivalent in the context of symmetric reciprocity is the *jocha*. On reciprocity in the Andean world, see Alberti and Mayer 1974.

20 The word *llucho* comes from Quichua and means nude, very poor. *Callomicuc* and *rocoto* are adaptations between the two languages; the former means "eater of *callos*" referring to the pork innards. *Rocoto* is a corruption of Quichua and refers to a variety of chilli (Capiscum Violaceum H.). *Mitayo* refers to the Indians who had to respect forced labor obligations (mitas) and *traposo* means dressed in torn and dirty cloths. Documentation in the parish civil office archive contains reports of quarrels among townsfolk, dated between 1920s and 1940s, that were motivated by insulting and disrespectful exchanges between people perceived to be of different rank. Among the most common insults cited in the claims appeared words such as *chagra*, *rocoto*, *indio*.

21 In Sanganao, the chagras lived in their own anejo. After the agrarian reform, Sanganao became a mixed chagra-Indian community.

22 According to records, Julio Teodoro Salem took possession of the area's two haciendas in 1935, and the lawsuit was filed in 1937.

23 My reconstruction of the process of mobilization in Tixán is based on several interviews I conducted with elders from the communities of La Pacifica, La Merced, Pachagsí, Yacupungo, and Pachamama.

24 My reconstruction of Ambrosio Laso's struggle is primarily based on several in-depth interviews I conducted with Taita Pedro Marcatoma. Taita Pedro is no longer alive, but a more extensive text of these interviews was published in *Pueblos Indígenas y Educación* 24 (1992): 39–62.
25 For a discussion of types of haciendas and their processes of dissolution, see Inter-American Committee for Agricultural Development 1965 and Guerrero 1991a.
26 A deliberation of *reversión* would give land to commoners without requesting any payment, whereas *expropiación* would request a payment fixed by IERAC authorities based on the property's estimated value.
27 This refers to the properties of the Asistencia Pública, which became property of the state after the Liberal Revolution (led by Eloy Alfaro at the beginning of the twentieth century) as a result of expropriation of church properties, which had been rented out to private individuals (arrendatarios).
28 See Prieto 1980.
29 See chapter 4.
30 Among the measures taken to protect the indigenous population were the 1918 legislation abolishing debt peonage and imprisonment and the ministerial decrees of 1923 that eliminated taxes on rural property.
31 I analyze these conflicts in chapter 4.
32 Pishillig San Francisco, Urtzuquís, Pishillig Yacupungo, and the Farm Worker's Association of Yanayacu.
33 Currently named La Merced, La Pacífica, and Pachagsí, part of the haciendas of La Pacífica, San Carlos, and Ermita, belonging to Pacífica Salem, Mercedes Salem, and Julia Salem, respectively. The people of the Pachagsí community worked as sharecroppers on Salem property and on the land of some tixaneños.
34 Throughout the country, the plots given to the huasipungueros as compensation tended to be the worst and least productive land of the haciendas (Pallares 2002).

Chapter 2: Tixán Becomes Modern

1 According to archival records in the Tixán parish civil office, members of the Salem family had contracted debts with the Banco Provincial de Chimborazo for the purchase of luxury goods. In 1963 the bank took legal action against José Antonio Calderón Salem and Angel Banderas Salem, and embargoed nine stacks of threshed barley. According to record no. 712 of the IERAC archives in Chimborazo, when Rosa Matilde Salem died, her properties were divided between her husband and her six legitimate children, but all these properties were already mortgaged to the Banco Provincial de Chimborazo. Due to recurring debts, Angel Banderas had to face foreclosure.
2 For the dynamics of land acquisition, see chapter 4.
3 My reconstruction of the local process of change is based on testimonial ac-

counts of the postreform period by indigenous and nonindigenous elders, the parish priest, and other actors involved in that process.

4 The station in Tixán was closed because landslides and falling rock often resulted in the suspension of the service. Today the rail line between Quito and Cuenca is primarily a tourist attraction (see Clark 1998).

5 As I explain in chapter 3, compadrazgo relations were established between two families on the occasion of a baby's baptism and of a marriage.

6 See chapter 5.

7 Sharecropping relationships regulated access to resources for landless comuneros within indigenous communities. In the case of indigenous communities with no communal lands, such as Gusniag and Chalahuán, sharecropping relationships involved indigenous workers and townsfolk.

8 I explain below that in the case of the chagras, both class and social status are essential to the whitening of their racial identity.

9 During the hacienda period, the bulls were given by the landowner.

10 Unlike in Bolivia and Colombia, where indigenous groups based their land-rights claims on written land titles even during the colonial period, in Ecuador there was a lamentable absence of written documentation that indigenous people could use for their land-rights claims. As a result, those anejos that had legal recognition under the 1937 legislation could not claim any specific tract of land as their patrimony.

11 This form of reciprocity obliges whoever receives it to return it at some future time. With both the formal request for help and the actual realization of the work, the person requesting the help must provide food and drink.

12 Many young men migrate to the coast during the local harvest season or to the cities, especially to Quito and Guayaquil, where they work primarily as masons.

13 Indigenous activists attribute to urbanization the spread of STDs and domestic abuse in their societies, which in turn affected women.

14 Most of the staff working in the nurseries as teachers, cooks, and managers were women. For many indigenous women, this experience in nurseries functioned as a structural opening toward their preparation to become leaders or by which they gained access to further education, paid labor, and even the market economy (see CEPLAES 1998).

15 Even if market-oriented monoculture did not eliminate crop diversification, traditional crops not requested on the market such as the melloco and oca became rare and available almost exclusively for household subsistence. The Ecuadorian NGO Center of Social Study and Communication (CEDIS) implemented two productive agricultural projects with Canadian funds on behalf of the Inca Atahualpa that addressed monoculture and deforestation, the area's leading problems. For a discussion on the racial implications of food and agricultural production see Weismantel 1988.

16 For a discussion of similar impacts of agrarian reform and state-led modernization in Bolivia, see Lagos 1994.

17 For a thorough discussion on the Catholic Church in Latin America and its effects in the Andean region, see Orta 2004.

18 The Shuar Federation is one the first grassroots indigenous federations based on ethnic identity, and was created with the active participation of Salesian missionaries, in 1968.

19 In Tixán, *tierras de arriba* and *tierras de abajo* refer, respectively, to areas that are located in the páramo between 3,600 and 4,200 meters and to the more temperate ecosystems between 3,500 and 2,800 meters. The parish capital is located at 2,900 meters. This distinction also connotes differences in livelihood, culture, and ethnicity. Pastoralism is the principal productive activity in the páramo, and páramo people are considered brave and more traditional.

20 As chroniclers of the precolonial period have shown, in the Andean indigenous world the rivalry between upper and lower groups addressed by the Inca Atahualpa's formation case is not new (see Duviols 1973; Bouysse-Cassagne, Cereceda, Harris, and Platt 1987; Molina 1989). Tristan Platt (1986a, 1987c) has amply demonstrated that the political structure of Andean societies responds to a logical division into moieties, *hanan* and *urin*, literally meaning "up" and "down," which have their symbolic expression in complementary but not necessarily symmetric pairs of opposites (such as masculine and feminine, left and right).

21 I offer a more detailed explanation of this action in chapter 5.

22 Father Torres's participation in this process is examined in greater detail in chapter 6 with the discussion of the harvest festival.

Chapter 3: Invisible Victories

1 This chapter is based on two years of participant observation during which I interacted with indigenous people, chagras, and tixaneños and received their comments and points of view as part of our everyday conversations.

2 De Certeau 1988; Eriksen 1992; Hanchard 2006; Kelley 1994; Scott 1985; Scott 1992.

3 García and Chávez 2004; Pallares 2002; Postero 2007; Rappaport 1990, 2005.

4 The meaning of the Quichua term *ñaupa* is complex; it means the one who leads by walking both in front and behind. For the Quichuas, the past is both behind and ahead of human beings to guide them.

5 As Raúl Prada Alcoreza points out, memory "is an accumulative return . . . a successive analogous recovering of collective experiences. . . . ; but memories are indeed juxtaposed" (1992, 69, 71).

6 The progressive arm of the Catholic Church used the image of awakening to justify political mobilization of indigenous peasants. The name of the first highland regional federation founded in 1976, ECUARUNARI is an acronym for "the awakening of the Ecuadorian Indian." See discussion in Pallares 2002.

7 See the discussion of Wolf in Thurner 1993, 41.
8 See Burga 1988; Flores Galindo 1987; Ossio 1973.
9 See chapter 6.
10 I understand the term "historic accumulation" not as a continuity of practices, but rather as the continuity of a habitus of defensive attitudes that informs the sociality of interethnic conflict (Ramón Valarezo 1990, 41).
11 The rocola is where tixaneño men gathered to drink, play cards, and listen to *pasillo* (a rhythm derived from the bolero). In urban settings, rocolas are frequented by the working class; they are also widespread in the rural areas.
12 For a discussion on the politics of aversion and black politics in the United States, see Hanchard 2006.
13 The 1990 uprising meant the official confirmation of indigenous activism at the national level (see chapter 4).
14 One of the claims presented by the Movimiento Indígena de Chimborazo (MICH) to the provincial authorities during the 1990 uprising demanded adherence to established transportation fares.
15 Such as, for example, the Saraguros, Otavaleños, Salasacas, and Chibuleos in other provinces, and the Puruhaes in Cacha, a northern area of the province of Chimborazo.
16 See discussion on language in chapter 5.
17 The rate of interethnic compadrazgo involving chagras with either tixaneños or Indians did not increase.
18 In chapter 4 I examine the substantial impact of these labor relations on the formation of social hierarchies within indigenous and chagra communities.
19 The comedor project, proposed by a Canadian volunteer, Ameliè, and endorsed by the Inca Atahualpa, was financed by INSOTEC, an Ecuadorian institution that provides financial support to small businesses.
20 I analyze this tournament further in chapter 6.

Chapter 4: When the Hills Turned Red

1 As I analyze later, the demand for land formulated nationally by lowlands indigenous activists was expressed in terms of territoriality, which generated debate among state representatives about the constitutionality of such a demand.
2 The agrarian laws also contributed to the process of formation of indigenous organizations. According to the law, only legalized first-grade organizations (communities) or second-grade organizations (associations, cooperatives, or grassroots organizations) could claim hacienda lands.
3 Loans were provided by Banco de Fomento and FODERUMA.
4 Income from extrarural activities sustained household economies, providing funds for children's education, healthcare, and purchases of property.

5 Of the 59 analyzed cases, 33 were still unsolved in 1991. Of the remaining 26 cases, only 4 were resolved with agreement acts in favor of the indigenous plaintiffs (*Acta Transactional*).

6 For the analysis of these cases, I took into account the official documents relevant to the procedures and testimony from members of the communities involved in the disputes.

7 Pertinent documentation for the Pomacocho case was not available from IERAC; I derived information for this case from the documentation gathered by the Inca Atahualpa. Since the property was still occupied at the time of my fieldwork, and due to the difficult situation, I was not able to interview those directly involved belonging to the Pomacocho Workers Association.

8 This was confirmed by testimony and by the IERAC report.

9 This mechanism of solidarity is similar to the one reported in the uprisings that took place over the centuries and drew hundreds of Andean indigenous people together around a common cause. Major uprisings—including the Túpac Amaru rebellion in Peru, in 1781, and the Fernando Daquilema rebellion in Yaruqui, in 1871, in Chimborazo Province—contained messianic elements that proved to be strongly cohesive. For the Ecuadorian case, see Moreno Yánez 1985.

10 The various reasons and causes of such problems are beyond the scope of my discussion. According to some NGO personnel, this type of problem did not always occur due to the dishonesty of indigenous representatives. Requirements of funding agencies were often unrealistic and not based on the reality of indigenous communities. Furthermore, at the onset, indigenous commoners were not experienced with accounting and project management, making it difficult to meet expectations regarding financial reporting.

11 See for example Gow 1973; Izco 1991; Lentz 1986; Platt 1986a, 1987c; Seligman 1991.

12 Priostazgo and ritual obligations, the "pasar fiestas," are also relevant among nonindigenous people as a mechanism for building political prestige. By "good," Taita A. V. means "generous."

13 A cabildo is comprised of five authority figures: president, vice president, secretary, treasurer, and at least one substitute, *vocal*. All of them are elected by the community members every two years.

14 Such as carrying the baton (*vara*), an insignia of traditional leadership.

15 In the hacienda period, the arrimados had a lesser status than did huasipungueros, and agrarian reform did not accord them rights or access to land.

16 In 2002 A. L. realized one of his dreams; he obtained funds from the International Canadian Cooperative to open a local radio station named Zotaurko and has become its sole director.

17 See Korovkin 1997; Manning Nash 1989.

18 The heading on this page translates as One thought! One heart! One fist! This was the motto of the 1990 uprising.

19 See *Sismo étnico en el Ecuador* (CEDIME 1993), *La revolución del Arco Iris* (Bolivar Torres 1993).

20 Cecilia Chacón Castillo, *El Día*, 9 June 1990. This resonates with the image of indigenous awakening adopted by the regional organization ECUARUNARI, whose name itself means "the awakening of the Ecuadorian Indian."

21 Ileana Almeida 1991, 99; Macas 1991, 17; Perez 1991, 37; Pacari 1993, 113.

22 See articles in *Kipu* 1990.

23 The only indigenous organizations that did not participate in the uprising were evangelic federations, which at the national level represent a small minority within the indigenous movement. They sided with the military against the rebellion.

24 Hale (1994) applies the concept of contradictory consciousness, derived from Antonio Gramsci, to his analysis of revolutionary Nicaragua and the antirevolutionary alignment of Miskitu Indians.

25 "Documento de la CONAIE es inacceptable pues busca crear un estado paraleleo," 23 August 1990, official communiqué of the Presidency of the Republic in Kipu 15, 56.

26 See also Zamosc 1994.

27 Governor, prefect, major, provincial deputy, health provincial chief, provincial chief of the ministry of agriculture, district chief of the National Institute of Energy and Hydraulic Resources (INHERI), provincial director of the ministry of social welfare, representative of the fourth zone of the ministry of public work, and bishop. INHERI is responsible for irrigation waterways and adjudication of water flowing in the countryside.

28 A detailed discussion of development policies and indigenous communities is beyond the scope of this book. With the term *development*, I refer to a body of ideological constructs and practices around matters of economic and social changes that have been sponsored by states and multilateral agencies ever since the post–Second World War period and the end of historical colonial regimes of the twentieth century. According to this discourse, the world was divided into First, Second, and Third World countries, more recently renamed as developed and developing countries, and international funds (whether proceeding from industrialized countries or multilateral agencies such as the International Monetary Fund) have been channeled toward developing countries in order to promote their economic and social advancement. Nongovernmental organizations have played a pivotal role in the administration of those funds and more recently in the definition of development policies and trends which have been constantly redefined over the decades. For more details on the debate around development discourses, see Bretón 2000; Escobar and Alvarez 1992; Gardener and Lewis 1996; Gupta 1998; and Lewis and Wallace 2000, among others.

Chapter 5: Words and Scars

1 See discussion on constitutional reforms in chapter 7. See also Goodale 2008; Van Cott 2000; Yrigoyen 2004.

2 For the Ecuadorian case, see Fernando García 2002; García and Chávez 2004; Iturralde 1993; Wray 1993.

3 Fernández Osco 2000; Goodale 2006a; Poole and Das 2004; Poole 2006; Rappaport 2005.

4 These are two chagra communities, Pishillig San Francisco and Urtzuquís; one indigenous community, Pishillig Chico Yacupungo; and one agricultural workers' association, called Yanayacu and consisting mainly of chagras. According to some elders from Yacupungo, in 1984 they decided to separate due to the mistreatment and arrogance of the chagras of the locality.

5 In Pachamama Chico, for example, Taita E. V., who was not a member of the cabildo, still carried the baton, the traditional insignia of power, and was always consulted in disputes. He became president of the Inca Atahualpa in 1993.

6 As explained before, *camari* refers to a gift made in the context of asymmetric reciprocity by an inferior to a superior. The asymmetry can be determined by a difference in social status or simply by the momentarily disadvantageous position of the gift-giver.

7 For other cases of indigenous justice among Quichuas, see Fernando García 2002.

8 Since the opening of the casa comunal, in 1996, the Inca Atahualpa's previous headquarters remained as a mill and storage place.

9 "At that time Indians were very brutish. They did not know how to read and write and understood very little Spanish, only Quichua" (Don D. B., 1992).

10 In daily life, written messages never work: they never reach their destination or at least are never taken into account. Radio broadcast is used instead and is a widespread means of communication.

11 I discuss some of the impacts of these changes in chapter 4, in relation to the formation of a new modern indigenous leadership.

12 Tinterillos were ambiguous characters, very common in rural towns. Although they did not have law degrees, they acted as lawyers and wrote *actas* (claims and documents) for illiterate indigenous people, over which their customers had no control.

13 The tension involved the hostility shown by the vice president and secretary toward the president because of his illiteracy.

14 A group of volunteers including myself formed the "equipo técnico." Luc and Amelié were volunteers from Quebec working with the Inca Atahualpa on two different projects (a irrigation system and early childhood care). Javier worked with the Inca Atahualpa on other productive projects on behalf on the Ecuadorian NGO CEDIS. Alfonso was an agronomy student working as a volunteer with the organization.

15 The four indigenous SGOs in the canton of Alausí at the time were the Inca Atahualpa; the ATAMZICH; the Federation of Indian Communities of Achupallas, from Achupallas parish; and the General Rumiñahui Indian Federation, from Alausí. Of these, the oldest is the Achupallas Federation. The others were created later to provide for the basic needs of the communities in the area. The ATAMZICH and the Inca Atahualpa had the highest number of affiliated communities and the most prestige. The fame of the Inca Atahualpa crossed provincial ethnic borders, having acquired two indigenous communities from the southern province of Cañar as affiliates.
16 See chapter 2, on the arriba and abajo rivalry.
17 The interrogations were filmed to provide indisputable evidence of the propriety of the Inca Atahualpa's proceedings.
18 In present times, an indigenous justice principle of supposed Incaic origin and widespread among the Quichua population is "Don't be a thief, don't be lazy, don't be a liar" (*Ama shua, ama quilla, ama llulla*), which references the three most common offenses.
19 It seems that this particular measure is adopted in major cases as an ultimate exemplary punishment. It had once been used in the punishment of the chagra cattle thieves.
20 Punishment became public only when one of the four competing organizations first challenged the legitimacy of the Inca Atahualpa. Public performance of justice thus served to retell the truth in order to extend the jurisdiction of the challenging organization.
21 See Goodale 2006a, 2008; Harris 1996; Poole and Das 2004; de Sousa Santos 1995.
22 The 1998 and the 2008 constitutions recognize the legitimacy of traditional authorities without defining the areas in which they are allowed to operate, other than simply mentioning internal cases, that is, cases at the community level.

Chapter 6: Celebrating Diversity

1 Benavides 1989; Rasnake 1988. For San Juan festivals, celebrations of patron saints, the Mama Negra fest in Cotopaxi Province, and the Yumbada in Pichincha Province in Ecuador see Crain 1989; Crespi 1981; Guerrero 1991b; Guerrero Arias 1993; Salomon 1981a; Thurner 1993; and Weismantel 2003.
2 My discussion of the festival focuses on the first one I attended, in 1992, a celebration that the Inca Atahualpa leaders at the time considered to be the most beautiful they had ever organized. I also attended the 1993 and 1994 celebrations and discuss the changes that were incorporated from year to year.
3 Judges and prize donors were recruited from among locally prominent people, such as members of NGOs that worked with the Inca Atahualpa, and cantonal and parish authorities.
4 Colchas are colorful textile compositions, embroidered on velvet, that depict

bullfighting. Their beauty is in the selection of vivid colors and shining stones used in the decoration. Colchas are tied to the bulls' backs and are won by the bullfighters who are able to pull them off the animals. The alcancías are offerings given to all festival participants. They can be, for example, souvenirs, drinks, or anything else that can be distributed or thrown to persons in the streets or neighbors in the district. In the case of the harvest festival, they are thrown from the arena to the spectators before the bullfighting begins. According to testimonies, chicha's ceremonial use in rituals has been replaced by trago, or *aguardiente* (sugarcane alcohol) consumption, while chicha is prepared only for special occasions such as Carnival and the harvest festival. Canelazo, a hot drink made of aguardiente, cinnamon tea, lemon, and sugar, was drunk publicly and privately during town festivals. The word *trago* can also refer to any alcoholic drink.

5 Whether performed on household or collective lands, mingas always have a sponsor or host who offers food and drink to the workers. The landowner was the host during the hacienda times.

6 In Quichua the word *paqui* refers to something broken. In Patricio Guerrero Arias's interpretation, the paqui, as leader of the jahuay, "breaks" the silence (1994, 31).

7 For a visual reference of jahuay chanting in Chimborazo see, "Música tradicional de la provincia de Chimborazo, Ecuador," http://www.youtube.com/watch?v=LuMvd2GC058/.

8 Chimborazo and Carihuairazo are the two sacred, snow-covered volcanoes in the province.

9 From *punta* (first) and *purij* (the noun form of the verb *purina*, "to walk").

10 The zamarro is worn mostly in the páramo for riding horses and for protection against the cold. In everyday life, it is also worn by chagras.

11 In chapter 3 I explained how this practice functioned as a weapon of the weak in hacienda times, when workers often stole sheaves, risking punishment by tight-fisted landowners.

12 Or *punllay*, in the local Tixán variant, from the verb *pugllana*, which means "to play."

13 For a discussion of chagra identity, see Cervone 2010.

14 "Ñucanchic Pachamamamanta, Pachmama sinchi runacuna, así cantamos y saludamos las communidades." In Ecuador to greet implies acknowledgment; if one is not greeted, it means that his or her presence has not been recognized. Greetings even by acquaintances are important to Quichuas as a sign of respect.

15 On many occasions, white townsfolk expressed their disappointment in the current policy of international cooperation. They felt that only "Indians" received attention from international agencies while local nonindigenous people were neglected.

16 Dedication to the indigenous cause earned Father Torres many enemies among

white mestizos in town and throughout the entire province. Military and local authorities considered him a subversive.

17 The criteria on which the Quichuas base their differences are linguistic, evidenced by their different accents and by their dress, its color more than its form.

18 This type of dance was popular especially among chagras and tixaneños. Popular verbenas, in fact, were one of the main events during the town festivals for San Juan, although on those occasions they had live bands and a *disco móvil* (a disc jockey with equipment).

Chapter 7: Beyond Recognition

1 Although this chapter examines the process of indigenous political empowerment nationally until the political "crisis" that followed the Lucio Gutiérrez debacle (or the "gutierrazo"), the conclusion offers an update about the current movement under Correa's mandate.

2 Connolly 1996; Goldberg 1995; Gordon and Newfield 1996; Hale 2002, 2005; Kymlicka 1995; Postero 2007; Rappaport 2005; Taylor 1994; I. Young 1996; Žižek 1997.

3 The term multiculturalism has found widespread usage in social-science discourse in Australia and the Americas. The term also has been used in many European countries to characterize changes ensuing from the extensive immigration that started in the 1980s.

4 In the United States, discussions on multiculturalism have emphasized the role that formal education has in fostering a profound and non-ethnocentric understanding of cultural diversity. A progressive understanding of multiculturalism has promoted curricular reforms in schools and colleges that since the late 1980s have introduced new literary and artistic forms and traditions other than the Judeo-Christian (see Goldberg 1995).

5 Charles Hale calls the intervention of Latin American states in this process "neoliberal multiculturalism" (Hale 2005).

6 I refer here to the protests that led to the fall of Presidents Bucaram (1997), Mahuad (2001), and Gutiérrez (2005) in Ecuador, and of President Sánchez de Lozada (2003) in Bolivia. For a detailed analysis of social protest in Bolivia, see Postero 2007.

7 Zamosc (2004) argues that recent indigenous mobilization in Ecuador, which started in 2000, has brought back to the fore the importance of class in the analysis of indigenous politics.

8 I disagree with interpretations that attributed this lack of vision to the ethnic dimension of indigenous politics (Santana 2004; V. José Almeida 2005).

9 For a more detailed discussion of this process, see Van Cott 2005.

10 The establishment of the council was the result of intense debate between indigenous activists, mostly of CONAIE, and the cabinet of Abdalá Bucaram.

Joanne Rappaport (2002) underscores the ambiguity of being both within and outside the state structure in the case of the ethnic movement in Colombia. In 1998, as result of a restructuring process pushed by indigenous leaders affiliated with CONAIE, the national council changed its name to Consejo de Desarrollo de las Nacionalidades y Pueblos del Ecuador (CODENPE).

11 1998 Political Constitution of the Ecuadorian Republic, title VIII, chap. 1, art. 191, emphasis added.

12 A comparable understanding of interculturalidad is expressed by indigenous intellectuals in Colombia (see Rappaport 2005).

13 This phase of politicization of ethnic identity pushed scholars to develop new interpretative frameworks to analyze political mobilizations, which in turn led to the formulation of the politics of identity and the new social movements frameworks that often highlighted the empowering potential that ethnic identity had for minority groups struggling for their rights (Escobar and Alvarez 1992; Urban and Sherzer 1991). Neither scholars nor activists at that time could have clearly foreseen the dilemmas that those political processes would later pose.

14 Becker 2008; Clark and Becker 2007; Mattiace 2003; Nash 2001; Pallares 2002; Postero 2007; Rappaport 2005; Postero and Zamosc 2004.

15 The Ecuadorian case parallels those of aboriginal mobilizations in Canada, New Zealand, and Australia.

16 An entity ascribed to the presidency of the republic, CONAM is in charge of the modernization of the Ecuadorian state. It is the principal entity promoting the privatization and deregulation of state-owned companies. During this period, modernization and decentralization initiatives were supported and funded by the Inter-American Development Bank. The Law of Modernization of the State of 1993 prepared the ground for decentralizing policies.

17 Data on indigenous alcaldías were collected in 1996 for a consultancy on indigenous municipalities, which I conducted on behalf of the Inter-American Development Bank. Data from Huamboya were collected by Carlos Viteri Gualinga. The data on Suscal, however, were gathered in 1997 in the context of a project on indigenous female leadership, which I coordinated for CEPLAS.

18 Before the law of decentralization was passed, members of the *juntas parroquiales* were nominated locally. After the law was passed, they came to be elected via administrative elections. The 1998 constitution also disposed the abolition of the figure of the teniente político by transferring its functions to the junta and substituting for it a justice of the peace. Yet, as declared in the Organic Law of Municipal Regimes of 2001 and reiterated in the new 2008 constitution, in practice the abolition of the teniente político cannot be enforced until the promulgation of a law which regulates the attribution of the justice of the peace.

19 New laws were issued in 2010, the Organic Law of Citizen Participation (Ley Orgánica de Participación Ciudadana) and the Organic Code of Territorial

Organization (Código Orgánico de Organización Territorial), which regulate forms of civil society's participation in local administrations and organize the local territory. Ethnic and cultural diversity is transversally incorporated in both these laws. In my last trip to Tixán in June of 2011, indigenous activists were working with the local junta in order to design viable local models for these forms of participation and territorial jurisdictions. Therefore, new forms of administration and participation are a work in progress.

20 Although beyond the scope of this book, such ecological concerns also relate to the process of consolidation of transnational indigenous politics, what Goodale (2006b) defines as indigenous cosmopolitanism (see also Brysk 2000; Selverston-Scher 2001).

21 The political alliance with Lucio Gutierrez, which I discuss later, is an example of this political expansion.

22 See Executive Decree 1833-A, *Official Bulletin* No. 378, 15 July 2004.

23 Established in 1968, FENOCIN was intended primarily to be a national federation of peasants, but it later incorporated the ethnic component to acknowledge the cultural specificity of indigenous peasants. Established in 1989, FEINE was specifically an indigenous federation of evangelical organizations. In chapter 4 I discuss the extent to which evangelical indigenous forces opposed the 1990 levantamiento and often worked to undermine CONAIE's political actions.

24 Based on data that I collected in 1998 from conversations with indigenous activists from different regional organizations. The reconfiguration of the CONAIE board by nationality had already been discussed at that time.

25 "Los indígenas se pelean el CODENPE," *El Comercio*, 20 October 2003.

26 "TLC: Oxy y la asamblea hacen el milagro de resuscitar a la Conaie," *El Comercio*, 18 November 2005.

27 "Movilización nacional en defensa de la vida: ¡Sí a la vida! ¡No al TLC! ¡Fuera Oxy! ¡No al plan Colombia!," *Llacta!*, March 2006, http://www.llacta.org.

28 "Los Mestizos no estamos de acuerdo con que paralicen la ciudad: Enrique Proaño," *El Comercio*, 6 April 2006.

29 "Manifestantes piden para sus provincias UDS 1 por barril de crudo: Serrano recibió a los dirigentes," *El Comercio*, 9 May 2006.

30 In February 2006, EnCana sold its rights to the Chinese oil company Andes Petroleum.

31 See "Oxy: Palacio no irá a Miami por declaraciones de Jewell," *El Comercio*, 26 May 2006.

32 "Pachakutik teme otro fracaso," *El Comercio*, 3 April 2006.

33 See chapters 2 and 3.

34 See interview, Maldonado 2003.

Conclusion

1 The other cantonal federations are also still active, although some have changed their names. A new organization was formed in 2003 with the name of Union of Organizations INDAÑAN.

2 Yet it provided training, and with the help of PRODEPINE, many of the men and women who were involved in the project opened saving accounts that still assist them in managing the cash they need for their wool production.

3 The administrative level that formerly was called canton is now called municipality; for example, the canton of Alausí is now the municipality of San Pedro de Alausí.

4 The return of the jahuay celebration within the harvest festival is part of this same process.

5 Puruhaes, Cachas, Calpis, Achambas, Columbis, Cubijies, Guanandus, Guanus, Guamotes, Licanis, Lictus, Liribamba, Muyucanchas, Ucputis, Tiquizambis, Pallatangas, Pangores, Penipis, Pungalaes, Punies, Quimiaces, Tiucajas, Ilapos, Zibambis, Cicalpas, and Zicaos. See "Los 22 Pueblos de la Nacionalidad Puruhá piden la inmediata derogatoria del Decreto 1833-A," *Llacta!*, 5 August 2004, http://www.llacta.org.

6 Class-based movements, for example, have been fragmented around different political ideologies. I am thinking here of the Italian labor movement in which ideological distinctions informed the creation of multiple workers unions and federations (Italian General Confederation of Labor, Italian Confederation of Labor Unions, and Italian Union of Labor, respectively affiliated to the Communist Party, the Socialist Party, and the Christian Democrat Party).

7 Other people from NGOs who have been working with the Inca Atahualpa for a long time have expressed the same perplexity that A. L. had.

8 According to A. L., local nonindigenous small farmers also participated in the protest, while nonindigenous urban residents of Riobamba did not.

9 The rental fee ranges from $10 to $12 per hour.

10 See, among others, Escobar and Alvarez 1992; Hooker 2005; Mattiace 2003; Pallares 2002; Postero 2007; Zamosc 2004.

11 This law is no longer in force. It has been replaced by new laws issued between 2009 and 2010 that have incorporated the multicultural recognition of the 2008 constitution (see for example the Organic Law of Citizen Participation of April 2010 and the Organic Code of Judicial Function of March of 2009).

12 See Executive Decree 1585, published in *Official Bulletin* No. 539 of 3 March 2009.

13 See Executive Decree 1780, published in *Official Bulletin* No. 620 of 25 June 2009.

References

Abercrombie, Thomas. 1991a. "Articulación doble y etnogénesis." *Reproducción y Transformación de las Sociedades Andinas*, vol. 1, ed. Segundo Moreno and Frank Salomon, 197–212. Quito: Abya-Yala.

———. 1991b. "To Be Indian, to Be Bolivian: 'Ethnic' and 'National' Discourses of Identity." *Nation-States and Indians in Latin America*, ed. Greg Urban and Joel Sherzer, 95–130. Austin: University of Texas Press.

Aguirre, Carlos, and Charles Walker, eds. 1990. *Bandoleros, abigeos y montoneros: Criminalidad y violencia en el Perú, Siglos XVIII–XX*. Lima: Instituto de Apoyo Agrario.

Alberti, Giorgio, and Enrique Mayer, eds. 1974. *Reprocidad e intercambio en los Andes Peruanos*. Lima: Instituto de Estudios Peruanos.

Albó, Xavier. 2002. "Bolivia: From Indian and Campesino Leaders to Councillors and Parliamentary Deputies." *Multiculturalism in Latin America, Indigenous Rights, Diversity, and Democracy*, ed. Rachel Sieder, 74–102. London: Palgrave.

———. 1989. *Para comprender las culturas rurales en Bolivia*. La Paz: MEC.

Almeida, Ileana. 1991. "El movimiento indígena en la ideología de los sectores dominantes Hispano-Ecuatorianos." *Indios*, by ILDIS, 293–318. Quito: ILDIS / El Duende / Abya-Yala.

Almeida, Ileana, and Nidia Arrobo Rodas, eds. 1998. *En defensa del pluralismo y la igualdad: Los derechos de los pueblos indios y el estado*. Quito: Abya-Yala.

Almeida, V. José. 2005. "The Ecuadorian Indigenous Movement and the Gutiérrez Regime: The Traps of Multiculturalism." *Political and Legal Anthropological Review* 28.1: 93–111.

———. 1993. "El levantamiento indígena como momento constitutivo nacional." *Sismo etnico en el Ecuador*, by CEDIME, 7–28. Quito: CEDIME / Abya-Yala.

Alvarez, Sonia E., Evelina Dagnino, and Arturo Escobar. 1998. *Cultures of Politics/ Politics of Cultures: Re-Visioning Latin American Social Movements*. Boulder: Westview.

Anderson, Mark. 2009. *Black and Indigenous: Garifuna Activism and Consumer Culture in Honduras*. Minneapolis: University of Minnesota Press.

Asad, Talal, ed. 1973. *Anthropology and the Colonial Encounter*. New York: Ithaca Press.

Assies, Wilem, Gemma van der Haar, and Andre Hoekema, eds. 1999. *El reto de la diversidad pueblos indigenas y reforma del estado en America Latina*. Zamora, Michoacán, Mexico: El Colegio de Michoacán.

Barkan, Elazar. 2001. *The Guilt of Nations: Restitution and Negotiating Historical Injustices*. Baltimore: Johns Hopkins University Press.

Barre, Marie-Chantal. 1983. *Ideologías indigenistas y movimientos indios*. Madrid: Siglo XXI.

Barsky, Osvaldo. 1988. *La reforma agraria Ecuatoriana*. Quito: Corporación Editora Nacional.

Becker, Marc. 2008. *Indians and Leftists in the Making of Ecuador's Modern Indigenous Movements*. Durham: Duke University Press.

———. 1997. "Class and Ethnicity in Rural Movements in Cayambe, Ecuador." Paper presented at the Latin American Studies Association Meeting, Guadalajara, Mexico.

Benavides, Gustavo. 1989. "Religious Articulations of Power." *Religion and Political Power*, ed. Gustavo Benavides and M. W. Daly, 1–12. New York: State University of New York Press.

Benhabib, Seyla. 2002. *The Claims of Culture: Equality and Diversity in the Global Era*. Princeton: Princeton University Press.

Benjamin, Walter. 1969. *Iluminations*. Edited by Hannah Arendt. New York: Schocken.

Berreman, Gerald D., Gutorm Gjessing, and Kathleen Gough. 1968. "Social Responsibilities Symposium." *Current Anthropology* 9.5: 391–436.

Bigenho, Michelle. 2002. *Sounding Indigenous: Authenticity in Bolivian Music Performance*. New York: Palgrave.

Bolivar Torres, Cesar. 1993. *La revolución del Arco Iris*. Quito: De Parra.

Borja, Luis Alberto. 1953. *En pos de la mujeres*. Buenos Aires: De Peuser.

Botasso-Gnerre, ed. 1989. *Del indigenismo a las organizaciónes indigenas*. Quito: Abya-Yala.

Botero, Luis F. 1991a. "La fiesta Andina." *Compadres y priostes*, ed. Luis F. Botero, 11–64. Quito: Abya-Yala.

———, ed. 1991b. *Compadres y priostes*. Quito: Abya-Yala.

Bourdieu, Pierre. 1991. *El sentido práctico*. Madrid: Taurus.

———. 1990. *The Logic of Practice*. Stanford: Stanford University Press.

———. 1977. *Outline of a Theory of Practice*. Cambridge: Cambridge University Press.

Bourque, Nicole. 1995. "Savages and Angels: The Spiritual, Social, and Physical Development of Individuals and Households in Andean Life-cycle Festivals." *Ethnos* 6.1–2: 99–114.

Bouysse-Cassagne, Thérèse, Veronica Cereceda, Olivia Harris, and Tristan Platt. 1987. *Tres reflexiones sobre el pensamiento Andino*. La Paz: HISBOL.

Bretón, Víctor. 2000. *El desarrollo comunitario como modelo de intervención en el medio rural*. Quito: CAAP.

Bromberger, Christian. 1991. "Per una etnologia dello spettacolo sportivo." *Identitá culturali*, 150–76. Milano: Franco Angeli.

Brush, Stephen. 1974. "Conflictos intercomunitarios en los Andes." *Allpanchis* 5: 29–41.

Brysk, Alison. 2000. *From Tribal Village to Global Village: Indian Rights and International Relations in Latin America*. Stanford: Stanford University Press.

Burbach, Roger. 2010. "Ecuador's President Correa Faces Off with Indigenous and Social Movements." *NACLA*, 28 January, http://nacla.org.

Burbano, Felipe. 2005. "La caída de Gutiérrez y la rebellión de Abril." *Íconos* (FLACSO-Ecuador) 23: 19–26.

Burga, Manuel. 1988. *El nacimiento de la utopía, muerte y resurección de los Incas*. Lima: IAA.

Burgos, Hugo. 1977. *Relaciones interétnicas en Riobamba*. Mexico City: Instituto Indigenista Interamericano.

Burke, Timothy. 1996. "Sunlight Soap Has Changed My Life: Hygiene, Commodification and the Body in Colonial Zimbabwe." *Clothing and Difference: Embodied Identities in Colonial and Post-colonial Africa*, ed. Hildi Hendrickson, 189–212. Durham: Duke University Press.

Canetti, Elias. 1984. *Crowds and Power*. New York: Farrar, Straus, and Giroux.

———. 1979. *Earwitness: Fifty Characters*. New York: Seabury.

Carrasco, Eulalia. 1982. "Descripción y breve análisis de la fiesta religiosa Andina." *La fiesta religiosa campesina*, ed. Marco V. Rueda, 45–67. Quito: PUCE.

Carrasco, Hernán. 1993. "Democratización de los poderes locales y levantamiento indígena." *Sismo etnico en el Ecuador*, by CEDIME, 29–70. Quito: CEDIME / Abya-Yala.

Casagrande, Joseph B. 1981. "Strategies for Survival: The Indians of Highland Ecuador." *Cultural Transformation and Ethnicity in Modern Ecuador*, ed. Norman Whitten, 260–77. Urbana: University of Illinois Press.

Castillo, Julio. n.d. *La Provincia de Chimborazo en 1942*. Riobamba: Castillo-Paredes.

CEDIME. 1993. *Sismo etnico en el Ecuador*. Quito: CEDIME / Abya-Yala.

CEPLAES. 1998. *Mujeres contracorriente: Voces de líderes indígenas*. Quito: CEPLAES.

Cervone, Emma. 2010. "Celebrating the Chagras: Mestizaje, Multiculturalism, and the Ecuadorian Nation." *The Global South Journal* 5.1: 94–118.

———. 2007. "Building Engagement: Ethnography and Indigenous Communities Today." *Tranforming Anthropology* 15.2: 97–110.

———. 2004. "Neoliberal Politics and Ethnic Recognition in Ecuador." Paper presented at the Latin American Studies Association Meeting, Las Vegas, 17–19 October.

———. 2003. "Beyond Recognition: Indigenous Politics in Contemporary Ecuador." Paper presented at the American Anthropology Association meeting, 11–23 November.

———. 2002. "Engendering Leadership: Indigenous Women Leaders in the Ecuadorian Andes." *Gender's Place*, ed. Janice Hurtig, Charo Montoya, and Lessie Jo Frazier, 179–96. New York: Palgrave.

———. 1999. "Los desafíos de la etnicidad: Luchas del movimiento indígena en la modernidad." *Journal of Latin American Anthropology* 4.1: 46–73.

———. 1998. "Festival Time, Long Live the Festival: Ethnic Conflict and Ritual in the Andes." *Anthropos* (Germany) 93: 101–13.

Cervone, Emma, and Fredy Rivera, eds. 1999. *Ecuador racista: Imágenes e identidades*. Quito: FLACSO-Ecuador.

Clark, A. Kim. 1998. "Race, Culture and Mestizaje: The Statistical Construction of Ecuadorian Nation, 1930–1950." *Journal of Historical Sociology* 11: 185–211.

———. 1992. *Indians and the State in Liberal Ecuador*, mimeo.

Clark, A. Kim, and Marc Becker. 2007. "Indigenous Peoples and State Formation in Modern Ecuador." *Highland Indians and the State in Modern Ecuador*, ed. A. Kim Clark and Marc Becker, 1–21. Pittsburgh: University of Pittsburgh Press. 1–21.

Clastres, Pierre. 1980. *Cronaca di una tribù*. Milano: Feltrinelli Editore.

Colloredo-Mansfeld, Rudolf Josef. 1999. *The Native Leisure Class: Consumption and Cultural Creativity in the Andes*. Chicago: University of Chicago Press.

CONAIE. 2010. "Resolución del Congreso Extraordinario de Ambato," 26 February. Quito: CONAIE.

———. 1993. *Declaración política de los pueblos indígenas del Ecuador*. Fourth Congress. Quito: CONAIE.

———. 1992. *Proyecto Político de la CONAIE*. Quito: CONAIE.

———. 1990. *Mandato por la defensa de la vida y los derechos de las nacionalidades indígenas*. Quito: CONAIE.

———. 1989. *Las nacionalidades indigenas en el Ecuador: Nuestro proceso organizativo*. Quito: Abya-Yala / Tincui.

Connolly, William. 1996. "Pluralism, Multiculturalism and the Nation-State: Rethinking the Connections." *Journal of Political Ideologies* 1.1: 53–73.

Coordinadora Provincial del Levantamiento Indígena y Campesino de Chimborazo. 1990. *Demandas Organizaciones Indígenas y Campesinas de Chimborazo*. Riobamba, Coordinadora Provincial del Levantamiento Indígena y Campesino de Chimborazo.

Cordero, Luis. 1989. *Diccionario Quichua*. Quito: Corporación Editora Nacional, Proyecto EBI.

Costales, Alfredo, and Piedad de Costales. 1962. "El chagra." Special issue, *Llacta* 11. Quito.

Crain, Mary. 1989. *Ritual, memoria popular y proceso político en la sierra Ecuatoriana*. Quito: Abya-Yala.

Crespi, Muriel. 1981. "St. John the Baptist: The Ritual Looking Glass of Hacienda Indian Ethnic and Power Relations." *Cultural Transformation and Ethnicity in Modern Ecuador*, ed. Norman Whitten, 477–505. Urbana: University of Illinois Press.

Das, Veena. 2007. *Life and Words: Violence and the Descent into the Ordinary*. Berkeley: University of California Press.

de Certeau, Michel. 1988. *The Practice of Everyday Life*. Berkeley: University of California Press.

de la Cadena, Marisol. 2000. *Indigenous Mestizos: The Politics of Race and Culture in Cuzco, Peru, 1919–1991*. Durham: Duke University Press.

de la Cadena, Marisol, and Orin Starn, eds. 2007. *Indigenous Experience Today*. Oxford: Berg.

de la Peña, Guillermo. 2005. "Social and Cultural Policies toward Indigenous Peoples: Perspectives from Latin America." *Annual Review of Anthropology* 34: 717–39.

———. 2002. "Social Citizenship, Ethnic Minority Demands, Human Rights and Neoliberal Paradoxes: A Case Study in Western Mexico." *Multiculturalism in Latin America: Indigenous Rights, Diversity and Democracy*, ed. Rachel Sieder, 129–56. New York: Palgrave.

de Sousa Santos, Boaventura. 1995. *Towards a New Common Sense: Law, Science and Politics in the Paradigmatic Transition*. New York: Routledge.

de Sousa Santos, Boaventura, and Cesar A. Rodriguez-Garavito, eds. 2005. "Law, Politics and the Subaltern in Counter-Hegemonic Globalization." *Law and Globalization from Below*, ed. Boaventura de Sousa Santos and Cesar A. Rodriguez-Garavito, 1–26. Cambridge: Cambridge University Press.

Díaz-Polanco, Héctor. 2006. *Elogio de la diversidad: Globalización, multiculturalismo y etnofagia: Sociología y política*. Mexico City: Siglo XXI.

Dietz, Gunther. 2004. "Beyond Victimization: Maya Movements in Post-War Guatemala." *The Struggle for Indigenous Rights in Latin America*, ed. Nancy Grey Postero and Leon Zamosc, 32–80. Sussex, U.K.: Sussex Academic Press.

Dubly, Alain, and Alicia Granda. 1991. *Desalojos y despojos*. Quito: CEDHU / El Conejo.

Duviols, Pierre. 1973. "Huari y Llacuaz: Agricultores y pastores: Un dualismo prehispánico de oposición y complementariedad." *Revista del Museo Nacional* (Lima) 39: 153–92.

ECUARUNARI. 2002. *Acuerdos y Resoluciones*. Otavalo, mimeo.

Enriquez Bermeo, Francisco, ed. 1989. *Leonidas Proaño el obispo de los pobres*. Quito: El Conejo.

Eriksen, Thomas. 1992. *Us and Them in Modern Societies*. Oslo: Scandinavian University Press.

Escobar, Arturo, and Sonia Alvarez, eds. 1992. *The Making of Social Movements in Latin America: Identity, Strategy and Democracy*. Boulder: Westview.

Fabian, Johannes. 2001. *Anthropology with an Attitude*. Stanford: Stanford University Press.

Falk, Richard. 2001. "The Right of Self-Determination in International Law: The Coherence of Doctrine Versus the Incoherence of Experience." *The Self-*

Determination of Peoples: Community, Nation, and State in an Interdependent World, ed. Wolfgang Danspeckgruber, 47–63. Boulder: Lynne Rienner.

Fanon, Frantz. 1986. *Black Skin, White Masks*. London: Pluto.

Fernández Osco, Marcelo. 2000. *La ley del ayllu: Prácticas del jach'a justicia y jisk'a justicia (justicia mayor y justicia menor) en comunidades Aymara*. La Paz: PIEB.

Fields, Karen. 1985. *Revival and Rebellion in Colonial Central Africa*. Princeton: Princeton University Press.

Flores Galindo, Alberto. 1987. *Buscando un Inca*. Lima: Instituto de Apoyo Agrario.

Foote, Nicola. 2006. "Race, State and Nation in Early Twentieth Century Ecuador." *Nation and Nationalism* 12.2: 261–78.

Foucault, Michel. 1976. *Vigilar y castigar*. Madrid: Siglo XXI.

Fox, Richard Gabriel, and Orin Starn. 1998. "Between Resistance and Revolution." *Times Literary Supplement* 4995: 28.

———. 1997. *Between Resistance and Revolution: Cultural Politics and Social Protest*. New Brunswick: Rutgers University Press.

Fraser, Nancy. 1997. *Justice Interruptus: Critical Reflections on the "Postsocialist" Condition*. London: Routledge.

Friedman, Jonathan. 1994. "The Past in the Future: History and the Politics of Identity." *American Anthropologist* 94.4: 837–59.

García, Fernando. 2002. *Formas indígenas de administrar justicia: Estudios de caso de la nacionalidad Quichua Ecuatoriana*. Quito: FLACSO / Sede Académica de Ecuador.

García, Fernando, and Gina Chávez. 2004. *El derecho a ser: Diversidad, identidad y cambio: Etnografía jurídica indígena y afroecuatoriana*. Quito: FLACSO / Petroecuador.

García, Maria Elena. 2005. *Making Indigenous Citizens: Identity, Development and Multicultural Activism in Peru*. Stanford: Stanford University Press.

Gardner, Katy, and David Lewis. 1996. *Anthropology, Development and the Postmodern Challenge*. London: Pluto.

Geertz, Clifford. 1990. "Ritual y cambió social: Un ejemplo javanés." *La interpretación de las culturas*, ed. Clifford Geertz, 131–51. Barcelona: Editorial Gedisa.

Glave Miguel. 1989. *Trajinantes: Caminos indígenas en la sociedad colonial siglos XVI–XVII*. Lima: IAA.

Gluckman, Max, and Cyril Daryll Forde. 1962. *Essays on the Ritual of Social Relations*. Manchester: Manchester University Press.

Goldberg, David Theo, ed. 1995. *Multiculturalism: A Critical Reader*. Malden, Mass.: Wiley-Blackwell.

———. 1990. *Anatomy of Racism*. Minneapolis: University of Minnesota Press.

Goldstein, Daniel M. 2004. *The Spectacular City: Violence and Performance in Urban Bolivia*. Durham: Duke University Press.

Goodale, Mark. 2008. *Dilemmas of Modernity: Bolivian Encounters with Law and Liberalism*. Stanford: Stanford University Press.

———. 2006a. "Legalities and Illegalities." *A Companion to Latin American Anthropology*, ed. Deborah Poole, 214–29. Malden, Mass.: Blackwell.

———. 2006b. "Reclaiming Modernity: Indigenous Cosmopolitanism and the Coming of the Second Revolution in Bolivia." *American Ethnologist* 33.4: 634–49.

Gordon, Avery, and Christopher Newfield. 1996. *Mapping Multiculturalism*. Minneapolis: University of Minnesota Press.

Gough, Kathleen. 1968. "New Proposals for Anthropologists." *Current Anthropology* 9.5 (December): 403–7.

Govers, Cora, and Hans Vermeulen. 1997. "From Political Mobilization to the Politics of Consciousness." *The Politics of Ethnic Consciousness*, ed. Cora Govers and Hans Vermeulen, 1–30. New York: St. Martin's.

Gow, David D. 1973. "El impacto de la reforma agraria sobre el sistema de cargos." *Allpanchis* 5: 131–57.

Greene, Shane, ed. 2009. "'Entre Lo Indio' y 'Lo Negro': Interrogating the Effects of Latin America's New Afro-Indigenous Multicuturalism." Special issue of *Journal of Latin American and Caribbean Anthropology* 12.2.

Gross, David, and Stuart Plattner. 2002. "Anthropology as Social Work: Collaborative Models of Anthropological Research." *Anthropology Newsletter* (American Anthropological Association) 43.8: 4.

Guaman Poma de Ayala, Felipe. 1988. *Primer nueva coronica y buen gobierno*. Edited by John Murra, Rolena Adorno, and Jorge Urioste. Madrid: Siglo XXI.

Guerrero, Andrés. 1994. "Una imagen ventrílocua: El discurso liberal de la 'desgraciada raza indígena' a fines del siglo XIX." *Imágenes e imagineros*, ed. Blanca Muratorio, 197–252. Quito: FLACSO.

———. 1993. "La desintegración de la administración étnica en el Ecuador." *Sismo etnico en el Ecuador*, by CEDIME, 91–112. Quito: CEDIME / Abya-Yala.

———. 1991a. *De la economía a las mentalidades*. Quito: El Conejo.

———. 1991b. *La semántica de la dominación: El concertaje de Indios*. Quito: Libri Mundi.

———. 1989. "Curagas y tenientes políticos: La ley de la costubre y la ley del estado (Otavalo 1830–1875)." *Revista Andina* 2: 1–43.

———. 1983. *Haciendas, capital y lucha de clases Andina*. Quito: El Conejo.

Guerrero Arias, Patricio. 1994. "Música y danza en Chimborazo." *Revista CCE Nucleo Riobamba* 19: 11–36.

———. 1993. *El saber del mundo de los cóndores*. Quito: Abya-Yala.

Guillet, David W. 1974. "Transformación, ritual y cambio socio-político en una comunidad campesina Andina." *Allpanchis* 5: 143–59.

Gupta, Akhil. 1998. *Postcolonial Developments: Agriculture in the Making of Modern India*. Durham: Duke University Press.

Gupta, Akhil, and James Ferguson. 1992. "Beyond 'Culture': Space, Identity and the Politics of Difference." *Cultural Anthropology* 7.1: 6–23.

Gustafson, Bret. 2009. *New Languages of the State: Indigenous Resurgence and the Politics of Knowledge in Bolivia*. Durham: Duke University Press.

———. 2002. "Paradoxes of Liberal Indigenism: Indigenous Movements, State Processes and the Intercultural Reform in Bolivia." *The Politics of Ethnicity: Indigenous Peoples in Latin American States*, ed. David Maybury-Lewis, 267–306. Cambridge: Harvard University Press.

Gustafson, Lowell S., and Satya R. Pattnayak. 2003. *Economic Performance under Democratic Regimes in Latin America in the Twenty-First Century*. Lewiston, N.Y.: Edwin Mellen Press.

"Hablan paramilitares y comuneros." 1992. *Punto de Vista* 520: 8–10.

Hale, Charles. 2008a. "Introduction." *Engaging Contradictions: Theory, Politics and Methods of Activist Scholarship*, ed. Charles Hale, 1–28. Berkeley: University of California Press.

———. 2008b. *More than an Indian: Racial Ambivalence and Neoliberal Multiculturalism in Guatemala*. Sante Fe: School of American Research Press.

———. 2005. "Neoliberal Multiculturalism." *Critical Perspectives on Human Rights and Multiculturalism in Neoliberal Latin America*, ed. Maria Teresa Sierra and Shannon Speed. Special issue of *Political and Legal Anthropology Review* 28.1: 10–19.

———. 2004. "Rethinking Indigenous Politics in the Era of the 'Indio Permitido.'" *NACLA* 38.2: 16–20.

———. 2002. "Does Multiculturalism Menace?: Governance, Cultural Rights and the Politics of Identity in Guatemala." *Journal of Latin American Studies* 34.3: 485–524.

———. 2001. "What Is Activist Research." *Social Science Research Council Bulletin* 2, nos. 1–2: 13–15.

———. 1997. "Cultural Politics of Identity in Latin America." *Annual Review of Anthropology* 26: 567–90.

———. 1994. *Resistance and Contradiction: Miskitu Indians and the Nicaraguan State, 1894–1987*. Stanford: Stanford University Press.

Hale, Charles R., Kay B. Warren, and Jean E. Jackson. 2004. "Review of Indigenous Movements Self Representation and the State in Latin America." *Journal of Latin American Studies* 36.1: 193–95.

Hall, Stuart. 1995. "Negotiating Caribbean Identities." *New Left Review* 209: 3–14.

Hanchard, Michael. 2006. *Party/Politics: Horizons in Black Political Thought*. New York: Oxford University Press.

Hardt, Michael, and Antonio Negri. 2004. *Multitude War and Democracy in the Age of Empire*. New York: Penguin.

Harris, Olivia, ed. 1996. *Inside and Outside the Law*. London: Routledge.

———. 1986. "Complementary and Conflict: An Andean View of Women and Men." *Sex and Age as Principle of Social Differentiation*, ed. J. S. La Fontaine, 21–39. London: Routledge.

———. 1985. "Ecological Duality and the Role of the Center: Northern Potosi." *Andean Ecology and Civilization: An Interdisciplinary Perspective on Andean Eco-*

logical Complementarity, ed. Shozo Masuda, Izumi Shimada, and Craig Morris, 311–55. Tokyo: Tokyo University Press.

Hendrickson, Hildi, ed. 1996. *Clothing and Difference: Embodied Identities in Colonial and Post-colonial Africa*. Durham: Duke University Press.

Heredia Garzón, Angel Arturo. 1985. *Tixán: Monografía*. Riobamba: CCE.

Hill, Jonathan, ed. 1996. *History, Power and Identity*. Iowa: University of Iowa Press.

Hill, Jonathan David, and Fernando Santos-Granero. 2002. *Comparative Arawakan Histories: Rethinking Language Family and Culture Area in Amazonia*. Urbana: University of Illinois Press.

Hobsbawn, Eric. 1959. "The Social Bandit." *Primitive Rebels*, by Eric Hobsbawn, 338–39. Manchester: Manchester University Press.

Hodgson Dorothy. 2002. "Precarious Alliances: The Cultural Politics and Structural Predicaments of the Indigenous Rights Movements in Tanzania." *American Anthropology* 104.4: 1086–97.

Hooker, Juliet. 2005. "Indigenous Inclusion/Black Exclusion: Race, Ethnicity and Multicultural Citizenship in Latin America." *Journal of Latin American Studies* 37: 85–310.

Hopkins, Diane. 1982. "Juego de enemigos." *Allpanchis* 17.20: 167–88.

Ibarra, Hernán. 1992. *Indios y cholos: Orígenes de la clase trabajadora Ecuatoriana*. Quito: El Conejo.

ILDIS. 1991. *Indios*. Quito: ILDIS / El Duende / Abya-Yala.

Inca Atahualpa. 1992. "Unión de Organizaciones Populares 'Inca Atahualpa.'" Tixán, mimeo.

———. n.d. "Proyecto de convenio de funcionamiento de los centros de cuidado diario infantil en las comunidades rurales de la matriz de Alausí y Tixán." Tixán, mimeo.

Instituto Nacional Estadisticas y Censos. 2001. *Census de población y de vivienda*. Quito: INEC.

Inter-American Committee for Agricultural Development. 1965. *Tenencia de la tierra y desarrollo socio-ecónomico del sector agrícola en el Ecuador*. Washington: OEA.

Iturralde, Diego. 1993. "Usos de la ley y usos de la costumbre: La reinvindicación del derecho indígena a la modernizacíon." *Derecho, pueblos indígenas y reforma del estado*, ed. Alberto Wray and J. C. Ribadeneira, 125–50. Quito: Abya-Yala.

Izko, Javier. 1991. "Poderes ambiguos: Ecología, política y ritual en el altiplano central de Bolivia." *Poder y violencia en los Andes*, ed. Henrique Urbano, 299–339. Cuzco: Centro de Estudios Bartolomé de las Casas.

Karakras, Ampam. 1990. *Las nacionalidades indias y el estado Ecuatoriano*. Quito: CONAIE.

Kearney, Michael. 1996. *Reconceptualizing the Peasantry Anthropology in Global Perspective*. Boulder: Westview.

Kelley, Robin. 1994. *Race Rebels: Culture, Politics, and the Black Working Class*. New York: Free Press.

Kipu: El mundo indígena en la prensa ecuatoriana, nos. 14–15. 1990. Press reports. Quito: MLAL / Abya-Yala.

Korovkin, Tanya. 1997. "Indigenous Peasant Struggles and the Capitalist Modernization of Agriculture: Chimborazo, 1964–1991." *Latin American Perspectives* 24.3: 25–49.

Kymlicka, Will. 1995. *Multicultural Citizenship: A Liberal Theory of Minority Rights*. Oxford: Clarendon.

Kymlicka, Will, and Norman Wayne. 2000. *Citizenship in Diverse Societies*. Oxford: Oxford University Press.

Lagos, Maria. 1994. *Autonomy and Power: The Dynamics of Class and Culture in Rural Bolivia*. Philadelphia: University of Pennsylvania Press.

Langer, Erik. 1985. "Labor Strikes and Reciprocity in Chuqisaca Haciendas." *Hispanic American Historical Review* 65.2: 255–77.

Langer, Erik, and Elena Muñoz, eds. 2003. *Contemporary Indigenous Movements in Latin America*. Wilmington, Del.: Scholarly Resources.

Larson, Brooke. 1991. "Explotación y economía boral en los Andes del Sur." *Reproducción y transformación de las sociedades Andinas, siglo XVI–XX*, 2 vols., ed. Segundo Moreno and Frank Salomon, vol. 2:441–80. Quito: Abya-Yala.

Lentz, Carola. 1986. "De regidores y alcaldes a cabildos: Cambios en la estructura socío política de una comunidad Indígena de Cajabamba/Chimborazo." *Ecuador Debate* 12: 189–212.

León, Jorge. 1994. *De campesinos a ciudadanos diferentes*. Quito: CEDIME / Abya-Yala.

———. 1991. "Las organizaciones indígenas: Igualdad y diferencia." *Indios*, by ILDIS, 377–418. Quito: ILDIS / El Duende / Abya-Yala.

Lewis, David, and Tina Wallace. 2000. *New Roles and Relevance: Development NGOs and the Challenge of Change*. Sterling, Va.: Kumarian Press.

Liebre Ilustrada. 1988. "Tixán, Azufre, Tren y Rebeldía." No. 189, 17 July. Quito.

Lucero, José Antonio. 2003. "Locating the 'Indian Problem': Community, Nationality, and Contradiction in Ecuadorian Indigenous Politics." *Latin American Perspectives* 30: 23–48.

Macas, Luis. 1991. "El levantamiento indígena visto por sus protagonistas." *Indios*, by ILDIS, 17–36. Quito: ILDIS / El Duende / Abya-Yala.

Maldonado, Luis. 2003 *Ciudadanía, desarrollo y cooperación internacional en tiempos de globalización: una visión autocrítica sobre el Movimiento Indígena en Ecuador*. Interview by Daniel Mato. Quito, 30 July, 2003; Colección Entrevistas a Intelectuales Indígenas, No. 2. Caracas: Programa Globalización, Cultura y Transformaciones Sociales. Available at http://www.globalcult.org.ve/entrevistas.html.

Martinez Novo, Carmen. 2005. *Who Defines Indigenous?: Identities, Development, Intellectuals, and the State in Northern Mexico*. New Brunswick: Rutgers University Press.

Marzal, Manuel. 1988. *Estudios sobre religión campesina*. Lima: CONCYTEC.

Massey, Doreen, ed. 1994. "General Introduction." *Space, Place and Gender*, ed. Doreen Massey, 1–16. Minneapolis: University of Minnesota Press.

Mattiace, Shannan L. 2003. *To See with Two Eyes: Peasant Activism and Indian Autonomy in Chiapas, Mexico*. Albuquerque: University of New Mexico Press.

Mayer, Enrique. 1974. "Las reglas del juego en la reciprocidad Andina." *Reciprocidad e intercambio en los Andes Peruanos*, ed. Giorgio Alberti and Enrique Mayer, 37–65. Lima: Instituto de Estudios Peruanos.

McAdam, Doug, John McCarthy, and Mayer Zald. 1988. "Social Movements." *Handbook of Sociology*, ed. by Neil J. Smelser, 695–737. Newbury Park, Calif.: Sage.

Meisch, Lynn. 2002. *Andean Entrepreneurs: Otavalo Merchants and Musicians in the Global Arena*. Austin: University of Texas Press.

Melucci, Alberto, and Mario Diani. 1992. *Nazioni senza stato*. Milan: Feltrinelli Editore.

MICH. 1984. "Movimiento indígena de Chimborazo." Riobamba, mimeo.

Mignolo, Walter. 2000. *Local Histories/Global Designs: Coloniality, Subaltern Knowledges, and Border Thinking*. Princeton: Princeton University Press.

Millones, Luis, ed. 1990. *El retorno de las Huacas: Estudios y documentos sobre el Taki Onqoy*. Lima: Instituto de Estudios Peruanos / SPP.

Mintz, Sidney W., and Eric Wolf. (1950) 1995. "Análisis del parentesco ritual. Compadrazgo." *Cosmos, hombre y sacralidad: Lecturas dirigidas de antropología religiosa*, ed. Marco V. Rueda and Segundo Moreno, 371–412. Quito: PUCE / Abya-Yala.

Molina, Cristóbal de. 1989. "Relación de las fábulas y mitos de los Incas." *Fábulas y mitos de los Incas*, ed. Henrique Urbano and Pierre Duviols, 47–134. Madrid: Historia 16.

Moraña Mabel, Enrique Dussel, and Carlos A. Jáuregui, eds. 2008. *Coloniality at Large: Latin America and the Postcolonial Debate*. Durham: Duke University Press.

Moreno Yánez, Segundo. 1985. *Sublevaciones indigenas en la audiencía de Quito*. Quito: PUCE.

Moreno Yánez, Segundo, and Jorge Figueroa. 1992. *El levantamiento indígena del Inti Raymi de 1990*. Quito: FESO / Abya-Yala.

Murra, John. 1989. *La organización económica del Estado Inca*. 5th edn. Mexico City: Siglo XXI.

———, ed. 1975. *Formaciones económicas y políticas del Mundo Andino*. Lima: Instituto de Estudios Peruanos.

Murray Li, Tania. 2000. "Articulating Indigenous Identities in Indonesia: Resource Politics and the Tribal Slot." *Comparative Studies in Society and History* 42.1: 149–79.

Nader, Laura. 1991. *Harmony Ideology: Justice and Control in a Zapotec Mountain Village*. Stanford: Stanford University Press.

Nash, June. 2001. *Mayan Visions: The Quest for Autonomy in an Age of Globalization.* New York: Routledge.

Nash, Manning. 1989. *The Cauldron of Ethnicity in the Modern World.* Chicago: University of Chicago Press.

North, Liisa, and Cameron, John D., eds. 2003. *Rural Progress, Rural Decay: Neoliberal Adjustment Policies and Local Initiatives.* Sterling, Va.: Kumarian.

Obarrio, Juan. 2010. "Remains to Be Seen: Third Encounter between State and 'Customary' in Northern Mozambique." *Cultural Anthropology* 25.2: 263–300.

OPIP. 1990. "Acuerdo sobre el derecho territorial de los pueblos Quichua, Shiwar y Achuar de la provincia de Pastaza a suscribirse con el estado Ecuatoriano." 5 August. Puyo, mimeo.

———. "50 Años de Resistencia India 1990 Territorio y recursos Naturales." Paper for the First Continental Indigenous Conference, Quito.

Orlove, Benjamin. 2002. *Lines in the Water: Nature and Culture at Lake Titicaca.* Berkeley: University of California Press.

———. 1990. "La posición de los abigeos en la sociedad colonial." *Bandoleros, abigeos y montoneros: Criminalidad y violencia en el Perú, siglos XVIII–XX*, ed. Carlos Aguirre and Charles Walker, 277–305. Lima: Instituto de Apoyo Agrario.

———. 1973. "Abigeato: La organización social de una actividad ilegal." *Allpanchis* 5: 65–82.

Orta, Andrew. 2004. *Catechizing Culture: Missionaries, Aymara, and the "New Evangelization."* New York: Columbia University Press.

———. 2002. "'Living the Past Another Way': Reinstrumentalized Missionary Selves in Aymara Mission Fields." *Anthropological Quarterly* 75.4: 707–43.

Ortiz, Pablo. 1991. "Frente al control y la represión." *Punto De Vista* 459: 12–13.

Ortiz, Santiago. 2004. *Cotacachi: Una apuesta por una democracia participativa.* Quito: FLACSO-Ecuador.

Ossio, Juan. 1973. *Ideología mesiánica del mundo Andino.* Lima: Prado.

Pacari, Nina. 1993. "Levantamiento Indigena." *Sismo étnico en el Ecuador*, by CEDIME, 169–86. Quito: CEDIME / Abya-Yala.

Pallares, Amalia. 2002. *From Peasant Struggles to Indian Resistance: The Ecuadorian Andes in the Late Twentieth Century.* Norman: University of Oklahoma Press.

Parking, David. 1982. "Introduction." *Semantic Anthropology*, ed. David Parking, xi–li. London: Routledge.

Perez, Ignacio. 1991. "El levantamiento visto por los hacendados." *Indios*, by ILDIS, 37–89. Quito: ILDIS / El Duende / Abya-Yala.

Platt, Tristan. 1987a. "The Andean Soldiers of Christ: Confraternity Organization, the Mass of the Sun and Regenerative Warfare in Rural Potósi (18th–20th Centuries)." *Journal de la Societe des Americanistes* 73: 139–92.

———. 1987b. "Calendarios tributarios e intervenciòn mercantil: La articulaciòn estatal de los ayllus de Lipez con el mercado minero Potosino." *La participación indígena en los mercados Surandinos: Estrategies de reproducción social siglos XVI a XX*, ed. Olivia Harris, Brooke Larson, and Enrique Tandeter, 471–557. La Paz: Centro de Estudios de la Realidad Económica y Social.

———. 1987c. "Entre Chaxwa y Muxsa: Para una historia del pensamiento político Aymara." *Tres reflexiones sobre el pensamiento Andino*, ed. Thérèse Bouysse-Cassagne, Veronica Cereceda, Olivia Harris, and Tristan Platt, 61–122. La Paz: HISBOL.

———. 1986a. "Mirrors and Maize: The Concept of Yanantin among the Mancha of Bolivia." *Anthropological Histories of Andean Polities*, ed. John Murra, Nathan Wachtel, and Jacques Revel, 228–59. Cambridge: Cambridge University Press.

———. 1986b. "El rol del allyu Andino en la reproducción del régimen mercantil simple en el norte de Potosí (Bolivia)." *Identidades Andinas y lógicas del campesinado*, by Lucy Briggs, 25–83. Lima: Mosca Azul.

———. 1982. *Estado Boliviano y ayllu Andino: Tierra y tributo en el norte de Potosí.* Lima: Instituto de Estudios Peruanos.

Ponce, Javier. 2000. *Y la madrugada los sorprendió en el poder*. Quito: Editorial Planeta.

Ponciano del Pino, Horacio. 1998. "Family, Culture and 'Revolution': Everyday Life with Sendero Luminoso." *Shining and Other Paths: War and Society in Peru, 1980–1995*, ed. Steve J. Stern, 158–92. Durham: Duke University Press.

Poole, Deborah, ed. 2006. *A Companion to Latin American Anthropology*. Malden, Mass.: Blackwell.

———. 1994. *Unruly Order: Violence, Power, and Cultural Identity in the High Provinces of Southern Peru*. Boulder: Westview.

———. 1991. "El folklore de la violencia en una provincia alta del Cusco." *Poder y violencia en los Andes*, ed. by Henrique Urbano, 277–98. Cuzco: Centro de Estudios Bartolomé de las Casas.

———. 1988. "Landscapes of Power in a Cattle-rustling Culture of Southern Andean Perú." *Dialectical Anthropology* 12: 367–98.

Poole, Deborah, and Veena Das. 2004. *Anthropology in the Margins of the State*. Santa Fe: School of American Research Press.

Postero, Nancy Grey. 2007. *Now We Are Citizens: Indigenous Politics in Postmulticultural Bolivia*. Stanford: Stanford University Press.

Postero, Nancy Grey, and Leon Zamosc. 2004. *The Struggle for Indigenous Rights in Latin America*. Sussex, U.K.: Sussex Academic Press.

Povinelli, Elizabeth A. 2002. *The Cunning of Recognition: Indigenous Alterities and the Making of Australian Multiculturalism*. Durham: Duke University Press.

Prada Alcoreza, Raúl. 1992. *Análisis sociodemográfico poblaciones nativas*. La Paz, Bolivia: Ministerio de Hacienda, Instituto Nacional de Estadística.

Prieto, Mercedes. 1980. "Haciendas Estatales: Un Caso de Ofensiva Campesina, 1926–1948." *Ecuador: Cambios en el Agro Serrano*, by Facultad Latinoamericana de Ciencias Sociales and Centro de Planificación y Estudios Sociales, 101–32. Quito: FLACSO / CEPLAES.

Proaño, Leonidas. 1991. *Los indígenas, la Iglesia viva y la nueva sociedad*. Quito: CEDEP.

———. 1989. *La Iglesia, los pobres y la opción de una comunidad*. Quito: CEDEP.

Quijano, Anibal. 2000. "Coloniality of Power, Eurocentrism and Latin America." *Nepantla* 1.3: 533–80.

Radcliffe, Sarah A., Nina Laurie, and Robert Andolina. 2002. *Indigenous People and Political Transnationalism: Globalization from Below Meets Globalization from Above?* Oxford: University of Oxford.

Rahier, Jean Muteba. 1998. "Blackness, the Racial/Spatial Order, Migrations, and Miss Ecuador 1995–96." *American Anthropologist* 100.2: 421–30.

Ramón Valarezo, Galo. 2000. "El racismo en el Ecuador ensaya sus cantos." *Boletín ICCI-Rimay no. 13 April 2000, online publication http://icci.nativeweb.org/boletin/abri12000/ramon.html.*

———. 1993. *El regreso de los runas*. Quito: COMUNIDEC.

———, ed. 1992. *Actores de una década ganada*. Quito: COMUNIDEC.

———. 1990. "Identidad India y modernización." *Difusión Cultural* 10: 36–41.

Rappaport, Joanne. 2007. "Civil Society and the Indigenous Movement in Colombia: The Consejo Regional Indígena del Cauca." *Social Analysis* 51.2: 107–123.

———. 2005. *Intercultural Utopias: Public Intellectuals, Cultural Experimentation, and Ethnic Pluralism in Colombia*. Durham: Duke University Press.

———. 2002. "Imagining Andean Colonial Culture." *Ethnohistory* 49.3: 687–701.

———. 1994. *Cumbe Reborn: An Andean Ethnography of History*. Chicago: University of Chicago Press.

———. 1990. *The Politics of Memory*. Cambridge: Cambridge University Press.

Rappaport, Joanne, and David Gow. 2002. "The Indigenous Public Voice: The Multiple Idioms of Modernity in Native Cauca." *Indigenous Movements, Self-Representation, and the State in Latin America*, ed. Kay B. Warren and Jean E. Jackson, 47–80. Austin: University of Texas Press.

Rasnake, Roger Neil. 1988. *Domination and Cultural Resistance: Authority and Power among an Andean People*. Durham: Duke University Press.

Roseberry, William. 1994. "Hegemony and the Language of Contention." *Everyday Forms of State Formation: Revolution and the Negotiation of Rule in Modern Mexico*, ed. Gilbert M. Joseph and Daniel Nugent, 355–66. Durham: Duke University Press.

Rosero Garcés, Fernando. 1991. "Defensa y ocupación de la tierra: Campesinado, identidad etnocultural y nación." *Indios*, by ILDIS, 419–48. Quito: ILDIS / El Duende / Abya-Yala.

Rueda, Marco V., ed. 1982. *La fiesta religiosa campesina*. Quito: PUCE.

Salomon, Frank. 1981a. "Killing the Yumbo: A Ritual Drama of Nothern Quito." *Cultural Transformation and Ethnicity in Modern Ecuador*, ed. Norman Whitten, 162–210. Urbana: University of Illinois Press.

———. 1981b. "Weavers of Otavalo." *Cultural Transformation and Ethnicity in Modern Ecuador*, ed. Norman Whitten, 420–47. Urbana: University of Illinois Press.

Saltos Galarza, Napoleón. 2001. "Movimiento indígena y movimientos sociales: Encuentros y desencuentros." *Boletín ICCI-Rimay* 3.27 (June).

Sánchez Parga, José. 1985. "Matrices espaciales y comunidad Andina." *Cultura, Revista del Banco Central del Ecuador* 21: 95–122.

Santana, Roberto. 2004. "Cuando las elites dirigentes giran en redondo: El caso de los liderazgos indígenas en Ecuador." *Ecuador Debate* 61 (April 2004): 235–258.

Sawyer, Suzana. 2004. *Crude Chronicles: Indigenous Politics, Multinational Oil, and Neoliberalism in Ecuador*. Durham: Duke University Press.

Scott, James. 1992. *Domination and the Art of Resistance: Hidden Transcript*. New Haven: Yale University Press.

———. 1985. *Weapons of the Weak: Everyday Forms of Peasant Resistance*. New Haven: Yale University Press.

———. 1976. "Peasant Moral Economy as a Subsistence Ethic." *The Moral Economy of the Peasant*, ed. James Scott, 1–11. New Haven: Yale University Press.

Seligman, Linda. 1995. *Between Reform and Revolution: Political Struggles in the Peruvian Andes, 1969–1991*. Stanford: Stanford University Press.

———. 1991. "La ley y el poder en la sociedad Andina: La reforma agraria de 1969." *Poder y violencia en los Andes*, ed. Henrique Urbano, 361–78. Cuzco: Centro de Estudios Bartolomé de las Casas.

Selverston-Scher, Melina. 2001. *Ethnopolitics in Ecuador: Indigenous Rights and the Strengthening of Democracy*. Coral Gables, Fla.: North-South Center Press at the University of Miami.

Shapiro, Ian, and Will Kymlicka. 1997. *Ethnicity and Group Rights*. New York: New York University Press.

Sieder, Rachel, ed. 2002. *Multiculturalism in Latin America. Indigenous Rights, Diversity and Democracy*. New York: Palgrave.

Smith, Gavin. 1991. *Livelihood and Resistance: Peasants and the Politics of Land in Peru*. Berkeley: University of California Press.

"Somos Ecuatorianos." *Punto de Vista* 421, 11 June 1990, 8.

Speed, Shannon. 2008a. "Forged in Dialogue: Towards a Critically Engaged Activist Research." *Engaging Contradictions: Theory, Politics and Methods of Activist Scholarship*, ed. Charles R. Hale, 213–36. Berkeley: University of California Press.

———. 2008b. *Rights in Rebellion*. Stanford: Stanford University Press.

———. 2005. "Dangerous Discourses." *Critical Perspectives on Human Rights and Multiculturalism in Neoliberal Latin America*, edited by M. T. Sierra and Shannon Speed. Special issue of *Political and Legal Anthropology Review* 28.1: 29–51.

Spivak, Gayatri. 1988. "Can the Subaltern Speak?" *Marxism and the Interpretation of Culture*, ed. Cary Nelson and Lawrence Grossberg, 271–315. Urbana: University of Illinois Press.

Starn, Orin. 1999. *Nightwatch: The Politics of Protest in the Andes*. Durham: Duke University Press.

Stavenhagen, Rodolfo. 1990. *The Ethnic Question: Conflicts, Development, and Human Rights*. Tokyo: United Nations University Press.

———. 1971. “Decolonizing Applied Social Sciences.” *Human Organization* 30: 333–57.

Stern, Steve. 1992. “Paradigms of Conquest: History, Historiography, and Politics.” *Journal of Latin American Studies* 24: 1–34.

———. 1987a. “The Era of Andean Insurrection, 1742–1782: Una Reinterpretación.” *Resistance, Rebellion, and Consciousness in the Andean Peasant World, Eighteenth to Twentieth Centuries*, ed. Steve Stern, 50–96. Madison: University of Wisconsin Press.

———. 1987b. “Nuevas aproximaciones al estudio de la conciencia y las rebeliones campesinas: Las implicaciones de la experiencia Andina.” *Resistance, Rebellion, and Consciousness in the Andean Peasant World, Eighteenth to Twentieth Centuries*, ed. Steve Stern, 25–49. Madison: University of Wisconsin Press.

———, ed. 1987c. *Resistance, Rebellion, and Consciousness in the Andean Peasant World, Eighteenth to Twentieth Centuries.* Madison: University of Wisconsin Press.

Stoler, Ann. 2002. *Carnal Knowledge and Imperial Power: Race and the Intimate in Colonial Rule*. Berkeley: University of California Press.

Suess, Paulo. 1993. “Culturas indígenas y evangelización.” *Hacia una teología de la inculturación*, by Paulo Suess, 7–48. Quito: Abya-Yala.

Sutton, David. 1998. *Memories Cast in Stone: The Relevance of the Past in Everyday Life*. New York: Berg.

Sylva, Paola. 1986. *Gamonalismo y lucha campesina*. Quito: Abya-Yala.

Tamayo, Eduardo. 1991. “Crónica de una muerte anunciada.” *Punto de Vista*, No. 463:8–11.

Tamayo, Eduardo, and Helga Serrano. 2005. “Ecuador: La revuelta de ‘los forajidos.’” *América Latina en Movimiento* 395.

Taussig, Michael. 1987. *Shamanism, Colonialism, and the Wild Man*. Chicago: University of Chicago Press.

Taylor, Charles. 1994. *Multiculturalism: Examining the Politics of Recognition*. Edited by Amy Gutmann. Princeton: Princeton University Press.

Thomas, Nicholas. 1994. *Colonialism’s Culture*. Princeton: Princeton University Press.

Thurner, Mark. 1993. “Peasant Politics and Andean Hacienda in the Transition to Capitalism: An Ethnographic History.” *Latin American Research Review* 28.3: 41–82.

Tilley, Virginia. 1997. “The Terms of the Debate: Untangling Language about Ethnicity and Ethnic Movements.” *Ethnic and Racial Studies* 20.3: 497–521.

Turner, Victor. 1970. *The Forest of Symbols: Aspects of Ndembu Ritual*. Ithaca: Cornell University Press.

Urban, Greg, and Joel Sherzer. 1991. *Nation-States and Indians in Latin America*. Austin: University of Texas Press.

Van Cott, Donna Lee. 2005. *From Movements to Parties in Latin America: The Evolution of Ethnic Politics*. Cambridge: Cambridge University Press.

———. 2002. *Constitutional Reform in the Andes Redefining Indigenous: State Relations*. Basingstoke, U.K.: Palgrave MacMillan.

———. 2000. *The Friendly Liquidation of the Past: The Politics of Diversity in Latin America*. Pittsburgh: University of Pittsburgh Press.

van Gennep, Arnold. 1960. *The Rites of Passage*. Chicago: University of Chicago Press.

Vargas-Cetina, Gabriela. 2003. "Representations of Indigenousness." *Anthropology News* 44.5: 11.

Velasco, Juan de. 1979. *Historia del reino de Quito en la América meridional*. Vol. 3. Quito: CCE.

Viatori, Maximilian. 2010. *One State, Many Nations: Indigenous Rights Struggle in Ecuador*. Santa Fe: SAR Press.

Wachtel, Nathan. 1976. *Los vencidos: Los indios del Perú Frente a la Conquista Española (1530–1570)*. Madrid: Alianza.

Walsh, Catherine. 2002. "The (Re)articulation of Political Subjectivities and Colonial Difference in Ecuador: Reflections on Capitalism and the Geopolitics of Knowledge." *Nepantla: Views from the South* 3.1: 61–97.

Warren, Jonathan W. 2001. *Racial Revolutions: Antiracism and Indian Resurgence in Brazil*. Durham: Duke University Press.

Warren, Kay. 1998. *Indigenous Movements and Their Critics: Pan Maya Activism in Guatemala*. Princeton: Princeton University Press.

Warren, Kay B., and Jean E. Jackson. 2005. "Indigenous Movements in Latin America, 1992–2004: Controversies, Ironies, New Directions." *Annual Review of Anthropology* 24: 549–73.

———, eds. 2002. *Indigenous Movements, Self-Representation, and the State in Latin America*. Austin: University of Texas Press.

Weismantel, Mary J. 2003. "Mothers of the Patria: La Chola Cuencana y la Mama Negra." *Millennial Ecuador: Critical Essays on Cultural Transformations and Social Dynamics*, ed. Norman Whitten, 325–34. Iowa: University of Iowa Press.

———. 2001. *Cholas and Pishtacos: Stories of Race and Sex in the Andes*. Chicago: University of Chicago Press.

———. 1988. *Food, Gender, and Poverty in the Ecuadorian Andes*. Philadelphia: University of Pennsylvania Press.

Whitten, Norman, ed. 2003. *Millennial Ecuador: Critical Essays on Cultural Transformations and Social Dynamics*. Iowa City: University of Iowa Press.

———, ed. 1998. "The Ecuadorian Levantamiento Indígena of 1990 and the Symbol of 1992." *History, Power and Identity: Ethnogenesis in the Americas, 1492–1992*, ed. Jonathan D. Hill, 194–217. Iowa: University of Iowa Press.

Williams, Raymond. 1977. *Marxism and Literature*. New York: Oxford University Press.

Wogan, Peter. 2001. *Magical Writing in Salasaca: Literacy and Power in Highland Ecuador*. Boulder: Westview.

Wray, Alberto. 1993. "El problema indígena y la reforma del estado." *Derecho, pueblos indígenas y reforma del estado*, ed. Alberto Wray and J. C. Ribadeneira, 11–70. Quito: Abya-Yala.

Yashar, Deborah. 2005. *Contesting Citizenship in Latin America: The Rise of Indigenous Movements and the Postliberal Challenge*. Cambridge: Cambridge University Press.

———. 1998. "The Post-Liberal Challenge in Latin America." Paper presented at the American Political Science Association conference, Boston.

Young, Iris Marion. 1996. "Polity and Group Difference: A Critique to the Ideal of Universal Citizenship." *Theorizing Citizenship*, ed. Ronald Beiner, 175–207. Albany: State University of New York.

Young, Robert. 1996. *Colonial Desire: Hybridity in Theory, Culture and Race*. New York: Routledge.

Yrigoyen, Raquel. 2004. "Legal Pluralism, Indigenous Law and the Special Jurisdiction in Andean Countries." *Beyond Law* 27: 32–49.

Zamosc, Leon. 2004. "The Indian Movement in Ecuador: From Politics of Influence to Politics of Power." *The Struggle for Indigenous Rights in Latin America*, ed. Nancy Grey Postero and Leon Zamosc, 131–157. Sussex, U.K.: Sussex Academic Press.

———. 1995. *Estadísticas de las areas de predominio etnico de la sierra Ecuatoriana*. Quito: Abya-Yala.

———. 1994. "Agrarian Protest and the Indian Movement in the Ecuadorian Highlands." *Latin American Research Review* 29.3: 37–68.

———. 1993. "Protesta agraria y movimiento indígena en la sierra Ecuatoriana." *Sismo etnico en el Ecuador*, by CEDIME, 273–304. Quito: CEDIME / Abya-Yala.

Zibechi, Raúl. 2006. "Indigenous Movements: Between Neoliberalism and Leftist Governments." Center for International Policy Americas Program, 3 May, http://www.cipamericas.org.

Žižek, Slavoj. 1997. "Multiculturalism, or the Cultural Logic of Multinationalism." *New Left Review* 225: 28–51.

Index

Emma Cervone is an assistant professor of anthropology at Johns Hopkins University.

Library of Congress Cataloging-in-Publication Data
Cervone, Emma.
Long live Atahualpa : indigenous politics, justice, and democracy in the Northern Andes / Emma Cervone.
p. cm.
Includes bibliographical references and index.
ISBN 978-0-8223-5175-7 (cloth : alk. paper)
ISBN 978-0-8223-5189-4 (pbk. : alk. paper)
1. Indians of South America—Political activity—Ecuador—Chimborazo.
2. Political activists—Ecuador—Chimborazo.
3. Social conflict—Ecuador—Chimborazo.
4. Social movements—Ecuador—Chimborazo.
I. Title.
F3721.3.P74C47 2012
303.48′4—dc23 2011048243